Theatrical Anecdotes

Peter Hay

THEATRICAL
ANECDOTES

Oxford University Press

NEW YORK   OXFORD

OXFORD UNIVERSITY PRESS

Oxford   New York   Toronto
Delhi   Bombay   Calcutta   Madras   Karachi
Petaling Jaya   Singapore   Hong Kong   Tokyo
Nairobi   Dar es Salaam   Cape Town
Melbourne   Auckland

and associated companies in
Berlin   Ibadan

First published in 1987 by Oxford University Press, Inc.,
200 Madison Avenue, New York, New York 10016
First issued as an Oxford University Press paperback, 1989

Oxford is a registered trademark of Oxford University Press

Library of Congress Cataloging-in-Publication Data
Hay, Peter.
Theatrical anecdotes.
Bibliography: p.   Includes index.
1. Theater—Anecdotes, facetiae, satire, etc.
2. Entertainers—Great Britain—Anecdotes, facetiae, satire, etc.
3. Entertainers—United States—Anecdotes,
facetiae, satire, etc.   I. Title.
PN2217.H39   1987   792'.02'9   86-28442
ISBN 0-19-503818-5
ISBN 0-19-506078-4 (pbk)

2 4 6 8 10 9 7 5 3
Printed in the United States of America

For Martin Esslin
raconteur extraordinaire,
in warm appreciation
of our long friendship,
following the friendships
of our fathers
and of our grandfathers
who worked on the same
newspaper in Budapest.

Preface

Anecdotes are almost as old as theatre. Throughout much of its twenty-five centuries of recorded history, the stage has been blessed with real characters as fascinating as any invented by a dramatist. Spinning stories around them became the players' chief form of entertainment. Plagued by poverty, the excesses of liquor, and every other known infirmity, holed up in flea-ridden lodgings and shabby green rooms, these colorful vagabonds kept alive the peculiar glories and miseries of their calling. And, incidentally, they provided us with a motherlode of curious traditions and entertaining table-talk, piquant gossip and instructive anecdotes.

Kinship between the anecdote and the drama is evident in the form of each. Both depend on human character, quick depiction, a simple but memorable incident, dialogue, and verbal wit. The typical anecdote begins almost like a fairy tale; the scene is then set with the introduction of characters; the plot unfolds and, in Bottom's succinct phrase, "so grows to a point." The ending is often a brief homily, like in so many classic tragedies and comedies. This recognizable form imposes its own tyranny on any collection and can quickly produce surfeit instead of the ideal prescription suggested by an eighteenth-century writer, that anecdotes should "stimulate the appetite for reading, and create it where deficient."

I have attempted in this volume a pointillist portrait of the stage, which has always held a mirror to society, not only to nature, recording the morals and manners of an age, while revealing the unchanging human emotions under the costumes. And just as theatre can instruct, outrage, and move the spirit to tears or laughter all in the same evening, I have tried within the covers of a book to give the reader a range of distilled experiences that might otherwise be considered too trivial for a consequential history.

My aim has been to preserve, wherever possible, the original words rather than impose my own style. I made minimal alterations in texts, mainly for brevity and intelligibility; American spelling is used except in material of British origin. I used interviews and colloquial sources, rather than literary memoirs. I have tried to provide a perspective, not just from the stalls but also from "the gods," the wings, and backstage. I selected material to appeal both to practitioners and to lovers of theatre, and the topical arrangement should allow them to find quickly the chapters that may interest them the most. Within a chapter or section, the anecdotes follow the evolution of a tradition or practice. However, working more in the manner of a documentary, I have often used juxtaposition and contrast rather than chronological progression; to date a story, even roughly, the reader may have to consult the bibliographic notes.

All anthologies are governed by a private sensibility, and the selections unavoidably reflect my cultural background. Despite severe limitations of space, I have tried to give a sense of theatre in different ages and countries. But this book is almost entirely about the Western stage tradition, which happens to be richly anecdotal. The abundance of English and French stories from the seventeenth to nineteenth century can be explained by an exceptional interest, during this period, in the anecdotal genre. The relatively short shrift given to the American theatre will be remedied in a later book of Broadway anecdotes.

There are many stellar figures of the stage today for whom I found no roles, and many obscure players of the past whose stories I kept because they seemed archetypal and thoroughly modern. I was interested not in the particular players but in the topic and in the quality of the anecdote. I tried to strike a balance between chauvinism about the present and nostalgia for the past. Anecdotes tend to gather around certain figures in every age, but I also wanted to pay tribute to the near-anonymous, common players without whom stars could not be stars, and theatre would not exist. This selection of vignettes— about people who were famous once but may be forgotten now, and some who were never famous—may serve as a reminder that performance is but for the moment, not for all time, and that among the unchanging imperatives in an actor's life it is more important to be busy than to be great.

Los Angeles
November 1986

P.H.

Acknowledgments

I owe much to many people, only some of whom are identified in the text. My parents brought me up in the theatre and in a culture famed for its anecdotal tradition. (As Clifton Fadiman observed: "I have rarely met a Hungarian who was not either the subject of good anecdotes or himself a repository of them.")

I feel great gratitude to my editors and the staff at Oxford University Press in New York: to Sheldon Meyer for his faith and wise guidance, and to Leona Capeless for her exacting standards. Stephanie Sakson-Ford has been an understanding copyeditor.

A book such as this could not exist without the cooperation of the patient people who work in the permissions departments of publishing companies, many of whom performed detective feats in tracking down out-of-print titles and extinct imprints.

I owe a very special debt to Laurence Evans, the chairman of International Creative Management in London, for obtaining permissions on behalf of his distinguished clients: Dame Peggy Ashcroft, Sir John Gielgud, Lord Olivier, and the late Sir Ralph Richardson's estate represented by Lady Richardson. I am grateful to John Casson (the estate of Dame Sybil Thorndike); to Joan Hirst and Lady Rachel Redgrave; to Peter Rosati of Michael Imison Playwrights Ltd., for permission to quote from the late Sir Noel Coward; and to Gillon Aitken and Ronald Harwood for their understanding. Thanks also to Jerome Lawrence, Tom Milne, Roy Moseley, John Osborne, John Neville, Diana Raymond, Pauline Swan, and George Speaight for their generous help.

David Parrish helped me with preparing the manuscript for press. My friends and colleagues at the Sundance Institute, First Stage, UCLA, and USC gave me strength, support, and many useful leads. In addition to the names mentioned in the sources I want to thank: Laurence and David Ambrose, Anthony Anderson, Michael Brewer, Didi Conn, Paul D'Andrea, Gautam Dasgupta, Molly Fowler, Michael Gearin-Tosh, William A. Gregory, Kati and Miklós Gyárfás,

Michael Hackett, Evan Handler, Leonora and David Hays, Jeffrey Henderson, Theodore Hoffman, Paul Jarrico, Agnes Kenyeres, Susan LaTempa, Paul Lieber, Grace McKeaney, Donald Margolis, Bonnie Marranca, Max Mayer, Virginia Morris, Rosanne Rich, Marsie Scharlatt, Arthur Seelen, David Shire, Herbert Shore, Eve Tettemer Siegel, Elizabeth Sweeting, Julie Taymour, Gwenn Victor, J. T. Walsh, April Webster, Norman Welsh, and John York.

This book would not have been possible without the resources of many libraries, especially collections at the University of Southern California, the University of California at Los Angeles, the Huntington Library, the Bodleian Library, and the Performing Arts Library at Lincoln Center. I am grateful to countless bookstores in many countries for locating rare and hard-to-find books, and especially to Gerard Kahan of Theatricana in Athens, Georgia. I want to thank my students for bringing several anecdotes to my attention and for being willing listeners to mine.

Finally, the two women in my life: my mother, Eva Hay, for her help and unfailing moral support, and to my wife, Dorthea Atwater, who was my stage manager and lighting designer when we met twenty years ago, and who still manages to put up with me and continues to light up my life.

Contents

CHAPTER VII   OUTWARD SHOW

CHAPTER VIII   DRAMATISTS

CHAPTER IX   WORDS, WORDS, WORDS

CHAPTER X   MANAGERS AND PRODUCERS

CHAPTER XI   DESIGN

CHAPTER XII   DIRECTORS

CHAPTER XIII   AUDIENCES

CHAPTER XIV   CRITICS

CHAPTER XV   THEATRE AND SOCIETY

CHAPTER XVI   BACKSTAGE

CHAPTER XVII   DISASTERS AND BEYOND

Theatrical Anecdotes

[CHAPTER I]

Actors and Acting

[1] CURTAIN RAISERS

Actor and Liar

The word "Thespian" commemorates the first Greek actor whose name has been preserved. Thespis of Icarus is supposed to have made his debut at the dramatic festival of Dionysus in 534 B.C. In Greek the actor was called "the answerer," because he talked back to the chorus. In English we derive the word "hypocrite" from it: no wonder that politicians have tended to see actors as competition. The power of drama to create illusion bothered some thinking Greeks before Plato, who wanted to ban plays from his ideal Republic. Plutarch tells this story of Solon, the great lawgiver, accusing Thespis, the great actor, of lying.

Thespis was beginning to act tragedies, and the people flocked to see the novelty, though there were no dramatic competitions yet. Solon's nature was attracted to hearing and learning new things, and now in old age, he had the leisure to enjoy life, with a little music and wine. So he went to see Thespis act. After the play, Solon went backstage and asked the actor if he was not ashamed to tell so many lies before such a large crowd. When Thespis replied that it was no harm to do so in a play, Solon vehemently struck his staff against the ground: "Ah, but if we commend lying on the stage, some day we will find it in politics."

The Greatest Roman of Them All

Quintus Roscius, a Roman actor, was so celebrated upon the stage that every actor of superior eminence to his contemporaries has been since called "the Roscius." It is said that he was not without some personal defects, in particular, his eyes were so distorted that he always appeared upon the stage with a mask; but the Romans frequently constrained him to take it off and overlooked the deformities of his face, that they might better hear his elegant pronunciation.

5

Not Altogether Fool

Richard Tarleton was the most famous comic actor and clown of the early part of Queen Elizabeth I's reign. It was an age that enjoyed bear-baiting and dog-fights along with the tragedies of Marlowe and Shakespeare.

Tarleton's nose was flattened by a blow which he received whilst parting some dogs and bears. This misfortune he turned into merriment by noticing that it did not affect him, for that he had still sagacity enough to smell a knave from an honest man.

The King's Jester

Thomas Killigrew, who received the patent of the King's Company, and who built the old theatre at Drury Lane, became page to Charles I and followed the Prince of Wales into exile. At the Restoration, Charles II made him a groom of the bedchamber, and he became known as the King's jester. During the troubles between his son the Duke of Monmouth, and the Duke of York, his Majesty, who loved both his son and brother, behaved with so much indifference and negligence in the business, that it was with great difficulty he could be persuaded to attend the council, or dispatch any affair whatever. One day, when the council had met and waited long for him, a member came to his apartments, but was refused admittance. His Lordship complained to Nell Gwyn of his dilatoriness, upon which she wagered him a hundred pounds that the King would that evening attend the council.

Accordingly she sent for Killigrew, naturally a buffoon, but a free favourite with his Majesty, and desired him to dress himself in every respect as if for a journey, and enter the King's apartments without ceremony. As soon as his Majesty saw him: "What, Killigrew! are you mad? Why, where are you going? Did not I order that nobody should disturb me?" "I don't mind your orders, not I," said Killigrew, "and I am going as fast as I can." "Why? Where?" said his Majesty—"where are you going?" "Going! why to hell," said Killigrew. "To hell, and what to do there?" "To fetch back Oliver Cromwell, to take some care of the national concerns, for I am sure your Majesty takes none."

This expedient had the desired effect, for the King immediately went to council.

Lord, What Fools These Mortals Be!

John Rich, the first Harlequin on the English stage, spent large sums over his favourite pantomimes at Covent Garden. He was also the fortunate producer of John Gay's *The Beggar's Opera*, which was facetiously said to have made Rich gay, and Gay rich. He took so little interest in what is termed the "regular drama" that he is reported to have exclaimed, when peeping through the curtain at a full house to witness a tragedy—"What, you are there, you fools, are you!"

A Valuable Actress

In the year 1728 Lavinia Fenton (afterwards Duchess of Bolton) was tempted by Rich from the Haymarket in Lincoln's Inn Fields by a salary of fifteen shillings per week. On the success of *The Beggar's Opera*, to secure this valuable actress, he raised it to thirty shillings. Such was the rage of the Town respecting her, that she was obliged to be guarded home every night by a considerable party of her confidential friends, to prevent her being run away with.

The Methusaleh of the Stage

Charles Macklin killed a fellow actor who had taken a wig of his without permission, by one thrust of a cane which entered the brain through the eye. He was the Methusaleh of the stage, born about 1700 or even earlier* and living until 1797—his last appearance being in 1789. Macklin, an Irishman whose family name was McLaughlin, took leading roles in Dublin and in various theatres in London. His greatest part was Shylock, but he also played in Fielding's farces and in Garrick's *Lethe*. Though kindly and indulgent at home, he was quarrelsome in his profession, once causing a riot through the aggressive loyalty of his friends and once occasioning a violent disturbance by merely appearing on the stage.

Declamation

John Kemble's conversation often flowed into blank verse, and his more famous sister, Mrs. Sarah Siddons, was legendary for her dramatic persona.

* Some sources give 1690.

"The gods do not bestow such a face as Mrs. Siddons's on the stage more than once in a century," says Sidney Smith. "I knew her well, and she had the good taste to laugh at my jokes. She was an excellent person, but she was not remarkable out of her profession, and never got out of tragedy even in private life. She used to stab her potatoes; and said, 'Boy, give me a knife!' as she would have said on the stage, 'Give me a dagger!' Many pleasant stories were current at the time about Mrs. Siddons's stately fashion and tragic tone, heard in shops and at dinner-table: 'Will it wash?' as though she were speaking to Macbeth about the dreadful bloodstains; her blank verse to the Scotch provost, 'Beef cannot be too salt for me, my lord!' and to an attendant at the dinner-table: 'You've brought me water boy; I asked for beer.' Sir Walter Scott (an excellent mimic) was fond of repeating this tragic exclamation."

Taking Off

Samuel Foote, eighteenth-century actor and writer, the father of the burlesque, took off many of his contemporaries.

One night, at his friend Devalal's, one of the party would suddenly have fixed a quarrel upon him for his indulgence of personal satire. "Why, what would you have?" exclaimed Foote, good-humouredly putting it aside. "Of course I take all my friends off, but I use them no worse than myself. I take myself off." "Gadso!" cried the gentleman, "that I should like to see." Upon this, Foote took his hat and left the room.

Foote had a cork leg, as a result of a riding accident. Dr. Johnson obviously disliked him, and he had an ingenious explanation why Foote left him out from his wide repertory of spoofs.

Boswell: Foote has a great deal of humour." *Johnson:* "Yes, sir," *Boswell:* "He has a singular talent for exhibiting character." *Johnson:* "Sir, it is not a talent, it is a vice; it is what others abstain from. It is not comedy, which exhibits the character of a species, as that of a miser gathered from many misers; it is farce, which exhibits individuals." *Boswell:* "Did not he think of exhibiting you, sir?" *Johnson:* "Sir, fear restrained him; he knew I would have broken his bones. I would have saved him the trouble of cutting off a leg; I would not have left him a leg to cut off."

Digestion

The Duke of Cumberland came one night into the green room. "Well, Foote," said he, "here I am, ready, as usual, to swallow all your good things." "Really," replied Foote, "your royal highness must have an excellent digestion, for you never bring up any again."

The Wages of Sin

The greatest of the Restoration actresses was Mrs. Elizabeth Barry. She went on the stage as a protégée of the Earl of Rochester, by whom she later had a child. Colley Cibber admired her extravagantly.

Mrs. Barry in characters of greatness, had a presence of elevated dignity; her mien and motion superb, and gracefully majestic; her voice full, clear, and strong, so that no violence of passion could be too much for her: and when distress or tenderness possessed her, she subsided into the most affecting melody and softness. In the art of exciting pity she had a power beyond all the actresses I have yet seen, or what your imagination can conceive.

Mrs. Barry was middle-siz'd, and had darkish hair, light eyes, dark eyebrows, and was indifferently plump. The gossips all agreed that she was irresistibly attractive to men and that her lovers were beyond numbering. They asserted that she was hard, miserly, mercenary and vicious. Said Tom Brown, "Should you lie with her all night, she would not know you next morning, unless you had another five pounds at her service." Davies ascribed her death to the bite of a favourite lapdog, who had been seized, unknown to her, with madness.

Personality

Sarah Bernhardt:

The artist's personality must be left in his dressing room; his soul must be denuded of its own sensations and clothed with the base or noble qualities he is called upon to exhibit. I once had an Italian chamber-maid who, returning one evening from seeing me in *Phèdre*, said: "Oh! Madame was so lovely that I didn't recognize Madame!" And no compliment ever went more direct to my heart.

Natural Acting

Lord Chesterfield once said to Mr. Garrick, "David, you are an actor everywhere but upon the stage."

Envy

Mrs. Clive was one night seen standing at the wing, alternately weeping at and scolding Garrick's acting. Angry at last at finding herself so affected, she turned on her heel, crying, "D— him, he could act a *gridiron*."

Thin Ice

The summer of 1919 was hotter than usual, and Tallulah Bankhead decided not to wear stockings on the stage. Audiences were shocked by her immodesty. At matinees she was hissed by outraged ladies. Producer Lee Shubert pleaded with her to wear stockings. She said she was too hot. She became the subject of scandalized gossip all over New York . . .

She wore her fingernails an inch long and had them lacquered in Chinese red. She would ride through Central Park in a hansom cab, with a spray of purple lilac in her fingers, while she recited fragments of *Cynara,* by Ernest Dowson. Her beauty was simply breathtaking. John Barrymore, who was then the idol of every young woman, was awed by it and asked to be introduced to her. "Lord," he was heard to murmur, "isn't she a beautiful thing!" One of the loveliest actresses of the time, introduced to Miss Bankhead at the Algonquin, refused to join the group, saying, "I can't sit at the same table with this girl. She makes me look so terribly plain."

In the early 1920s Tallulah Bankhead went to London; playing opposite Sir Gerald du Maurier in The Dancers *she was an overnight sensation.*

She became the craze in London. There were Tallulah hats, Tallulah dresses, Tallulah coiffures. Adolescent females dyed their hair blonde. . . One critic remarked, "A first night in London of a Tallulah Bankhead play is a wild orgy of emotion." Lines queued up forty-eight hours in advance for the unreserved seats. On one occasion two thousand admirers stormed the stage door of the Lyric Theatre and the police were called to disperse the rioters. . . .

Upon being asked why Tallulah was such a success in London, Mrs. Pat Campbell explained, "She's always skating on thin ice—and the British public wants to be there when it breaks."

Jealousy

When John Kemble was living at Lausanne he used to feel rather jealous of Mont Blanc; he disliked hearing people always asking, "How does Mont Blanc look this morning?"

[2] ART AND PASSION

Rules

Baron, who was the French Garrick, had a most elevated notion of his profession: he used to say that tragic actors should be nursed on the laps of queens! Nor was his vanity inferior to his enthusiasm in his profession, for according to him the world might see once a century a Caesar, but it required a thousand years to produce a Baron. "Rules," said this sublime actor (thus he is called), "may teach us not to raise the arms above the head, but if Reason carries them it will be well done;—Passion knows more than Art."

A Striking Actor

Thomas Betterton was a son of Charles the First's cook. A humble lad, born in Tothill Street before monarchy and the stage went down, he had a royal funeral in Westminster Abbey, after dying in harness almost in sight of the lamps. Mr. Booth, who knew him only in his decline, used to say he never saw him—off or on the stage—without learning something from him, and frequently observed that Betterton was no actor, that he put on his part with his clothes and was the very man he undertook to be till the play was over, and nothing more. So exact was he in following nature that the look of surprise which he assumed in the character of Hamlet astonished Booth, when he first personated the Ghost, to such a degree that he was unable to proceed with his part for some moments.

Robert Wilks, acting in *The Maid's Tragedy* with Betterton, was so much struck by the actor's dignity that he could hardly speak. Betterton, remarking his confusion, said, "Young man, this fear does not ill become you—a horse that sets out at the strength of his speed will soon be jaded."

A Strict Observer of Nature

Thomas Doggett was a first-rate low comedian in the eighteenth century, immensely popular with the pit and gallery. He was, in the general opinion of the world, an original actor, a close copier of Nature, and so sensible of what his natural abilities could effect that he never ventured upon any part to which they were not well adapted. He is praised for the exactitude with which he dressed his characters, and also in colouring the different degrees of age—a circumstance which led Sir Godfrey Kneller to tell him one day that he was a better painter than he. "I," said Sir Godfrey, "can only copy Nature from the originals before me, while you vary them at pleasure, and yet preserve the likeness."

His Very Stick Acted

David Garrick was the greatest actor of eighteenth-century England and the first modern superstar.

"Mr. Murphy, sir, you knew Mr. Garrick?" "Yes, sir, I did, and no man better." "Well, sir, what did you think of his acting?" After a pause: "Well, sir, *off* the stage he was a mean sneaking little fellow. But *on* the stage—throwing up his hands and eyes—"oh, my great God!"

Jack Bannister was behind the scenes of the theatre when Garrick was playing Lear, and said that the tone in which Garrick uttered the words, "O fool, I shall go mad!" absolutely thrilled him. "In *Lear* Garrick's very stick acted," Bannister said. "The scene with Cordelia and the physician, as Garrick played it, was the most pathetic I ever saw upon the stage."

Move Others, Not Yourself

"Garrick roused the feelings more than any actor on record, and most probably suffered as much from their exertion." A gentleman once making the above remark to Tom King, the comedian, received this reply: "Pooh! he suffer from his feelings! Why, sir, I was playing with him one night in *King Lear*, when, in the middle of a most passionate and affecting part, and when the whole house was drowned in tears, he turned his head round to me, and putting his tongue in his cheek, whispered—'Damn me, Tom, it'll do.' "

No Feelings, Please

Henry Irving was the most controversial actor in late Victorian England. Edward Gordon Craig, who was Ellen Terry's son, started in Irving's company and later wrote a book in which he probed the secret of his art.

Spontaneity Irving valued, but seldom indulged in: what he did he did by design. He did not respect that artlessness which fails to reveal art. He was not merely fond of his art—his art of acting was his religion. To be playful and go-as-you-please about it—to be spontaneous, unless by the grace of God—was to him a sign of idiocy. There seems to have been a day when, after witnessing what is called "an inspired performance of genius," "full of feeling," he took himself aside and said: "My boy, listen to me. In the next twenty or thirty years you may be called upon to perform some eight thousand times, and as you may possibly not feel inspired each time you perform you may, during the course of a very stren-u-ous role, not feel inspired for more than—er—let us say—um—ten minutes per act. I think, therefore, you will do well to remember that by taking great pains you can, shall we say—um—design a part, a role, so carefully that, inspired or not, you'll be demmed interesting. The less 'feeling' the better. See what I mean, my boy?"

Good Acting

Joseph Jefferson, the nineteenth-century American actor, when he was asked his opinion about the so-called Coquelin controversy (Coquelin believed that an actor shouldn't feel anything at all, and Irving believed that the actor should appear to be feeling the very things he's talking about), said very meekly: "As for me, I find that I act best when my heart is warm and my head is cool."

Sarah Bernhardt was a friend of both Coquelin and Irving.

I made enemies of Irving and Coquelin because I said in private conversation that Coquelin was a remarkable actor but not an artist,
while Irving was a mediocre actor, but a great artist.

Simile

"Kean is original; but he copies from himself," Coleridge said. "To
see him act, is like reading Shakespeare by flashes of lightning."

A Chameleon

*Charles Mathews (the Elder) was a friend of Coleridge's and was cele-
brated for his mimicry.*

It was a winter's day: the snow began to fall, and doubts arising as to
the possibility of Mrs. Gilman's making her way under such circumstances, Mathews with his inimitable talents of entering into the mind
as well as the manner of others, walked up and down the drawing-
room, and began to imitate Coleridge by anticipation, somewhat as
follows: "My dear Mr. Mathews, such was the inveteracy of the angry element in its fleecy descent, that to encounter it was barely possible to Mr. Gilman and myself. For one of the softer sex the affair was
altogether impracticable. Mrs. Gilman, after making several efforts,
was obliged to desist, and Mr. Gilman and I have therefore made our
appearance without her." Scarcely had we ceased to laugh at this exhibition when the gatebell rung, and—as the demon of imitation would
have it—the two men made their appearance, and Coleridge began,
"My dear Mr. Mathews, such was the inveteracy of the element,"
&c . . . and concluded almost in the language of the benevolent
banker who had just discounted his oration. You may imagine the
effect this produced upon our risible organs, which we with difficulty
restrained."

In 1806 Mathews appeared in Hook's farce of Catch Him Who Can
at the Haymarket.

So admirable was the rapidity with which Mathews, as the nobleman's servant, assumed some six or seven disguises, and so complete
his personation, that the audience on the first night, fairly taken in,

failed to recognise his identity, and received him with perfect silence. The applause was of course rapturous on the discovery of the deception.

Acting Simplified

Sir Frank Benson told how, in his early days, certain actors never studied any parts but their own, and that only from mysterious bits of paper called "scrip." The sight of a book was anathema to them. "Text, text? I've never heard of it," they would say. "What the hell is text? All I want, laddie, is first the bizness, then the cues, and I bet my last bob I get a bread-and-butter notice."

Passion

Edmund Kean was notoriously a passionate-tempered man. One night he went to hear Fuller, a mimic, give representations of the leading actors, including Kean. The tragedian frequently rapped his applause during the performance; but when Fuller came to the imitation of Kean, he paused. Kean looked with approval, and Fuller commenced. In a few moments Kean threw a glass of wine in his face. There was a fight, after which Kean, by way of apology, said that if he thought he was such a wretch as Fuller represented him he would hang himself.

Kean acted at Birmingham once, where his benefit was a total failure. The play was Massinger's *New Way To Pay Old Debts*. Allusion is made to the marriage of a lady. Kean suddenly exclaimed, "Take her, sir, and the Birmingham audience into the bargain."

It's Called Acting

Bill Woodman was serving on the jury of the Irene Ryan Awards given to promising students by the American College Theatre Festival. The actress who established the scholarships had played the mother in a successful television show, *The Beverly Hillbillies*, and she wanted to give back something of her wealth to the theatre. A week before the ceremonies in the spring of 1973, Irene Ryan died suddenly and the Festival called Helen Hayes at the last minute to substitute. Miss Hayes gave a moving speech about the late Miss Ryan, the great trouper and jewel to her profession. It was a wonderful personal tribute from one actress to another which had everybody sobbing.

Backstage afterwards Bill Woodman congratulated Miss Hayes on the speech and offered his condolences on losing such a good friend. "I don't know who the heck she was," replied the first lady of the American theatre, "they called me when the old girl kicked off and asked whether I'd come down; and I told them that I'd go anywhere for a trip."

[3] PHYSIQUE

Short Giants

Many people today are surprised to find their stage or movie idols are smaller in real life than they imagined. It was ever thus.

"What a pity it is," said a lady to Garrick, "that you are not taller!" "I should be happy, indeed, Madam," replied Garrick, "to be higher in your estimation."

Long before Kean's triumph in London Mrs. Jordan was starring at a provincial theatre in *The Wonder*. "Who," said she at rehearsal, "is to be my Don Felix?" "That gentleman," said the manager, pointing to the shortest member of the company. "Oh, I can't act with him, he's too little!" The "little" actor gave her one look and walked away. Some years later, when all London was talking of Edmund Kean, Mrs. Jordan, amongst others, was anxious to be introduced to him. In the green room at Drury Lane they met. "Great heavens!" she exclaimed, "the little man with the eyes!" She said afterwards the eyes haunted her—she had never forgotten their reproachful look.

Too Tall

Great actors overcome their physical limitations, but they rarely ignore them. Sir Michael Redgrave recounts how he came to play Uncle Vanya.

Before the war I had been asked to go to the Old Vic and do, amongst other things, a Chekhov play. I chose *Uncle Vanya* because I could see certain things that reminded me of Tusenbach [a character in

Chekhov's *Three Sisters*]. I thought that if I could do Tusenbach I could certainly do Uncle Vanya; and it was agreed that I should do it. So I decided to go across to Paris, to see a retired Russian actress who had been a great help to Michel Saint-Denis with his production of *Three Sisters*; and this woman, I was told, was very thrilled to know that I was coming. I had brought an interpreter with me and we went into her room, but she took one look at me and said, "Non, non, non, no Vanya! no Vanya! Astrov! Astrov!" That put me off for quite a time. Anyway she said "non" all the time. She wanted me to play the part of the doctor, Astrov, because of my size, six foot two and a half inches. And so I was delighted when Olivier rang me up, two or three years ago, for the Chichester Festival, and asked if I would play Vanya; by then I had got over the feeling of being too tall.

Too Thin

When Jack Bannister, who began his career as a tragic actor, said to Garrick that he proposed to attempt the hero of Sotherne's drama, *Oroonoko, an African Prince,* he was told by the great little man that, in view of his extraordinarily thin person, he would "look as much like the character as a chimney-sweep in consumption!" It was to Bannister, on this same occasion, that Garrick uttered the well-known aphorism, "Comedy is a very serious thing!"

And Fat

Edmund Tearle was married to Kate Clinton. Edmund as Hamlet, a mastodon in tights, was always good for an unscheduled laugh when he soliloquized, "O, that this too, too solid flesh would melt." Kate, squeezed into costume as Portia, equaled him as a provoker of laughter when she complained, "My little body is a-weary of this world."

Their voices matched their girth. One story tells how Edmund was appearing in a Lancashire town one night while Kate stayed up in a hotel opposite the theatre waiting for him to return. When he got back after his performance, she had some disturbing news. "You were not in good voice tonight, my dear," she said. "I kept the window open, but I couldn't hear a word from where I was sitting."

Too Much

Madame Suzanne Lagier was a good actress, but extremely stout. One night she was enacting a part in a melodrama with Taillade, the original Pierre of *The Two Orphans*, and this actor had at one moment to carry her, fainting, off the stage. He tried, with all his might, to lift the fat heroine, but although she helped her little comrade by standing on tip-toe in the usual manner, he was unable to move her an inch. At this juncture, a boy cried out from the gallery, "Take what you can, and come back for the rest!"

Comic Nose

Sometimes an actor's physiognomy renders him unsuitable for certain parts, a fact often difficult to accept. In the case of Constant Coquelin, the creator of Cyrano de Bergerac, Sarah Bernhardt had to break the news to him.

Coquelin's was a voice both magnificent and complete. It ranged over all the scales, and had every shade of resonance. If Coquelin had had an ordinary nose, he would certainly have succeeded in some tragic parts. During a tour we made together in America, he confided to me one day of his disappointment.

"Tell me," he remarked, "why I have not succeeded in dramatic parts."

"But, Coquelin," I answered, "it is because of your nose; it gives you a comical physiognomy in greatness and in sorrow."

"How stupid! Listen, I will recite Néron to you."

I listened to him. To be sure it sounded very well, and his conception of Néron was interesting; but it would not have done to look at him. The wrinkled forehead, knit brows, fine and piercing glance were not enough to mitigate the comicality of that nose open to all winds, sniffing up the joy of living, and contradicting by its aspect the dramatic expression of the forehead and the eyes.

Overdrawn

John Kemble, from a family of great actors, overcame several disadvantages to become one of the preeminent actors of the early nineteenth century.

Away from the lamps he was a mere private gentleman, and to most persons must have appeared an exceedingly dull one. His mind was not obtuse, but his extreme slowness gave him all the appearance of obtusity. In allusion to his asthma, he was wont to say that no one else of his family knew the misery of "drawing on their own chest, and finding the cheque dishonoured."

[4] LEARNING

The Great Tradition

Roscius set up the first school for actors in ancient Rome, but professional training did not become widespread until our century. Most actors acquired their skills through experience, working as extras (or "general utility" and "walking gentlemen" as they were quaintly called); they learned by observing more experienced actors. Acting styles change with every generation, but something is transmitted from the great actors of the past.

Forbes-Robertson was very fortunate because quite early in his career the famous Shakespearean player Samuel Phelps took a fancy to him, engaged him, and coached him in all his parts. In this way he learnt the technique that had been handed down from Garrick, through Mrs. Siddons and Macready, to Phelps, whose influence and teaching, Robertson affirmed, were mainly responsible for his own achievements. "I may boast of a good histrionic pedigree," he said. "There is the good old school and the bad old school and the former is the best school for any time."

The School of Life

Lady Constance Benson:

We watched experienced actors to see how they got their effects, how they achieved their "makeup" for certain parts, how they changed their walk to suit the character they portrayed. I remember Sir Henry Irving saying to me, "Watch, watch always, and if you see nothing worth copying, you will see something to avoid"; and Ben Greet, in a letter of kindly advice, wrote, "See as much acting as you can, good and bad."

The Master

Everybody inside the theatre referred to Noël Coward as The Master, because he so readily dispensed advice and wit to younger aspirants.

Early in 1962 Noël was the guest of honour one Sunday at a dinner given by the Gallery First-Nighters' Club. Beginning his speech, "Desperately accustomed as I am to public speaking," he continued, "you ask my advice about acting? Speak clearly, don't bump into people, and if you must have motivation think of your pay packet on Friday."

Learning To Laugh

Noël Coward remembers how Sir Charles Hawtrey, after engaging him at the age of eleven, took in hand his theatrical education.

I used to stand at the side of the stage, watching him and he used to teach me—he taught me how to laugh. I remember him standing over me at rehearsal, in front of the whole company and saying, "Now, boy, you've got to laugh. Now start with this. Ho, ha, ha, ha, ha, ha. But put your breath right." And he stood over me till I did it. He said, "now smile with it a bit," and I'd go, "Ha, ha, ha." And he said, "Now give way," and I'd go "Ha, ha, ha, ha." That was entirely technical and, of course, it was an enormous help; he could laugh on the stage indefinitely. He taught me also to use my hands and my arms and swing them without looking as though I were acting at all.

Cured of the Giggles

A few years later Noël Coward had a chance to repay his education by teaching the young Laurence Olivier, who could not stop giggling on stage. He had lost one job because of it and was almost fired for the same offense at the Birmingham Repertory Theatre, where he got his first real break. Finally he was cured of this dangerous habit during the run of Private Lives.

Noël saw that I was a giggler and said, "Right, I'll cure you," and he brought me round to his dressing-room one day and said, "Look, if you ever giggle again, I'm going to make you very sorry indeed. I'm going to train you not to giggle. Now, you've got three months in London, you've got four months in New York with this play. By the end of that time, that's seven months, I'll have cured you." And he said, "I'll tell you how I'm going to do it. I'm going to make you giggle. I'm going to make you, make you, make you, make you, make you giggle." And what he and Gertrude Lawrence didn't get up to, to make me giggle in that breakfast scene at the end of *Private Lives* is nobody's business. For one thing he invented a dog called Roger . . . Then, when Gertrude Lawrence as Amanda had to splutter over the coffee, I had to slap her too hard on the back. One day she choked and turned round and said, "You great clob." And Noël said, "Clob?" and she said, "Yes, clob." And Noël said, "The man with the clob foot." You know, it sounds too silly, but on the stage those things are as funny as they are in church.

Acting School

Olivier did actually attend a drama school. He auditioned for Elsie Fogerty, at the Central School; she was to have a lasting influence on him.

I did the "Seven Ages of Man." Afterwards she said, "Come down, boy, come down," and she sat me beside her and she said, "I think you've got a little too strong an idea of the importance of action." It's rather funny that anybody could say that about me then, aged seventeen. She said, "It is not really necessary to make fencing movements when you are saying 'Sudden and quick to quarrel.'" And then she did a marvellous thing, an unforgettable thing, she said, "You have a weakness here," and she took her little finger and placed it vertically down the middle of my forehead. It's funny, I must have shown some sort of shyness, and been beetle-browed, and she said, "You have a weakness here and remember that." Well, *something* made me slap all that putty on my face for years and years afterwards, and I dare say it was that.

Priceless Advice

Laurence Olivier was already a famous actor when he almost quit his profession. Fortunately he ran into Tyrone Guthrie at the right moment.

On one occasion Guthrie gave me the most priceless bit of advice I've ever had from anybody, and that was a great surprise to me. Guthrie and John Burrell had restarted the Old Vic and Ralph Richardson and I opened our first play, *Arms and the Man*, at the Opera House, Manchester. Ralph and I had been got out of the Navy in order to do this work, and we opened and it was all right. The next day Ralph and I went along to the pub, next to the stage door, and we had half a pint, or something. On the way back he bought a paper and, looking over Ralph's shoulder going along the street towards the Midland Hotel I remember seeing, "Mr. Ralph Richardson was a brilliant Bluntschli. Mr. Laurence Olivier, on the other hand . . ." and I thought, "That's it. That's it. I've had this now for nearly twenty years. I'm going back to the Navy. I can't stand it . . . I cannot stand criticism, I can't bear it any more." Well, that night Tony Guthrie came to see the performance, and as we came out of the stage door and turned the corner underneath the canopy outside the theatre, Tony, from his great height, looked down at me and said, "Liked your Sergius very much." I snarled and said, "Oh, thank you very much, too kind, I'm sure." And he said, "No, no. Why, what's the matter?" And I said, "Well, really, don't ask . . . no, please." And he said, "But don't you love Sergius?" And I said, "Look, if you weren't so tall, I'd hit you. How do you mean, how can you love a part like that, a stupid, idiot part? Absolutely nothing to do but to conform, to provide the cues for Shaw's ideas of what was funny at the time. How can you possibly enjoy or like a part like that?" And he said, "Well, of course, if you can't love Sergius, you'll never be any good in him, will you?" Well, it clicked, and something happened, I suppose, that gave me a new attitude, perhaps an attitude that had been completely lacking in me, up to that time, towards the entire work of acting.

Shamed into School

Drama schools, as a prerequisite of the profession, are a relatively recent development. It used to be common for stage-bound youths to apprentice themselves backstage with a theatre company, hoping to be used in small parts and thus get noticed. Mr. W. Duncan Ross, who has directed some major drama schools in England, Canada, and the United States, remembers the sort of incident that has happened in practically everybody's career.

I was working at the Nottingham Playhouse in the 1950s and we were looking for an apprentice who would perform those myriad odd jobs that need to be done in the theatre. A striking youth with fair hair and blue eyes "auditioned" for the position. It was obvious that he had a burning ambition to act and was too talented to be used as a "go-fer." The young man left with a look of bitter disappointment.

Three years later, I was at the Bristol Old Vic watching a production of *The Matchmaker* in which the same youth was causing a buzz in the tiny part of the coachman. Afterwards, I went backstage to congratulate him and asked him what he had done since that interview in Nottingham. The young Peter O'Toole replied: "I went and auditioned at once for RADA [the Royal Academy of Dramatic Art]; that experience shamed me into getting properly trained as an actor."

The Golden Rule

Paul Muni was a struggling actor in Philadelphia when W. C. Fields came backstage after a matinee.

"You'll never make it as a juggler, m'boy," Fields told Muni. "Your eyes are too sad." Muni's eyes must have looked extra-sad, because Fields added: "But don't listen to me, kid. My entire success is based on one rule: never take advice from anybody!"

CHAPTER II

Seven Ages
of Acting

Mr. Smith Is Stage-struck

Many an acting career was launched when a visiting troupe came to town. Sol Smith, who later became one of America's most respected actor-managers, was a young store clerk in Albany, New York, when the players came to town in the 1810s. He did not have the money for a ticket, but he simply had to see Richard the Third.

About six o'clock I entered the back door, which happened to be un-guarded at the time, and went up to my old quarters in the carpenters' gallery. I felt my way in the dark until I found something which appeared to be a large box, into which I popped without the least hesi-tation, and closed the lid. For more than an hour I lay concealed, safe, as I thought, from discovery. At length the bustle of the carpenters and tuning of instruments in the orchestra announced that the opera-tions of the evening were about to commence. The curtain rose, and I ventured to peep down upon the stage. I was delighted; I could see all that was going on, myself unseen. The second act was about to be-gin, and I was luxuriating in the pleasure I should derive from the "courting scene" of Richard and Lady Anne, when I heard four or five men making their way directly to my hiding-place. I had barely time to enter my box and close the lid, when I found, to my utter dis-may, that the box was the object of the search; in short, as you will al-ready have anticipated, *I was shut up in King Henry's coffin!* Here was a situation for a stage-struck hero!

The coffin was taken up, the men remarking "it was devilish heavy," and I felt myself conveyed down stairs and placed upon the bier. Since I had been carried so far, I made up my mind to carry the joke a little farther. So I lay as quiet as the "injured king" would have lain had he been in my place, and was carried by four strong supernumer-aries on the stage, followed by the weeping Lady Anne and all the court. Little did the lady imagine she was weeping over a living corpse! For my part I perspired most profusely, and longed for an opportunity to escape. When I was carried off "to Whitefriars" to be interred, the supers were desired to replace the coffin in the carpenters' gallery. Being awkward (did you ever see supernumeraries who were not?), and finding their load rather heavy, they turned and tumbled it about in such a way that I could not bear it any longer, and was obliged to call out. The men dropped their precious burden and ran away in affright, which gave me an opportunity to make my escape from the coffin and my exit through the back door.

I afterward heard that the affair had made a great noise in the theatre at the time of its occurrence—the four men declaring that a hollow voice had issued from the coffin bidding them "put it down and be d—d to them!" and the carpenters affirming, on the contrary, that when they opened the coffin they had found it empty. The four supernumerary gentlemen never visited the playhouse again, but immediately joined the Church. One of them, I believe, has become a notorious preacher, and never spares the theatre or theatrical people in his sermons, telling his hearers that he had a most mysterious warning when he was a young man!

Getting Started

C. B. Cochran later became one of the greatest English impresarios.

At sixteen I got an engagement at the Royal Clarence Music Hall, Dover, but one song was enough for them. The manager, in fact, refused to pay me. At eighteen I went to the United States. The producer asked, "Who is the child?" I looked round for the child—but he meant me! My first job was seven different parts in a revue called *Round the World in Eighty Days*. I was a policeman, waiter, Red Indian, gentleman, and any other thing they happened to be short of. One Middle-West critic said, "All he can do well is to chew the paint off the scenery." But I was ready to do anything. If a manager asked, "Are you an acrobat?" I would say, "Yes, sure!" Just before I got the revue job the sole of my boot had come off as I tramped round New York.

Getting a Break

Dame Sybil Thorndike:

We were at home at Claverton Street and a brougham drove up and a bell rang and down I went and there was a lady and she said, "Will you come and speak to my sister?" And I went out and it was Ellen Terry. And she asked me if I would come and play Mistress Ford to her Mistress Page on the halls. Then I went to see Ellen at her house in the Kings Road and she said to me, "Well, now what wages, child?" And I said—I like my answer as much as I like her question—I said to her, "I've never had more than five pounds a week, Miss Terry." Imagine anybody saying that today! And she said, "I shall give you fifteen and take it off the man."

Getting Hired

The story of how Ralph Richardson got his first professional break already features a bicycle, a forerunner of the series of famous motorcycles on which Sir Ralph would terrorize London and the English countryside well into his seventies.

There was a chap that used to come to Brighton once a year, Charles Doran, and in those days he had quite a famous company, the Charles Doran Shakespeare Company. And as the Shakespeare plays that we did very much interested me, I wrote to him, told him what I was doing, asked him if he would give me an interview with the idea of my getting a job with him. I got a reply, he was very good in that way, and he asked me to go over and see him in Eastbourne, after the matinee of *The Merchant of Venice* the following Wednesday. "Oh, my goodness," I thought, "what a wonderful thing." I got out my bicycle and gave it an extra clean—I had the cleanest bicycle, it was so clean that if there was only a spot of rain I never dared to take it out, I'd walk. I put on my cycle clips and away over the downs I went and I saw part of the show. I was nervous as a cat, I'd never been really behind the scenes of a professional theatre before. It was the Devonshire Park in Eastbourne. However, Doran came off the stage as Shylock and his dresser said, "Come in, the Guv'nor 'll see you." He was taking his make-up off, and he hardly looked at me. He could just see me in the mirror and he said, "Oh yes, Richardson, let's hear you spout something to get an idea what kind of voice you've got." I'd thought this was probably coming, so I had learnt Mark Antony's funeral oration from *Julius Caesar*. "Yes," said Doran, "stand over there will you, just over there so that I can get a look at you." So I stood over at the back of where his street clothes were hanging and he was watching me in the mirror. So he said, "Go on, start away." I said, "Friends, Romans, countrymen, lend me your ears. I come to bury

Caesar, not to praise him," and I went on with the speech, "Remember on the feast of Lupercal," becoming then quite dramatic, and he said, "Stop, stop, pack it up." So I said, "Isn't it any good, Mr. Doran? Isn't it any good, don't you like it?" And he said, "It's fine, it's fine, but you're standing on my trousers."

[6]   CHILD ACTORS

Just as there are many children who act on stage and the screen today, young people have performed in the threatre for several centuries. Children's companies flourished in Elizabethan and Jacobean London. Ben Jonson perpetuated in doggerel verse the memory of one of the children of Queen Elizabeth's Chapel, named Salomon Pavy, who died in his thirteenth year and was particularly well known for playing old men. Many famous actors began their stage careers at a tender age. In the nineteenth century, the American actor Joseph Jefferson engaged in a stage combat at the Park Theatre with broadswords at age six; Madame Ristori, first carried on the stage in a basket at two months, was at the age of four playing children's parts in her native Italy. But that century is more noted for the extraordinary children stars who briefly commanded greater attention than rock stars today, and then faded into obscurity.

The Infant Phenomenon

William Henry West Betty, known as Young Roscius, was in his eleventh year when he first saw a play, *Pizarro*, with Mrs. Siddons in the part of Elvira. With this character he was captivated: he repeated her speeches, imitated her manner, copied her accents, and studied her attitudes. From that moment drama became his chief study, the master passion of his soul, and he frankly informed his father that he "should die if he were not permitted to become a player."

He was introduced to Mr. Atkins, the manager of the theatre at Belfast, and on August 1, 1803, as a child of less than twelve years, he appeared for the first time in the tragedy of *Zara*. After performing in many provincial theatres he made his debut before a London audience, at Covent Garden Theatre, on the first of December, 1804. He was engaged for twelve nights at fifty guineas a night, while he agreed to perform at Drury Lane during the intervening nights, an arrangement unprecedented in the history of the stage. It would be impossible to describe the enthusiasm which he excited; it seemed an epidemic mania. At the doors of the theatre where he was to perform for the evening the people crowded as early as one o'clock in the afternoon, and when the hour of admittance came, the rush was so dreadful that numbers were nightly injured by the pressure.

Young Betty was presented to the king, and noticed by the rest of the royal family and the nobility as a prodigy. Prose and poetry were put in requisition to celebrate his praise; prints of his person were circulated throughout the kingdom. It was even in public contemplation to erect statues to him; and Opie painted a full-length portrait of him, in which the Young Roscius was represented as having drawn inspiration from the tomb of Shakespeare.

After performing a host of tragic characters at fifty and a hundred guineas per night, the Young Roscius retired from the stage with an ample fortune, at an age when other boys are only at the point of entering a public school.

And the Bubble Bursts

Master Betty created an instant fad for young performers to play adults, until one of Shirley Temple's prototypes proved too much for an audience.

In November 1805, a Miss Mudie, called "The Theatrical Phenomenon," made her debut at Covent Garden, as Miss Peggy, in *The Country Girl*. A child apparently about eight years of age, but with a figure remarkably diminutive even for her years, she had in the preceding season played first-rate comic characters at Birmingham, Liverpool, Dublin and other theatres.

She repeated the words correctly, and her performance as an infant was surprising, but as an infant, the illusion was completely lost. In the first scene, the sentiments of the house were good-naturedly expressed; when Moody promised "to send her back into the country," the audience expressed their concurrence by loud applause. In the succeeding scenes when Miss Peggy came to be talked of as a "wife", as a "mistress," as an object of love and jealousy, the scene became so ridiculous that loud hissing and laughing ensued. When Peggy was with her guardian, Mr. Murray, who was not very tall, he was obliged to stoop to lay his hand on her head, to bend himself double to kiss her, and when she had to lay hold of his neckcloth to coax and pat his cheek, he was obliged to go almost on all fours. In the third act

Miss Peggy is seen walking in the Park, dressed in boy's clothes, when instead of appearing as a young man who ought to be "shown the town," she looked shorter than before, and even too little to be safely put into jacket and trousers. Yet Mr. Brunton, as her lover Belville, pursues her and is transported to find her under this disguise, while Mr. Murray, her pretended husband, is thrown into an agony of despair at the idea of another man taking her by the hand. The absurdity was too great to be endured; and there was a burst of censure from all parts of the house.

Miss Mudie, who was certainly no infant in assurance, and whose energy was not in the least damped by the marked disapprobation of the house, now walked to the front of the stage, with great confidence, though not without some signs of indignation, and said, "Ladies and gentlemen, I have done nothing to offend you, and as for those who are sent here to hiss me, I will be much obliged to you to turn them out." This bold speech, from such a baby, astonished the audience. Some laughed, some hissed, others called "off, off!," and many applauded. A loud cry for the manager succeeded, when the first tragedian of his day, Mr. Charles Kemble, appeared, to supplicate that the child might be allowed to finish the play. The audience, however, were inexorable, the part of Miss Peggy was transferred to a young lady whose age corresponded with the character, and Miss Mudie was withdrawn.

A Dwarf

Sometimes adults played the parts of children.

In the production of *Pizarro* in which Macready was playing, the child was in reality a dwarf, nearing forty years of age. Macready, however, did not know this. In making his way through the raging torrent with the "infant" perched on his shoulder, the great tragedian happened to stumble, whereupon a 'Cockney voice rasped his ear: "For Gawd's sike, cully, don't you go an' drop us!"

Getting On

Olive Logan related an American incident involving Dora, *a play based on Tennyson's poem.*

When the lady who plays the part of Mary Morrison made her exit to bring on her little Willie of four years, she was shocked to find a lubberly boy of at least fourteen, and as he was the only Willie at hand, on he must go, though he was well nigh as big as his mother. The Farmer Allen of the play, being equal to the emergency, instead of inquiring, "How old are you, my little man?" endeavored to remedy the matter by saying, "How old are you, my strapping boy?" But he failed, for the boy, who was instructed to say "four to six," said it in such a coarse, sepulchral tone as to drive the good-natured grandfather to exclaim, "Forty-six! You look it, my boy, you look it!"

Life Begins at Forty

Many actors who begin too young are robbed of their childhood, as was Mrs. Kendal, a famous actress in the latter part of the nineteenth century.

Little Madge Robertson was only three when she first put her tiny foot upon the stage. On this occasion she played the part of a blind child, but espying her nurse in the distance, she rushed to the wings, exclaiming: "Oh, Nannie, look at my beautiful new shoes!"

"I was grown up at ten," exclaimed Mrs. Kendal, the former Madge Robertson, "and first began to grow young at forty."

[7] STRUGGLES

Darned Socks

James Quin was one night going upon the stage in the character of Cato, when Mrs. Cibber pulled him back, to tell him he had a hole in his stocking. "Darned stockings I detest," said Quin, "that seems premeditated poverty."

A Rake's Progress

This portrait of a dissolute eighteenth-century actor, Thomas Weston, shows that some things have not changed very much in the theatre.

His debts increased, and before even the summer season was over he could never show his head in public unless on a Sunday. He then lived at Newington, in Surrey, and stole into the theatre, when he wanted, by a way few would have thought of. The doors of the Haymarket were always beset by bailiffs, and the back way, by Mr. Foote's house in Suffolk-street was also not safe; he therefore went into the Tennis-court, James-street, and getting out at the top of the building, entered the theatre by the upper windows of the dressing-rooms. This road he pursued for a whole season unsuspected, Dick Hughes always going before him as an advance-guard, to see that the coast was clear.

To avoid the inconvenience and danger of getting caught by the bailiffs, Weston moved into the Haymarket Theatre.

During this recess he kept close except on Sundays, and as the dressing-rooms wherein he lived were rather dark and dull, after dinner he usually brought a table into the lobby, and shutting the half-door, which had spikes on the top of it, took the air and smoked his pipe without fear of the bailiff. Once, indeed, he was outwitted; a man, whose face he was unacquainted with, came to the hatch, and having some clothes covered with green cloth, like a tailor, asked if Mr. Foote was at home. Tom unsuspectingly answered yes, and opened the hatch, where the bailiff entered and acquainted him that he had a writ against him. "Very well," said the delinquent, coolly, "follow me to Mr. Foote, who will settle it either by paying the money or giving security." The bailiff followed to the passage leading to the stage, behind the boxes, which was very dark, and along which he groped slowly; but Tom, knowing the way, soon got to the door, which had spikes also to it, and bolted it, then crossing the stage, went through Foote's house into Suffolk-street and escaped. He returned when the coast was clear, and was never after off his guard.

But the bailiffs got smarter, too.

Debts were continually on the increase, and the managers of Drury Lane had more than once released Weston; but the frequent repetition of his arrests made them resolve to do so no more. One day, when his name was in the bills, he being seized by a Marshalsea-court officer for a small debt, which the managers refused to have any thing to do with, Tom prevailed with the two officers to go to the play with him, and placed himself in the front of the two-shilling gallery. When the play was to begin, a performer came forward to make an apology for him, as being ill and unable to attend, hoping the audience would accept a substitute. On this Weston got upon the bench, and cried out that it was entirely false; that he was not ill, that he was ready to do his business on the stage, but that at present he was in the custody of a couple of bailiffs for a small debt, for which he had sent to the managers in the morning to give security, that he might have his enlargement; that they had refused, and that he submitted the whole to the consideration of the audience. This trick was successful, the managers sent for him, and the matter was settled.

More Bailiffs

Weston was by no means alone with his problems or the solution. John Palmer's embarrassed circumstances caused him at one time to live in his dressing room in the Drury Lane Theatre.

When the Haymarket re-opened for the summer season, at which he was engaged, the fear of arrest suggested the expedient of conveying him with a cart full of scenery, in one of the cabinets used in *The Prize*, and in this manner he actually was removed from one theatre to the other.

A similar story is told of William Phillips, a famous Harlequin and contemporary of Garrick. He was arrested for a debt, and lodged in a sponging-house. Having liberally treated the bailiff to drink, he pretended that he had a dozen bottles of wine ready packed at his house, which he begged permission to send for, to drink while he was in custody, offering to pay sixpence a bottle for the privilege. The bailiff acceded to his request, and the wine was ordered to be brought. When a porter presented himself with the load, the turnkey called to his master that the porter and hamper had come. "Very well," answered the bailiff; "then let nothing but the porter and hamper out." The porter acted his part well: came heavily with an empty hamper, and went lightly out with Phillips on his back.

The Acting Life

The struggles and privations of the actor have pathetic illustration in the story of Benjamin Webster's early career. Alas! he was unwise enough to marry at the age of nineteen a widow with a family. The necessity of setting to work in right good earnest was thus brought home to him. He could not travel for lack of means, but he walked many weary miles to many different towns in the hope of securing the post of a walking gentleman in some company. Failure succeeded failure, and he got deeper and deeper into debt:

"I had heard that Mr. Beverley of the Tottenham Street Theatre was about to open the Croydon Theatre for a brief season. I applied to him for walking gentleman. 'Full.' For little business and utility. 'Full.' For Harlequin and dancing. Don't do pantomime or ballet.' For orchestra. 'Well,' said he, in his peculiar manner, 'just now you were a walking gentleman!' 'So I am, sir; but I have had a musical education, and necessity sometimes compels me to turn it to account.' 'Well, what's your instrument?' 'Violin, tenor, violoncello, double bass, and double drums.' 'Well, by Nero!'—he played the fiddle, you know—'here, Harry' (calling his son), 'bring the double—no, I mean a violin—out of the orchestra.' Harry came with the instrument, and I was requested to give a taste of my quality. I began Tartini's 'Devil's Solo' and had not gone far when the old gentleman said that would do, and engaged me as his leader at a guinea a week.

"Had a storm of gold fallen on me it could not have delighted Semele more than me. I felt myself plucked out of the slough of despond. I had others to support, board myself, and to get out of debt. I resolved to walk to Croydon, ten miles every day, to rehearsal, and back to Shoreditch on twopence a day—one pennyworth of oatmeal, and one pennyworth of milk—and I did it for six weeks, Sundays excepted, when I indulged in the luxury of shin of beef and oxcheek. The gentlemen in the gallery pelted the orchestra with muttonpies. At first indignation was uppermost, but on reflection we made a virtue of necessity, and collecting the fragments of the not very light pastry, ate them under the stage."

Christmas on Stage

Ben Webster became one of the most prosperous managers of the nineteenth century.

A *Christmas Carol* became standard Christmas fare at the Adelphi. J. L. Toole, a famous comedian in the making, habitually played Bob Cratchet. He recounted that "Every night at 8 o'clock for forty nights I had to serve a goose and plum pudding. Mr. Webster provided a real goose and a real plum pudding, which were served smoking hot for the Cratchets' Christmas dinner." It became apparent that Tiny Tim, an ethereal, skin-and-bones little girl, was accounting for about three man-sized helpings every night, as she sat huddled on her little stool on the hearth. Watchers were strategically placed to try and solve the puzzle. They at last discovered that she was smuggling the food to a relay of small brothers and sisters, children of one of the stagehands, who were carefully concealed behind the fireplace.

Actor's Luck

Comedian Joe Frisco, a big spender, was advised by his agent to save some. "Use your bean: put away ten thousand dollars a year for the next ten years, and you'll have a hundred thousand in the bank. When the next depression hits us, you'll be sitting pretty." "Not me," scoffed Frisco. "With m-m-m-my luck, we wouldn't have any next depression, and there I'd be s-s-stuck with a hundred thousand bucks."

[8] THE GREAT ROLE

Lady Macbeth Shops in Byzantium

Ellen Terry's flaming Norse Queen was also an ardent woman, not at all in the "fiend-like" Siddons tradition, and she aroused furious argument. It is easy to visualize how she looked from Sargent's flaming picture of her in the glittering beetles'-wings dress. Oscar Wilde drily remarked: "Lady Macbeth seems an economical housekeeper, and evidently patronised local industries for her husband's clothes and the servants' liveries; but she takes care to do her own shopping in Byzantium."

The Role of Her Life

Many great actors long for a great role all their lives, especially one that they can create for the first time. Olivier claims to have had only one such part in his entire career: Archie Rice in John Osborne's The Entertainer. *Sir Ralph Richardson could never quite forgive himself for turning down a chance to play in the first English production of* Waiting for Godot. *Both of them were middle-aged by then. Others have been more lucky or determined. Here Sybil Thorndike describes how she and her director-husband, Lewis Casson, looked for and found the role of her life.*

We commissioned dear Laurence Binyon to write a play for us. I'd always wanted to play St. Joan, because I adored her. Then we suddenly saw in the newspaper that Shaw was writing one too. So Lewis wrote to him and said, "Here, Laurence Binyon's going to write the play for Sybil and me," and he said "Nonsense," on a postcard, "Nonsense, Sybil is playing my Joan, let so-and-so play Binyon's." You see, Shaw had seen me in *The Cenci*. Now in *The Cenci* there is this wonderful trial scene, and he went back to his wife Charlotte and said, "I'll write the play now; I've found the woman who can play it."

As usual, when Shaw was finished with the script, he held a reading. Dame Sybil recalls:

We went down with Bronson Albery and Cherry Garrard, the South Pole man, and we sat in Shaw's little room and he read it to us. I thought I'd *die*. It was that first scene; I thought, "God in heaven, you've given me something which I never dreamed that I was ever going to be asked to play." He read the first three scenes and then he came to the Tent Scene. Just before he read that he said, "Now the play really begins, the rest is all flapdoodle." But Shaw himself was a perfect Saint Joan; he could have played it far better than any of us.

   Shaw said to me, "Have you read all the histories?" I said, "Every single one of them." So he said, "Forget them. I'll tell you what to say." And when he read his play I knew they were all the things I passionately wanted to say. And to prove it, that's the only time, on a first night, that I haven't had one nerve. I was exalted. God was there and I didn't care a hoot for anything, except getting over what Shaw had written. Oh, what a wonderful man. I must tell you, he gave me a book, my book that I'd been rehearsing with, and he wrote in the beginning of it, "To Saint Sybil Thorndike from Saint Bernard Shaw."

Building a Part

It was Richard III, *at the Old Vic in 1944, that established Olivier as the preeminent Shakespearean actor of his generation.*

First of all I had heard imitations of old actors imitating Henry Irving; and so I did, right away, an imitation of these old actors imitating Henry Irving's voice—that's why I took a rather narrow kind of vocal address. Then I thought about looks. And I thought about the Big Bad Wolf, and I thought about Jed Harris, a director under whom I'd suffered *in extremis* in New York. The physiognomy of Disney's original Big Bad Wolf was said to have been founded upon Jed

Harris—hence the nose, which, originally, was very much bigger than it was finally in the film. And so, with one or two extraneous externals, I began to build up a character, a characterization. I'm afraid I do work mostly from the outside in. I usually collect a lot of details, a lot of characteristics, and find a creature swimming about somewhere in the middle of them. . . . Some people start from the inside, some people start from the periphery. I would say, at a guess, that Alec Guinness is what we would call a peripheral actor. I think I'm the same. The actor who starts from the inside is more likely to find himself in the parts he plays, than to find the parts in himself; perhaps not necessarily in himself, but simply to find the parts, go out to them and get them, and *be* somebody else.

Whose Role Is It Anyway?

When Laurence Olivier first played Hamlet in 1937, John Gielgud went backstage after the opening night and said, "Larry, it's one of the finest performances I have ever seen, but it's still my part."

Work-out

The young John Neville played Hamlet in 1957.

I remember when I first joined the Old Vic, Richard Burton was playing Hamlet and I was playing Fortinbras, which is nothing, no strain at all. He used to say that on the days when you're playing Hamlet—this is in repertoire, of course—you wake up in the morning and you know that that night you're going to play Hamlet, it hangs over you the entire day. I didn't really believe this was quite true until I actually played it myself, and it is quite true. It's such an enormous work-out, you use everything. You use your own personality, and if you play the role properly, you must use everything of your being; you are completely and utterly drained. I played it emotionally, I don't know any other way to play it, because there's a great deal of emotion in the role. It's very taxing indeed and I think you need to be something of an athlete both mentally and physically. I remember quite vividly the very first night I played it in London, it was quite a big first night for us all, I was actually physically sick at the end of the performance, I came straight off from the curtain calls and was violently sick.

Camp

Asked whether he might still play in Shakespeare, Noël Coward replied:

I think I've left it a bit late. I might play the nurse in *Romeo and Juliet.*

[9]   OLD AGE

Age Cannot Wither

Sarah Bernhardt played Joan of Arc with her wooden leg when she was seventy.

The curtain rose on her trial scene. She was discovered standing with her face to the backdrop. The first words spoken were an inquisitor's "How old are you?" "Eighteen." She said the word almost defiantly, then swung her face toward the audience, challenging them to disbelieve that she was the youthful and inspired Maid of Orleans.

The Old Trouper

In 1784 Charles Macklin accepted an engagement to perform in Dublin. He was then, at the lowest computation, eighty-five, but by strong probability, ninety-five; yet at this extraordinary age, by either computation, did he engage to visit a distant land, and to perform at least twice a week two of the most difficult parts. He fulfilled not only his engagement with spirit but visited Liverpool and Manchester in the course of his journey; performed at each some of his principal characters and continued, with scarcely any declension in his powers, till November 28, 1788, when he first experienced a decay in his memory. Next year, on January 10, 1789, his recollection again failed; his last attempt on the stage was on the seventh of May following, when he tried Shylock for his own benefit, which the manager, knowing the state of the old man's finances, had granted, but to prevent disappointment, had another actor to study the part, for he dreaded the veteran's infirmities.

Macklin, having dressed himself with his usual accuracy, went into the green room, and coming up to the late Mrs. Pope said, "My dear, are you to play to-night?" "Good God! to be sure I am; don't you see I am dressed for Portia?" "Ah, very true, I had forgot;—but who is to play Shylock?" The feeble sadness with which he who was dressed for the part of the Jew said this depressed all who heard it. Mrs. Pope, however, answered, rousing herself, "Why, you; are not you dressed for the part?" He put his hand to his forehead, and said, pathetically, "God help me!—my memory has, I fear, left me!"

The whole range of the invented drama has few more mournful scenes; the poor old man, ninety-two or a hundred and two years old, went upon the stage and delivered two or three speeches, but evidently did not understand what he was repeating; after some time, however, he recovered, but it was only a flash from the burnt-out candle in the socket. Nature could go no farther; he paused, a poor, weak, and despised old man, and looking helplessly around, said, "I can do no more," and retired from the stage for ever.

Bring Me a Pickled Elephant

Lester Wallack, from a long line of actors, heard this story from his father, James William Wallack.

Poor Elliston at last was so overcome with the gout that he could not act at all. He was then lessee of Old Drury Lane, and my father was the stage manager, appearing in Elliston's old parts. At that time at Exeter Change an elephant went mad, and became so dangerous that he had to be killed. It was nearly the first elephant ever exhibited alive in England, and naturally the incident was in everybody's mind. It was Elliston's habit to go to the theatre every night, particularly if one of his own celebrated characters was to be performed, and being wheeled down to the prompter's place in an invalid chair, he would sit and watch all that was going on. In the mad scene in *The Belle's Stratagem* (then playing), Dorincourt, who is feigning madness, has a little extravagant "business," and at a certain exit, utters some wildly absurd nonsense, such as: "Bring me a pigeon pie of snakes." On the night in question, when the town talked of nothing but the dead elephant, my father, on his exit after the mad scene, shouted: "Bring me a pickled elephant," to the delight of the easily pleased house, but to the disgust of the sensitive Elliston, who, shaking his gouty fist at him, cried: "Damn it, you lucky rascal; they never pickled an elephant for me when I played Dorincourt!"

Wheel of Fortune

The last years of George M. Cohan's life were embittered by the thought that the parade had passed him by, and that lines and devices for which people had cheered him in happier days were now regarded as "corny" and obvious. A succession of failures sharpened his resentment. Then came *Ah, Wilderness!* and a chance to star in a sure-fire hit. Cohan appeared in another author's play for the first time in years. The first-night audience gave him an ovation, and the critics sang his praises to the sky. Was Cohan happy? He was not! When a friend said, "Well, George, this is something like again, isn't it?" Cohan shook his head dejectedly and grumbled, "Imagine my reciting lines by Eugene O'Neill! Why, he ought to be on the stage reciting lines by me!"

Mrs. Pat

Sir John Gielgud tells the story of his effort to find a play suitable for Mrs. Patrick Campbell towards the very end of her career. He eventually found one he felt might work: in it she was to play an ex-opera singer who took pupils in a mountain chalet. This lady spent the first act making pasta and singing snatches from her past triumphs. In the second act her daughter was forced to disguise herself as the Virgin Mary and hide in a church, to escape the wrath of the local peasants after having had an affair with one of their number. Mrs. Pat was not taken with the idea: "I suppose you want me to play the daughter," she said, aged seventy and portly with it.

[10]   RETIREMENT

Mrs. Woffington Repents

It is related of Peg Woffington that, having heard a sermon which turned on sins similar to her past errors, she was so filled with sorrow at the manner in which she had lived, that she resolved to quit the theatre and endeavour to improve her life—a resolution which she carried strictly into effect; and without the airs of a devotee or the cant of a Methodist, continued in her penitence with exemplary propriety to the end. After her retirement her conduct is spoken of, by all who have expressed an opinion of her, as something like a phenomenon. It was simple, graceful and pious. It partook of all that was blameless in her previous life. The stage alone she regarded with some degree of aversion, because it had ministered to her early vices, and professed to teach virtue, but was far otherwise in effect. In this respect, some of those who were offended with her retirement, thought they could perceive affectation; but their own spleen deceived them—for she was one of those few penitents who condemn their follies, but do not let their contrition corrode their amiable qualities.

Remembrance of Things Past

After she left the stage Mrs. Siddons, from the want of excitement, was never happy. When I* was sitting with her of an afternoon she would say, "Oh, dear! this is the time I used to be thinking of going to the theatre; first came the pleasure of dressing for my part, and then the pleasure of acting it; but that is all over now." When a grand public dinner was given to John Kemble on his quitting the stage, Mrs. Siddons said to me, "Well, perhaps in the next world women will be more valued than they are in this." She alluded to the comparatively little sensation which had been produced by her own retirement from the boards, and doubtless she was a far, far greater performer than John Kemble.

Contentment

The actor J. L. Toole visited Macready after his retirement to Cheltenham.

It had been said that he was not over-polite to some of his profession, and that, in a general way, he was exclusive and difficult to approach. I found him the opposite of this; a fine, distinguished old man, white hair, very courteous, and with a most pleasant smile—a trifle melancholy perhaps—a touch of Werner, but a gentle and human touch. We had a long chat; he spoke of his last appearance, and I said how I honoured him for making it his last when he said it was, the more so that I knew that he had had tremendous offers to induce him to reappear. And, of course, this was very honourable in Macready, seeing that he had managed Drury Lane often at a loss, in the interests of art, and only retired just in time to keep a remnant of his fortune to live on in a quiet way. Considering that he was not rich, there was

* Samuel Rogers.

something very dignified in refusing offers of great and certain sums to appear again, especially in the face of examples of ladies and gentlemen, operatic and otherwise, taking not one farewell, but half-a-dozen . . . He said he did not believe in an actor remaining on the stage after his powers were at an end; he thought a man should retire in the zenith of his strength; and he believed that he had played Macbeth on that last night as well as ever he had played it. I confirmed this; and it pleased him very much when I told him that I had stood at the entrance of Drury Lane on his farewell appearance for five hours.

Give My Regards to Broadway

In 1952 Ethel Merman married Robert Six, then the president of Continental Airlines. Miss Merman settled into a huge mansion in Denver and tried to live, as many actresses before and a few since, as a private person. Columnist Leonard Lyons visited the actress in her retirement.

Dusk was settling over the Rockies, and it was time to leave. The last songs of the album were George M. Cohan's "45 Minutes from Broadway." Ethel sang along, but the transplanted Broadway star sang it "45 Hours from Broadway." Then it ended, with the record and the hostess singing "Give My Regards to Broadway," and the Sixes drove me to the airport.

In a corner of the room I'd noticed two copies of *Variety*. And as we drove through Ethel Merman's new home-city, Denver, I remembered a story about Lylian Tashman, who had said that stardom palled and expressed a wish to get far away from all show business. "I want to retire to a faraway desert island," Miss Tashman had sighed. "A beautiful desert island, with a stretch of sea and sand and moonlight—just enough moonlight to read *Variety* by."

[11] EXIT LINES

The Epilogue

After Nell Gwyn had died in some character and the servants of the stage were preparing to carry her off, she started up and exclaimed—

Hold off, you d——d confounded dog!
I am to rise and speak the epilogue.

Death Scene

Mr. Powell, so eminent for his tragic powers, may be literally said to have felt "the ruling passion strong in death." When he was on his death-bed, and Mrs. Powell had left the room, Mrs. Hannah More, who sat by his bedside, was alarmed by observing his cheek suddenly assume a lively colour. He at the same time threw himself into the proper attitude, and exclaimed, "Is that a dagger that I see before me?" A moment after this, as if sensible of his danger, he cried out, "O God!" and instantly expired.

Lucid Interval

Mrs. Mountford, who was the identical fair beauty on whom Gay founded his celebrated ballad of Black-eyed Susan, was an actress of considerable fame. After her retirement from the stage, love and the ingratitude of a bosom friend deprived her of her senses, and she was placed in a receptacle for lunatics. One day, during a lucid interval, she asked her attendant what play was to be performed that evening, and was told it was *Hamlet*. Whilst on the stage, she had been received with rapture as Ophelia. The recollection struck her and with the cunning which is so often allied to insanity she eluded the care of the keepers and got to the theatre. There she concealed herself until the scene in which Ophelia enters in her insane state; she then pushed on the stage, before the lady who performed the character could come on, and exhibited a more perfect representation of madness than the utmost exertions of mimic art could effect; she was in truth Ophelia herself, to the amazement of the performers and astonishment of the audience.

Nature having made this last effort, her vital powers failed her. On going off, she exclaimed, "It is all over!" She was immediately conveyed back to her late place of security, and a few days after—

Like a lily drooping, she hung her head, and died.

Heritage

Talma, the greatest French actor of the Napoleonic era, had his first success in Voltaire's play Mahomet. *He died with the playwright's name on his lips.*

"Voltaire . . . ! comme Voltaire . . . toujours comme Voltaire . . ."
He left behind only a collection of costumes, which were bought by a
provincial actor so that he could advertise: "Monsieur Delaistre will
appear this evening in Talma's costume."

Farewell Dream

The last performance of Edmund Kean was at Covent Garden, March
25, 1833, in *Othello*, his son Charles sustaining the part of Iago. On
arriving at the third act Edmund became faint and swooned away in
the arms of his son. Warde, another actor, was called in to finish the
part. Removed to Richmond, Kean did not live long. About two
hours before his death, a friend who was keeping sleepy watch by his
bedside was startled by hearing him shout: "A horse! A horse! My
kingdom for a horse!" and seeing him spring up from his couch. It
was the farewell dream of his earthly greatness.

Tribute

The actress Fanny Kemble upon the death of Edmund Kean:

Kean is gone, and with him are gone Othello, Shylock, and Richard.
I have lived among those whose theatrical creed would not permit
them to acknowledge him as a great actor; but they must be bigoted
indeed who would deny that he was a great genius—a man of most
original and striking powers, careless of art, perhaps because he did
not need it, but possessing those rare gifts of nature without which
art is as a dead body . . . If he was irregular and unartist-like in his
performance, so is Niagara compared with the waterworks of Versailles.

Epitaphs

On Mr. King, late of Drury Lane:

> Here lies a crownless monarch, though a King,
> Sans lands, sans subjects, and sans everything.

On Samuel Foote, the mimic:

> Foote from his earthly stage, alas! is hurled;
> Death took him off, who took off all the world.

Thomas Jackson, who was a favorite provincial actor, lies buried in the church-yard of Gillingham, Norfolk, with the following curious epitaph inscribed on his tombstone:

Sacred to the memory of Thomas Jackson, Comedian, who was engaged December 21, 1741, to play a comic cast of characters in this great Theatre, the World, for many of which he was prompted by nature to excel. The season being ended, his benefit over, the charges all paid, and his account closed, he made his exit in the Tragedy of "Death," on the 17th of March, 1798, in full assurance of being called once more to rehearsal; when he hopes to find his forfeits all cleared, his cast of parts bettered, and his situation made agreeable by Him who paid the great stock-debt for the love he bore to performers in general.

Final Respects

Henry Irving was buried in Westminster Abbey. On the day of his funeral, all the London cabbies tied a black bow on their whips.

Life on Stage

[12]   REHEARSALS

Lesson

John Coleman was a young actor when he had an opportunity to play on the same stage with the Eminent Tragedian of his day, William Macready.

It is scarcely possible to convey an idea of what we, the youth of that day, gained by being brought into contact with Macready at rehearsal. He poured forth knowledge in reckless, never-ending profusion. Our only difficulty in following his directions was that sometimes they were given sotto voce and in a growl. In rehearsing the last scene of *Werner,* he said to me: "Sir, will you be good enough to—err—to do me the favour when I say—err—err—to stand—err—err—and don't move hand or foot till I lift my—err—err—you understand?" "Not quite, sir." "Good God, sir, am I not speaking the English language?" expostulated the great tragedian. "I presume so, sir, but as it is my misfortune not to clearly understand, if you will kindly tell me intelligibly where I am to stand when you say, 'err—err,' I won't move hand or foot until you lift your err—err." He looked at me dubiously and even angrily for a moment and then repeated the directions with clearness and precision.

Her Own Audience

One day Rachel, alone on the stage, was going through her great scene of *Angelo.* I* had slipped quietly into my stage-box. Not a living soul was near us. At her last line I leaped upon the stage and embraced her. "You were sublime," I said, "as if Aeschylus and Corneille themselves were sitting in the pit, and still there was no one there." "I beg your pardon, dear friend, you were there." "And if I had not been there?" "There would still have been myself."

* Arsène Houssaye, director of the Comédie-Française in the middle of the nineteenth century.

Getting His Point Across

At a rehearsal of *Venice Preserved*, when a new actress highly recommended to Garrick was to make her debut as Belvidera, she repeated the tender exclamation, "Would you kill my father, Jaffier?" with so much sang-froid, that Garrick whispered to her in the ear, and in much the same tone: "Can you chop cabbage, madam?"

Low Form

Henrietta Hodson was rehearsing in a play written and produced by W. S. Gilbert. One day she made a move that Gilbert had expressly asked her not to make and went to sit on a chair center stage. Inadvertently she missed the chair and landed heavily on the floor instead. "Very good!" shouted Gilbert from the stalls, "I always knew you would make an impression on the stage one day."

Double Entendre

The actor-manager Robert Atkins was having a read-through of his next *al fresco* Shakespeare production on the grass in Regent's Park when one young actress failed to come in with her line. Atkins, seeing her sitting cross-legged and dejected, with her head in her lap, snapped at her: "It's no good looking up your entrance, dear. You've missed it."

Freudian Slip

In the Old Vic production of Hamlet in 1937, Guthrie and Olivier were much influenced by Freudian theory. Ernest Jones, Freud's English biographer and author of a book called Hamlet and Oedipus, advised on the production. The following year, Olivier was to play Iago to Ralph Richardson's Othello, and he tells the famous story of how he got carried away with some of Jones's suggestions.

Nobody has ever really disputed what makes up Othello, but they've certainly wondered about Iago, what makes him such a thoroughly beastly fellow as he is; and Jones's theory was that Iago was subconsciously in love with Othello. Well, Tony Guthrie and I were completely sold on this idea. Ralph wouldn't hear of it at all. However, there came one moment in rehearsal, so the story goes, and I don't remember this—that losing all control of myself, I flung my arms round Ralph's neck and kissed him. Whereat Ralph, more in sorrow than in anger, sort of patted me and said, "Dear fellow, dear boy," much more pitying me for having lost control of myself than despising me for being a very bad actor.

The whole production proved to be a disaster.

After the performance Richardson was to be seen wandering forlornly up and down the corridor outside his dressing-room, enquiring of passers-by, "Has anyone seen my talent? It was always small, but it used to be shining."

Big Bad Wolfit

Ronald Harwood's The Dresser *has popularized on stage and film the formidable actor-manager Sir Donald Wolfit on whom the character of "Sir" is based. This picture of Wolfit at rehearsal is from the biography by Ronald Harwood, who had in fact been Wolfit's dresser.*

To Wolfit, rehearsals were the means of getting the externals right; his own interpretation was conceived in private, and developed by playing the part repeatedly. He therefore mumbled his speeches in order to give time to the other characters; this method had grave drawbacks. When breaking-in, for example, a new Edgar in *King Lear*, Wolfit would recite the King's part *sotto voce e molto prestissimo*, cut to cue perhaps, so that when the new actor was confronted on the opening night with a Lear of the first magnitude, poor Tom, inadequately rehearsed by any standards, would flounder and falter through the complexities of the character.

The Clash of Titans

William Redfield played Guildenstern in the famous Gielgud-Burton production of Hamlet *that ran on Broadway in 1964. His book about the rehearsals,* Letters from an Actor, *is full of delicious gossip and insights, including this vignette of the competition between the director, John Gielgud, and the star, Richard Burton.*

As our rehearsal time passes, one senses a tension between the two men. There can be no doubt of their mutual affection and respect, but some of Gielgud's manner and conversation implies the helpless resig-

nation of a man whose leadership is being denied. Mr. Burton is entirely courteous, but two of his remarks are worth quoting. To one of
Gielgud's suggested readings involving heavy emphasis on the word
"I," Burton replied, "John, dear, you are in love with pronouns, but I
am not." It caused a good deal of jocund laughter, Gielgud's included,
but it must have stung a bit. Another time, when Sir John proposed a
rather elaborate staging around a table during one of his soliloquies,
Burton rested his chin in one hand and murmured, "It is a possibility,
of course, but so is sitting still."

[13] NERVES

Contempt

Sir Frank Benson was fond of telling the story of the junior member
of his company who was once overwhelmed with stage fright. The
young actor came on and was immediately at a loss for words. All he
could remember was that his character was to show contempt for the
hero—and contempt he certainly showed when he strode up to him,
looked at him blankly for a moment, then spat in his face. Without
saying a word, the young actor then swaggered off.

Foreknowledge

*Ellen Terry was notorious for forgetting her lines, a problem often
compounded by opening night nerves that most actors experience.
The designer W. Graham Robertson tells this story about her.*

Always nervous on a first night, Miss Terry was more than usually so
in *Henry VIII* and suddenly swept in upon me on the very day of the
production in a highly distraught condition exclaiming, "I've just
come in to tell you that I'm going to break down tonight. I can tell
you the very line—it's in the scene with the two cardinals. I'm going
to dry up—dead!"
  "But if you know the line—why dry up?"
  "I can't tell you why, but I know I shall," she said. And she did.

Coping

Carol Channing stays up all night before an opening, going over every word. Sir Laurence Olivier did this on the night before his first

Richard III at the New Theatre in 1944. During the dress rehearsals, Olivier had suffered some alarming lapses of memory, which, for one who enjoys almost photographic recall of the text, was a very sinister omen. He was filled with a superstitious fear that the play would be the ugly duckling of the repertoire and that he would experience a really crucifying failure. The night before the opening he and Vivien Leigh and Garson Kanin went over the whole part again and again in a suite at Claridge's. The rest is history.

Some actors feel sick, quite literally sick, like Bob Hoskins who has been sick on first nights so many times that he gets worried if he isn't sick, and then somehow has to contrive to make himself sick before he can act. Alec Guinness develops a crippling pain in his knees and back. George Arliss would walk round the theatre several times before he dared enter, not only on first nights, but every night. José Ferrer, by a monumental effort of mind, convinced himself that everybody in the audience was a personal friend. Al Jolson did likewise, which was a little easier in his case as many of them were, and those who weren't, felt that they were. It was a thousand pities that he could never muster the nerve to cross the Atlantic and perform in England. Money beyond the dreams of Solomon was laid at his feet for a brief London season, and, after his films were released, his fan mail from England could have left him in no doubt as to the warmth of his reception there, but he regarded foreign appearances as very bad luck, and the thought of appearing in front of a strange audience filled him with superstitious terror. "If there's just one guy who ain't enjoying the show," he once said in explanation, "I'll know it and that'll kill me."

Who's Noivous?

On the opening night of *Annie Get Your Gun* in New York, Ethel Merman stood casually in the wings of the Imperial Theatre listening to the overture and waiting for the curtain to rise. Some say that she was chewing a stick of Juicy Fruit gum, and I wouldn't be a bit surprised, since the lady's relaxation is as notorious as her performing. Nearby, a chorus girl—less than twenty years old—was busily grinding her dance slippers into a resin box and alternately bouncing up and down in second position. She was candidly terrified and apparently trying to bump and grind her fears away. Eventually she forgot her horrors long enough to notice Miss Merman: dead-pan, fist-on-hip, jaws-slowly-working-gum, and looking altogether like a well-fed policeman off duty. "Oh, Miss Merman!" the girl cried. "You look so, so—unperturbed! Aren't you nervous?" Miss Merman removed a wad of exhausted gum from her mouth and dropped it precisely into a trash can. "Why should I be nervous?" she said. "I know my lines."

Sleeping

The other extreme is to be so totally devoid of nerves that one could even sleep on stage, as Sarah Bernhardt recalls here.

I have seen Coquelin sleeping soundly on the stage sheltered by supers during two or three minutes when he had nothing to say. A young actor named Chabert, who was very attached to him, would wake him up, and Coquelin, refreshed by three minutes of absolute isolation, would resume his part with zest.

[14] LINES

When in Rome

Of Colley Cibber the following incident is recorded. Playing one night in a Roman comedy, and coming to the words, "I was then in Rome," he stuck fast. He looked for assistance from the prompter, and not getting it he rushed to the wings, seized the fellow by the collar, dragged him to the footlights, and exclaimed, "Hang you, you scoundrel, what was I doing in Rome? Why don't you tell me?"

The Prompter

In the modern theatre the prompter has become almost obsolete, though in some European houses the box downstage center is still inhabited. Through the centuries, actors sometimes supplemented their income by prompting, or failed aspirants resigned themselves to the vicarious glory of the stage through such close proximity. Unfortunately, some of them developed embittered, vengeful personalities.

It is told of Old Barry, as he was called, formerly prompter in the Dublin Theatre, that he was so entirely independent of, and abstracted from the portion of the text actually going on, that on an actor's "sticking" one night, and looking anxiously toward Barry at the wing for the "word" (as it is called), Barry, who was, of course, engaged in some other business at the time, and his thoughts far away, took not the slightest notice of the appeal; till the actor at last, in despair, called out: "Barry, give me the word, will you?" To which Barry, with the imperturbability of a prompter, and the exquisite unconsciousness of an Irishman, replied, loud enough for the audience to hear: "What word, my boy?" and coolly wetting his thumb, began turning over the leaves to catch up with the unfortunate defaulter.

Too Much Help

Everybody knew of Ellen Terry's inability to memorize. When studying for one of her greatest roles in Irving's production of Madame Sans-Gêne, *she withdrew to a quiet seaside resort. She never did learn her lines.*

On the opening night there were prompters concealed at every entrance, behind the window curtains and in the fireplace; the moment she paused a volley of mutters and hisses would come from every part of the stage at once. Finally, in complete bewilderment, she stopped dead, clapped her hands together, and said in ringing tones, "Will *nobody* give me the word?"

Lapse

Sarah Bernhardt here describes the actor's nightmare.

On one occasion I had a very serious lapse of memory on the stage, of which I was not aware at the time. It occurred in London at the Gaiety Theatre. The previous evening I had been ill; overwork had brought on such a hemorrhage that Doctor Vintras and Parrot refused to let me play in the evening my part in *L'Etrangère* of Alexandre Dumas. I took no notice. The opium which they gave me in a potion left my head a little heavy. I went on the stage, almost unconscious but delighted with the reception I received. I walked in a dream and had difficulty in distinguishing my surroundings. The sound of my voice sounded to me very far away. I was in that delicious stupor that one experiences after morphia, opium, or hasheesh.

The first act passed off very well, but during the third act, just when I was relating to the Duchesse de Septmonts (played by Croizette) all the ills that had befallen me, Mrs. Clarkson, in my life, just as I should have commenced my interminable story, I could not remember anything at all. Croizette whispered my first words, but I could only see her lips moving without hearing a word. I then said quite calmly: "The reason I sent for you here, Madame, is because I wanted to apprise you of my reasons for acting as I have done . . . I have thought it over, and have decided not to tell you them to-day."

Sophie Croizette stared at me terrified, rose and left the stage, her lips trembling and her eyes fixed on me. "What is the matter?" they said to her, when she sank almost breathless into a chair.

"Sarah has gone mad! I assure you she has gone quite mad! She has cut out the whole of her scene with me.—How!—She has cut out two hundred lines! Why? I do not know. She seemed quite calm."

All this conversation, which was subsequently retailed to me, took less time than it takes to write it down. Coquelin was warned and he went on the stage to finish the act. After the curtain had fallen, I remained dazed and gloomy at what I had been told. I had been aware of nothing. Under the influence of opium, I had lost my memory for a moment. Happily I recovered it for the few things I had to do in the fifth act, in which I acquitted myself perfectly. I hardly dare confess that the audience did not notice the accidental cut.

Memory

Robert Wilks was, in all his parts, perfect to such exactitude, that in forty years he rarely changed or misplaced an article in any one of them. In a new comedy, he once happened to complain of a crabbed speech in his part, which gave him more trouble to study than all the rest, and he applied to the author to soften or shorten it. The dramatist, that he might make the matter quite easy to him, fairly cut it all out; but when Wilks went home from the rehearsal, he thought it such an indignity to his memory that any thing should be deemed too hard for him that he actually made himself perfect in that speech, though he knew it was never to be spoken.

Charles Macklin had an excellent memory well into his eighties. One day he was boasting at his favorite tavern that he had trained his memory to such perfection that he could recite anything after hearing it once. Samuel Foote happened to be present jotting something down.

Foote handed Macklin the following sentences, desiring he would read them once, and then repeat them: "So she went into the garden to cut a cabbage-leaf, to make an apple-pie; and at the same time a great she-bear coming up the street, pops its head into the shop. 'What! no soap?' So he died, and she very imprudently married the barber; and there were present the Picninnies, and the Joblillies, and the Garynlies, and the Grand Panjandrum himself, with the little round button at top; and they all fell to playing the game of catch-as-catch-can till the gunpowder ran out of the heels of their boots."

The laugh was not with Macklin.

Another actor with an astonishing memory was John Henderson, much admired in the latter half of the eighteenth century. His skills were tested by a Professor Dugald Stewart.

In the philosopher's presence he took up a newspaper, and after reading it once, repeated such a portion of it as to Mr. Stewart seemed marvellous. When he expressed his surprise, Henderson modestly replied, "If you had been like me—obliged to depend during many years for your daily bread on getting words by heart, you would not be so much astonished at habit having produced this facility."

Association

Macready was once victimised in the play *Virginius*. The actor playing the character of Numitorius could not remember his own name. "You will remember it, sir," said the tragedian, carefully pronouncing it for him, "by the association of ideas. Think of Numbers, the Book of Numbers." Numitorius did think of it all day, and at night produced, through "the association of ideas," the following effect:

Numitorius: Where is Virginia? Wherefore do you hold that maiden's hand?

Claudius: Who asks the question?

Numitorius: I, her uncle—Deuteronomy!

Acting by Rote

It is not enough to memorize the lines; an actor also has to be on the ball.

Mr. Bransley (a comedian, some years since, on Drury-lane boards) could never vary in the least from the text of the author; and, if any other person on the stage with him fell into that error, Bransley generally produced some whimsical effect, by adhering too closely to the original words. He was playing one night, and this question being put to him—"Are you this young lady's father?"—had to say—"I am." The person who had to put the interrogatory varied the words, but strictly preserved the sense. He said, "Is this young lady your daughter?" to which Bransley very pompously replied, "I am!"

Adapting Shakespeare

Julia Marlowe, as Olivia, forgot the rest of her lines in the scene with the Friar in *Twelfth Night*. Without a hint of anxiety, she turned to the actor and said:

> Then lead the way, good father—And heavens so shine,
> I can't remember another blessed line.

Leveling

On one occasion George Grossmith forgot the words of a song he had been singing for nearly a year: it was the Lord Chancellor's song in *Iolanthe*. "There were two verses very nearly alike," says Mr. Grossmith, "and this is always a ticklish task for any singer. My prompter was not there, and I broke down. I did not lose my temper, though the situation was trying. I said to the audience: 'I have been singing this song 300 times, and it is so long since I learned it that I have forgotten the words.' This was received with roars of laughter, and I commenced again, and broke off once more at the same place. The people were very much amused, and I said: 'If you don't mind waiting for a moment I will go and see if there is such a thing as a prompter.' And so I went off, found the book in the side wing, refreshed my memory by a glance, and returned to render the song."

The whole thing was such a success that Mr. Grossmith often said he would do it again.

Word Perfect

Noël Coward had a disconcerting habit of turning up to a first rehearsal absolutely word perfect, even if it was not his own play.

I believe that learning the part and each cue with a postcard over the page, which I do relentlessly, is the most horrible drudgery. And if I make one mistake on a page I go right back to the beginning again, until I've not only learnt it with this part of my mind, but with that part. I don't worry about whether I'm getting at the right meaning at this point. When I get up on the stage, the words give me the meaning; you can't know it better than the words. It's not only knowing it by heart, it's more than that. It's knowing it inside, getting to what the Lunts call the silky stage.

Coward was equally demanding of others.

During rehearsal he was criticising an actress for being very slow with her lines in a scene they were playing together. Finally, very worked up, the actress screamed: "If you go on like that I'll throw something at you." Coward replied sweetly: "You might start with my cues."

On another occasion an actor continually fluffed a French phrase in rehearsal. At last The Master asked the actor if he could speak French. "Un petit peu," was the reply. "I never think that's really quite enough," said Coward.

Claudette Colbert was having trouble with her lines when rehearsing a live TV show of *Blithe Spirit* in New York. Tempers were beginning to blaze one morning when Miss Colbert said apologetically: "I'm sorry. I knew these lines backwards last night." "And that's exactly the way you are saying them this morning," snapped the usually urbane playwright.

[15] IN THE VINEYARDS OF THE LORD

The Old Excuse

In ancient Greece theatre was celebrated in honor of Dionysus, the god of wine. The connection has been cherished by individual members of the profession ever since.

The celebrated Ned Shuter delighted to exhibit his eccentricities among the lowest company in St. Giles's, where he has been known more than once to treat a dozen of the rabble with drams and strong beer. His sober apology for such absurdities was that in his walk of drama it was necessary that he should know life from the prince to the beggar in order to represent them as occasion might require.

The Morning After

Kean had gone to dine somewhere about ten miles from town with
some players. Temptation and the bottle were too strong for him; he
outstayed his time, drank to excess, and lost all recollection of Shakespeare, Shylock and Drury Lane. His friends, frightened at the indis-
cretion they had caused, despatched Kean's servant with his empty
chariot and a well-framed story that the horses had been frightened,
the carriage had been upset, and the tragedian's shoulder dislocated.
This story was repeated from the stage by the manager; and the rising
indignation of the audience was instantly calmed down into commis-
eration and regret. The following morning Kean was shocked and bewildered at discovering the truth of his situation. But how must his
embarrassment have increased on learning that several gentlemen had
already arrived from town to make anxious inquiries after him? Luckily
his old associates, the actors, had with great presence of mind and
practised effrontery, carried on the deception of the preceding night.
The village apothecary lent himself to it, and with a grave countenance confirmed the report; and Kean was obliged to become a part,
nolens volens, to the hoax. His chamber was accordingly darkened, his
face whitened, and his shoulder bandaged. No one discovered the
cheat; and to crown it completely, he appeared in an incredibly short
time on the boards of old Drury again, the public being carefully informed that his respect and gratitude towards them urged him to risk
the exertion, and to go through his arduous parts with his arm in a
sling!

What Greatness Here Is O'erthrown!

*Many theatrical careers have been ruined by alcohol. "Er trank und
sank" ("He drank and sank")—a pithy epitaph for a German comedian in Leipzig called Klager—could grace a number of famous actors'
tombstones. Sol Smith describes the ravages of drinking on one of his
most brilliant contemporaries.*

I was acquainted with Junius Brutus Booth for about a quarter of a
century. When I first knew him (in 1827) he was a truly great actor,
and continued so to be until he fell into bad company in New Orleans, and took to hard drink. Then he became undependable, and,
"putting an antic disposition on," made many believe that he was

crazy. I never believed him to be a crazy man except when he was excited by liquor, and that was pretty often—nearly all the time, in fact. After Tom Flynn broke his nose he was a different man and an indifferent actor. His face, which had been beautiful and intellectual, became almost disgusting to see; his voice, which had been of great power and sweetness, became harsh and nasal—he was completely changed. The present generation had not seen the Booth that I knew.

Me? Drunk?

There are many extant versions of the following. This is Sir Cedric Hardwicke's.

The touring Shakespeareans always played *Richard III* on Saturday nights, after they had been handed their pay on Saturday afternoon so that they could settle up with their landladies before they moved on to the next town. One Saturday, the actor playing the Duke of Gloucester devoted his money to a more gratifying cause than paying for his lodgings. He made his entrance in *Richard* swaying like a ship at sea. The rowdies in the audience took only one look at him before they started yelling, "Get off; you're drunk!" Gloucester steadied himself and straightened out his assumed hump back. At full height and in a voice that reached the gallery, he intoned, "What? Drunk? Me? Just wait 'til you see Buckingham."

Playing Drunk

Lekain and Garrick were excellent friends, and each fancied the other his superior. One day Garrick and Lekain amused themselves in the Champs-Elysées by counterfeiting drunkenness to the great amusement of a crowd of bystanders. Lekain at length said: "Well, my friend, do I perform it well?" "Yes," replied Garrick hiccuping, "very well; you are drunk all over, except your left leg."

Unusual Role

The Duke of Norfolk was much addicted to the bottle. On a masquerade night he asked Samuel Foote what new character he should go in. "Go sober," said Foote.

A Prayer

Most drinking stories are about men, but at least one actress was fa-
mous for her drinking.

It is true that Tallulah "adores" all liquids containing alcohol, regardless of proof, with the exception of Scotch. She likes mint juleps, Du-
bonnet, Rhine wine, vermouth cassis, bourbon and soda, rye old-
fashioned, champagne, beer, cognac, ale, or stout—and she likes them
in quantity. One of her favorites is a little witches' brew called a
French 75—brandy laced with champagne. She can polish off six
French 75's without losing her invariable sang-froid. At Sardi's, where
she often lunches, her favorite meal—which is not on the table d'hôte—
is a bowl of vichysoisse and four daiquiris.

  . . . In connection with her drinking habits, she goes through a
quaint ritual in her dressing room a few moments before she makes
her first entrance on the opening night of a new play. She kneels
down before gold-framed photographs of her mother and father which
rest on her dressing table. She crosses her heart and silently prays,
"Dear God, please don't let me make a fool of myself tonight." Then
she swallows a glass of champagne.

[16] PULLING LEGS

Ad Lib

Like students, actors love practical jokes. Standard pranks include mis-
laid costumes or props, booby traps laid for unwary novices, or faked
letters of adulation to vain members of the cast. H. Allen Smith, who
wrote the book on practical jokes, mentions such sophomoric tricks as
holding an oyster or a ball of cold cream when having to shake hands
with another character on stage. He calls the stage a ribber's paradise.

There is the story about Eve Arden and a stage telephone. She was
playing in a summer theatre and was in the midst of a long and important speech when the telephone rang. It wasn't supposed to. She
stopped and glanced at the actor who was on stage with her. There
was just enough of a smirk on his face to tell her that he had arranged
the rib. She stepped quickly to the telephone, answered the call, then
turned to the actor and said, "It's for you." His efforts to ad lib a tele-

phone conversation were quite unconvincing and when he finished his poor performance, Miss Arden resumed her speech as if nothing happened.

The practice of veering from the script and inserting ad-lib remarks, thus messing up cue lines, also has a long history in the theatre. Playing King Lear, the great Edwin Booth addressed Edgar: "What's your study?" Edgar replied, quite properly, "How to prevent the fiend, and to kill vermin."

Booth then dead-panned a line that Shakespeare forgot to write: "Skeeters and sitch?"

It took Edgar quite a little while to get back on the track.

A Sneezing Actor

While Tom Flynn, the comedian, was at the Bowery Theatre, New York, the celebrated Junius Brutus Booth played an engagement there, during which *Julius Caesar* was produced—Booth as Cassius; Hamblin (the manager), Brutus; and John Woodhull as Mark Antony. Hamblin, after dressing, repaired to the green room, and, having a bad cold which somewhat impaired his speech, asked Flynn what he could do for it. Tom, who never lost the chance for a joke, let it hit where it would, said, "Use my remedy." "What's that?" asked Hamblin. "Why, get some vinegar in a tea-cup, put some snuff in it, mix the two together, pour it into your hand, and inhale it through your nose."

Hamblin, not thinking of the consequences, took a sufficient quantity to produce a fit of sneezing, which he found very difficult to overcome. After going upon the stage, he saluted the audience with a sneeze, and struggled hard to smother the effects of the snuff, but without avail. He began—"What is that you would (sneeze) impart to me? If it be aught toward the general good (d——— the snuff) set honour in one eye (sneeze) and death in the other; and I will look (sneeze) on both indifferently. For let the gods so speed me, as I love (sneeze) the name of (sneeze) honor more than I fear death (curse that Flynn)." All his efforts to check the effects of Flynn's remedy, which proved worse than the disease, were unavailing. The sneezing became contagious with the Bowery boys, for immediately after one of Brutus's convulsions, an immense sneeze would echo from the audience. Flynn sat in the boxes enjoying Hamblin's discomfort. What rendered the affair more ridiculous was that Hamblin several times attempted to sneeze, but failing, the audience did it for him, and then,

when they expected the actor would remain quiet, he would give another sneeze, which would cause the whole house to roar with laughter, thus converting the tragedy into a laughable farce.

After the play, Hamblin rushed into the green room, and said to
Flynn, "What in the name of heaven did you advise me to take that
infernal mess for?" Tom, standing before the grate with his hands under his coat-tails, replied with the utmost coolness, "Why, it always
cures me of a cold in the head, Mr. Hamblin, when I take it," and as
the sneezing Brutus left the green room, Flynn turned to Booth, who
had been standing in one corner of the room enjoying the joke, and
said "Why, Junius, my boy, I never thought before that your performance of Cassius was to be sneezed at."

Alas, Poor Yorick!

*George Vandenhoff, the nineteenth-century actor, recalls the follow-
ing in his* Dramatic Reminiscences (1860).

There was a low comedian, familiarly called Dick Hoskins, whom I
occasionally encountered at several of the small country theatres in
the North of England, and who was an inveterate and practical joker
on the stage. He was always very well behaved with me; but when he
came in contact with a tragedian for whose talents he entertained a
contempt, or whose person or manners displeased him, woe to the unhappy subject of his fun!

He played the Grave-digger one night at the Rochdale Theatre, in
Lancashire, to the Hamlet of a Mr. C——, a most solemn and mysterious tragedian, of the cloak-and-dagger school. The theatre was
built on the site of an old dissenting chapel, in which a preacher
named Banks had held forth, and in the small graveyard attached to
which the Doctor—for he was popularly dubbed Doctor Banks—had
been buried some twenty years ago; and his name was familiar yet. So,
after answering Hamlet's question—"How long will a man lie in the
earth ere he rot?" Dick proceeded in due course to illustrate his answer by Yorick's skull; and taking it up, he said, in the words of the
text—

"Now here's a skull that hath lain in the earth three-and-twenty
years. Whose do you think it was?"

"Nay, I know not," replied Hamlet in his sepulchral, tragedy-tone.

"This skull, sir," said Dick, pursuing the text thus far, and then making a sudden and most unlooked-for alteration—"this was Doctor Banks's skull!"

And the word skull he pronounced like bull. Of course the house was in an uproar of laughter and confusion. The victimised tragedian stamped and fumed about the stage, as well he might, exclaiming, "Yorick's, sir, Yorick's!"

"No," said Dick coolly, when the tumult had subsided, taking up another skull, and resuming the text, "this is Yorick's skull, the king's jester, but t'other's Doctor Banks's, as I told you."

This was the last straw on the tragedian's back; he jumped into the grave, seized the (very) low comedian by the throat and a most fearful contest ensued, in which Dick held his own bravely and succeeded at length in overpowering, in a double sense, the worsted tragedian whom he held down in the grave with one hand, while he flourished Doctor Banks's skull in triumph above his head.

The curtain was dropped, amidst roars and shrieks of laughter, in which King, Queen, monk and courtiers—who, in the vain hope of arresting the row, had been sent on with Ophelia's empty coffin—were compelled to join, forming a tableau which finished the play for that night.

Corpsing

As the young Olivier knew only too well, there is nothing easier than to get the giggles on stage and few things harder to stop. Quite apart from regular and unexpected occasions which can set one off, there is a tradition and sport within the profession known as "corpsing." Specifically, this refers to a situation so funny that an actor, who is supposed to lie dead on stage, would start rocking with laughter.

When Garrick first came upon the stage, one very sultry evening in the month of May, and performed the character of Lear in the first four acts he received the customary tokens of applause; at the conclusion of the fifth, when he wept over the body of Cordelia, every eye caught the soft infection, big round tears ran down every cheek. At this interesting moment, to the astonishment of all present, his face assumed a new character, and his whole frame appeared agitated by a new passion; it was not tragic, for he was evidently endeavouring to suppress a laugh. In a few seconds, the attendant nobles appeared to be affected in the same manner; and the beauteous Cordelia, who reclined upon a crimson couch, opening her eyes to see what occasioned the interruption, leaped from her sofa, and with the Majesty of England, and the gallant Kent, ran laughing off the stage. The audience could not account for so strange a termination of a tragedy in any other way than by supposing the cast to be seized by a sudden frenzy; but their risibility had a different source.

A Whitechapel butcher, seated in the centre of the first bench of the pit, was accompanied by his mastiff, who, being accustomed to sit on the same seat as his master at home, thought naturally enough that he might enjoy the same privilege here. The butcher sat back, and the quadruped, finding a fair opening, got upon the bench, and fixing his forepaws on the rails of the orchestra, peered at the performers with as upright an head, and as grave an air as the most sagacious critic of the day. The corpulent slaughterman was made of "melting stuff" and, not being accustomed to a play-house heat, found himself much oppressed by the weight of a large and well-powdered Sunday peruke, which, for the gratification of cooling his head, he pulled off, and placed on the head of the mastiff. The dog, being in so conspicuous a situation, caught the eye of Garrick and the other performers. A mastiff in a church-warden's wig was too much; it would have provoked laughter in Lear himself at the moment he was most distressed—no wonder that it had such an effect upon his representative.

Easy Bet

More often "corpsing" refers to active efforts on stage to make fellow actors laugh. Lady Benson remembers Alice Denvil, an old actress in the Benson company.

Though possessed of a strong sense of humour, she had the greatest abhorrence of joking on the stage, and used to boast that nothing would make her laugh during a performance. We therefore made a bet with her that before the week was out we would spoil her record. With this object in view, during a "front" scene in *The Rivals*, I blacked out two of my front teeth, and turning my back to the audience, grinned in her face. To my great chagrin, she went steadily on with her words without a glimmer of a smile, and when she had finished her speech, murmured, "It's more inartistic than funny, and an easily earned five shillings."

Closing Nights

Last nights of a play are particularly prone to various pranks.

On the last night of a production of Arthur Miller's *All My Sons* in Seattle, Washington, the leading man reached for his pack of cigars and found they had been replaced with cocktail sausages. On the last night of a student production of Oscar Wilde's *Salomé* in Oswego, New York, John the Baptist's head was brought on covered by a napkin. When Salomé removed the napkin, she discovered not the head of the saint but a pile of ham sandwiches.

Actors' Jokes

Like Jewish jokes, actors' humor reflects the grim reality of their existence.

The old mummer, travelling as he did, with a very limited wardrobe, and occupying lodgings where bathrooms were usually non-existent, was often none too cleanly in his person. It is told of one comedian that, having a part in which black stockings were required, and these forming not part of his wardrobe, he blackleaded his legs. After the show he asked the stage-manager, "Do we play this piece again?" "Yes," was the reply, "next week." "Good," said the comedian; "then I needn't wash my legs."

Two comedians, somewhat down on their luck, had obtained an engagement at Dublin, but having got as far as Holyhead, they found their remaining funds were insufficient to pay the passage. They searched round and found a kindly skipper of a cargo boat who offered to take them over at a nominal rate. Arrived at Dublin, the ship was hailed by the Customs Officers, who asked of what the cargo was composed. "A load of guano and two actors," was the reply. "Good gracious, Bill," said one comedian to the other, "aren't we ever going to top the bill?"

Agents

Many current actors' jokes are about agents, a favorite target of their frustrations.

The actor comes back from an audition and finds his house burned to the ground. He goes up to the cop at the corner and asks: "What happened?" The cop says: "Well, apparently your agent came over to the house, raped your wife, clubbed her to death, murdered your two children and then burned the house down."

An incredulous smile passed over the actor's face: "You mean, he came to my house . . . ?"

The agent was sitting in a cafe with a colleague when one of his clients passed by. "There goes that bastard," said the agent, "who takes 90% of everything I earn."

[17] CROWDS AND EXTRAS

Comic Relief

This from the Herald *published at Stratford-upon-Avon, in April 1883.*

During a performance of *King Lear* at the Memorial Theatre on Monday evening last an incident occurred which created a good deal of laughter. One of the supernumeraries, who was rather slow in making his exit from the stage, allowed one of the scenes to come down upon his head and, continuing its course, he and his spear became separated, he being on one side of the curtain and his weapon on the other. The incident following a scene of great tragic power caused some little relief among the audience.

Anything for Money

Once, when the Benson Company was playing in a Scotch town, the fairies required in the play were engaged locally. Lady Benson saw a crowd of stout elderly females round the stage door, all engaged in animated and acrimonious discussion, and told the stage manager that they must not wait outside, but could return later for their children. "Mothers? Why, those are the fairies," said the manager.

When Herbert Tree first produced *The Merchant of Venice* he found his recruits for the crowd in the East End; the pay for each appearance was two shillings. In one scene the Christians pretended to spit at the Jews. After the first night one of the crowd asked to see Tree. "Make it a round guinea a week, guv'nor," he pleaded, "and those —————— Christians may really spit at me."

The Tedium Is the Message

The British actor William Terriss was assassinated outside the stage-door of the Adelphi in 1897 by Richard Price, a recently dismissed walk-on. Usually these unappreciated drones took their revenge with less violence.

An ambitious but not overly talented young actor was employed in Sir Donald Wolfit's travelling Shakespeare company as the final messenger in *Macbeth* who has to run on stage, stammer out "My Lord, the queen is dead," and then run away. For many seasons he did just this, and then he became bored and asked Sir Donald if he could play a larger part. Wolfit refused. The actor continued to ask and Wolfit continued to refuse. The young actor became increasingly depressed and the matter developed into an obsession. Thoughts of revenge filled his waking hours and one evening he decided to sabotage the play. That night he ran onto the stage. "My Lord," he shouted, "the queen is *much better and is even now at dinner*." He then ran off, leaving the astonished actor-manager to deal with the situation as best he could.

Compliment

James O'Neill was playing Sheridan Knowles's *Virginius* one night, and after a great scene and the curtain, he turned and saw one of the supers drop on the stage. Going over to the man who had by this time resumed an upright position, O'Neill asked what the trouble was. The super replied, "Mr. O'Neill, I just could not help it. Your acting at the end was so terrific, I could not stand it, and I fainted away."

This O'Neill considered quite a compliment, and later he handed the super a five-dollar bill. The next night and at the same place, all the supers dropped to the stage, but they did not get any fives from Jim.

Crowd Scene

Edward Gordon Craig is considered one of the geniuses of the modern theatre, a view he would have heartily endorsed. A son of Ellen

Terry, it was natural that he should have started as an actor. There is a rough justice in the theatre, though at times it gets to the wrong man.

Craig was never noted for his modesty, and he was not the most popular actor in the theatre, especially with the supers. In the battle scene of *Cymbeline* he and Ben Webster had to fight their way, shoulder to shoulder, through serried ranks of embattled walk-ons. One night Ben became aware that he was being prodded from behind with a spear, bashed on the head with an ax, pushed and jostled by the troops at his rear beyond the call of duty. At last he turned around and hissed furiously, "What the hell do you think you're doing?" The army wavered and stopped. "Very sorry, sir," whispered one of them. "We thought you was Mr. Craig."

Thanks but No Thanks

Orlando Day, a fourth-rate actor in London, was once called in a sudden emergency to replace a star for a single night. Even though the play had been running, he sent telegrams to sundry critics, as well as to J. M. Barrie, the author of the play, announcing "Orlando Day presents Allen Ainsworth's part tonight at the Criterion." Barrie's reply has survived. He wired back to the ambitious actor: "Thanks for timely warning."

[18] AMATEURS

Quintessential

Many of the great figures in the theatre began as amateurs. John Drinkwater, playwright and poet, was a founder with Barry Jackson of the Birmingham Repertory, one of the most important English theatres earlier this century. Before that he was an amateur actor, and he gives the essence of the amateur attitude in his reminiscence.

When a young man, I met Barry Jackson in Birmingham—a man of my own age. We were devoted to the theatre and together formed The Pilgrim Players, a group of amateurs different from most, in that members had to devote every night in the week to rehearsals. We both acted. I suppose I played sixty or seventy parts of all kinds, but

I was not a good actor—when I disliked a part, I had a desire to explain to the audience, "This isn't really me, you know."

A Very Good Fishmonger

A singular elopement once took place at the Edinburgh Theatre. A fishmonger named Stirling, who was ambitious to display his powers in the character of Hastings, obtained leave from the manager to gratify his vanity. When he had got nearly half through the part, amidst the din of catcalls, hisses, and roars of laughter, he retired, but it was supposed he would return to finish the part which he had so ludicrously represented. When, to the utter disappointment of the laughter-loving critics, Mr. Bland, uncle of Mrs. Jordan, made his appearance, and thus addressed the audience:

> Ladies and Gentlemen, Mr. Stirling, a very good fishmonger, has been so much mortified by your disapprobation of his performance in Hastings that he has not only made his escape suddenly from the Theatre, but I vow to God, Ladies and Gentlemen, he has taken with him Mr. Ross's best pair of breeches.

Attacking the Prompter

An amateur who later commanded a crack Highland regiment was upon one occasion not particularly perfect in the text of his part. To put it in theatrical language, he had not "swallowed his cackle." The prompter, therefore, had long innings—but unfortunately prompted "not wisely but too well." Imagine the delight of the audience, upon hearing the interpolation (accompanied by a pugnacious gesture at the man in the box) from the actor, of "Confound you—*I know that!*"

Then we have the old, old story of the Messenger in *Macbeth*, when Macready was playing the Thane of Cawdor. The novice had been coached in the lines by the prompter, and duly gave utterance as follows:

"My lord, as I did stand my watch upon yon 'ill, I looked at Burmah and methought I sore the woods begin a movin'!" (all in a breath). But at the words "Liar and slave!" from Macbeth, the unfortunate super flopped on his knees, exclaiming, " 'Pon my soul, Mr. Macready, 'e"—pointing off to the prompter—"told me so!"

Another amateur was playing the Ghost in *Hamlet* at a theatre in Ireland. His appearance aroused the mirth of the gallery, and one of them called out, "Och, bedad an it's Tim O'Rafferty! Look at 'em, boys, 'tis robbed a tinker's shop he has!" Whereupon the Ghost, advancing to the footlights, angrily retorted: "Asy now, Phil Rooney, till I get out of this, when I'll be afther warmin' the wax in yer ears!"

Oxford Amateurs

Scores of famous actors and directors have come out of the fine amateur tradition of Oxford and Cambridge. This is a typical picture of a production by O.U.D.S. (the Oxford University Dramatic Society) of Shakespeare's King John, *in 1891.*

Although we attained smooth and successful performances, the first night had rather more than its usual share of *contretemps*. When the combined British and French forces, to the number of some sixty performers, were all on the stage, their only proper means of exit was by means of a drawbridge into the town. This drawbridge spanned the moat when lowered, and rested on a parapet, thus forming a step by which to pass over through the gate. It happened that, for purposes of rapid scenic change on the second occasion of its use, this parapet was to be removed by lines worked from the side. An over-zealous carpenter worked this during the first dark change, in consequence of which the whole army was imprisoned, and the drop curtains had to be let down prematurely, leaving the "First Citizen" kneeling with the keys of the town in front of the act drop (from which he had to exit kneeling, as the stage critic in Sheridan says).

"One hitch," writes Nugent, "occurred on the first night. I had written a wedding march for the procession into the walls of Angiers; but the drawbridge stuck, and the music had stopped long before the last soldier had entered. Mackinnon was left alone on the stage, and the first words he uttered were, 'Mad world, mad kings, mad composition!' "

In another act, the arms of H. B. Irving (King John), and W. H. Goschen (King Philip), while both were in chain armour, became in an inexplicable manner fettered to one another by the links of the chain. The apparent brotherly affection had to be maintained through the stormy quarrel scene, and they left the stage like Siamese twins.

CHAPTER IV

Life Among
the Players

How To Get Ahead

When someone was lamenting Samuel Foote's unlucky fate of being kicked by a horse in Dublin, Dr. Johnson said he was glad of it: "He is rising in the world. When he was in England, no one thought it worth while to kick him."

And So He Became a Playwright

George Farquhar was described as an amiable young man, much esteemed by his friends, and indulgently considered by the audience; but an accident, rather than want of success, induced him to retire from the stage. In a scenic combat he happened to take a real sword instead of a foil, and in the encounter wounded his antagonist— although not mortally—in so dangerous a manner that his recovery was long doubtful. This affair, entirely an accident, affected him very deeply; he suffered from it painful remorse, indeed, to such a degree that he quitted the stage, although he was then but seventeen years of age.

Lady of *Fashion*

Fashion (the play by Anna Cora Mowatt) created an excitement in the theatrical world that had not been known for years before. The comedy was produced at the Park Theatre in New York on March 24, 1845. Mrs. Mowatt had never been behind the scenes of a theatre until she was taken to witness a rehearsal of *Fashion* the day before its production. Her second passage through a "stage door" was when she had her single rehearsal of *The Lady of Lyons*, in which she made her debut, becoming an actress, and a triumphant one, three weeks after her determination to go upon the stage was formed. Her house was crowded, the applause was genuine and discriminating, and one gentleman, wholly unprejudiced and of great experience, publicly pronounced it "the best first appearance" he ever saw. During the first year she was upon the stage she acted more than two hundred nights, and in almost every important city in the United States, playing Lady Teazle, Mrs. Haller in *The Stranger*, Lucy Ashton in the *Bride of Lammermoor*, Katharina in *The Taming of the Shrew*, Julia, Juliet, and all of the then most popular characters in the line of juvenile tragedy and comedy. The amount of labor, physical and mental, she endured during this period must have been enormous; and the intellectual strain alone was enough to have destroyed the strongest mental constitution. In the history of the stage in all countries there is no single instance of a mere novice playing so many different parts so many nights before so many different audiences, and winning so much and such merited praise, as did this lady during the first twelve months of her career as an actress.

Career Choice

In 1935 Laurence Olivier was directing his first play, when he got a higher call.

About this time, an accident happened which made a big difference to me. I had just got engaged by H. M. Tennant and Hugh Beaumont to play in a play by Frederick Lonsdale with Edna Best, and I had obviously been thinking a lot about "higher things"—you know, Shakespeare. It was beginning to eat at me a bit. My present standard of work, my present kind of work was beginning to dissatisfy me rather violently. And it only took two days of rehearsal of this play to make me give the part up. Now it was a very unfortunate circumstance, it always is when an actor wants to give a part up. He has to rely greatly on the kindness and the understanding of the manager. Well, H. M. Tennant was an awfully good sort of man and the author, Frederick Lonsdale, was extremely kind and I said, "I'm terribly sorry, I somehow no longer feel this is my sort of work. I don't know why I'm saying this, but I feel I ought to be playing Romeo now."

Two days later Olivier received an offer from producer Bronson Albery saying that John Gielgud wanted him to alternate with him in the parts of Romeo and Mercutio.

There Is a Tide

Arletty, the French film actress, was also famous as Blanche in Jean Cocteau's adaptation of *A Streetcar Named Desire* by Tennessee Williams. Her early career in music-hall and operetta began when she walked into a theatre by chance and auditioned for a revue by singing "It's a Long Way to Tipperary." She later claimed that had she been passing the high-minded Théâtre Odéon that morning, she might just as easily have become a classical actress.

[20] SUCCESS AND FAILURE

Fame

Richard Burbage, the great actor of Shakespeare's principal characters, we are told was so eminent in his profession that no country gentleman thought himself qualified for conversation without having a previous acquaintance with Dick Burbage.

Burbage made his name in *Richard III*, and his acting in the final scene when Richard dies, furious and despairing, on Bosworth Field, was much admired. Indeed there was a story current a generation or two later that when a Bosworth inn-keeper used to show visitors the battlefield, he would point out to them the place where *Burbage* cried: "A horse! A horse! My kingdom for a horse!"

Garrick's first appearance was at Goodman's Fields Theatre in the year 1741, in *Richard III*. With such rapidity did his fame spread, that, notwithstanding the distance of Goodman's Fields from the fashionable part of London, the long space between Temple Bar and Goodman's Fields is said to have been nightly blocked by carriages of the nobility and gentry waiting to see him act.

Overnight Success

Edmund Kean was born in London, and in early life was adopted by his aunt (Miss Tidswell), an actress in the Drury Lane Company. In childhood he played children's parts, and as a boy served a sort of apprenticeship with the prince of showmen, Richardson of *Bartelmy*

Fair fame. He then visited the provinces, married an Irish girl—a member of the company at Cheltenham—and after touring Ireland, settled at the Theatre Royal, Exeter. From Exeter Kean's fame travelled up to London at a time when the fortunes of the Old Drury were running low.

Lord Byron had a council assembled, and it was resolved unanimously to despatch the acting manager (Mr. Arnold) to Exeter to judge of the merits of this reported wonder. Arnold arrived at Exeter in time to be present at Kean's benefit, when he saw the great actor demonstrate his versatility by playing Shylock in the *Merchant of Venice* and Harlequin in the pantomime of *Mother Goose*. His report was: "If the Shylock of the west is right, the Shylocks of the great metropolis have all been wrong," but he advised the committee to get another opinion. Upon this, Lord Byron induced Dr. Drury of Harrow to visit the western city and report upon the actor's powers. Dr. Drury saw Kean in *Othello* and returned to London full of glowing praise. The result was an offer of an engagement at eight pounds per week, which was joyfully accepted. Leaving Mrs. Kean and his child to await results, after a farewell benefit he repaired to London to fulfill his engagement. Unfortunately for Kean, though the agreement secured him eight pounds a week once he started, there was no date named for his first appearance, and no arrangement as to salary in the meantime. Nor was there apparently any disposition on the part of the Drury Lane management to proceed to business. Kean was left hanging about doing nothing and finding it impossible even to get an interview with "Blustering Raymond," the stage manager.

Three months were wasted in this absurd manner, and hope delayed not only made the heart sick but the purse light. About this time R. W. Elliston became lessee of the Olympic, and he offered Kean a three years' agreement at eight, nine and ten pounds per week, his first appearance to be made the following Monday. This offer was eagerly accepted, but an injunction was applied for by the Drury Lane management, and again the actor was disappointed. Despairing and mortified, the poor actor now applied to his friend Hughes to advance him enough money to take him back to the country; but Hughes did better than that—he called on Lord Byron and through him secured for Kean an interview with the stage manager. "Well," said the manager, "you're a nice youth to enter into another engagement with Elliston, knowing at the same time you were under articles here." "Well," said the nice youth, "I cannot live on air, therefore I embraced the first offer that presented itself, to replenish my long-exhausted exchequer." "Well," said the manager, "we will appoint your debut for next Monday. What have you thought of to open with, eh?" "Shylock," said the trembling actor. "Shylock!" repeated the manager with a derisive laugh. "Why, my good young man, you had better put your head in a sack and throw yourself into the Thames than run the risk of such a dangerous experiment as that." But Kean was firm. Kemble might have tried it without commercial success; Huddart might have performed it without attracting a house; but as for him, it was Shylock or nothing, and he emphasized his ultimatum by striking the table with his hand and then leaving the room. Recalled to the manager's apartment, he said: "Only give me the chance; I will rush the breach."

The day came, the night, the hour—January 26, 1814. Hazlitt was among the critics in the front row. Kean was greeted with a slight recognition on his entrance, but he did not produce any visible effect until he uttered the passage: "If you tickle us, do we not laugh? If you prick us, do we not bleed?" At the conclusion of the scene, the people in the pit mounted their seats, waving hats and handkerchiefs, and Shylock was thrice called before the curtain. Lord Byron was among those who personally congratulated Kean on his success. The trial scene produced a marvellous effect. The audience refused to allow the fifth act to proceed as Shylock finished at the end of the fourth. Kean had taken the theatrical world of London by storm, and the result was Old Drury was lifted from poverty and ruin to luxuriance and prosperity. Kean filled the treasury with twenty-five thousand pounds in one season, and his salary was increased to twenty pounds per week.

The day following his great triumph Kean visited the theatre, when the hall-porter, who had treated him with insolent rudeness during the three months in which he was vainly seeking an interview with the stage manager, jumped from his seat, rushed at the door, and was about to open it for him when Kean gently put his hand aside, saying: "Pray do not trouble yourself; I am quite perfect in this part. You have given me enough rehearsals."

How To Take a Flop

Oscar Wilde arrived at his club one evening, after witnessing a first performance of *Lady Windermere's Fan*. "Oscar, how did your play go tonight?" asked a friend. "Oh," was the lofty response, "the play was a great success, but the audience was a total failure."

Some Don't Fly

"Not all your plays are successes, I suppose, Sir James," someone remarked to J. M. Barrie at a dinner party. In the manner of one imparting a confidence, Barrie leaned toward him and said, "No, some Peter out and some Pan out."

Imagination

Ruth Gordon once described to George Kaufman a new play in which she was appearing: "In the first scene I'm on the left side of the stage, and the audience has to imagine I'm eating dinner in a crowded restaurant. Then in scene two I run over to the right side of the stage and the audience imagines I'm in my own drawing room." Kaufman listened, then mused: "And the second night *you* have to imagine there's an audience out front."

And I Can Fail Again

Oscar Hammerstein, after a succession of flops, finally wowed 'em with *Oklahoma!*. In 1944 he took a memorable ad in *Variety* telling show biz, "I'VE DONE IT BEFORE AND I CAN DO IT AGAIN!" And instead of listing *Oklahoma!* or any of his previous successes, Hammerstein's self-kidding ad reprised some of his undistinguished but highly memorable flops, such as *Very Warm for May* (seven weeks), *Ball at the Savoy* (five weeks), *Sunny River* (six weeks), *Three Sisters* (six weeks), and *Free for All* (three weeks).

Giving Up the Ghost

An unfortunate débutant who made his appearance as the Ghost in *Hamlet* was so rudely treated by the audience that in the midst of his scene he took off his visor and put the audience in perfect good humour by saying, "Ladies and Gentlemen, it was my hope to please you; if I have failed, I must give up the Ghost."

[21] GENEROSITY AND MODESTY

Ready Money

James Quin enjoyed an unusual reputation for generosity

What generous humour in his reply to half-starved Winston (for whom he had procured an engagement, and an outfit, to enable him to enter on with decency), who timidly asked, under the impulse of hunger, what he should do for a little ready money for the next few days. "Nay," exclaimed Quin, "if you're in want of money, you must put your hand in your own pocket!" And when Winston did so, after Quin had left, he found a ten pound note, which Quin had placed there.

Their Brothers' Keepers

Because most of them have known poverty and struggle in their early careers, successful actors are often generous, especially to less fortunate members of their profession. There are several prominent nineteenth-century names in the following story.

J. B. Buckstone and Sydney Cooper, the one as "general utility" and the other as scenic artist, made their first essay in dramatic life at Hastings. The season proceeded with varying success until Wombwell's Menagerie entered the town and presented a rival attraction, and then receipts fell off and fortunes ran low. Cooper, always a prudent lad, had accumulated savings to the amount of five pounds, which in the form of a note, he kept inside the case of the large, old-fashioned, silver watch he wore. When fortune was at its lowest, the scenic artist woke up one morning to find both watch and note had disappeared. The company was assembled, and the serious nature of the financial position considered, and it was determined to put on a celebrated melodrama then playing the Surrey Theatre, in the hope of retrieving fortune. In this Buckstone was cast for an important part, to perfect himself in which he used to wander away to the neighboring downs for privacy and quiet.

Here, on one occasion, he met a gentleman, actually on the same errand bent, who, noticing the lad's earnest attention to his book, and perhaps divining the cause, asked him the subject of his reading.

The boy handed the book to the stranger, and told him that he was a member of the company then performing at Hastings. The gentleman said that he had a great taste for dramatic works, particularly Shakespeare's tragedies. "Ah!" said the rustic actor, "William Shakespeare is not a gentleman of my acquaintance yet, but I hope in time to be on speaking terms with him." "Very good," said the stranger, and then proceeded to inquire as to the business done at the theatre, eliciting the tale of misfortune with which the reader has already been made familiar. The gentleman next suggested that he should like to look over the theatre, and the young actor offered himself as guide. The gentleman's person was decorated by a blue coat with brass buttons, light pants, and Hessian boots with corresponding tassels. After visiting the theatre, the unknown was about to depart, when a post-chaise drove hastily up to the door. Out jumped R. W. Elliston, then manager of Drury Lane Theatre, and taking the stranger by the hand, said: "My dear Kean, you must return with me tomorrow; since your absence the business has been ruinous. I must announce you for *Richard the Third* for Monday." "Oh, no, said Edmund, "I came hither with your consent to study my part in the new tragedy." "Never mind the new part; we can put that off," said Elliston. "Well," said the great tragedian, "I will make a compact with you. If you will remain here and perform with me for the benefit of our unfortunate brethren tomorrow night, I will return with you the following morning." The terms were joyfully accepted.

The morrow came. The bill included *The Merchant of Venice*—Shylock by the Roscius of the world—and the farce, *The Liar*, with Elliston in the character of Wildrake. The house was crammed to suffocation, and the performance resulted in money enough being taken to pay all back salaries, not forgetting the lost watch and its contents, and to furnish the company with sufficient means to take them on with comfort to Dover.

Martyrdom

Most great actors are painfully aware of their own limitations. John Philip Kemble was one of the great tragedians of the nineteenth century.

John Kemble was not equally successful in comedy. Meeting him for dinner in the city, not long after he had performed Charles in the *School for Scandal*, our flattering host asserted that this character had been lost to the stage since the days of Smith, and added that Kemble's performance of it should be considered as Charles's Restoration. To this a less complimentary guest replied, in an undertone, that in his opinion it should rather be considered as Charles's Martyrdom. Our witty critic, however, did not speak so low but that the great tragedian heard him; when to our surprise and amusement, he smiled and said: "Well, now, that gentleman is not altogether singular in his opinion. A few months ago, having taken a glass too much, I inadvertently quarrelled with a gentleman in the street. The gentleman called on me the following morning for an explanation, 'Sir,' said I, 'when I commit an error, I am always ready to atone for it; and if you will only name any reasonable reparation in my power—' 'Sir,' interrupted the gentleman, 'at once I meet your proposal, and name one. Solemnly promise, in the presence of this my friend, that you will never play Charles Surface again, and I am perfectly satisfied.' Well, I did promise, not from nervosity, as you may suppose, gentlemen; but because, though Sheridan was pleased to say that he liked me in the part, I certainly did not like myself in it; no, no more than that gentleman who has just done me the favour to call it Charles's Martyrdom."

Camaraderie

In the theatre there are often rivalries, but most actors will help their fellows whenever they can. Fred Ross, a minor actor in nineteenth-century San Francisco, tells this story that involves Eugene O'Neill's father.

There was grand and fine comradeship in those good old days which I do not think is equalled at all today. For instance, one day after rehearsal I stood on the stage of the Baldwin Theatre talking to James O'Neill. The rest of the company had left the theatre. Tom Keene, rival leading man of the California Theatre, walked in. The two leading men shook hands, Jim saying, "Hello, Tom. What are you doing over here?" Tom replied, "Well, Jim, you know I am leaving here soon for the Boston Theatre, and they have sent me my opening part to play. I find it is the play of *L'Assommoir*, and recalling you had played Copeau in it here at the Baldwin, I thought you could give me some pointers on the part."

Jim said, "Of course I will. Have you the part with you?" Tom said, "Yes, and the manuscript as well." Jim turned to me and said,

"You hold the book, Fred, and Tom you give me the part, for I do not remember all the lines now."

Then Jim went all through the play and showed Tom every bit of business in it. I was only too proud to be with these two great leading men. It is doubtful if today one of our modern leading men would be so glad to assist a rival in such a manner. Weeks followed, and one day O'Neill came to rehearsal and opened a telegram which he said had been sent him by Tom Keene from Boston. In the wire, Tom said, "A great success; eleven curtain calls at the end of *delirium tremens* scene."

Kind to Stagehands

Most of the stories about Mrs. Patrick Campbell are not to her credit; her kindnesses were less amusing than her tantrums. The adoration a star gets from the public is often more fleeting than how she is remembered backstage. Margaret Webster, the director, recalls a conversation about Mrs. Pat in the late 1930s with a stagehand at the Shubert Theatre in New Haven.

He told me that they "spoke of her in a jolly sort of way—she must have been what we call a good fellow sort of woman." In San Francisco, they said, she engaged the finest doctors to attend an electrician who was ill. Years later, in London, this same man met her, walking along Piccadilly; she recognized him instantly and embraced him.

My Fur Lady

In the winter of 1940/41 George Devine tried to form the Actors' Company, which needed £700 for its first production, an adaptation of Great Expectations *made by Alec Guinness. The two were unwilling to ask money from other actors but finally, at their wits' end, they decided to consult Edith Evans, who was touring with* The Importance of Being Earnest. *Sir Alec recalls this in his autobiography.*

There was no question of asking her for money; the object of our visit was, I suppose, to seek sympathy, encouragement and possibly a commonsense opinion. We called on her as soon as the curtain fell after a mid-week matinee and explained what we were trying to do. She sat at her dressing-table, in Lady Bracknell's wig and hat, listening to us very seriously. When George, who was the spokesman, had finished speaking a long silence fell. Her elderly dresser, who was called Potter, offered us tea. We shook our heads. Then Edith turned to Potter, saying, "Potter, how much did I pay for the fur coat I bought last week?" "Seven hundred pounds, Miss Evans." "Potter, bring me my checkbook." George and I stood silently, a little apprehensive, certainly embarrassed. Edith wrote a cheque for £700 and handed it to us, saying, "Can't have actors out of work for the sake of seven hundred pounds when I buy a coat for the same amount."

[22] RIVALRIES

Envy

Garrick's success made him many enemies, and brought him plenty of ill-natured criticisms. Other actors became jealous of the popular favour showered upon him, and some adopted unworthy means of counteracting it. Quin, who had made himself somewhat famous in the character of Othello, resented Garrick's adoption of the part, and succeeded in bringing it into ridicule. Hogarth had recently published his famous series of prints, illustrating *Marriage à la Mode,* in one of which he had depicted a negro foot-boy entering an apartment carrying tea. This suggested to Quin a means of discomfiting Garrick, who was short of stature, and in *Othello* wore a black face. So on the entrance of Garrick in third or fourth act, Quin exclaimed loudly enough to amuse the pit: "Here is Pompey, but where are the tea-things?" The story was, of course, circulated widely outside the theatre, and so wounded Garrick's sensitive nature that he never played the part again.

Meanness

The most constant bane of Garrick's life was the satirist Samuel Foote. Garrick was known for his love of money, as Doctor Johnson relates.

Foote had a small bust of Garrick placed upon his bureau. "You may be surprised," said he, "that I allow him to be so near my gold; but you will observe he has no hands."

He Knew He Was Beaten

John Kemble declined for a long time to see Kean act, but at last was prevailed upon to witness a performance of *Othello*. Cribb, the picture-dealer who sent him an order for a box, met Kemble in the street shortly after, and asked him if he had seen Kean. "No, sir, I did not see Mr. Kean. I saw Othello; and further, I shall never act the part again."

Famous Whisper

The following anecdotes about Mrs. Pat's tongue originated with Alexander Woollcott, the Algonquin wit, who remarked that in her decline she was like "a sinking ship firing on her rescuers."

I remember a night in Katharine Cornell's dressing room. It was during Miss Cornell's season in *Dishonored Lady*, and she was rather hoping that the chaste austerity of her backstage life (just a few good etchings and a book of poems) would favorably impress a sorrowing great-aunt who was horrified enough at her young relative's being on the stage at all, let alone appearing in the role of a murderous nymphomaniac. Unfortunately, the great-aunt's visit to the dressing room was interrupted by the chance and separate arrivals of three such weird sisters as Theda Bara, Mrs. Leslie Carter, and Mrs. Patrick Campbell. Such a horrid confluence wrecked Miss Cornell's aplomb, so I tried to do the honors. "Ah, you're a famous critic!" cried Mrs. Campbell at the sight of me. "Tell me who *should* have played *Dishonored Lady?*" I tried to mask this glancing blow by a flurry of introductions. Surely the great Mrs. Campbell knew the great Mrs. Carter. "Honored, honored!" Mrs. Campbell boomed, and then, without relinquishing the infuriated hand of Mrs. Carter, she confided to me in a whisper that rattled the theater, "I thought she was dead."

That whisper of hers! It sounds like wind in the chimney of a haunted house. It can fill an entire theatre, particularly when she is in the audience. Thus at *The Cherry Orchard* I could not help hearing her try drown out Nazimova. I thought this was naughty of her, and as the curtain fell on the first intermission, I tried to scowl a reproof in her direction. Unabashed, she held me in the aisle with inquiries about Dorothy Parker, whom she admires enormously, but whom she usually refers to, for some mysterious reason of her own, as Dorothy Warren. Mrs. Campbell told me she had been having great success in her lectures by reciting one of Mrs. Parker's lovelorn poems which ends with the lines:

> There's no edgèd thing in all this night,
> Save in my breast.

By this time the whole audience was watching us, and I felt a thousand pairs of eyes critically surveying my contours as she cried out with considerable archness. "There's no use denying it. I'm sure *you* are the edgèd thing in her breast!"

To a Young Actress

Minnie Maddern Fiske, the American star whose mere name was enough to bring tears of adoration into the eyes of the critic Alexander Woollcott, did not take the success of younger rivals too gracefully. Standing in the wings one day with her young niece, Emily Stevens, while Blanche Yurka rehearsed an emotional scene, Mrs. Fiske remarked in a most audible stage whisper, "My dear, I hope you will let this be a lesson to you. Act if you must, but never Yurk!"

Miaow

An actress noted for her risqué lines opened in a new theatre. "They'll never hear her in that barn," said a critic, "the acoustics are terrible." "How nice," commented Ethel Barrymore. "Now she can be obscene but not heard." Later Miss Barrymore had acquired a new husband, and had made a full confession of her past life to him. "What honesty! What courage!" marveled the critic. "What a memory!" added Miss Barrymore.

[23] PRIVATE LIVES

Fickle Love

Soon after Garrick's first appearance on the stage of Drury Lane, an elderly woman called at his apartments and desired to speak with him on particular business. She told him that a young lady of great beauty and fortune, having seen him act Chamont, Lothario, and several other characters, was so charmed with his person and performance that she was willing to give him her hand, with her portion, which was at her own disposal. "But are you sure, Mr. Garrick, that you can prove a good husband?" His answer was that he did not doubt of his proving to be such a husband as the young lady would wish to have: "I beg to have the honour of waiting upon her."

She promised to call in less than a fortnight and to fix a day of meeting. In vain did Garrick wait for the performance of her promise. A considerable time had elapsed when he met her by chance in the street and asked her the reason she did not keep the appointment. "Oh dear!" said the good woman, "it is all over; the young lady has subsequently seen you play Abel Drugger, and her love is all gone."

Family Feud

Sometimes the drama in the lives of theatrical folk takes place off stage. Richard Sheridan's father was the well-known Irish actor-manager, Thomas. They were not always on speaking terms.

The first night *The Rivals* was brought out at Bath, Sheridan's father came and he refused to have anything to say to his son. It is related, as an instance of Richard's filial affection, that during the representation he placed himself behind a side scene opposite the box in which his father and sisters sat, and gazed at them all the time. When he returned to his house and wife, he burst into tears, and declared that he felt it too bitter that he alone should have been forbidden to speak to those on whom he had been gazing all the night.

Frequent Father

John Palmer was the celebrated creator of Joseph Surface in Sheridan's The School for Scandal.

His invariable excuse for every omission of punctuality, for every neglect of duty, for every postponement of engagement, was his wife. With handkerchief in hand, he would sigh, "My best of friends, this is the most awful period of my life. I cannot be with you, for my beloved wife, the partner of my sorrows and my joys, is just confined." Someone calculated that his wife rendered him a happy father once every two months.

Recognition Scene

The following event, though strange, is nevertheless true and happened in the Glasgow Theatre in the year 1793. Mrs. Cross, who played the previous winter at Covent Garden Theatre, went in the summer to Scotland to play with Mrs. Esten. When the season concluded at Edinburgh, the company went to Glasgow. On one occasion the Provost paid the theatre a visit and as soon as Mrs. Cross came on the stage he exclaimed loudly: "Stop the play till I speak with that woman!" The anxiety he manifested occasioned the manager instantly to suspend the performance. The curtain was dropped and the Provost went round to Mrs. Cross's dressing room. After a very few inquiries he found her to be his wife from whom he had been separated nearly twenty years. They each had supposed the other dead.

The husband immediately took her home, and the next evening, by way of showing that she had not forgotten the profession by which she had formerly existed, she made her appearance in the theatre as a spectator.

Irving's Wife

Henry Irving was always at his worst on first nights, and one of the reasons was the presence of his wife in the stage box. Although they had parted in 1871 on rather less than amicable terms, and although they never again spoke to each other, Irving continued to discharge what he felt to be his marital duty (or was it a secret masochism rising from God only knows what sense of guilt?) by giving her seats for all his premieres. She would sit there gazing at him with cold, implacable hatred, willing him to fail, and although he was very shortsighted, he never failed to see her.

Irving's Actresses

The women in his life, not only Ellen Terry, were warm, vital, merry, loving. It is hard to believe that so great an actor can have been so chilling as a man. Some biographers adduce the Victorian proprieties and Irving's concern for the dignity of the theatrical profession to support their point of view. They claim an equally frigid, platonic status for Eliza Aria, the dear and close friend of Irving's last years. This has greatly astonished her family, who, while devoted to "Aunt

Eliza," never thought of her as a platonic type. Her niece, Pamela
Frankau, went to see her aunt on the day of Ellen Terry's death and
found her in floods of tears; understandable indeed, she thought, on
the passing of so old a friend. But her proffered condolences were
swept aside. "Oh no, it isn't *that!*" wailed Aunt Eliza, "but she'll get
to Irving first!"

Catharsis

*Sybil Thorndike had a very long, normal, happy home life. Playing
awful characters on stage helped.*

I believe that within us we've got the germ of every other sort of
person. If I can play a terrible part which I can find somewhere inside me, then, but for the grace of God, I might have been that person. I can never forget that after playing Medea, I felt as though
I'd been in a bath. You can get rid of all sorts of embryo awfulness
and throw them off. All the foul tempers, wanting to knock my husband's block off, to spank the children, I got rid of them all. The
family used to say I was angelic after playing Medea.

My Daughter Electra

*This brings to mind Sara Adler, the great Yiddish actress, who said
this about her actress daughter, Celia.*

You know *Electra?* Well, *Electra* is like one day in my daughter's
life!

[24] ECCENTRICITIES

Strange Daughter

*Colley Cibber, actor-manager and much-ridiculed poet laureate of
the early eighteenth century, author of the most gossipy theatrical
autobiography of the age, never mentions his daughter, Charlotte,
Mrs. Charke, who also went on stage.*

From her childhood she had been wild, wayward and rebellious; self-
taught, as a boy might be, and with nothing feminine in her charac-

ter or pursuits. She was weak enough to be won by a knave with a sweet voice, whose cruel treatment drove his intractable wife to the stage, where she failed to profit by her fine opportunities. Mrs. Charke loved to play male characters. At the Haymarket Theatre, in 1745, she played Captain Macheath and other masculine parts, before she attempted to pass herself off upon the world—or hide herself from it—as a man.

She is said to have once given imitations of her father on the stage; to have presented a pistol at, and robbed him on the highway, and to have smeared his face with a pair of soles out of her own basket.

That Way Madness Lies

On his return from America, Kean told me* he had been mad at Montreal or Quebec for several days, and related an incident which proved it, namely, his having mounted a fiery horse, dressed in the full costume of the Huron tribe of Indians, of which he had been elected chief, and after joining them in their village or camp, haranguing them, parading them, and no doubt amusing them much, being carried back by some pursuing friends to the place whence he came, and treated for a considerable time as a lunatic.

Delusion

William Dowton, a great character actor in the first half of the nineteenth century, was known for his oddities.

Dowton undervalued Edmund Kean, whose merit he never could be induced to acknowledge. When the vase was presented to that great actor, he refused to subscribe, saying, "You may cup Mr. Kean, if you please, but you sha'n't bleed me." Amongst other eccentricities, Dowton fancied (a delusion common to comedians) that he could play tragedy, and never rested until he obtained an opportunity of showing the town that Edmund Kean knew nothing of Shylock. But the experiment was, as might have been expected, a total failure. The great point of novelty consisted in having a number of Jews in court, to represent his friends and partisans, during the trial scene; and in their arms he fainted, when told he was, perforce, to become a Christian. The audience laughed outright, as a commentary on the actor's conception.

* The narrator is T. C. Grattan (1833).

No Joy

Sir Johnston Forbes-Robertson used to say that he would rather be a painter than anything else in the world. Asked why he went on the stage, he replied, "Six guineas a week, from Phelps." Irving's heart and soul were in his work: the theatre was his life. But Robertson declared that he very rarely enjoyed himself when acting, that he was not temperamentally suited to his calling, and that "Never at any time have I gone on the stage without longing for the moment when the curtain would come down on the last act."

A Good Reason Not To Play Lady Macbeth

During the thirties, when Dame Edith Evans was enriching the theatre with a superb Katharina and a marvelous Rosalind, she was asked if she would like to play Lady Macbeth. "It's absolutely out of the question," she replied in that unique voice, "I could *never* impersonate a woman who had such a *peculiar* notion of hospitality."

Shakespeare Before Swine

Lillah McCarthy tells of Lord Lucas that "he wanted me to play a season of Shakespeare and knew how much I wished it; and one day he came to the theatre with a cheque. 'Here's the money for Shakespeare. I've sold my pig-farm. I like his pearls better than my pigs!'"

Nothing in Excess

Soon after John Neville moved from England to Canada in the early 1970s, critic Don Rubin conducted a lengthy radio interview with him for the Canadian Broadcasting Corporation. After exhaustive questions about the actor-director's long and distinguished career, Rubin wound up the interview with a final question:

"Mr. Neville, I've been burning to ask you all this time: why are you wearing that ring in one ear?" There was a long pause, and then John Neville answered in his quiet, thoughtful manner:

"Because I thought two earrings might look effeminate."

How To Prevent a Long Run

Tallulah Bankhead was asked by a journalist if she ever tired of a long run.

I like people to make a decent profit; six months is rather nice. But if a play is a downright failure the sooner it comes off the better. Once when the play was bad and *I* was very bad indeed, I used to walk past the end of the queue with my dresser and remark loudly, "This ghastly play, my dear! Too awful; and that terrible woman Tallulah Bankhead—simply dreadful!"

Carny Knowledge

Joseph Papp, the New York producer and director, sometimes breaks the ice of first rehearsal by trying to guess the weight of his actors. "I'd say you are 140," and when the actor replies, "I'm 160," he would snap back, "I didn't count all those clothes and shoes you've got on!" Papp had worked as a youth at carnivals and his job included guessing people's weight. Legend is silent on how well he did then.

[25]   THEATRE TALK

Exeunt Omnes

An anonymous English actor from the nineteenth century is the narrator of this tale.

The story was related to me by little Delaney, who was playing general utility in a country town in the North. Buskin was the leading man, and having attained that eminence within a few months after playing walking gentleman at Manchester, he seems to have imbibed rather large ideas of his own dignity and importance. *Hamlet* was put up for a certain evening with Buskin as the melancholy Dane; Delaney being cast for Horatio. At rehearsal, when D. taking the poisoned cup, said, "I'm more an antique Roman than a Dane—there's yet some liquor left," Buskin interrupted him loftily with "We don't say that!" "Don't say what?" inquired the astonished Horatio. "We cut that speech," replied Buskin, with a lordly wave of the hand. "Omit it, my dear fellow." In vain Delaney represented that it was usual to give the speech and cited the examples of Macready, Kean, Barry Sullivan, and other celebrities in support of his argument. No; the fiat had gone forth; the great Buskin had spoken; the speech was doomed. "Very well," said little Delaney, with the calmness of exasperation; "No speech, no Horatio!" "What do you mean?" demanded Buskin. "That I speak those lines, or I don't play the part." "You shall not speak the lines." "I shall!" "Indeed! we shall see." "We *shall* see." Night came; the tragedy commenced; everybody were in their places; Hamlet and Horatio exchanged glances of defiance when not before the footlights, but entered into no explanations. And now came the final scene; Laertes was killed, the Queen poisoned, the King slain, and Hamlet mortally wounded. The supreme moment had arrived. Horatio seized the poisoned cup. "I'm more an antique Roman than a Dane," he exclaimed; "there's yet some liquor left!" Did Hamlet break in with "As thou'rt a man, give me the cup; let go; by heaven I'll have it!" No. "Do you know what Buskin did?" said Delaney appealing to me. I answered in the negative. "He died!" said my informant in disgust; "Died, and left me with the cup in my hand!" "Atrocious!" I answered. "Now what would you have done under the circumstances?" inquired little D. I confessed that my resources would have been utterly unequal to so tremendous an emergency. "Well," said D., "I had taken up the poisoned cup; I had said 'I am more an antique Roman,' &c.; I had, in a manner of speaking, given the audience my word that I would take the poison. To have done aught alse would have been to show the white feather. So I *drained the cup, and died too!*"

Lingo

H. L. Mencken in his Dictionary of the American Language *wrote that "the theater, which is one of the chief sources of popular slang, also has a florid argot, and in part it is almost esoteric enough to amount to a cant. . . ." He reprinted a specimen dialogue between two vaudeville actors who met by chance on Broadway earlier this century.*

FIRST VAUDEVILLIAN: How they comin', Big Boy?

SECOND V: Not so hot, not so hot. I'm playin' a hit-and-run emporium over in East New York.

FIRST V: Gettin' much jack?

SECOND V: Well, the storm and me is cuttin' up two and a half yards, but when the feed bill and gas for the boiler is marked off, they ain't much sugar left.

FIRST V: Why don't you air her and do a single?

SECOND V: I guess I should; every one that's caught us says that the trick is a hundred per cent me. I had them howling so forte last night the whole neighborhood was in a uproar. What are you doing these days?

FIRST V: I just closed with a turkey that went out to play forty weeks and folded up after ten days. Believe me, them WJZ and WEAF wise-crackers ain't doin' show business any good. In the West now they are even gettin' the rodeo by radio.

SECOND V: Why don't you get yourself a partner and take a flyer?

FIRST V: Well, if I could get a mama that could do some hoofin' and tickle a uke, I think I would.

SECOND V: Well, ta ta, I gotta go now and make comical for the bozos. If you get a chance come over and get a load of me, but remember, Capt. Kidd, lay off my wow gags.

Actor-Talk

Actors have a unique and often peculiar perspective on plays. Here Laurence Olivier recalls a memorable and critical discussion with Anthony Quayle about the most difficult part in Shakespeare.

When I was on tour in Europe one time doing *Titus Andronicus*, and Anthony Quayle was playing Aaron, we had a little interval together, about five minutes. It was very hot in that part of Europe and we didn't bother to go to our dressing-rooms, with those huge stages, we sat at the back on a sofa and used to talk a little bit. One day he said to me, "Is this a very bad one for you, this Titus Andronicus?" and I said, "Yes, awful, awful," and I said, "But you've played Macbeth too. I think you'll agree that Macbeth is the worst." And he said, "You haven't done the black one yet, have you?" And I said, "No—why? Is that terrible?" He said, "Terrible. The worst parts, the most difficult ones to bear, are the ones that are complaining all the time, the ones that moan. Macbeth is all right because he is positive," he said, "but you know what you hate about the Titus, he's always going 'oh, oh, oh, look at—fancy them doing that to me, oh, oh, oh.' And how many ways are there of saying 'oh, oh.' It's very tough on your imagination, it's very tough on your resourcefulness of variations of all kinds, and, therefore, it's also a very great strain physically." He said, "Othello is all of that and you have to black up as well."

CHAPTER V

On the Road

Go and Blow Your Nose Elsewhere

A country actor so much persecuted John Rich that he permitted him to make his debut at Covent Garden Theatre as Hamlet. The man showed himself disqualified for the part from the first scene; but when he came to the celebrated soliloquy of "To be, or not to be," he unfortunately wanted to blow his nose. Being unfortunately provided with no pocket handkerchief, he had recourse to his usual habit of the fingers, which set the audience in such a roar of laughter, that it was with great difficulty the rest of the play could be got through. Rich, who was on tenter hooks at the side of the scene through the whole course of the representation, said nothing until the play was over. Then, going up to the performer, he exclaimed, "Mr. ———, I believe you to be a very good kind of a man, and know you to be a good companion; but as to acting, Mr. ———, you must go and blow your nose at some other theatre."

Kill That Actor

*Bernard Shaw once wrote that "the stock actor is a stage calamity."
But of course without such infantry there would have been no army;
it was on their shoulders that the great stars stood. However, the
relationship often aroused emotions other than gratitude.*

His name was Phillips, actor and prompter; on the stage he was not a distinguished personage and seldom did justice to the characters allotted him, but was an admirable prompter, and by nature a genuine comic genius. It is told that once when Edwin Forrest, the tragedian, came among the list of "stars," Phillips was assigned the part of Horatio in *Hamlet*. At rehearsal, during the first act a difficulty arose, from Phillips being unable to give the emphasis Forrest wished conveyed to Horatio's line, "I warrant it will." The progress of the rehearsal was interrupted, and many times the following dialogue repeated, without producing the desired effect:

HAMLET: I will watch to-night,
           Perchance 'twill walk again.
HORATIO: I warrant it will.

"No, no, no," roared Forrest; "deliver it in this way, Mr.–, Mr.–, Mr.–Phillips." Forrest repeated the instruction a dozen times; finally, Phillips, looking at the stage manager with a very serious countenance, remarked, "My salary is eight dollars per week, and –" Forrest, enraged, interrupted him, exclaiming, "Sir, we are not here to discuss salaries; can you or can you not speak that line in this way?" Then giving the line with the required force and expression, he paused and glared at Phillips, who very coolly and deliberately answered, "No, Sir, if I could deliver it that way, my salary would be five hundred dollars per night." The humour of the remark was too much for Forrest's gravity even; with a characteristic grunt (such as only Forrest could utter) the tragedian walked to the "prompt table," and with a smile said to the manager, "Let Mr. Phillips salary be doubled at my expense during my engagement." Night came, and poor Phillips, elated with good fortune, and over-anxious to please Forrest, ruined everything. "I will watch tonight," said Hamlet. "Perchance 'twill walk again," quickly replied Horatio, taking the sentence out of Hamlet's mouth. Forrest with difficulty restrained his passion, and when he came off the stage, fuming with rage, roared, "I will give one hundred dollars per week for life to any one who will kill Mr. Phillips."

Hee-Haw

John E. Owens, a nineteenth-century American actor-manager, used to tell the following good one, at his own expense. Many years ago he was touring the West. The night following a performance of *Solon Shingle and the Live Indian* in an Indiana town, the company took the train for Indianapolis. A hayseed, who had evidently witnessed the performance the night before, spotted Owens, and, after sundry remarks about the weather, asked whether he belonged to the "show." Owens answered that the "show" belonged to him, which amounted to the same thing. Hayseed remarked: "I thought I knowed you, that's why I spoke. You acted the clown fust rate. I've got a boy to hum that 'ud make a fust-rate clown, and I just thought I kinder inquire if you couldn't give him a job. He's just full of comic capers, and last night when me and the old woman was a lookin' at you cuttin' up monkey-shines, Martha said to me: 'Reuben, that's wot our boy ought to be a doin'.' An that's why I mention it. I'm sure Rube would make a fortin' among you clowns, for he's a reglar sort of a natoral born dam fool anyway."

[27] STOCK THEATRE

Mixed Up

The general public seldom realise the terrible amount of work that devolves upon a country actor (especially a beginner) when he is called upon to support a star with an extensive repertoire, and many are the blunders that spring from a confusion of parts on the brain. One actor, indeed, when playing two characters a night during a week's visit of the late Charles Mathews, became so hopelessly "at sea" on the Saturday that, in the second piece, after vainly trying to pull through with the assistance of the prompter and the star, he finally succumbed with the following few words to the audience, delivered in bewildered bursts: "Ladies and gentlemen, this is the twelfth part I've had to study and play this week. I'm completely 'mixed.' I don't know what I'm about, what the piece is about, or what business of the piece I ought to be about, and I think about the best thing I can do is to go in peace—about my business!" which he did, leaving Mr. Mathews master of that situation, but losing, I fear, his own.

Stock Joke

These situations must have been very common in stock theatre, and they were embroidered upon by generations of touring actors. It finally got attached to John Barrymore in this form.

John Barrymore used to tell of the confusion that prevailed in an old stock company with which he had once played in repertory. The vast number of plays, the frequency and inconsistency with which they were performed rendered confusion more or less inevitable. One evening Barrymore found himself unable to remember his lines. Faking a piece of business, he sidled over into the wings and hastily called to the director: "What's the line, what's the line?" The director sighed wearily and asked: "What's the play?"

Experience

For many generations before acting schools and studios, actors picked up their craft by touring with stock companies. Margaret Webster describes the typical conditions her mother, later Dame May Whitty, faced at the start of her career.

She had read that Squire Bancroft had played three hundred and forty different parts during a three-year apprenticeship with stock companies, and Irving, so it was said, nearly a thousand before he made his first London success. She wanted to learn and she wanted to be somebody in her own right. Surreptitiously, she began to look for another job.

When it came, she was amazed at her own temerity in taking it. A small-time stock-manager named William Neebe was getting together a company to play two weeks in the London suburb of Edmonton, followed by a short tour of "the smalls" not far away. The repertoire consisted of the Sheridan-Boucicault axis with a farce or two thrown in. They would do twelve plays in the first two weeks and May would play the lead in eleven of them: Lady Teazle, Lydia Languish, Kate Hardcastle, the heroines of *London Assurance* and *The Shaugraun,* not to mention *East Lynne.* She would be paid two pounds a week. Since almost all the company were veterans of this kind of thing, there would be no preliminary rehearsals. Each play would be rehearsed once and played that night. . . .

Her letters continued daily, chronicles of desperation; one cannot imagine how she found time to write them. "I am feeling horribly seedy today. . . . I've been rehearsing 2 parts for tonight. I don't know either of them and feel too ill and tired to learn. I have still Lady Gay and Lady Isabel [in *East Lynne*] to study for Friday and Saturday night. Mon. night went off pretty well—I almost knew my part and so tried to act a little and made passionate love to Elmore, who didn't know his and in consequence didn't return it."

Unmixed Doubles

At a cocktail party, a very gushing "county" woman cornered Donald Wolfit. "Oh, I do think you're so clever the way you play eight parts in a week. I can't think why you don't get mixed up. Why, for example, when you're playing Lear, don't you speak bits of

Hamlet?" "Madam," Wolfit replied sternly, "if you are invited to play golf you do not take your tennis racket."

Forced To Tour

Wolfit, to replenish his coffers, had to tour again, eliciting no doubt, Hermione Gingold's famed comparison: "Olivier is a *tour de force*, and Wolfit is forced to tour."

But Robin May traces this story back to the 1930s.

Lilian Braithwaite was playing a part in Ivor Novello's *Party*, which was firmly based on Mrs. Patrick Campbell. Mrs. Pat, who was about to go off on tour with *The Thirteenth Chair*, ran into Lilian Braithwaite and said: "Oh, Lilian, I hear you are a perfect *tour de force* playing me! And here I am forced to tour!" (Mrs. Pat later played herself in *Party* in New York.)

The Lavatory Players

Laurence Olivier:

I got a job at one time with a troupe called the Lena Ashwell players. We used to play in swimming baths in Deptford, Ilford, Watford, Islington, Shadwell, paying our own fares—I was nearly starving getting £2 10s a week. We had to dress in the cubicles and sometimes in the lavatories, and so we became known as the Lavatory Players. Well, I had an opportunity with them when I was playing Flavius in *Julius Caesar*. There was a couple of very dreary wreaths pinned to the curtain, and the great thing to do was to tear them down angrily, and, if possible, tear down the curtain as well, to see the naked behinds of the girls dressing at the back; that was a big laugh. And one day Marullus was standing on a little beer box as a rostrum and saying, "Knew you not Pompey," and he had long pants and they came off underneath his toga and folded over his beer box so he couldn't move, couldn't get off. Well, I laughed so much I had to leave the stage: and the next morning I was fired.

The Earth Moved

Young Jack Barrymore, already known for his slovenly appearance and lazy habits, was trying to sleep through the San Francisco earthquake during a tour of the West. He was thrown out of bed by one of the shocks, spun around on the floor and left gasping in a corner. Finally, he got to his feet and rushed for a bathtub, where he stayed all that day. The next day he ventured out. A soldier, with a bayonet on his gun, captured Barrymore and compelled him to pile bricks for two days.

Barrymore was recounting his terrible experience in the Lambs' Club in New York. "Extraordinary," commented Augustus Thomas, the playwright. "It took a convulsion of nature to make Jack take a bath, and the United States Army to make him go to work."

[28]   BOONDOCKS

A Human Prop

Crassus, the Roman consul, was defeated and captured in 55 B.C. by the Parthian general Pomaxathres. The Romans looked upon the Parthians as barbarians, but according to this story in Plutarch, they were civilized enough to amuse themselves with The Bacchae of Euripides *in which the hapless Crassus ended up playing an important prop.*

The tables were just taken away, and one Jason, a tragic actor, of the town of Tralles, was singing the scene in *The Bacchae* of Euripides concerning Agave. He was receiving much applause, when Sillaces, coming down the hall, and having made obeisance to the king, threw down the head of Crassus into the midst of the company. The Parthians receiving it with joy and acclamations, Sillaces, by the king's command, was made to sit down, while Jason handed over the costume of Pentheus to one of the dancers in the chorus. Then, taking up the head of Crassus and acting the part of a bacchant woman in her frenzy, in a rapturous impassioned manner he sang the lyric passages:

> We've hunted down a mighty chase today,
> And from the mountain bring the noble prey—

to the great delight of all the company. But when the verses of the dialogue followed:

> What happy hand the glorious victim slew?
> I claim that honour to my courage due—

Pomaxathres, who happened to be there at the supper, started up and would have got the head into his own hands. "For it is my due," said he, "and no man's else." The king was greatly pleased and gave them presents according to the custom of the Parthians, and to Jason, the actor, gave a talent. Such was the burlesque that was played, they tell us, as the afterpiece to the tragedy of Crassus's expedition.

Son of a Gun

Frederick Warde emigrated from England and became a star of the American stage. He kept touring, and tells the following story from the 1880s.

Sedalia, Missouri, at the time of which I write, was a small town, its population composed almost entirely of railroad employees and their families, it being an important division point. The alleged "Opera House" at Sedalia was a long, narrow hall upstairs and over two stores facing the railroad station. It had a gallery at one end and a small stage at the other. The triangles formed by the proscenium were the only dressing rooms.

The audience was a comparatively large one and the play of *Virginius*, with its intense human sympathy and admirable construction, interested them greatly. It may be recalled that Virginia, daughter of Virginius, is claimed and seized by Vibulanus as a slave. The claim is contested by Virginius with all the indignation of an outraged father, and the cause is brought before Appius Claudius as chief Decemvir for trial. The unjust judge decides against the father and orders the girl to be given into the possession of Vibulanus. As this decision means the dishonor of his daughter, Virginius seizes a whittle from a butcher's stall and stabs his daughter to death before the assembled multitude. He afterwards strangles Appius Claudius to death and dies himself from grief and the excitement of the terrible tragedy; but, Vibulanus, the subordinate villain of the story is not disposed of by the dramatist and the play concludes with the death of Virginius.

At the conclusion of the play in Sedalia the audience remained in their seats while I and the other actors in the mimic tragedy went to our dressing rooms to remove our make-up and transform ourselves from ancient Romans to modern American citizens. I had removed my toga, tunic, and upper garments and was busily engaged with soap, water, and towel when a knock came to my dressing room door. I inquired, "Who's there?" A voice replied, "Me the manager." "What's the trouble?" I asked. "The people won't go out," he replied. "I am sorry," I said, "but the play is ended," and suggested that he put out the footlights to indicate that the entertainment was concluded, and continued my ablutions.

A few moments later he came again to my door, saying, "I turned out the lights but they won't move. What shall I do?" "Go in front of the curtain and tell them the performance is over," I suggested. "I wouldn't go in front of that curtain for a hundred dollars," he protested. The novelty and humor of the situation then appealed to me and I volunteered: "Wait a minute and I'll go and tell them myself."

I still had on my fleshling tights and Roman sandals, so I put a bath towel round my neck and enveloped myself in a long Ulster overcoat. My face being ruddy with the recent friction of the towel and my hair gloriously disheveled from the same cause, my general appearance must have indicated Puck grown up and in winter clothes.

I stepped before the curtain still impressed with the humor of the occasion, and addressed the audience: "Ladies and gentlemen, the play is over. I am dead, Virginia is dead, Dentatus is dead, Appius Claudius is dead—" when a voice from the back part of the gallery exclaimed in clear, bell-like tones that reached every corner of the building: "What have you done with that other son of a gun?"

I disappeared and the audience dispersed.

One-Night Stand

A road company at the end of the nineteenth century and its financial resources arrived in Waco, Texas, hoping to stay for a while and recoup. They failed to take the town by storm, which was put into perspective the next morning in the local paper: "Rain-storm in Galveston, lasted twenty minutes. Hail-storm in Beaumont, ten minutes. Wind-storm in Langtry, two days. Barn storm in Opera House, one night."

The American Tour

American tours for British and European stars became obligatory from the early part of the nineteenth century. It was often profitable but rarely a glamorous experience, as typically illustrated by Ben Webster and his company's stopping for a one-night stand in Chattanooga during the first decade of this century.

At one particularly derelict house they found these words painted on the back of the asbestos curtain: "We know the theatre's terrible. How's the show?" There was the classic gag about arriving actors who invariably remarked: "What a godawful theatre! Where's the mail?" and its companion piece about the notice underneath the mailboxes which said: "After you've read your mail please tear it up and throw it on the floor. We have nothing to do but pick it up."

In Chattanooga there had been a lynching the day before they arrived and there were rumors that the theatre would be blown up that night. All the liquor stores were closed, all the hardware stores crammed with men buying guns, the box office besieged by a crowd of people returning their tickets, no stagehands to be found. The company got the scenery in place and the curtain up by ten p.m. There were a dozen people in the house and two or three backstage. Suddenly a revolver shot was heard. And everybody left. The actors got the scenery down again and walked back to their hotel through pitch-dark streets in solid formation. The next morning they entrained thankfully for the next town.

The Secret of Success

Marc Connelly:

Billy Bryant, on whose floating theatre Edna Ferber did much of her research for *Show Boat*, was once asked why a production of *Hamlet* which he admitted was appallingly bad had enjoyed great success up and down the river for years. "The reason is simple," said Bryant. "In the towns we play, people will go anywhere there are chairs."

[29] LANDLORDS AND LANDLADIES

The Importance of Remaining Earnest

Charles Mathews used to tell a story that when he was starring in Edinburgh, his landlord, who seldom attended any other public meeting save the "kirk," asked Mathews if he would oblige him with "a pass for the playhoose." This favour being readily granted, the "gude mon" donned his cheerful black suit, and witnessed Mr. Mathews's two great performances, namely Sir Charles Coldstream in *Used Up*, and Plumper in *Cool as a Cucumber*, both considered to be certain "side-splitters." Meeting his landlord on the stairs as he proceeded to his own room after the performance, he was cordially thanked by that gentleman, of whom he then inquired how he had enjoyed the entertainment. "Weel," said the Northerner, "it pleased me vara much, ye ken, and I conseeder you played unco' naturally; but hey, mon, *I'd a hard matter to keep frae laughing!*"

Scottish Sabbath

As the nineteenth century progressed, the Scots failed to warm to theatre folk. Lady Benson wrote this about her early experiences.

The tour started at Falkirk. After an all-night journey on my arrival at Waverley Station, I met Herbert Ross, who was also joining the Company. Arrived at Falkirk, we set out to see if, at so early an hour (it was about seven a.m.) we could find some place for breakfast. After a considerable time, we persuaded a cottager to give us food and a wash. The latter we were only allowed to have in a bucket in the back yard, as our hostess informed us we were breaking the Sabbath, and could not perform our ablutions under her roof.

After a meal, cooked with great reluctance by this stern Sabbatarian, we set out to hunt for rooms. I was directed to a desolate-looking house, which styled itself a Temperance Hotel, and after some persuasion, the landlady consented to take me in. While in the bedroom, unpacking my bag, I heard the lock turned in the door, and a harsh voice shouting, "Ye'll no raise the blinds, nor come out of the room, until the Kirk is over. I wouldna hae the neighbours ken I had a low play-actress in ma hoose!" It was hopeless for me to explain that I was icy cold and had travelled all night; all the reply I got was, "Say your prayers, and dinna fash yersel, ye'll come out when the Kirk is scaled." So there I remained, shivering, until the godly lady saw fit to open the door, some hours later. Oh, they were very religious in Scotland in those days. The piano was always locked on the "Sawbath," but there was generally a cheerful aroma of whisky about the house.

Fleas

Lady Benson:

It was generally in the big northern towns we found the worst rooms. Stephen Phillips told me he got into a terrible place in Liverpool, and complained to the landlady, that, for obvious reasons that he mentioned, he could get no sleep. However, not being able to get other rooms, he remained there for the whole week. On Saturday, the woman asked him, "How do you find the fleas now?"

"I caught ten last night," said Phillips.

"That's good," replied the woman, "they're going fast!"

More Fleas

H. J. Byron, the Victorian dramatist and wit, was once staying in the provinces, where he was superintending the rehearsals of one of his plays. He had cause to complain of being assailed in bed by fleas.

"Fleas, Mr. Byron!" said the indignant proprietress of the apartment house where the dramatist was staying. "Why, there isn't a single flea in the house!"

"No," was Byron's lugubrious retort, "they're all married and have large families."

Good Address

Alexander Woollcott enjoyed a close friendship with Eleanor and Franklin D. Roosevelt. While in Washington during the run of *The Man Who Came to Dinner*, he resided at the White House. He later advised Ethel Barrymore to seek similar accommodations when in that city, assuring her, "Mrs. Roosevelt runs the best theatrical boardinghouse in Washington."

CHAPTER VI

Techniques and Methods

Out of Control

An actor in ancient Antioch was playing the part of the mad Ajax, and got so excited with his part that he tore the clothes of a fellow actor, hit Ulysses over the head with a flute, and then jumped from the stage and sat down in the senators' seats between two men of consular rank, who barely escaped being beaten with his whip, like the rams in that play. But afterwards he was so ashamed of his extravagance, that when members of his company wanted him to play Ajax again, he replied: "It is enough to have been mad once."

Presence

A great actor inspires others on the stage. Charles Young never forgot a production of Coriolanus.

I remember Mrs. Siddons coming down the stage in the triumphal entry of her son Coriolanus, when her dumb-show drew plaudits that shook the house. She came alone, marching and beating time to the music; rolling (if that be not too strong a term to describe her motion) from side to side, swelling with the triumph of her son. Such was the intoxication of joy which flashed from her eye, lit up her whole face, that the effect was irresistible. She seemed to me to reap all the glory of that procession to herself.

Physical Feats

Some actors have, through training and practice, achieved a high degree of physical control, which is very much part of acting. Here an anonymous critic describes the "unique and inimitable method" of Junius Brutus Booth and his extraordinary "control over the vital and involuntary functions."

He could tremble from head to foot, or tremble in one outstretched arm to the finger-tips while holding it in the firm grasp of the other hand. The veins of his corded and magnificent neck would swell, and the whole throat and face become suffused with crimson in a moment, in the crisis of passion, to be succeeded on the ebb of feeling by an ashy paleness. To throw the blood into the face is a comparatively easy feat for a sanguine man by simply holding the breath; but for a man of pale complexion to speak passionate and thrilling words pending the suffusion is quite another thing. He commanded his own pulses, as well as the pulse of his auditors, with most despotic ease.

If a trick was involved, it was already known to Thomas Betterton two centuries earlier.

Although his countenance was ruddy and sanguine when he performed Hamlet, through the sudden and violent emotion of amazement and horror at the presence of his father's spectre, instantly turned as white as his neckcloth, while his whole body seemed to be affected with a strong tremor; had his father's apparition actually risen before him, he could not have been seized with more real agonies. This struck the spectators so forcibly, that they felt a shuddering in their veins, and participated in the astonishment and the horror so apparent in the actor.

Mannerisms

Macready was frequently criticized for gesturing too much and in an effort to curb his mannerisms he took to rehearsing with his body bound with strings of worsted. When these strings broke he knew that the particular gesture was indispensable to his performance.

Suit the Action to the Words

Herbert Tree could be as witty as he enjoyed being silly, and some of his comments on people and things were unusually shrewd. A company of Sicilian actors, headed by Signor Grasso, was a nine-day wonder in London, and Tree went to see them in *Othello*. There was no restraint in Grasso's performance of the Moor, which was a sweeping, tornadic display of primitive and almost epileptic passion. In the great scenes of jealousy his eyes rolled in frenzy, he foamed at the mouth, and bellowed like a bull. "Very fine, very remarkable," said Tree, "But hardly Shakespeare's conception. You see, Grasso's Othello would never have wanted a pocket-handkerchief."

Epilepsy

The supremely physical actor of our era has been Laurence Olivier, whose complete mastery of movement, breath, and voice has been the subject of endless praise and criticism. His perilous backward tumble down a flight of stairs in Titus Andronicus *is still talked about, and Martin Esslin recalls how Olivier used his makeup in* Othello.

During the early performances at Chichester people were wondering of course how far the extraordinarily black makeup went. At first you could only see his face and neck; then gradually he revealed one arm and his legs, but you still did not know how far up he was blacked up. He must have known that this was creating its own tension, and even Shakespeare knew, or he might not have obliged with that scene with the epileptic fit, which gave Olivier an opportunity to roll all over the stage and finally show *everything*. This was very characteristic of the way he would use even his makeup to build the part physically.

Poetry and Motion

John Gielgud:

When I first worked with Laurence Olivier in *Romeo and Juliet*, we alternated the parts of Mercutio and Romeo. I was directing and I bullied him a great deal about his verse-speaking, which, he admitted himself, he wasn't happy about. I was rather showy about mine, and fancied myself very much a verse-speaker, and I became very mannered in consequence. But I was so jealous, because not only did he play Romeo with tremendous energy but he knew just how to cope with it and select. I remember Ralph Richardson saying to me, "But you see, when Larry leans against the balcony and looks up, then you have the whole scene, immediately." Because he has this wonderful plastique, which is absolutely unselfconscious, like a lithe panther or something. I had been draping myself around the stage for weeks, thinking myself very romantic as Romeo, and I was rather baffled and dismayed that I couldn't achieve the same effect at all.

How He Got Slapped

When Alfred Lunt and Lynn Fontanne, a notably devoted husband and wife, started rehearsing *At Mrs. Bean's*, a play in which it was necessary for Miss Fontanne to strike Mr. Lunt in the face, she found she couldn't hit him. She pulled her hand back and let go—and then stopped dead before she struck. Her husband begged her to do it, but after thirty minutes she still couldn't. Finally Mr. Lunt shouted: "For God's sake, Lynn, you're the lousiest actress I've ever played opposite!"

The Fontanne hand made a direct hit. Mr. Lunt yelped with pain, then grinned. But when they put on the show he had to whisper, "Don't be lousy, dear," each time before she would hit him.

[31] MIMICRY

Parmenon's Pig

The Greeks loved animal imitations of all kinds, and actors had their own specialty. Parmenon was famous for his pig, which became proverbial.

When people tried to compete with him, others would say, "Yes, but what's this compared to Parmenon's pig?" So one of the amateurs one day hid a real piglet under his arm and made it squeal during his performance. And when they said, "Yes, but what's this compared to Parmenon's pig?", he let the piglet out to prove his point that the judges were making their decision according to what seemed to be the truth, not the truth itself.

Stick to Cows

Mr. James Boswell, the friend and biographer of Dr. Johnson, when a youth, went to the pit of Covent Garden Theatre, in company with Dr. Blair, and in a frolic imitated the lowing of a cow; and the universal cry in the galleries was, "Encore the cow! encore the cow!" This was complied with, and in the pride of success, Mr. Boswell attempted to imitate some other animals, but with less success. Dr. Blair, anxious for the fame of his friend, addressed him thus: "My dear sir, I would confine myself to the cow."

Power of Mimicry

When Samuel Foote was acting in Dublin, he introduced into one of his pieces the character of Faulkner, the printer, whose manners and dress he so closely imitated that the poor fellow could not appear in public without meeting with scoffs and jeers from the very boys in the streets. Enraged at the ridicule thus brought upon him, Faulkner one evening treated to the gallery all the devils* of the printing-office, that they might hiss Foote off the stage. Faulkner placed himself in the pit, to enjoy the actor's degradation, but when the objectionable scene came on, the unfortunate printer was excessively chagrined to find, that so far from a groan or a hiss being heard, his gallery friends partook of the laugh. The next morning he inveighed against them for having neglected his injunctions, and demanded some reason for their treachery. "Arrah, master," said the spokesman, "do we not know you?—sure 'twas your own swate self that was on the stage; and shower light upon us, if we go to the play-house to hiss our worthy master."

Burlesque

Dr. Straus in his Reminiscences *described one of the great nineteenth-century mimics, Frederick Robson, taking off Madame Ristori's performance of Medea.*

The wonderful little man's comic play and utterances had in them, maybe unconscious to actor and audience alike, a subdued undercurrent of sobs and tears, as did also the loudest burst of laughter that greeted his performance. I remember Robson's truly marvellous performance of the part of Medea in Robert Brough's burlesque. Before the piece began, I went behind the scenes with the author, where we found Robson in a state of extreme nervousness, as it had been creditably reported that the lady tragedian, whom he was about to imitate (not to travesty, mind, for there truly was nothing of the buffoon pure and simple in Frederick Robson), was actually in the theatre. Well, with this overpowering oppression upon him, he contrived to achieve a glorious success. His Medea was a truly grand tragic figure, gracefully draped in a light veil of burlesque. She who had created the intensely tragic character of ill-starred Medea was so deeply impressed by the little man's wonderful tragi-comic reproduction of her own

* Printer's apprentices were called devils.

creation—which she had been led to believe would turn out a farcical caricature—that she could not refrain from there and then presenting to the great actor the flattering tribute of her gratification and admiration. She came round, accordingly, at once, escorted by that most courteous of gentlemen Earl Granville, who joined the lady in overwhelming the shy man with well-merited compliments. When we had Robson to ourselves again, he cried like a child—partly with pleasure, partly with distress at his nervous awkwardness, which he said "must have made me look like a fool."

Inspiration

John Gielgud:

Once when I was rehearsing *Crime and Punishment*—it was a very hot day, I was walking through St. James's Park—I saw a tramp lying down, with his head buried in the dirty grass, filthy hands and everything, and he was absolutely relaxed. I thought, "This is the way that Raskolnikov must lie on the bed," and immediately it gave me a kind of line on the part.

Mimesis

Many years ago, as Richard Burton tells it, he was standing in a hallway amusing some fellow student-actors by "doing" Gielgud. At one point the faces of his auditors froze and the giggles went silent. Burton turned round to see Gielgud standing behind him, looking as fearfully imperious as Catherine of Russia. "Generally speaking," said Sir John, "very good impersonators do *not* make very good actors."

[32] METHODS AND METHOD

Blocking

Macklin was very particular as Shylock, so much so that he requested Bobby Bates, who performed the part of Tubal, not to speak until he saw him standing on a certain spot: "Nay," said Macklin, "not till you see me place my right foot on this nail," pointing with his stick to the head of a large nail which was driven into the stage. Bobby promised to remember the old man's instruction, and that he might have a better view of the nail, he marked it in a conspicuous manner with a piece of chalk. At night, Macklin had forgotten the nail; therefore, when Tubal entered and remained for some time without speaking, Macklin exclaimed, in an under voice: "Why the devil don't you speak?" "Sir," replied Bobby, "put your right foot upon the nail." This so disconcerted the veteran actor that it was with great difficulty he finished the part.

An Actor Prepares

Garrick had become acquainted with a man, whom he greatly esteemed, in Leman-street, Goodman's-fields. This old gentleman had an only daughter, about two years old, of whom he was dotingly fond. One day, as he stood at an open window dandling and caressing the child, it suddenly sprung from his arms, and falling into a flagged area was killed on the spot. His mind instantly deserted him—he stood at the window delirious, wild, and full of woe: the neighbours came flocking to the house, they took up the body and delivered it to him, thinking it might break the spell of his grief; but it had no effects, his senses were fled, and he continued bereft, filling the streets with the most piercing lamentations.

As he was in good circumstances his friends allowed him to remain in his house, under two keepers appointed by Dr. Munro, and Garrick went frequently to see the distracted old man, whose whole time was passed in going to the window, and there fondling in fancy with his child; after seemingly caressing it for some time, he appeared as if he dropped it, and immediately burst into the most heart-piercing cries of anguish and sorrow; then he would sit down with his eyes fixed on one object, at times looking slowly around, as if to implore compassion.

It is said that from this hint Garrick formed his unparalleled scene of the madness of Lear over the body of Cordelia; and certainly it is not easy to determine from what slight analogies genius derives the elements of the things it creates. In that exquisite performance, which touched the heart of the spectators with a sympathy more like grief than only sympathy, he had no sudden starts nor violent gesticulations; his movements were slow and feeble, misery was in his look, he fearfully moved his head, his eyes were fixed and glittering without speculation; when he turned to those around him he paused, seemed

to be summoning remembrance, and in every sad and demented feature expressed a total alienation of mind.

Underacting

Voltaire, though he was a very indifferent actor (even when he played
in his own pieces) possessed a good theoretical knowledge of the
stage, which he communicated to Lekain and from which he greatly
profited. In one of Lekain's journeys to Ferney (as we find in one of
his letters) Voltaire made him totally change the manner of playing
Ghengis Khan. On his return to Paris, it was the first character he
played. The public, at first astonished at the change, was for a long
time undecided whether to praise or blame it. They fancied the actor
was indisposed: there was nothing of the *fracas*, or of the resources,
or rather tricks of the art which had previously procured him so much
applause in this character. It was only after the fall of the curtain that
the public, motionless during the entire piece, felt that Lekain in fact
was right in substituting for rant and pomp and vulgar effect, accents
more simple, noble, terrible, and impassioned. The public opinion was
formed instantaneously and, by an electrical movement, it manifested
itself in long and loud applause. Lekain, going up to his box, hearing
the applause, leaning over the balustrade said to Rougeot, a servant of
the theatre: "What is all that?" "Why, Sir, it is you they are applauding; they have at length found out you were right."

Sleepwalking

According to Richard Burton, the late Diana Wynyard—a lovely-
looking woman as well as a dedicated and gifted actress—insisted
on playing Lady Macbeth's sleepwalking scene with her eyes closed.
Having done some Stanislavskian research on the subject, she discovered that sleepwalkers do not pursue their nightly rounds with their
eyes open, as most actresses playing Lady Macbeth would have us believe. Lady Diana was devoted to the truth and refused to make matters easy for herself. She closed her eyes and kept them closed. Un-
happily, this particular scene was staged along a rather narrow parapet
which jutted impressively into the audience. Miss Wynyard practiced
her sightless walk over and again, going through the dress rehearsal
without a hint of mishap. On opening night, however, she fell from
the ramp and broke everything in sight—including a disheartening
number of her own bones.

How Did I Do That?

Laurence Olivier has been considered the supreme technical actor of our century, but technique does not necessarily mean he always knows why he acts the way he does.

Cedric Hardwicke once said that theory is the backwash of success, and it's true. If you are successful in something, people ask you how you did it, and you have to find a reason. You might have been perfectly snug and comfortable in the dark about the true reasons for your instincts doing certain things. I remember Charles Laughton coming and giving me a reason when I was playing *Henry V*, and he came round to my dressing-room and said, "Do you know why you're so good in this part?" And I said, "No, please tell me." And he said, "You're England, that's all," and so when people came round aı.¹ said to me, "Tell me how," I said, "It's simple: I am England."

Alienation

Dame Peggy Ashcroft:

When we did the production of *The Good Woman of Setzuan*, we were lucky enough to have Helene Weigel [Brecht's widow] at some of the rehearsals and I asked her what her attitude to alienation was, because it seemed to me, when I had seen a Brecht play in Germany, that it is Brecht himself in the writing of the plays who performs this act of alienation. The actor has, as we say, to realize the character that he plays just as fully as in any other dramatist. But Brecht was not interested in psychological investigations of character, and so the actor has to make his effect with great economy of means, but the realization must be complete. I was rather relieved to find that Helene Weigel agreed with this.

Stanislavsky

Michael Redgrave:

When I first came across Stanislavsky (because nobody told me about him) I misused what I read in much the same way as the later disciples of what is now called The Method have misused it; that is to say, I thought it permitted me to do anything that came into my head, regardless of whether it was right for the play. Very shortly after I first started reading him, for instance, I was acting in a naturalistic play which took place in a very untidy room. I was only playing a supporting part, a doctor. Intoxicated as I was at that moment by Stanislavsky, I thought a doctor would probably be rather a neat, tidy person, and I began to use the untidiness of the room by picking up threads, tucking things away in a drawer. It wasn't my room, I was just visiting. I hadn't warned any of the other actors I was going to do these things, they thought I had gone quite mad, and in a way I had gone mad.

The Method

In America Stanislavsky's System was taught by a number of his pupils. It was adapted into what is known as The Method by Lee Strasberg, whose Actor's Studio has had an enormous influence on American acting. Although Strasberg was far from as dogmatic as his disciples, stories and jokes about Method-acting have become part of the American vernacular.

A favorite joke was built around the Method players' passion for analyzing their every act on stage: George S. Kaufman tells a "bothersome actor" to cross the stage and hold for four "beats" before speaking his next line. "What's my justification for holding four beats?" the actor asks the director. "Because I tell you to, that's why!" Kaufman screams in reply. Or a typical variation: "What's my motivation for moving on that line?" inquires the actor. "Your paycheck!" snaps the director . . . Before they started rehearsals for *Major Barbara*, Charles Laughton quite genially but firmly said to Eli Wallach, "I don't want any of that Stanislavsky shit from you!"

An earlier incident during the Studio's very first season involved Eli Wallach, who was taking Strasberg's class with the cast of *Brigadoon* and appearing on Broadway in Katharine Cornell's 1948 production of *Antony and Cleopatra*. Wallach played a messenger who appears in Act II to inform the queen that Antony has married Octavia. One day he heard Strasberg give a lecture on "action." "If you go on stage to do something, do it!" Strasberg exhorted his actors. Wallach was so stirred by the talk, he could hardly contain himself at that evening's performance. He rushed into the theatre and hurriedly put on his costume, makeup, and sword. He was so worked up by Strasberg's words that he could not wait to give Cleopatra the news of Antony's marriage. But Shakespeare wrote several long speeches for Cleopatra before the messenger reveals his message. Wallach would say, "Madame . . ." and Miss Cornell would reel off several lines of poetry. He would repeat, "Madame! . . ." and again she would speak at length. Finally, unable to contain his pent-up enthusiasm, he abruptly exclaimed, "Madame, would it please you hear me?"—and cut a good number of Miss Cornell's best lines. The astonished actress hauled off and hit him, then swept off stage. Wallach went to Strasberg's next class and said to him, "What the hell kind of Method is that?!" Strasberg told him, "Wait for your cues!"

Frenzy

Harold J. Kennedy:

I asked Jean Barrère, stage manager for Judith Anderson's highly acclaimed Broadway production of *Medea*, whether Miss Anderson used any particular acting method. "Judith has her own method," Jean said. "She drives herself into a frenzy before she walks on the stage." He pointed out that her very first entrance in the play, where she comes on shrieking "Death! Death!" is at an emotional peak few actresses are able to reach by the end of a normal third act. He then told me the story about Judith and her arch enemy, Florence Reed, who was co-starring in the play with her and John Gielgud. When Jean called "half hour" one night, Judith Anderson called him into her dressing room and said: "I want you to take this message to Florence Reed. You are to tell that old bitch that she is not to move a muscle, not a muscle, during my soliloquy. Now tell her that exactly." Jean then went and knocked on Florence's door. "Come in," said Florence in that deep Mother Goddam* voice. He opened the door and there was Florence, adjusting her chin straps and putting on a gallon of rouge. "I have a message from Miss Anderson," Jean said, and repeated the message verbatim. Florence gave one of the chin straps an extra tug. "Tell Judith," she said, "to go f—k herself." Jean did what we all do under those circumstances, which is nothing. He called "fifteen minutes," then "five minutes," and finally "places," and no questions were asked. Florence took her place on the stage and the curtain went up. Meantime Judith was pacing like a panther in the wings,

---

* Florence Reed played the original Mother Goddam on Broadway in *The Shanghai Gesture* in 1926.

waiting for her entrance. As she passed the stage manager's desk, she said to Jean, "Did you give Florence my message?"

"Yes, Miss Anderson," said Jean. "Warning. You're on."

"What did she say?" demanded Judith.

"You're on, Miss Anderson."

"Tell me what she said," hissed Judith, already in character.

"She said, Miss Anderson, that you should go f—k yourself."

"Death!" screamed Judith. "Death!" And plummeted onstage.

[33] TRICKS OF THE TRADE

Masking

May Whitty's first part was as Irving's daughter in *The Lyons Mail*, and in one scene she had to be dragged sobbing from his arms, leaving him in his prison cell, condemned to die. When they reached this point, May indicated that here some sobbing occurred and turned to ask where the exit was supposed to be. Irving raised a sardonic eyebrow. "Can't scream?" he said. "Voice bad? Pity. Ought to be able to scream." "Of course I can scream," retorted the old heroine of *East Lynne* indignantly, and forthwith split the rafters. Irving appeared satisfied. But on the opening night, as she clung in his arms distractedly, she became aware that he was thumping her head and muttering furiously in her ear, "Box! Dammit, box!" She stole a quick look and realized her crime: she had inadvertently obscured his face from the line of sight of the right-hand box.

Act in Your Pauses

Sir Cedric Hardwicke:

Later along in years, I heard Ellen Terry sum up in a sentence this everlasting distinction between the actor's art and the playwright's. "My boy," she said to me, "act in your pauses." At those moments, you are a creator, not a servant of playwrights.

Less Is More

Sir Michael Redgrave:

I remember Edith Evans saying to me, "When you hear me say that line" (which was just four words, 'perfectly, perfectly, Mr. Horner' in

The Country Wife) "put your hand on my diaphragm," and I did, and she said, "Perfectly, perfectly, Mr. Horner," but so that you could hear it through the whole house. And she said, "Do you realize I'm using more strength of voice just to say those whispered words, than I need for when I'm speaking loud?" That was a subtle way, I think, of telling me that I was occasionally dropping my voice, and that when I wanted to talk quietly I had to use more force and not less.

Relaxing

It took John Gielgud a long time to learn by experience the advice Komisarjevsky gave him to relax. He first played Hamlet at the Old Vic in 1929, directed by Harcourt Williams.

It was arduous because we played the entirety, without any cuts at all, for several performances; then we played a cut version; then we went back to the entirety; then we moved to the Queen's Theatre and did another cut version; so that we were always learning new bits. Curiously enough, I found the entirety less tiring, because the other parts are longer and Hamlet has a few more rests.

Thirty-five years later, directing the Broadway production of Hamlet, *Gielgud could pass on his experience.*

Rehearsing Richard Burton in *Hamlet*, I said to him, "Well this is going to be *your* Hamlet, you know, I'm not going to try and give you mine; but perhaps I can help you a bit with the technical side of it." After the first week or two he said, "The thing which I've got from you is that you've shown me where to save myself; I'm not exhausted at the end of this scene, or that scene, which used to kill me when I first played the part at the Vic." And I said, "Well, that's all I've learned over the years."

Enjoy What You Do

Noël Coward:

There are many tricks in the theatre that the comedians—not first-rate comedians, but quite excellent comedians—use. They like upstaging, which is one of the most archaic forms of acting, and quite nonsense, and they do little tricks to spoil somebody else's lines, not realizing that by doing so they are destroying themselves and the play. Now the Lunts are exactly the opposite. They would spend minutes to enable me to get a laugh when I stubbed a cigarette out, and I would do the same for them. The great thing is that you, as a comedian, must enjoy what you're doing. I hate this new solemnity in the theatre. If anybody says to me, "She's a dedicated actress," I'd like to strangle her. What is she dedicated about?

Training the Audience

The elder Mathews was always annoyed when playing some favourite character, by parties arriving late at the theatre, and the play half over. When playing the title part in Moncrief's *Monsieur Mallet* at the Adelphi and this annoyance occurred, it would seriously disconcert him. He would exclaim, on leaving the stage, "Look at those people. They have come to see Mallet, have book'd places to see Mallet; don't come to the theatre till Mallet is nearly over, and my best scene over. Sure to go away and say they've seen Mallet, haven't seen Mallet, know nothing about Mallet. What do they come for? Better stay away altogether; best plan."

At Plymouth, during one of his entertainments, a gentleman before him presented such a melancholy face that it so fidgetted Mathews he was obliged to advance and address the gentleman thus, at the same time giving one of his comical looks: "I beg your pardon, Sir, but if you don't laugh I can't go on." This was received by the audience with such roars that the unconsciously offending gentleman throughout the evening laughed louder than anybody else.

How To Win the Audience

Noël Coward:

Darling Yvonne Arnaud, who was one of the most brilliant comediennes I ever saw, could look at a script, read through the lines and decide: titter, laugh, drag, slight titter, big laugh, before she even started rehearsing. Her favourite thing was a bad Saturday matinee, a lot of old ladies who were rather comatose and wishing for their madeira cake and their tea. She'd say to herself, "I'll get you by the end of the afternoon," and she always did.

[34] VOICE

When in Doubt, Shout

Sir Cedric Hardwicke describes the old school of acting.

To be prepared when fate knocked on the dressing-room door for me,
I memorized every part in *The Monk*. I also took careful heed of the
advice that was continually being drilled into us by Mr. S. Major
Jones, the florid, bustling, sarcastic stage manager, whose military rank
was confined to his Christian name. "What you need for this type of
play is a good pair of lungs," he admonished us. "When in doubt,
shout—that's the motto." I had a ready-made way of developing my
voice. I walked by the mile on Hampstead Heath now that I had
moved my lodgings close by that desolate and surprisingly remote corner of London, shouting *King Lear* on the hills among the scrubby
trees against the wind.

Losing It

*Drama consists of language, and the voice is the actor's most impor-
tant instrument. It is easily strained or ruined. Most actors spend a
vast deal of time developing and training it. Here Sybil Thorndike describes what its loss can mean.*

I was playing at Princeton University and my brother Russell and I
were staying with Woodrow Wilson, who was then president of the
university. I was playing Good Deeds in *Everyman*—and I opened my
mouth and drew in my breath, and a piece of powder-puff which was
on my veil flew into my throat and got stuck round my vocal cords
and I couldn't speak. I did a lot of *acting*, but I couldn't say another
word! And that began my struggle with voice. I worked for nearly
three months in the open air with a false voice. Finally it got so bad
that Russell said, "Sybil's got to go home. She must see a doctor."

I came home and I saw a top specialist, Sir St. Clair Thompson,
who was King Edward's throat doctor. And he looked at my throat,
and said, "Are you a brave girl?" And I said, "Yes, I am." And he
said, "I'm afraid you won't speak on the stage again." Wasn't that
awful! And he said, "Your vocal cords are smothered with growths. I

can't see anything, I can't see a vocal cord at all. But if you could possibly be silent for six weeks, I might see if it's curable." Not a word did I speak—I practised the piano, I went for long walks in the country. I was staying at the vicarage of course, with my father and mother. And then, when I went back to the specialist in six weeks, he looked at my throat, and I was sitting in perfect terror. He said, "You've got the constitution of an ox, those growths have all gone, your vocal cords are clear. Now," he said, "you've got to be jolly careful." Then I went to a person and worked. He was quite a quack, but he knew how to get me over the first difficulties and so I got back my voice again.

Later she was overworking and got into trouble again.

I was using my voice wrongly, overstraining it, trying to push too hard. If you strain, then you do something to your vocal cords, and Elsie Fogerty got me through difficult times. I never had to be off at all. She went through the whole thing of breathing; and relaxing was one of the first things she taught me. She had a wonderful way of focusing the voice and helping you to get all the notes. She said, "You must have your three octaves." Well, I did have my three octaves until I was over eighty and now I've only lost two notes.

Cocaine and Menthol

A more unconventional method of getting one's voice back is described by Tallulah Bankhead.

In London, when I had one of my frequent attacks of the actor's nightmare, laryngitis, Sir Milton Reese, the King's doctor, sprayed my throat with a solution laced with cocaine. It stimulated my larynx, relieved strain on my vocal cords, reduced my chances of becoming mute during a performance. At Boots, the London chemists, where I presented the prescription, I was given a bottle of pale little lozenges, labeled "Cocaine and Menthol." Obsessed with the desire to shock people, I whipped the vial out at every opportunity. I'd hold it out to my friends: "Have some cocaine?" "Tallulah, isn't it habit-forming?" "Cocaine, habit-forming? Of course not. I ought to know. I've been using it for years."

Velvet

When Olivier came to play Othello in 1964 he felt his natural voice was inadequate for the task.

I did go through a long period of vocal training especially for it, to in-crease the depth of my voice, and I actually managed to attain about six more notes in the bass. I never used to be able to sing below D, but now, after a little exercising, I can get down to A, through all the semitones; and that helps at the beginning of the play, it helps the violet velvet that I felt was necessary in the timbre of the voice.

Shaw's Advice

Michael Redgrave:

You can't do a rehearsal of *King Lear*, or for that matter *Uncle Vanya*, or anything, without adding a sufficient timbre to your voice and increasing your stamina. I think Shaw was right when he said that if anyone would sing for half-an-hour each day they'd be in much bet-ter health.

He Did It His Way

Today actors and singers have intensive voice training. One of the best-known teachers in America for a couple of generations has been Arthur Lessac. This is how he started his own system.

I was studying with Adelin Fermin at the Eastman School in Roches-ter, New York, and after my third year I went to see him and said, "I'm worried that my voice still can't get to the upper covered regis-ters, and so I won't be able to have a singing career." Fermin smiled reassuringly: "Believe me, one morning while you are washing your face the first note out of your mouth will have the upper covered reg-ister." I kept washing my face diligently, but the sound never came. So I didn't go back to a fourth year. In fact, that is how I started thinking about the problems of the voice, and it was the beginning of the Lessac Method.

Breathing

It was Mrs. Siddons who described applause as something akin to breath, because actors need it to stay alive. Breathing is an important part of the actor's training, as described here by Sarah Bernhardt.

There was a famous professor, a shareholder in the Comédie Française, M. Talbot by name, who was my first tutor and gave me excellent advice, but towards the end of his career he became a trifle eccentric. He would make his pupils lie flat; then he would place the marble slab of his mantelpiece on their stomachs, and say: "Now breathe . . . and say your part." The worthy Talbot perhaps exaggerated the proceedings a little, but his first method of respiration was excellent. The finest voice is not proof against shortness of breath. To master this instrument, it is essential to achieve perfection in breathing.

The Master's Voice

Asked about his singing voice, Noël Coward told *The Daily Mirror*: "I belong to the bullmoose set. We are people who go to the same vocal teacher in New York. His name is Alfred Dixon and his lessons are remarkable for their simplicity. We just sit and moo. It does wonders to the voice and it's remarkably easy—once you have learned how to moo."

CHAPTER VII

Outward Show

The Faithful Dresser

The original Lothario—in Rowe's *Fair Penitent* (1703)—was George Powell, an esteemed actor who won applause from Addison and Steele, but who appears to have been somewhat of a toper, and was generally reputed to obscure his faculties by incessant indulgence in Nantes brandy. The fourth act of the play over, the actor was impatient to be gone, and was heard behind the scenes angrily demanding the assistance of Warren, his dresser, entirely forgetful of the fact that his attendant was employed upon the stage in personating the corpse of Lothario. Mr. Powell's wrath grew more and more intense. He threatened the absent Warren with the severest of punishments. The unhappy dresser, reclining on Lothario's bier, could not but overhear his raging master, yet for some time his fears were surmounted by his sense of dramatic propriety. He lay and shivered, longing for the fall of the curtain. At length his situation became quite unendurable. Powell was threatening to break every bone in his skin. In his dresser's opinion the actor was a man likely to keep his word. With a cry of "Here I am, master!" Warren sprung up, clothed in sable draperies which were fastened to the handles of his bier. The house roared with surprise and laughter. Encumbered by his charnel-house trappings, the dead Lothario precipitately fled from the stage. The play, of course, ended abruptly.

Anachronisms

When *The Earl of Warwick* was first performed in Dublin, Mrs. Kelf, a most beautiful woman, and a fine actress in both tragedy and comedy, played Lady Elizabeth Grey. She dressed from a picture of Vandyke, and her appearance had a novel and most pleasing effect, it being quite a new thing to dress in the habits of the times or country when and where the scene was laid. Barry played Othello the Venetian Moor in a complete suit of English regimentals, and a three-

cocked, gold-laced hat! and Thomas Sheridan, in *Macbeth*, dressed in
scarlet and gold English uniform; and when King, he wore a Spanish
hat turned up before, with a diamond and feathers in the front. All
the characters in the play of *Richard III* appeared in the same modern
clothes as the gentlemen in the boxes wore, except Richard himself,
who dressed as Richard, and thus looked an angry Merry-Andrew
among the rest of the performers. In *Henry VIII* none wore the habits of the times but Henry himself: his courtiers were apparelled in the
dress only known two hundred years after.

How Did It Get Through Customs?

On one occasion, immediately after his return from America, William
Macready was playing Hamlet and John Cooper was playing the
Ghost. Macready, always particular about stage dresses, provided as
usual the costume for his adopted father's ghost, using the same suit
as had done duty in America. At the solemn moment when Hamlet,
seeing the ghost on the ramparts of Elsinore Castle, interrogates him,
Cooper started rubbing his neck as he said: "Thy father's spirit doomed
for a certain time to—" (a jerk of the ghostly head and then an exclamation). "What the devil is it?" Macready (glowing with rage, *sotto
voce*): "Go on, sir." "I cannot; I am ate up alive by something."
(Laughter in the audience.) Hamlet: "Get off, sir." Ghost: "Where's
the trap?" (to lead to sulphureous flames) feeling with his feet for it,
descends, rubbing his hands and saying: "Oh, remember me." Macready, exasperated beyond measure, rushing to the green room as the
act-drop fell, demanded an explanation. "Ask the cockroaches in your
infernal armour," replied the ghost. The costume had not been un-
packed since its use in America until that afternoon, and was found
to be swarming with cockroaches.

Mrs. Campbell Is Discovered

May Whitty attended the opening night of a new melodrama at the
Adelphi Theatre, *The Trumpet Call*. There was an unknown actress
in it, a handsome, gypsy creature with an odd name, Mrs. Patrick
Campbell. May didn't think much of either the play or the acting:
"awful rubbish—vilely acted all round," she wrote. But in the last act
Mrs. P. Campbell's skirt fell off. Any actress might have been excused
for rushing off the stage overwhelmed with shame and confusion; not
Mrs. P. Campbell. She gathered it up, wrapped it around her with all

the dignity of a Roman empress investing herself with the purple, and calmly went on with the scene. The tittering audience was hushed and held; a ripple of admiration widened through theatrical London.

Clothes Do Not an Actress Make

Jo Mielziner, one of the outstanding designers of the American theatre learned his craft from Robert Edmond Jones.

One morning Bobby told me to report early to the Eaves costume workshop instead of the studio as was usual. When I arrived, I was told to go to Fitting Room A. I knocked. I opened the door. There in front of me was the back of a seventeenth-century lady bent over in a deep and exaggerated curtsy. Her wig was rich with trimming, and the hand that held her train was loaded with period jewelry and roped with pearls. I glanced beyond this magnificent figure into the mirror. There, between the baroque pearl necklace and the rich hairdressing was Bobby Jones's eager face—black brows, piercing eyes looking through his glasses, and a broad grin under the clipped black mustache. He laughed. "You know, Jo," he said, "most actresses really don't know how to wear these things. I just had to see what it felt like." He moved about the room in the splendid gown. "It's wonderful, don't you think?"

Anatomy

In 1945 Ralph Richardson gave a famous Falstaff.

It's a bog part to tackle and I didn't think I could do it all. But my partner at that time, who was Laurence Olivier, said, "Nonsense, all parts are difficult. Don't be so coy, don't be so silly. Just have a go at it." So I did, and we did both parts of *Henry IV*. My costume was wonderful, it was Alex Stone who designed it. She created a complete anatomy for me in padding, I had two or three stomachs, two or three chests, and two huge arms. And over this she put a very light, revealing flannel material, so that you could see the anatomy of the creature; in other words, he wasn't a puffed-up football, as he has often been.

Shakespeare's Craft

Donald Wolfit's padding for Falstaff was a monstrous piece of old-fashioned engineering. Hot, heavy and Gothic, it caused the actor to sweat mercilessly. Between matinee and evening performances it would be hung from the flies with a powerful light shining on to it, in the hope that the heat would dry it. But the worst drawback of the padding was that it had to be removed entirely if the actor was to relieve himself during the performance. Falstaff, luckily, is off-stage for some length of time during the course of the play, and this provided Wolfit with the necessary opportunity. "Brilliant craftsman, Shakespeare. Knew the actor would want to pee and constructed the play accordingly. A master, a master!"

The Dressing Room

Roy Moseley began as a dresser to many stars, among them Vivien Leigh, whom he got to know during the London run of Duel of Angels *in 1958.*

Her dressing-rooms always looked as much like her home as she could make them. She would move in favourite paintings, familiar pieces from her boudoir and even her Corgi, Amando, and a Siamese cat. There was one glorious incident at the Apollo when I went back-stage one day and found the entire cast changing in her dressing-room. Someone on the staff had been letting the dressing-rooms out to prostitutes after the company had gone home. The cast were terrified of picking up certain unmentionable complaints, so they all piled into Vivien Leigh's dressing-room. With all her possessions inside it was the only one that was bolted, and the only uncontaminated by the ladies of the street. She loved it and was not the least put out by everyone stripping and changing in her room.

Tights

At the first dress rehearsal of the revue *Sigh No More* choreographer Wendy Toye was sitting next to Noël Coward when a young actor (his first job) sprang on to the stage as the Fourth Harlequin. He had obviously never worn tights before and didn't know what should have gone under them. "The sight was alarming," says Wendy. "Noël grabbed my hand and whispered piercingly: "For God's sake go and tell that young man to take that Rockingham tea service out of his tights.""

[36] WIGS

Black and White

The accounts still extant of the revels at court during the reigns of Elizabeth and James contain many charges for wigs and beards. Thus a certain John Ogle is paid "for four yeallowe heares for head attires for women, twenty-six shillings and eightpence," and "for a pound of heare twelvepence." And mention is made of a delivery to Mrs. Swee-go the silk-woman, of "Spanish silke of sundry cullers weighing four ounces and three quarters, at two shillings and sixpence the ounce, to garnish nine heads and nine skarfes for the nine muzes."

With the Restoration wigs came into general wear, and gradually the beards and moustaches which had literally flourished so remarkably from the time of Elizabeth were yielded to the razor. The actors appeared upon all occasions in the enormous perukes that were introduced in the reign of Charles II, and continued in vogue until 1720. The flowing flaxen wigs assumed by Booth, Wilks, Cibber, and others, were said to cost some forty guineas each.

But if the heroes of the theatre delighted in long flaxen hair, it was always held necessary that the stage villains should appear in jet-black periwigs. "What is the meaning," demanded Charles II, "that we never see a rogue in the play, but odds-fish! they always clap him on a black periwig, when it is well known one of the greatest rogues in England always wears a fair one?" The king was understood to refer to Titus Oates.*

A Historic Wig

Many actors in the eighteenth century had large and valuable wig collections. One was Richard Suett, the comic actor who appeared in the burlesque of Tom Thumb *wearing a large black peruke with flowing curls that had once been the property of Charles II.*

He had purchased this curious relic at the sale of the effects of a Mr. Rawle, accoutrement-maker to George III. When the wig was submitted for sale, Suett took possession of it, and, putting it on his

* Titus Oates was responsible for fabricating the so-called "Popish Plot" of 1678 which led to mass hysteria in London and the execution of dozens of prominent Catholics.

head, began to bid for it with a gravity that the bystanders found to be irresistibly comical. It was at once declared that the wig should become the actor's property upon his own terms, and it was forthwith knocked down to him by the auctioneer. The wig appeared upon the stage during many years, until at last it was destroyed, with much other valuable property, in the fire which burnt to the ground the Birmingham Theatre. Suett's grief was extreme. "My wig's gone!" he would say, mournfully, for some time after the fire, to every one he met.

Losing It

Mr. Bensley, the tragedian so much admired by Charles Lamb, and so little by any other critic, was playing Richard III in an Irish theatre. The curtain had risen, and he was advancing to the footlights to deliver his opening soliloquy, when an unlucky nail in the side-wing caught a curl of his full-flowing majestic wig, and dragged it from his head. He was a pedantic, solemn actor, with a sepulchral voice, and a stiff stalking gait. The loss of his wig must have occasioned him acute distress. For a moment he hesitated. What was he to do? Should he forget that he was Richard? Should he remember that he was only Mr. Bensley? He resolved to ignore the accident, to abandon his wig. Shorn of his locks, he delivered his speech in his most impressive manner. Of course he had to endure many interruptions. An Irish audience is rarely forbearing—has a very quick perception of the ludicrous. The jeering and ironic cheering that arose must have gravely tried the tragedian. "Mr. Bensley, darling, put on your jasey!" cried the gallery. "Bad luck to your politics! Will you suffer a Whig to be hung?" But the actor did not flinch. His exit was as dignified and commanding as had been his entrance. He did not even condescend to notice his wig as he passed it, depending from its nail like a scarecrow. One of the attendants of the stage was sent on to remove it, the duty being accomplished amidst the most boisterous laughter and applause of the whole house.

Beard

When Laurence Olivier directed and first played *King Lear* at the Old Vic in 1946, Hubert Griffith wrote in the *Sunday Graphic*: "He handicapped himself by wearing a beard and mane so stupendous that his voice came to me as though he were talking through a tree."

Carrot

When John Mills was playing in a play called *The Uninvited Guest* in London, a critic remarked: "Mr. John Mills wanders around the stage at the St. James's Theatre looking like a bewildered carrot." (John Mills says he was wearing what he thought was the best red wig that Wig Creations ever made.)

[37] MAKEUP

Special Effects

Some say that when Aeschylus introduced the chorus in the *Eumenides*, the masks worn by the Furies so frightened the audience that some infants died and women went into early labor.

Not Just Makeup

Hesketh Pearson:

Herbert Tree's genius for getting into the skin of a part, physically and mentally, was never better exemplified than in *Beethoven*. Louis Parker, who had adapted the play from the French, said that when Tree first appeared at the dress-rehearsal the entire company gasped with surprise. There entered "a short stocky, square-set little man, with dark eyes. His head was Beethoven's head." Tree was tall, lanky, blue-eyed, the very opposite to Beethoven in build and features; and I, too, experienced a shock when I found myself next to him at Covent Garden, where he was giving an act of the play at a charity matinee, because, though expecting his appearance, I completely failed to recognise him and was under the strong impression of looking down at a man whose eyes were normally on a level with my own. These metamorphoses were uncanny, and what made His Majesty's the most thrilling theatre in the world was that even when he was hopelessly miscast Tree's acting was so clever, so inventive, so varied, so intensely interesting, that for unalloyed entertainment one would rather see him in a bad play than anyone else in a good one.

Grease-paint

Once during a matinee at the Haymarket Theatre, Tree, made up as Falstaff, met Coquelin in the wings. The great French actor was tremendously impressed by the way Tree had made up his features. "Pardon me," he said, "but how do you pad your cheeks?" Tree invited him to touch them. Coquelin did so, and with a mild French oath exclaimed: "Why, there is nothing!" Tree's effects were gained not by padding and such like devices, but simply by sheer skill as a grease-paint artist.

Contrast

Not every actor takes the same amount of care with makeup. The designer W. Graham Robertson paints a contrast between Sarah Bernhardt and Mrs. Pat Campbell.

One evening I was sitting with Madame Sarah in her dressing-room at the theatre, watching her make up. This always fascinated me— it was absorbing to note the subtle touches with which she changed her own delicate features into the sensual, heavy-lipped face of Theodora, the olive-tinted mask of Lorenzaccio, or the fragile semblance of Napoleon's ill-fated son. This evening Sarah was gradually resolving into Cleopatra, and, as final details were being added, Mrs. Campbell entered.

Sarah was absorbed for the moment and could spare little attention: she was painting her hands, staining the finger-tips and palms with the dusky red of henna. Mrs. Campbell watched with some impatience; she had business to discuss and was in a hurry. "Why do you take so much trouble?" she said at last. "What you are doing will never show from the front. Nobody will see it." "I shall see it," replied Sarah slowly. "I am doing it for myself. If I catch sight of my hand it will be the hand of Cleopatra. That will help me."

Perfect Disguise

In order to play in *Rosemary*, John Drew shaved off his mustache, thereby greatly changing his appearance. Shortly afterward he met Max Beerbohm in the lobby of a London theatre, but could not just then recall who the latter was. Mr. Beerbohm's memory was better:

"Oh, Mr. Drew," he said, "I'm afraid you don't know me without your mustache."

Blood

Cedric Hardwicke:

For *Hamlet*, we hired the Alhambra itself for three performances and rehearsed on its stage. The climax of the melodrama which was being staged professionally during that week of rehearsing was the electrocution of the villain in an electric chair. The chair was a most ingenious prop. Each arm held a little cup of magnesium, which flared up to create the illusion of lethal current crackling through the victim. Inside the helmet, where it touched the culprit's head, was a sponge soaked with red dye, which trickled like blood down his face when the headpiece was clamped down on him.

Waiting for a cue one rehearsal, I sat myself in the chair and experimentally pulled on the helmet. My cue came up and I made my entrance unknowingly streaming with simulated blood. Ophelia shrieked; the rest of the company gaped in horror. For a stupefying moment I wondered if somehow the death chair had been wired in fact and I was doomed. But soap and water put an end to my fears, and we went back to rehearsing.

Noses

In London in July 1955, a stage adaptation of *Moby-Dick* was produced at the Duke of York's Theatre, starring Orson Welles as Captain Ahab, with Kenneth Williams as Elijah and Gordon Jackson as Ishmael. Welles always wore a false nose when he was working on stage, largely because he hated his own, and in one performance of *Moby-Dick*, while Ahab was delivering one of his big speeches, the nose began to fall apart. "Tell him his nose is falling off," Kenneth Williams hissed to Gordon Jackson. It was too late. The nose had beaten them to it and was already slipping down over Welles's mouth. As the great actor screamed, "Get that white whale, men!" the nose dropped off completely, landed at his feet, and was sent curling into the stalls with a deft drop-kick.

Vivien Leigh had shown similar dexterity four years before in the Festival of Britain production of Shaw's *Caesar and Cleopatra*. Miss

Leigh had to slap Elspeth March across the face. As the nurse Fata-
teeta, Miss March was wearing a false nose and on one unhappy occasion Cleopatra's slap sent the nose flying into the air. All was not
lost. Vivien Leigh fielded it brilliantly with her other hand and gave
it back to Miss March, who was able to make her exit holding her
hand to her face, without the audience having noticed a thing.

Beyond Makeup

*Paul Muni began his career in his teens in the Yiddish theatres of
New York. His name then was Muni Wiesenfreund, and like most
young actors he played mainly old parts, while young romantic leads
were the preserve of established actors pushing sixty. By the age of
thirty-one Paul Muni had worked for eighteen years and played three
hundred parts in Yiddish; his "overnight discovery" and transition
to the mainstream is one of those legends that exist in many versions.
This one is from the authorized biography,* Actor, *by the dramatist
Jerome Lawrence. In October 1926, producer Sam Harris urgently
needed a replacement for Edward G. Robinson, who was playing a
very old man in the Broadway-bound production of a play called* We
Americans *by William Herbert Gropper and Max Siegel.*

Sam Harris looked up at the youthful Muni when he walked in and
immediately dismissed him with a preemptory wave. "Too young. Are
you out of your minds? He's just a kid!" Muni turned to leave the
room. Siegel put up his hand to stop him. Muni looked back at Sam
Harris; then he bent over and tottered toward the producer's desk. He
wore no makeup, but his voice seemed as wise and ancient as time.
"Oh, sir, you're right. We old bastards shouldn't let any of those
young punks into the theater. What do they know—still wet in the
diapers, still shitting their pants?" Harris looked up, laughed, then
glanced over at the equally startled director. Forrest, who hadn't said
a word, now said just two: "Sign him."

[38]   IMPERSONATION

Boy Actresses

*The Elizabethan theatre was famous for its children's companies,
and several boy actors went on to specialize in adult female roles.*

Nathaniel Field was considered second only to Burbage as an actor; his father, John Field, was a Puritan preacher who thundered from his pulpit against the stage. Other names of well-known boy-actresses of the early seventeenth century include Robert Goffe, William Ostler (whose variant name, Hostler, some think, may be lurking under the mysterious "Mr. W. H." of Shakespeare's sonnets), and "Dickey" Robinson who was killed during the Civil War by one of the notorious Puritans. He was famous as a youth, praised in Ben Jonson's The Devil Is an Ass *as dressing "himself the best, beyond Forty of your very ladies."*

There's Dickey Robinson

A very pretty fellow, and comes often
To a gentleman's chamber, a friend of mine. We had
The Merriest supper of it there, one night
The gentleman's landlady invited him
To a gossip's feast: now he, sir, brought Dick Robinson,
Drest like a lawyer's wife, amongst them all:
I lent him clothes—But to see him behave it,
And lay the law, and carve and drink unto them,
And then talk bawdy, and send frolics! O,
It would have burst your buttons, or not left you a seam.

Ladies' Pet

Even when actresses took over female parts on the English stage, one female impersonator kept his popularity from pre-Restoration days. Colley Cibber as a young apprentice met Edward Kynaston, then already in his forties.

Kynaston at that time was so beautiful a youth that the ladies of quality prided themselves in taking him with them on their coaches to Hyde Park in his theatrical habit, after the play. Of this truth I had the curiosity to inquire, and had it confirmed from his own mouth, in his advanced age; and indeed to the last of him his handsomeness was very little abated; even at past sixty his teeth were sound, white, and even as one could wish to see in a reigning toast of twenty.

Shaving the Queen

Cibber is probably alluding to Kynaston in the following incident, involving Charles II.

The King coming a little before his usual time to a tragedy, found the actors not ready to begin, when his Majesty, not choosing to have as much patience as his good subjects, sent to them to know the meaning of it, upon which the master of the company came to the box, and, rightly judging that the best excuse for their default would be the true one, fairly told his Majesty that the queen was not shaved yet; the King, whose good humour loved to laugh at a jest as well as to make one, accepted the excuse, which served to divert him till the male queen could be effeminated.

Vice Versa

In the year 1780, Mr. Colman had recourse to a most whimsical and indecent mode of attracting visitors to his theatre in the Haymarket, viz. by travestying *The Beggars' Opera*, that is, by putting all the female performers in the male parts, and vice versa.

The Ideal Woman

There has been a tradition of female impersonators in American show business since the minstrel shows and vaudeville of the nineteenth century. That is how Bill Dalton began his career in Boston in 1905; five years later, under the stage name Julian Eltinge, he was the biggest star on Broadway, with a theatre named after him. Very much a "manly man" off-stage, his fan magazine published beauty secrets for a wide readership of women.

It took him a full hour and a half to prepare for each performance. He shaved his beard, applied flesh-tone grease-paints to his face, and finished off his complexion with powders. He formed his eyes into almond shapes, accenting the lids with blue and building up the lashes with black. "Lip rouge" completed his face. He rubbed his own white liquid preparation into his arms and shoulders, then powdered over the lotion to get the soft white effect he wanted. Trying to make his hands look smaller and more delicate, he powdered them white, rouged the fingers from the second knuckle to the tips and brightly painted his nails, which had the effect of tapering the fingers, and finally added blue pencil lines on the backs of his hands to make them look slender. He advised women never to hold the breadth of the hand toward the viewer. By presenting the narrow sides, the hands seemed longer and more delicate. Besides being two and a half sizes too small, his shoes were always satin, which shone under bright lights making the feet look tinier. Finally, he styled his wigs to look soft and fluffy around the face and the back of the neck. The result of all this, he hoped, was the "ideal girl," what one writer called women the way "they ought to be."

CHAPTER VIII

Dramatists

The Father of Tragedy

Aeschylus wrote ninety tragedies, forty of which were rewarded with the public prize, and yet only seven of them have been preserved. One of his plays nearly proved fatal to him; he was accused of impiety, and condemned to be stoned to death. The sentence was just going to be executed when his brother Amynias, with a happy presence of mind, throwing aside his cloak, showed the poet's hand which had been cut off when bravely fighting at the battle of Salamis, in defense of his country. The sight made such an impression on the judges, that touched with the remembrance of his valour and the friendship he showed for his brother, they pardoned Aeschylus. The poet, however, resented the indignity of this persecution so much, that he bade an everlasting adieu to his native place, and retired to the court of Hiero, King of Sicily, where he lived until his death.

Another tradition says that Aeschylus retired into Sicily because the seats "broke down" during the representation of one of his tragedies. Some have taken this literally, but according to the scholar Joseph Scaliger this was a phrase among the comedians: a piece that "broke down the seats" was one that could not stand, but fell to the ground. The truth was that the plays of Aeschylus had begun to be less pleasing to the Athenians than those of Sophocles, a younger and more polished writer.

Sophocles

Sophocles was twenty-five when he conquered his master, Aeschylus, in tragedy. Cimon, the Athenian general, had found the bones of Theseus and brought these noble relics with pomp into the city. A tragic contest was announced, as was usual upon extraordinary occasions. Aeschylus and Sophocles were the two rivals, and the prize was adjudged to Sophocles, although it was the first play he ever presented in public.

He once appeared on stage in the character of a mere servant, who had not a word to utter, but only to play at ball, in order that by his peculiar skill in the art, he might give the last finishing touch to the representation of the tragedy.

A Classicist

When Racine was a scholar at Port Royal he was so fond of reading Sophocles and Euripides that he committed the whole of their plays to memory, and delighted to repeat their most striking beauties. While thus studying the models of antiquity, he accidentally met with the Greek romance of *The Loves of Theagenes and Chariclea*, on which he afterwards founded his first tragedy. His perceptor surprised him in the act of reading, took the book and threw it into the fire. Racine found means to get another copy which underwent the same fate, but such was his fondness for it that he did not rest till he had procured a third copy, when, to provide against any repetition of the disaster, he got the whole by heart, and then taking the book to his master, said, "You may now burn this, as you burned the others."

Who Stole from Whom?

This from a letter by George Peel, an Elizabethan dramatist, about some of his distinguished contemporaries.

I never longed for thy company more than last nighte. We were all very merrye at the Globe, where Ned Alleyn (actor and founder of Dulwich College) did not scruple to affirme pleasantly to thy friend "Will" (Shakespeare) that he had stolen the speeches about the qualityes of an actor's excelencye in *Hamlet*, from conversations manyfold, which had passed between them, and opinions given by Alleyn touching the subject. Shakespeare did not take this tale in good sorte; but Jonson put an end to the strife by wisely remarking: "This needs no contention. Ned, you stole, no doubt; do not marvel. Have you not seen him act times out of number?"

One hardly knows which to admire most, Ben's wit or tact.

Plagiarism

When Voltaire's tragedy *Alzire* was first performed it was busily whispered that it was not his own work. "I wish it may not be," said a man of wit. "Why so?" "Because," the man answered, "we should then have two good poets instead of one."

A young playwright was describing his most recent play to Dorothy Parker, who felt that he had been copying her themes: "It's hard to sum it up—but it's a play against all isms." "Except plagiarism," said Mrs. Parker.

Two plays were written about Dorothy Parker—one by George Oppenheimer, the other by Ruth Gordon. Mrs. Parker once commented, "Now, I suppose, if I ever wrote a play about myself I'd be sued for plagiarism."

A Gentleman, Not an Author

Voltaire was anxious to see and converse with a brother dramatist of such celebrity as the author of *The Way of the World*. He expected to find a man of a keen satirical mind who would join him in a laugh against humanity. He visited Congreve and naturally began to talk of his works. The fine gentleman spoke of them as trifles utterly beneath his notice, and told him, with an affectation which perhaps was sincere, that he wished to be visited as a gentleman, not as an author. One can imagine the disgust of his brother dramatist. Voltaire replied that had Mr. Congreve been nothing more than a gentleman he should not have taken the trouble to call on him, and therewith retired with an expression of merited contempt.

Frank Words

Chekhov's plays annoyed Tolstoy, whose views on art were both independent and unorthodox. That rugged oldster once told Chekhov, "I cannot bear Shakespeare, you know, but your plays are even worse. Shakespeare takes the reader by the neck and leads him to a certain goal, and does not let him turn aside. And where is one to go with your heroes? From the sofa where they are lying to the closet and back."

Education of a Dramatist

Unlike most of his genteel Irish colleagues, Sean O'Casey lacked a formal education. Journalist James Hodson took this snapshot of the artist as a working stiff.

Sean O'Casey worked in those days in penny school exercise books, and then typed and re-typed until he got it right. He had to hold a manuscript three inches from his nose to read it. Sometimes he wrote a one-act play as diversion, but a three-act play—that took a long time and a great many ideas, he said.

He pulled on his heavy boots, a trench coat, and a cap down over his eyes and we walked down into the centre of Dublin together. He might have been a bricksetter's labourer, or a gunman. But he talked with remarkable wit, and insight, and was extraordinarily incisive in his opinions. He seemed to suffer from no doubts. Education? Education was a great drawback to a dramatist. He was half-starved till nine years old, living on dry bread and tea, he learnt his lessons in the streets of Dublin, taught himself to read at fourteen, and then earned four shillings a week in an ironmonger's; next year he was working fifteen hours a day for nine shillings a week at a news-vendor's. Afterwards he navvied, carried bricks and did odd jobs for fifteen years. For ten of those years he visited the Abbey Theatre—pit or gallery—read Shakespeare, and wrote plays that were rejected. Part of the time he was on the dole. His first success was *The Shadow of the Gunman*, written largely out of his own experience. But it wasn't until *Juno and the Paycock* caught on that he gave up his manual work. "I decided then," he said, "that one job is enough for any man."

Symbolism

At a meeting of the Playwrights' Company a foreign manuscript came under discussion in which the author's meaning was cloaked in symbolism and the general tone was abstruse. Sherwood commented: "I prefer the plays of Robert Emmet Sherwood. He hasn't got much to say but at least he does not try to say anything else."

Helpful Advice

Noël Coward had this to say about Bernard Shaw.

He was so kind when I was a young writer. He corrected my scripts for me, before I'd even met him. He took the trouble to help a young playwright and he wrote me a postcard saying, "Never read anything of mine again, so long as you live."

Narrative Drama

One of the most influential dramatists of the twentieth century was Bertolt Brecht, a controversial character and abrasive personality. My father, the Hungarian playwright Julius Hay, knew Brecht for more than thirty years and delivered a funeral eulogy at his grave in 1956. The story of how they met is characteristic of both writers.

One evening Micky [Hay's current girlfriend] came home in high spirits.

"Helly Weigel sends her regards."

I have always had a bad memory for names. "And who is Helly Weigel?"

"Actress. Bertolt Brecht's wife."

"Aha. And how does she know of my existence and of the fact that I can be sent regards through you?"

"I've just been having coffee with her. I told her about you. I told her you wrote plays. And what kind of plays."

"And what did she say to that?"

"She gave a very decent donation for MASch [a left-wing agitprop theatre group for which they were raising money]. And she said to tell you that if you want to write plays you ought to go and see Bert. He'll be glad to tell you how it's done. She says it's quite simple."

I was suddenly as arrogant as only meek people can be when they start to rue their meekness. "In that case he'd better come and see me and I'll tell him how complicated it is."

Soon the two met: they were drawn to each other by similar political views but continued to differ in their theories about drama.

These discussions with Brecht did not affect our friendship, though one did need a sense of humour to take his somewhat boisterous chaffing, as for example on the occasion of the dress rehearsal of my play *The New Paradise*. It was a magnificent production by Heinz Hilpert with a brilliant cast and everyone in the theatre business was there, including Brecht, with Helly and his "staff." With growing irritation they were obliged to take cognizance of the fact that the play—which incidentally had been written before my first meeting with Brecht—ran very much counter to his theories of the drama. The upshot was that Brecht, Helly, and "staff" left at the interval. I was so wrapped up in a bad case of dress rehearsal nerves that I did not even see them go.

Next day a slightly embarrassed Micky came to me and said, "Helly's on the phone. Greetings from Brecht, and would you mind telling him the rest of the play—they didn't stay till the end last night."

Fortunately I managed to keep my temper. "Tell her greetings from me too. There's *one* ticket left for tonight's performance. Brecht can go along himself and then he'll be able to tell the others what it's all about. I'm against narrative drama myself."

How To Become a Playwright

Somerset Maugham told students in a drama course at London University: "A sure formula for success is to write first a tragedy in five acts. Put it away in a drawer for six months, then change it into a comedy in three acts. Forget it for another year. Then reduce it to a curtain raiser. That done, rush right out and marry a rich American."

[40] HOW THEY WORKED

Exit Pursued by a Bear

Don Francisco de Quevedo describes an incident in his life of Paul, the Spanish barber: "When I was writing a play, the maid used to bring up my dinner and leave it there; and it was my way to act all I wrote, and talk aloud as if I had been on the stage. As the devil would have it, when the maid was coming up the stairs, which were dark and upright, with the dish of meat and plates in her hands, I was at the time composing a scene of hunting a bear; and being wholly intent upon my play, cried out as loud as I could:

Fly, fly the bloody bear! take heed, I say;
Alas! I'm kill'd, and you'll become its prey.

The poor wench hearing me roar that I was killed, and she in danger of becoming a prey to the bear, took to her heels, and treading on her coats in the confusion tumbled down all the stairs. The soup was spilt, the earthen pots broken, and she ran out roaring in the street, that a bear was killing a man!"

Fast Work

Of all the dramatic productions of Mr. Sheridan, the play of *Pizarro*, adapted from Kotzebue, was the most lucrative: the author received no less a sum than three thousand pounds for it. It is said that the last two scenes were not written when the curtain drew up for the commencement, and that Mr. Sheridan actually wrote them during the progress of the earlier part of the play.

Keeping Up with the News

Collective creation, in which a company writes the play rather than buying one ready-made from a playwright, became an important trend in the 1960s. Here is an example from a hundred years earlier.

Mr. Joseph Harker was traveling with a company at the time that President Lincoln was assassinated. The enterprising and up-to-date manager of the show at once demanded that a play should be written around the murdered President. The whole cast accordingly got to work and inside two days they produced a three-act play—each act written by a different actor—dealing with the President's life and death. It was a story of love and revenge, the jealous lover shooting the President, who figured in the unsavory role of a betrayer of women. In spite of its libelous character, the play was well received.

How I Wrote This Play

Bernard Shaw:

Although I was forty-four or thereabouts when I wrote *Caesar and Cleopatra*, I now think I was a trifle too young for the job; but it was not bad for a juvenile effort. When I wrote the play I was stumbling about on crutches with a necrosed bone in my foot that every-body believed would turn cancerous and finish me. It had been brought on by an accident occurring at the moment when I was plunging into one of those break-downs in middle-life which killed Schiller and very nearly killed Goethe, and which have led to the saying that every busy man should go to bed for a year when he is forty. In trying to come downstairs on crutches before I was used to them I shot myself into empty space and fell right down through the house on to the flags, complicating the useless foot with a broken arm. It was in this con-dition that I wrote *Caesar and Cleopatra*; but I cannot see any mark of it on the play. I remember lying on the top of a cliff in the Isle of Wight with my crutches in the grass beside me, and writing the lines

> The white upon the blue above
> Is purple on the green below

as a simple memorandum of what I saw as I looked from the cliff. The Sphinx scene was suggested by a French picture of the *Flight into Egypt*. I never can remember the painter's name; but the en-graving, which I saw in a shop window when I was a boy, of the Virgin and child asleep in the lap of a colossal Sphinx staring over a desert, so intensely still that the smoke of Joseph's fire close by went straight up like a stick, remained in the rummage basket of my mem-ory for thirty years before I took it out and exploited it on the stage.

Shaw believed that the part of Caesar provided a litmus test for acting.

Cleopatra is not a difficult part; Caesar is: whoever can play the fourth act of it can play anything. Whoever can't, can play nothing.

Journey's Start

R. C. Sheriff's play, Journey's End, *produced in 1929, was the great antiwar play about the First World War.*

I was over twenty-five before I thought of doing dramatic writing; and I decided to write a play before I'd ever read one! When I was nine or ten years old we produced *Black Magic* in our cellar—my first attempt to mystify an audience. One "magician" served in India during the war. When he came back three or four of us were fed up one night and talked of getting up an amateur dramatic club. Two were deputed to buy some plays. I was one of them. We didn't get quite what we wanted. Coming back in the train my friend said, "Why don't *you* write a play?" At that time I had only been to a theatre two or three times. However, I bought one or two plays by Galsworthy to see how he set the characters out, and thus instructed I wrote a comedy. It played for fifteen minutes and had twenty-five people in it. The idea behind having so many characters was to ensure that a lot of tickets were sold. The longer your speeches the more tickets you had to sell. I shan't ever forget my elation after that first performance; my feelings when the curtain came down on the first night of *Journey's End* weren't half so acute; you can't recapture that glamour.

Slow Writer

Toward the end of the thirties, a publisher discovered the hitherto unpublished *Life of Our Lord* by Charles Dickens. For three years before this, Marc Connelly had been telling George Kaufman about his alleged progress on his new play. With the appearance of the new Dickens book, Kaufman said: "Charles Dickens, dead, writes more than Marc Connelly alive."

[41] GETTING A HEARING

Literary Manager

James Quin for a while became a reader of plays at Drury Lane, replacing Theophilus Cibber in that position after they quarreled and even fought a duel. The actor proved not to be overly conscientious as a literary manager.

A poor poet had placed a tragedy in his hands one night behind the scenes, whilst he was still dressed for the character he had performed. Quin put the manuscript into his pocket and forgot it. The bard having allowed some time to elapse, sufficient for the reading of the piece, called one morning to know what was its doom. Quin gave some invented reasons for its not being proper for the stage; the author requested it might be given back to him. "There," said Quin, "it lies in the window." But Bayes, on going to take it up, found a comedy, and his was a most direful tragedy. "Well, then," says the actor, "if that be not it, faith, Sir, I have certainly lost your play." "Lost my play!" cried the astonished bard "Yes, by G–d! but I have: look ye, however, here is a drawer full of both comedies and trage-dies, take any two you please in the room for it."

Another author, after reading an extremely bad play to Quin, asked his opinion of it. He answered that it would not do by any means. "I wish," resumed the author, "you would advise me what is best to do with it." "That I can," said Quin; "blot out one half and burn the other."

This recalls a story of Jonathan Swift who helpfully returned a play to an aspiring dramatist with most of it actually blotted out.

If Only He Knew

When Mr. Boaden had read his unsuccessful drama *Aurelio and Miranda* in the green room, he observed that he knew nothing so ter-rible as reading a piece before such a critical audience. The actress Mrs. Powell who was present said she knew one thing much more terrible. "What can that be?" demanded the author. "To be obliged," said she, "to sit and hear it."

Whatever Did I Do To Deserve This?

John Nichols in his *Literary Anecdotes* relates that he happened to be in Bolt Court on the day that John Henderson, the justly celebrated actor, was first introduced to Doctor Johnson. The conversation turn-ing to dramatic subjects, Henderson asked the Doctor's opinion of the tragedy of *Dido* and its author, Joseph Reed. "Sir," said Johnson, "I never did the man injury, yet he would read his tragedy to me."

Bad Plays

Theatres are always claiming to be looking for plays and playwrights are always complaining about their lack of interest. Since most writ-ers only know about their own play and usually have a somewhat biased opinion about its merits, it is difficult for them to conceive of a perspective that comes from trying to read through hundreds of bad plays. As any script reader or editor in a publishing house knows, out of hundreds of unsolicited manuscripts that arrive in their office, distressingly few are any good. A sometime literary manager myself, I was amused to read of Lord Byron's amazement when he saw a pile of five hundred manuscript plays on the shelves at Drury Lane and decided that there must be something worthwhile in that slush-pile. He made a personal investigation.

I do not think that of those which I saw there was one which could be conscientiously tolerated. There never were such things as most of them! . . . Then the scenes I had to go through! The authors and authoresses, and the wild Irishmen, the people from Brighton, from Blackwall, from Chatham, from Cheltenham, from Dublin, from Dundee—who came in upon me! to all of whom it was proper to give a civil answer, and a hearing, and a reading. Mrs. Glover's father, an Irish dancing-master of sixty years, calling upon me to request to play Archer, dressed in silk stockings on a frosty morning to show his legs (which were certainly good and Irish for his age, and had been still better); Miss Emma Somebody, with a play entitled *The Bandit of Bohemia,* or some such title or production; Mr. O'Higgins, then resident at Richmond, with an Irish tragedy, in which the unities could not fail to be observed, for the protagonist was chained by the leg to a pillar during the chief part of the performance. He was a wild man of a savage appearance, and the difficulty of *not* laughing at him was only to be got over by reflecting upon the probable consequences of such cachinnation. As I am really a civil and polite person, and *do* hate giving pain when it can be avoided, I sent them up to Douglas Kinnaird, who is a man of business, and sufficiently ready with a negative—and left them to settle with him.

Migraine

Arsène Houssaye was director of the Comédie Française in the middle of the nineteenth century.

We have given a comedy of M. Viennet in order not to be obliged to play one of his tragedies. I should add that the piece was only in one act. It was called *Migraine,* and true to its title it has given headaches to both actors and spectators alike who were trying to find the comedy behind the words, and failed. What is more, they have never been able to find out whether the piece was in prose or in verse.

M. Viennet has religiously attended the rehearsals. One day, out of sheer politeness, I sat down by his side. All at once he gets up, very angry at hearing some one laugh during the rehearsal of a sentimental scene. "Take care," he says to Mlle. Judith, "'I am here in the pit." "That's all right," she shouts, "I knew it, only I thought you were asleep."

How To Avoid Reading Plays

Nestor Roqueplan was an eminent Parisian journalist, but his great ambition was to be a successful theatrical manager, and notwithstanding that he wrote for several newspapers, fought duels, and tried to force peculiarly-shaped hats into fashion, he always found time enough to be at the head of some theatrical enterprise or the other, and during his career was director in turns of the Variétés, Opéra and Châtelet.

One day a poor prompter, named Boulé, met Roqueplan and told him that he had written a piece. The peculiar director, anxious to get away, makes an appointment with him, and rushes off, determined not to keep it. But Boulé was on the watch; the next day he penetrates into the theatre, sneaks into Roqueplan's private room, unrolls his manuscript, and puts on the usual falsely gay and careless appearance of the author about to read a play. Roqueplan sees that all is lost, lights a cigar, and makes up his mind for the worst. Boulé begins, and, horrible to relate—Boulé stutters fearfully. When the tormentor is done, Roqueplan rises from his arm-chair, and addressing himself to the reader, who is anxiously awaiting his reply, "That is a very original idea of yours to make all the characters stammer." "But, my dear Sir!" says Boulé, "n-n-n-nobody st-st-st-stammers in my p-p-p-p-piece!" "Very well then," replies Roqueplan, taking his hat, "it is downright rubbish, for that was the only good notion in it!"

Early Shaw

Clothed in a fashion of his own and looking rather like a Viking, Shaw entered Charles Wyndham's office one morning to read *Candida*. Sitting down at the table, he thrust one hand into a pocket of his trousers and produced a small note-book, thrust the other hand into a pocket of his coat and produced a second note-book, fished a third note-book from another pocket, a fourth from yet another, and so on until Wyndham wondered whether he was witnessing a conjuring trick. Then said Shaw: "You appear surprised to see all these little pocketbooks. The fact is, I write my plays mostly on the tops of buses."

He might have added that such parts of his plays as were not written on the roofs of buses were composed in the Underground Railway, which may account for the fact that all the characters in his early works seem to be talking at the tops of their voices.

How To Get Produced

A persistent playwright forced the same manuscript on David Belasco seven times, always claiming that important revisions had made it the stuff from which sure hits were fashioned. "It's awful," Belasco said finally. "All the great playwrights combined couldn't doctor it sufficiently." "Isn't there some way you can put it on the stage?" persisted the playwright. "Yes," snapped Belasco, his patience exhausted. "Give me the script." He tossed it to his assistant and ordered, "Chop this up and use it as the snowstorm tonight."

[42] DRAMA AND TRAUMA

A Tragedy Called *Europe*

Cardinal Richelieu, at the height of his glory and power, wrote a tragedy entitled *Europe* and brought it on the French stage. As the piece was little more than a political dialogue between the European nations, in which the comparative state of their revenues, forces, etc. were brought forward, it was barely heard from respect to the writer; but when it was given out for another representation, a murmur of disapprobation arose, and *The Cid* of Corneille was loudly demanded by the audience. This hurt the right reverend dramatist so much that he actually contrived to have a long and regular critique, written by the academicians of Paris, on that ill-fated *Cid* which had been set up as a rival to the progress of his tragedy.

Fiasco

Schiller once wrote a play called Fiesko. *The title should have been enough.*

It failed because Schiller insisted on reading the manuscript of the play to Baron Dalberg, the manager of the Mannheim Theater, in front of the whole acting company. Schiller was an execrable reader, and nobody had any desire to hear anything more after the first act. It wasn't until decades after Schiller's death that the play was redis-covered and put on the stage.

Curt Rejection

Sir Herbert Beerbohm Tree, to a would-be dramatist:

> My dear Sir: I have read your play. Oh, my dear Sir!
> Yours faithfully, &c.

Competition

Perhaps the most prolific American playwright was the now almost completely forgotten Owen Davis, whose play Icebound *won the Pulitzer Prize in 1923.*

There never will be an exact count of how many plays he wrote. He wrote at least three hundred. Between the ages of twenty-seven and forty he remembers nothing but writing plays. Somehow, between scripts, he managed to get married. Also to raise a family. Didn't notice either until he was forty. Then took up golf.

Davis had a unique contract with A. H. Woods. It stated that for a period of five years he could write plays for Woods only. Also stated that during that period Woods couldn't produce any plays but his. During those years he wrote fifty-eight melodramas, or a play a month for five years.

He once was turning out so many plays that he had to write under seven different names. Two of the *noms de plume,* Robert Wayne and John Oliver, became well known. In fact, a Pittsburgh dramatic critic wrote a piece about John Oliver stating that "at last a man had come along to drive Owen Davis out of business."

The Old Story

Samuel Shipman, another prolific American playwright of the early twentieth century, studied playwriting at Columbia University.

Brander Matthews gave him a C minus. He asked that his mark be raised and Matthews asked why. Shipman then pulled out a contract for a play he had just sold. Matthews merely replied: "It's the old story. Theory is theory and practice is practice."

Tryout

George Kaufman would grow wild with indignation when amateurs proposed that only good plays be produced. The suggestion that reading the play might spare all concerned from the bother of doing a failure nettled him. "Is it their opinion," he once demanded, "that I sit down at the typewriter with the express intention of creating a flop?"

He was as conversant with failures as he was with success. "In Boston the test of a play is simple," he said. "If the play is bad, the pigeons snarl at you as you walk across the Common."

[43] PLAYWRIGHT IN THE HOUSE

Interpretation

Molière's company was preparing to stage *Titus and Bérenice,* a new play by Corneille. Michel Baron was playing the role of Domitianus and, memorizing his part, he could not figure out the meaning of a particular quatrain. He asked Molière what the four lines meant, but he just shrugged that he did not know. Then Baron went to Corneille himself. The poet read the lines a few times, and said: "I must admit, I don't know now what I meant." "What am I to do?" asked the actor. "Nothing," said Corneille, "just say the lines as written. There will be some in the audience who won't understand yet will deeply admire them."

Sneak Previews

It is said that Molière read his comedies to an elderly female servant, named Laforêt, and when he perceived that the passages which he intended to be laughable and humorous had no effect on her, he altered them. He also required the players to bring their children to the rehearsals that he might form his opinion of different passages from the natural expression of their emotions.

Brogue

When the comedy of *She Stoops To Conquer* was in rehearsal, Oliver Goldsmith took great pains to give the performers his ideas of their several parts. On the first representation he was not a little displeased to hear the actor playing Young Marlow play it as an Irishman. As soon as Marlow came off the stage, Goldsmith asked him the meaning of this, as it was by no means intended for an Irish character. "Sir," replied the comedian, "I spoke it as nearly as I could to the manner in which you instructed me, except that I did not give it quite so strong a brogue."

Because He Moves in Mysterious Ways

Richard Mansfield produced *The Devil's Disciple* in Albany on October 1, 1897, bringing it to the Fifth Avenue Theatre, New York, a few days later, where it enjoyed a long run. He then toured it with success. But something about Shaw's work, to say nothing of Shaw, irritated him, and when told by a senator that he ought to thank God nightly on his knees for such a play, he replied that he did, but that he could not help adding: "Why, O God, did it have to be by Shaw?"

Shaw's Advice

In 1944 Ralph Richardson played Bluntschli to John Gielgud's Sergius in Shaw's Arms and the Man; *this is Sir Ralph's portrait of Shaw aged eighty-eight.*

Shaw came a good deal to rehearsal and he helped me very much indeed. As you remember, when Bluntschli comes on at the beginning of the play, he had escaped from the enemy, and climbed up a drainpipe and in through a window in a terrible state of exhaustion. I tried to act the exhaustion and to show how utterly tired and shot to hell he was. We rehearsed this for a long time, and I thought it was rather a good effect, and that I was rather good in it. Then Shaw came to me and he said, "You know, Richardson, I'd like to have a word with you about your Bluntschli. It's going to be a very fine Bluntschli, I'm sure." He was a wonderfully courteous, wonderfully polite man, I think perhaps the most polite man I've ever met in my life, especially sensitive to actors. You know, he'd take you aside and talk to you very quietly, very gently, very encouragingly. "But," he said, "you know there's one thing the matter with your Bluntschli. When you come in, you show that you're very upset, you spend a long time with your gasps and pauses and your lack of breath and your dizziness and your tiredness it's very well done, it's very well done indeed, but it doesn't suit my play. It's no good for me, it's no good for Bernard Shaw." He said, "You've got to go from line to line, quickly and swiftly, never stop the flow of the lines, never stop. It's one joke after another, it's a firecracker. Always reserve the acting for underneath the spoken word. It's a musical play, a knockabout musical comedy." That taught me a lot about playing in his plays.

Gnashing of Teeth

Unlike Shaw, Henrik Ibsen was notoriously unhelpful to directors and actors about his plays. Albert Ranft, a Swedish actor-manager, sought his advice after reading Little Eyolf.

"Can't this line be interpreted thus, and spoken thus?" asked Ranft. "Oh, yes." "But how do you think it should be said?" "Oh, my dear fellow," replied Ibsen. "You say it how you please, it's all the same to me." . . . After Ibsen had attended a performance of *The Wild Duck* in Copenhagen the cast waited expectantly for his comments. "But it seemed as though he no longer knew what he had meant by the play. He went around asking us actors, as though we should know better."

Not that Ibsen was indifferent. Perhaps his own unhappy career in the theatre (he called it a "daily abortion") convinced him of the futility of trying to intervene. Julius Elias sat next to him during a particularly awful dress rehearsal of Rosmersholm *in Augsburg.*

He witnessed the performance with weeping and gnashing of teeth. Seated in the front of the stalls he winced in pain at every word uttered from the stage; with both hands clutching the plush of the orchestra rail, he groaned ceaselessly: "Oh, God! Oh, God!" In the third act John Rosmer conceived the grotesque idea of appearing with elegant *pique* spats over shining polished calfskin boots. When the man appeared, Ibsen reeled as though struck, and clasped my arm. "Look, look at that!" The Rosmer he had created was wearing bright yellow spats. We were convinced that Ibsen would prohibit the whole performance at the last moment, with some vehement outburst, but then, suddenly, he straightened himself and, with a gesture as though to brush away a bad dream, said, "I must forget my original conception. Then it isn't too bad."

No Leading Lady

W. S. Gilbert was asked about a leading lady with whom he was very disappointed. "I only have a misleading lady," was his reply.

On a Clear Day

Dame Edith Evans was having trouble rehearsing Noël Coward's *Hay Fever*. Her line was: "From this window, on a clear morning you can see Marlow." But Dame Edith constantly said: "On a very clear day you can see Marlow." Finally Coward interrupted: "Dear Edith, you spoil the rhythm by putting in a 'very.' The line is 'On a clear morning you can see Marlow.' On a *very* clear morning you can also see both Beaumont and Fletcher."

Deep Cuts

Eugene O'Neill is famous for the length of his plays. In rehearsals he made a few cuts, but never because of mere length. When an actor in The Iceman Cometh *threatened to cut a long speech on opening night, O'Neill warned him that if he left out a single line he would not permit a second performance. At the tryout of* Ah, Wilderness! *the curtain fell so late that the stagehands demanded overtime. To make matters worse, George M. Cohan, the star, was introducing new business at every performance.*

O'Neill did make one "cut" in Pittsburgh. The Theatre Guild thought the play was running about ten minutes too long and commissioned Russel Crouse, who was handling publicity for *Ah, Wilderness!*, to ask O'Neill to reduce the script's playing time by ten minutes. Crouse dutifully delivered the message but told O'Neill he anticipated his reaction and added that, as a matter of fact, he agreed with him.

"Right," said O'Neill. "To hell with them."

The next day Crouse was on his way out of his room at the Hotel Schenley, where O'Neill was also staying, when the telephone rang. It was O'Neill.

"Come down to my room right away," O'Neill commanded. Crouse said he couldn't, he was on his way to the theatre to supervise a press interview he had arranged for George M. Cohan.

"I have to see you right now," O'Neill insisted.

Crouse explained he would be back in an hour or so and would see O'Neill then.

"I have that ten-minute cut for you," said O'Neill.

Crouse was in O'Neill's room within seconds.

"Sit down," said O'Neill genially.

"I'm late," answered Crouse. "Just give me the script with the cuts marked."

"There isn't any script. Sit down," repeated O'Neill with a self-satisfied grin.

Crouse threw O'Neill a trapped and pleading look, and O'Neill finally relented. He explained that he had decided simply to telescope the first two acts into one, eliminating a ten-minute intermission.

Expert Advice

Eugene O'Neill did sometimes adopt suggestions. The day after *The Hairy Ape* opened in New York, an old sailor friend from the days when he roistered on the waterfront wrote him, "I liked the show a lot, but for God's sake tell that Number Four stoker to stop leaning his prat against that red-hot furnace."

Playwright to the Rescue

The first production of a play is usually wrought with constant revisions which test the actors' flexibility to the utmost. Cotter Smith played the title role in Mark Medoff's play The Majestic Kid *when it premiered at the Snowmass Festival in Colorado (1982).*

Medoff is a voracious rewriter and I told him that it was fine with me, he could bring as many changes as he wished. On the morning of the opening he brought me a long, brand-new monologue for the ending of the play and asked me whether I would substitute it for what I had already memorized. I agreed to try it, but I would also carry with me the written text just in case I went up. Mark agreed, feeling that he would rather have the new speech read than to hear the old one that did not work.

The moment for the monologue came. I went downstage, where I was to address the audience directly, and began the speech which, about a third of the way through, became hopelessly intertwined with the old version. So I stopped and proceeded to explain to the audience what had happened and that I would now read the rest. But in the intermission I had changed my jacket, and now I was searching all my pockets in vain. So there I stood alone on stage on opening night and didn't know what to do. For a while I was really lost and then got an inspiration: "Mark, are you out there?" I shouted into the dark void. And from the very back of the house Mark Medoff called out to his lead actor on stage: "Yes, I'm right here."

"Can you talk me through this new speech?" I asked. And he did, sentence by sentence, line by line. It was one of the most thrilling moments in my theatrical career. And the audience loved it, of course: they were really seeing a new play being created.

Wish You Were Here

It was Chekhov who observed that "When an actor has money, he doesn't send letters but telegrams." This is a story about an actor receiving one.

George S. Kaufman once sent a telegram to one of his leading men in the middle of a performance. When William Gaxton returned to his dressing-room during intermission of Kaufman's *Of Thee I Sing*, he found the telegram from the playwright. It read: "Am watching your performance from the rear of the house. Wish you were here."

[44] DRAMATIC ENDINGS

Greek Tragedies

There is a story, preserved through the centuries, about the death of Aeschylus in Sicily. An eagle had caught a tortoise and was circling for a convenient rock on which to crack it open. The Father of Tragedy happened to be going for a walk, and the eagle mistook his bald pate for a rock.

Euripides is reported to have been torn apart by mad dogs in his Macedonian exile, soon after he wrote *The Bacchant Women*, in which a group of women tear apart a king. When Sophocles was nearing ninety, his heirs dragged him into court and tried to claim his property by having him declared senile. The dramatist took out the manuscript of his unfinished play, *Oedipus at Colonus*, and began reciting. The case and the heirs were thrown out of court.

There are two versions of his death. One story goes that after Sophocles exhibited his last play and obtained the first prize, he fell into such a transport of joy as carried him off. But Lucian differs from the common report, and affirms that he was choked with a grape-stone like Anacreon. The first version recalls the debate whether Lear died of joy or grief; the latter, of course, brings to mind the recent death of Tennessee Williams, reported to have been caused by choking on a plastic wine-top.

Two of the more successful nineteenth-century American playwrights came to an unhappy end. Frank Murdoch, like Keats, was said to have been killed literally by the critics; there was also John Augustus Stone, author of Forrest's great hit, *Metamora*. Apparently he threw himself, in a fit of insanity, into the Schuykill River, when barely thirty years of age.

When we come to our own century, it seems like we have gone full circle, back to the Greeks. Apart from Tennessee Williams, there was the terrible murder of Joe Orton by his homosexual lover, described in such vivid detail in John Lahr's biography that a messenger in Greek tragedy could not have done better.

Grave Dispute

Shakespeare died a peaceful death, as far as we know. Yet his tomb contains strict instructions not to disturb his bones, as if he foresaw the controversies regarding the authorship of his plays. Molière is supposed to have died while performing the title role during the premiere of The Imaginary Invalid. *In fact, he passed away a few hours after the fourth performance. Although he was the most famous actor in France and a favorite of Louis XIV, the Church refused him a Christian burial, because he did not repent of being an actor before giving up his soul.*

The king, being informed that the archbishop of Paris would not permit Molière to be buried in consecrated ground, sent for the prelate and expostulated with him. But finding the archbishop inflexibly obstinate, his majesty asked how many feet the consecrated ground reached? This question coming by surprise, the archbishop replied, about eight. "Well," answered the king, "I find there's no getting the

better of your scruples; therefore, let his grave be dug twelve feet
deep, that's four below your consecrated ground, and let him be
buried there."

Fate

On June 1, 1938, Ödön von Horváth, the Austro-Hungarian author
of *Tales from the Vienna Woods* and other works, walked down the
Champs Elysées on the way to see Walt Disney's film, *Snow White
and The Seven Dwarfs*, when a freak storm broke out. The thirty-six-
year-old playwright took refuge under a chestnut tree; lightning struck,
causing a branch to kill him instantly. Nobody else under the same
tree was hurt. Horváth had been on the run from the Nazis, who had
him on their black list. His flight from Berlin had taken him to Amsterdam. A man of many superstitions, he consulted a clairvoyant,
who told him to go to Paris, where the greatest adventure of his life
would await him. A week later he was dead. His friend Franz Theodor
Csokor later recalled Horváth telling him a year before that he never
tried to go out on the last day of May or the first day of June because
he was certain that he would meet an accidental death on those days.
And the man who had escaped the Nazis said: "Why are most people
afraid in a dark forest? Why are they not afraid of simply walking
down the street?"

A Broken Heart

When Elisabeth Bergner, the great Austrian-born star of Max Rein-
hardt's theatre, fled to London from Nazi Germany in the 1930s, she
was wooed by several eminent playwrights. The diminutive actress
had the looks of a boy, which is why she excelled in such roles as Saint
Joan. Inevitably she also appealed deeply to the elderly Sir James Barrie, whose own sexuality (or lack of it) was as ambivalent as that of
his most famous character, Peter Pan. Barrie, who had by then long
stopped writing, invited Bergner to his luxurious apartment and during tea asked her: "What, my dear, has been the most important artistic experience you have had during the past five years?" The actress,
without giving the matter a great deal of thought, replied: "Not long
ago I was in Amsterdam and at the Rijksmuseum I saw Rembrandt's
wonderful painting *David Playing the Harp for Saul.*" "Oh, really?"
Barrie said mysteriously, and after she had picked up her bag to leave,
he whispered close to her ear: "You are my boy David."

Elisabeth Bergner put this down to an old man's eccentricity, but a few months later it was announced that Sir James had at long last taken up his pen and had written a play called *The Boy David* especially for the refugee actress. It was to be the sensation of the 1935 season, with the master impresario C. B. Cochran producing, Augustus John designing and many other great names associated with the production. Inevitably, the play could not live up to such expectations and despite reverent notices it died after two months. Bergner immediately left for a vacation in Switzerland, where she received a telegram summoning her back for a revival of the production as a Royal Command performance for George V and Queen Mary. The Austrian actress, who had been a recent immigrant to England, did not understand the meaning of a royal command. Telegrams flew fast and furious, but Bergner refused to break off her holiday and go back to a play she did not care about. In consequence the play was never revived and it was said that Barrie had died soon thereafter of a broken heart.

Last Wish

George Kaufman:

When I die, I want to be cremated and have my ashes thrown in Jed Harris's face.

Exaggerated Rumor

Actress Elizabeth Huddle was escorting Tennessee Williams to a performance of one of Edward Albee's plays at A.C.T. in San Francisco.

After the show Williams wanted to go backstage and say hello to Albee, but it so happened that Albee had missed his plane connection and the performance. Then Tennessee wanted to congratulate the cast, so I asked the stage manager to call everybody on stage to meet him. As he was being introduced to the leading actress, she became flustered and said to Tennessee Williams: "I'm sorry, but who did you say you were?" Without missing a beat, America's most famous dramatist replied: "I know, honey, I'm *not* dead."

Obituary

Writing about the death of Tennessee Williams in 1983, Los Angeles critic Dan Sullivan recalled a performance ten years earlier of *A Streetcar Named Desire* at the Ahmanson Theatre. A woman in the audience turned around to reprimand a man behind her for guffawing throughout the performance. Didn't he realize this was a serious play? The man was Tennessee Williams, who loved to laugh at his plays in the theatre. He told an interviewer: "My tragedies are funnier than my comedies. Some of these characters have to laugh. They've got to. Or they'll die."

CHAPTER IX

Words,
Words, Words

Human Nature

The American playwright Romulus Linney has remarked: "There are three primal urges in human beings: food, sex, and rewriting someone else's play."

Rewriting the Play

In 1905, Ben Webster, Margaret's father, was in his first American play, The Marriage of William Asche, *which was having its tryout in Philadelphia.*

. . . Ben began to learn several theatrical customs which had not yet reached England. One was "rewriting the play," an exercise which survived and was brought to the peak of perfection many years later by the Theatre Guild. Under the rules of this game, the author's script is treated as if it were a very tame bull in the tryout bull ring, where everyone is welcome to enlist as picador or matador and no weapons are barred. The laurels of victory go to him who can ultimately stab the poor, bleeding creature to the heart. The routine of cutting, transposing, inserting, altering and rewriting was already flourishing in 1905. Ben wrote in some bewilderment from Philadelphia: "We went on rehearsing till after 6 p.m.; Tuesday, the new Fourth Act; Wednesday the same, and tonight, more cuts . . . and the scene with 'Kitty,' composed of a bit of the original Fourth Act, a portion of the new one and three or four speeches which I had never seen before. It's rather exhausting." On Friday he asked Grace George which version she intended to play; she replied wearily, "Whichever I can remember when I get to it."

How To Tell What Shakespeare Wrote

Wolfit omitted the scene in *Twelfth Night* where Malvolio is imprisoned and visited by Feste pretending to be Sir Topas. The actor contended that the scene was the work of another pen. "I cannot learn it," he declared, "and if I cannot learn it, Shakespeare did not write it!"

Playwright's Protest

In the 1930s Elisabeth Bergner was much in demand, and Bernard Shaw, who thought that her Saint Joan was the best performance he had seen, went to see her to talk her into doing the part in English during the Malvern Festival. Citing her poor English, the tremendous length of the role and some of the speeches, she finally agreed on the condition that she could play the part more or less the way she had done it in German. Shaw made the theatre and the director agree to these terms and the play opened with cuts that the playwright had approved. But Bergner was tired of the part and to save energy she improvised further cuts of her own. At a matinee, when she was particularly prone to take things easy and had just skipped lightly over a long Shavian speech, there was a sudden thump heard in the auditorium. In the ensuing commotion it was discovered that the noise had been caused by Shaw himself, who happened to be watching from the back of the house: he had fainted to the ground.

Perspective

When *A Streetcar Named Desire* was the hit sensation of its decade, a Chicago company was formed and a long-out-of-work character actor was selected to play the small role of the doctor. This character appears in the final minutes of the play. He speaks few lines. He is there to take Blanche away to an institution, and he is gentle enough to cause her to say, "I have always depended on the kindness of strangers." When the actor playing this role arrived in Chicago, some long-unseen relatives called him to invite him to dinner. The gentleman accepted and was greeted royally by his relations. At one point during the festive dinner, one breathlessly inquisitive niece said to her uncle, "We've heard so much about this *Streetcar* play. Please would you tell us what the story is?" The old gentleman put down his soup spoon and smiled at the young lady (character actors are notoriously courtly) and said, "Of course I'll tell you what the story is, my dear. It's about a doctor who comes to New Orleans because he's received a telephone call from a young lady whose sister is having a nervous breakdown."

[46] SHAKESPEARE AND HIS CULT

Throw Them the Bard

When Woodward the actor resided in Dublin, around 1760, a mob one morning beset the parliament-house in that city in order to prevent the members of it from passing an unpopular bill. Such as were supposed to belong to the court partly experienced the grossest insults; and some of the ringleaders, thinking it necessary to make their representatives swear that they would not assent to the bill, surrounded Mr. Woodward's house, which was opposite to the parliament-house in College-green, and called repeatedly to the family to throw them a Bible from the window. Mrs. Woodward was greatly alarmed at the request; unluckily, not having at the time such a book in her possession. Her husband, however, in the midst of her agitation, snatched up with great presence of mind a volume of Shakespeare's plays, which tossing out of the dining-room window, he told the insurgents they were very welcome to. Upon this, they gave three cheers; and the ignorant rabble administered their oath to several of the Irish senators upon the works of the old English bard, which was afterwards returned by them, in safety, to the owner.

Bathos

The house in which the immortal Shakespeare lived at Stratford-upon-Avon was lately* inhabited by a butcher, who wrote over his door—

> Shakespeare
> Was born here.
> N.B.—A horse and cart to let.

Obscure Shakespeare

W. S. Gilbert was sitting one night at the Garrick Club in the company of several great lovers of Shakespeare, and they were discussing the poet. "Well, I don't care what you all say," said Gilbert, "I think he's a very obscure writer." "What?" they said, "Shakespeare obscure? Give us an instance." "Well," he replied, "what do you make of the following passage?

* Written in 1820.

I would as lief be thrust through a quickset
Hedge, as cry "plosh" to a callow throstle.

"There's nothing obscure in that," said one. "It's perfectly plain. Here's a man, a great lover of the feathered songsters, who, rather than disturb the carolling of the little warbler, prefers to go through the awful pains of thrusting himself through a thorny hedge. But I don't know that passage; in what play does it occur?" "In no play," said Gilbert; "I've just invented it!"

Our Shakespeare

There are literally dozens of Shakespeare Festivals in English-language countries where artists frequently clash with the local worthies. Nigel Playfair, a successful impresario and director, was invited in 1919 to produce As You Like It, *one of the perennial favorites at the Stratford Memorial Theatre. He found that both the Board and the inhabitants of Stratford-upon-Avon had definite ideas about producing Shakespeare.*

The play was to be given uncut, with only one interval. "I was determined," Playfair wrote some years later, "not to cut a single sentence . . . 'If they want the Bard,' I said to myself, 'they shall have him—whole and unadulterated.'" But when he arrived at the Memorial Theatre Playfair discovered that Stratford had numerous ideas about how a production of *As You Like It* should be put on, and they had nothing to do with respect for the Bard's text. Chief of these was the obligatory appearance of the stuffed Charlecote stag. Playfair looked at the moth-eaten animal and categorically refused to use it. He was met with stupefied disbelief. "Such a piece of iconoclasm," he wrote, "had apparently never been heard of in Stratford before . . . " Resolutely stag-less, the production opened. Sir Frank and Lady Benson were in the first-night audience to give gentle encouragement to their protégé. They saw a play transformed, with young actors playing young parts, with scenes flowing into scenes, lines spoken which they had always cut, a Rosalind (Athene Seyler) who was not the gracious womanly figure they were used to, but giggling and girlish . . . Among Stratford theatre-goers the reaction was one of outrage. "Outside the theatre," Playfair wrote, "the storm raged, and it attained a ferocity I would hardly have thought possible. When I came into my hotel . . . people turned their backs and got up and walked from the room . . . The rest of the cast fared little better; they were cut and cold-shouldered everywhere. When Lovat Fraser [the designer] was walking in the street, a woman came up to him and shook her fist in his face. 'Young man,' she said impressively, 'how dare you meddle with our Shakespeare?''

Ye Olde Tent

In 1952 a group of citizens from the Canadian town of Stratford, Ontario, approached Tyrone Guthrie with the idea of starting a Shakespeare Festival. There was no building, and the festival began the following year in a huge tent. Guthrie and his designer, Tanya Moiseiwitsch, were primarily concerned about constructing the right kind of stage.

Miss Moiseiwitsch and I had long dreamed of such a stage as was now to come into being. We were agreed that, while conforming to the conventions of the Elizabethan Theatre in respect of practicalities, it should not present a pseudo-Elizabethan appearance. We were determined to eschew Ye Olde. Rough sketches on the back of envelopes gave place to careful drawings. Like every good designer, Moiseiwitsch knows not only what she wants a thing to look like, but why; and also knows how it is made.

Guthrie began rehearsing Richard III *and* All's Well That Ends Well *with a company headed by Alec Guinness. They worked in a wooden shed on the fairgrounds, waiting for the tent to arrive from Chicago.*

The weeks wore on. The plays were nearly ready. But still there was no sign of the Tent. Anxiety began again. A king's ransom was spent on long distance calls to the tentmaker in Chicago. Fabulous numbers of women were reported to be stitching day and night.
   . . . On Saturday Skip Manley appeared. Skip was the Tent man. He travels the world putting up, looking after and taking down enormous tents. He had come from Iowa, where he had been in charge of a Gospel Tent. Nightly, several hundred people had plunged fully clad into a Baptismal Tank. After a season of Shakespeare with us he was booked to look after a Circus Tent in Venezuela.
   Mr. Manley was a friendly midwesterner of lean physique. He brought with him a ton of hardware and kept making calculations on odd scraps of paper. He referred to the tent as "She" and the

hardware—iron rings, chains, swivels and so on—were all parts of the apparatus that would raise "Her" from the ground. I never saw him except in working dress—he was a hard and dedicated worker—and for work in all weathers he wore a white panama hat, with a pink and gold ribbon; a pair of very very old trousers that had once been white; brown shoes of basketwork with pointed toes and an intricate design, and a shirt made of pink and silver brocade, the sort of garment which in Europe elderly ladies wear for evenings *en pension* at Bath, or Lucerne, or Wiesbaden. In Bath they call them Bridge Coatees. On the bony workworn fingers of the Tent Man, there flashed and flickered jewelled rings.

When at last She did arrive from Chicago half Stratford turned out to see Her put up. It was a sight worth watching. Four eighty-foot poles of Douglas Pine were moored in position by guys of steel wire. Skip directed this operation like Toscanini conducting a symphony. Each pole was drawn up and held in place by four guys. Two of these were operated by hand—two teams of fifteen men; the other two were attached to tractors. Skip would sign first to this group to pull so far, then to that; then, with the sweep of a jewelled hand, he would bring the first tractor into play, holding the remainder of his forces at the ready as though they were trombones waiting to make an entry. The whole tricky, delicate operation took a day and a half. Thereafter the great expanse of canvas was hoisted comparatively quickly and easily. In another day or two we were able to rehearse in the tent.

The Wooden O

There were already problems with the original Shakespearean theatre, the Globe.

Upon the site of what is now[*] Hollywell Lane, Shoreditch, during the Middle Ages, stood the Priory of St. John the Baptist; at the Reformation it shared the common fate of religious houses, and after lying in ruins for some time, one Giles Allen purchased the ground and leased it out for building. One of these plots was taken by James Burbadge, or Burbidge—the name is indifferently spelt—an actor in the Earl of Leicester's company, but a joiner by trade, in partnership with his father-in-law, John Braynes, and thereon they erected a circular wooden building, open to the sky, at a cost of £600 or £700,

[*] Written in 1904.

for theatrical and other amusements, which they named the Theatre, and which was opened to the public in the autumn of 1576.

The Theatre enjoyed but a brief career. In 1597, Giles Allen, the ground landlord, perhaps under pressure of the Puritan citizens, intimated to Messrs. Braynes and Burbage that he required the land for other purposes. Now, according to the stipulations of the lease, Burbage had the power to remove the building at the end of his term; but Allen denied this right, and evidently thought he had the power of evading it. One morning, however, the actors and some assistants set about pulling down the house, and, in spite of the armed resistance of the ground landlord, amidst a great tumult, succeeded in carrying off the materials to Bankside, Southwark, and the timber thus saved helped to erect another theatre, which was afterwards called the Globe . . . The Globe was a hexagonal building, and had for its sign Atlas supporting the world, and underneath was written, *Totus mundus agit histrionem*, which motto, as *As You Like It* was first produced at this house, probably suggested the famous speech commencing, "All the world's a stage."

Tragic Flaw

"The trouble with Shakespeare," wrote George Kaufman into the part of an old character actress, "is that you never get to sit down unless you're a king."

[47] LITERARY FIGURES

Found Out

The stage has always tempted writers who excelled in other branches of literature. A host of famous names—Alexander Pope, Henry Fielding, Charles Lamb, Henry James, Arnold Bennett—tried to succeed in show business but found to their regret that playwriting is a different metier.

In 1743 Garrick produced and performed the principal character in Fielding's comedy of *The Wedding Day*. He told Fielding he was apprehensive that the audience would make free with him in a particular passage, and remarked that as a repulse might disconcert him for the remainder of the night, the passage should be omitted.

"No," replied Fielding, "if the scene is not a good one, let the audience find that out." The play was accordingly produced without alteration, and, as had been anticipated, marks of disapprobation appeared. Garrick, alarmed at the hisses he had met with, retired into the green room, where the author was solacing himself with a bottle of champagne. He had by this time drank pretty freely, and glancing his eye on the actor, while clouds of tobacco issued from his mouth, cried out, "What's the matter, Garrick?" What are they hissing now?" "Why, the scene that I begged you to retrench," replied the actor; "I knew it would not do, and they have so frightened me that I shall not be able to collect myself again the whole night." "Oh," replied Fielding, with great coolness, "they have found it out, have they?"

The Company of Muses

One of the performers at the Haymarket Theatre was observing to Foote what a humdrum sort of a man Dr. Goldsmith appeared to be in the green room compared with the figure he made in his poetry. "The reason of that," said he, "is because the muses are better companions than the players."

Life Class

Charles Dickens not only had a lifelong passion for every aspect of the theatre, he was a very adequate and highly regarded amateur actor himself. J. B. Van Amerongen prefaces his volume The Actor in Dickens *(1926) with this sigh from an unnamed supernumerary: "Ah, Mr. Dickens, if it hadn't been for them books, what an actor you would have made!" He was also a shrewd judge of talent, writing after seeing a performance in 1840 that "there is a young fellow in the play, his name is Henry Irving, and if that young man does not one day come out as a great actor, I know nothing of art." It would be another thirty years before Irving proved Dickens (who died that year) right by becoming an overnight star with his performance in* The Bells. *The novelist found material for a number of his famous characters in the theatre, as the American actor Otis Skinner recalls.*

"And could Dickens act?" I asked.

"Oh, yes, he was pretty fair as an actor. Nobody could do much with the parts he had to play, and I guess Dickens didn't think it worth while to try hard with his. He always looked out of place in the queer costumes Davenport gave him to wear."

I asked Chapman if other people in Davenport's troupe were recognizable in the personnel of the Vincent Crummles's company who acted with Nickleby and Smike in the Dickens story.

"Every one of them except that there was only one young male Crummles instead of two. I'll swear our leading woman was Miss Snevellicci, and if our heavy man wasn't Dickens's Mr. Lenville, he was the very spit of him. Davenport's fat wife certainly had a 'charnel house voice' like Mrs. Crummles."

"How about the 'infant phenomenon'?"

"Absolutely."

"But Mrs. Lander," I said, "denied point-blank that she was the model for this character."

"Of course it was exaggerated," said Chapman, "but she was Crummles's daughter. Dickens dressed her up—that's all. The company often walked from town to town while the properties were carried in a rickety cart, drawn by a weary pony—Crummles's pony, whose mother had been on the stage and whose father was a dancer. As for Dickens, well, he might have been Nicholas Nickleby."

CHAPTER X

Managers
and Producers

The General's Secret

In ancient Athens a producer was called "choregos," or provider of the chorus. There was no financial gain involved; on the contrary, it cost the producer a great deal of money. However, it was considered both a civic duty and a high honor to be asked to produce plays at the dramatic festivals. So the ablest and the wealthiest citizens competed for the privilege.

Socrates was talking about Antisthenes the general and his great quality of always wanting to win. "Did you notice that when he was a producer, his chorus always won?" "Good heavens," Nicomachides exclaimed, "it is an entirely different matter to be leading an army from producing a play!" "And even though Antisthenes knows nothing about singing or how to rehearse a chorus," Socrates replied, "yet he could find the best people for the job."

The Thrifty Producer

Another Athenian general and statesman who produced plays was Phokion in the fourth century B.C.

One time an actor who was playing the role of the queen in a new tragedy asked the producer for a train of followers, all of whom would have had to be dressed in very expensive costumes. Phokion said no, and the actor threw a tantrum, refusing to perform. Melanthos, the chorus-leader, pushed him on to the stage and gave him a dressing down: "Don't you see that Phokion's own wife only has one servant waiting upon her, while you want to show off, and give a bad example to other women!" The audience overheard these words and gave them their thunderous approval.

The Manager's Stratagem

The playwright George Farquhar had been disappointed by his former
patron the Earl of Orrery, who, following the advice of the Duke of
Ormond, had given an army commission he had promised to Farquhar
to somebody else.

Robert Wilks endeavoured to cheer him, by representing that the
Earl was a man of so much honour, that he would not show nor even
harbour in his breast any resentment upon that account, especially
as the fault, if any had been committed, ought to be laid at the door
of the Duke of Ormond. He then gave him his best advice in his
kindest manner, and said there was but one way left for him to pursue, viz. "Write a play, and it shall be got up with all imaginable
expedition." "Write!" cried Farquhar, starting from his chair, "is it
possible that a man can write common sense who is heartless and
has not one shilling in his pocket?" "Come, come, George," replied
Wilks, "banish melancholy, draw your drama, and bring the sketch
with you to-morrow, for I expect you to dine with me. But as an
empty pocket may cramp your genius, I desire you to accept my
mite," and he presented him with twenty guineas.

When Wilks was gone, Farquhar retired to his study, and drew up
the plot of *The Beaux Stratagem*, which he delivered to Wilks the
next day, and the design being approved, he was desired to proceed
and not to lose a day with the composition. This comedy, which is
one of the best extant, was begun, finished, and acted in the space
of six weeks; but too late, with all that haste, for the advantage of
the author. On the third night, which was for his benefit, Farquhar
died of a broken heart.

Dubious Ethics

Augustin Daly was one of the famous managers in the cut-throat
theatre world of late nineteenth-century New York. Daniel Frohman,
who later took over Daly's Theatre, admired his predecessor's nego-
tiating technique.

When Clara Morris was the leading lady of his company she was
getting thirty-five dollars a week. She asked him one day whether she
couldn't receive more salary. He refused, and she intended to leave
the company, or so the papers announced. Daly came to the theatre

early one morning and, looking through the mail, he saw a letter addressed to Clara Morris from Wallack's Theatre Company. He surmised that Wallack was going to engage her so he took the letter out and told the doorkeeper that when Miss Morris came in to send her up to him, and then put the letter back when she had left the stage door. When she arrived, he agreed to give her the salary she asked, fifteen or twenty dollars more a week. She signed an agreement with him and then went down and got her mail. When she opened the letter from Wallack's, she found it offered her twice as much as Daly was paying her. So he kept her until she became a star in her own right, as many others of his company did.

God's Favorite

Few people have had as much impact on the course of modern theatre in England as a formidable and warm woman by the name of Lilian Baylis, who founded both the Old Vic and Sadler's Wells. She was the most unlikely candidate for the task and often turned to God for inspiration about what to do.

The early days at the Old Vic were very worrying. It was a coffee-music hall then, and we used to have a funny turn after the interval to attract the men back into the theatre from the bar. But when I got good turns other managers used to steal them. I started to show "movies"—we were probably the first theatre in London to give a full evening's entertainment of pictures. In two years I made £2,000 out of "penny pictures," and in the next two years I lost it all on symphony concerts. I gave up pictures because I couldn't get good ones; once I sat eight hours watching without finding a good one. Because of that difficulty I determined to try good plays and chose Shakespeare. I remember lying awake one night wondering distractedly, "What am I to do? How can I save the Old Vic?" Suddenly I heard a voice say quite clearly, "You must put on Shakespeare as you do operas." I am a religious woman—but not a Spiritualist—and I firmly believe the voice was Divine.

Bloody Thoughts

Laurence Olivier met Lilian Baylis many years before he inherited her position as manager of the Old Vic.

I was dragged along to see her by Tyrone Guthrie, to be presented as a possible leading man, and I went to see her in her office at the Old Vic which is now my dressing room.* I've still got her desk, I got it out of storage for sentiment's sake. She sat behind her desk, the dog in the corner snarling at me; I found that she was perfectly all right, no trouble at all. We got on very well, famously. During the dress rehearsal of *Hamlet*, which went on till five in the morning, I said, "My thoughts be bloody or be nothing worth." The rehearsal stopped again and she chuckled from her box and said, "I bet they couldn't be bloodier than they are, dear boy." She used to come to my dressing-room between the shows and wrap me up in Mrs. Sterling's eiderdown to give me good thoughts and that sort of thing. I once came to her with what I thought was a brilliant idea and I said, "Lilian, why don't we have a bar in the theatre, that would attract people much more. Why can't we have a bar?" She looked at me as though I'd shot her and said, "My dear boy, don't you realize if it hadn't been for drunken men beating their wives, we'd never have got this place?"

[49] MISERS AND TYRANTS

An Unpopular Manager

Drury Lane was rocking through a period of turbulence under different managers and different stars. In 1832 Macready and Edmund Kean finally played together—or rather, against each other. Kean was not vanquished, but the smell of defeat was in the air. In 1833 the egregious, notorious and much-detested Alfred Bunn became lessee and manager of the great national theatre.

Seldom can anyone have been so inappropriately named. He was a bejeweled, ample man of unquenchable assurance, a flamboyant impresario who fancied himself a poet. He bounded like a rubber ball between Drury Lane and the Bankruptcy Courts. His various tenures of office were marked by spectacular coups and utter debacles. In the season of 1833 he ran Drury Lane and Covent Garden in tandem. The most famous actors in the world could be seen in all their finery dashing madly across Bow Street in the rain on their frenzied way from an exit in one theatre to an entrance in the other. He made

---

* This interview in 1967 was before the National Theatre was built.

his money out of opera, circuses, even performing lions, all of which he preferred to drama. He subjected his actors to every sort of indignity and annoyance. Macready eventually became so exasperated that he stalked into Bunn's office and knocked him down. It was probably the most popular thing he ever did.

A Manager Outwitted

Dartois, the producer, had arranged with Dumas that if on the thirtieth representation of his play about Kean the total receipts reached 60,000 francs, the author should be paid an additional fee of two thousand francs. "A sou less," said Dartois, "and no extra fee!"

On the 29th night the receipts amounted to 57,999 francs, and Dumas felt tolerably confident. At nine o'clock he presented himself, not, of course that he wanted the money, but merely for curiosity, and, as luck would have it, the sum taken was 1,994 francs, making a total of 59,993—being seven francs short of the 60,000. "Very sorry," said Dartois, "but business is business, a sou less, you know." "Oh," gaily cried Dumas, "'tis the fortune of war, but in the meantime, as I have just emptied my pocket into that of a friend's, hand me twenty francs." "Here," said Dartois. Five minutes later three orchestra seats were taken for Kean, and the total receipts amounted to 60,005 francs. Dumas, you see, was a master of construction.

Poker

McKean Buchanan was quite famous as a tragedian of the barnstorming order in the second half of the nineteenth century. "Mac," as he was familiarly called, was a very successful poker player. It was his custom after paying salaries to his company to organize a friendly game of "draw" after the play. Needless to say, the salaries always found their way back to their original source. It is said that this peculiar managerial tactic enabled the tragedian to keep on the road in the face of very bad business. C. W. Couldock once met the tragedian at a small town in Ohio, and engaged in a friendly set-to after the show. Mac won Couldock's last dollar, then lent him twenty to continue his journey and took his note. As they were parting at the depot, Buchanan said: "Charley, I want to play in New York. I want to show 'em there what acting really is. Can't you give me a letter of introduction to some of the managers?" "Why, certainly," replied Couldock, and taking from his pocket the blank leaf of a letter, he penciled the following:

Wm. WHEATLEIGH, ESQ., MANAGER, NEW YORK
  CITY:

DEAR SIR:—This will introduce the eminent Western trage-dian, Mr. McKean Buchanan. He wants to play in New York. I have seen him play Macbeth, Richelieu and poker. He plays the latter best.

C. W. Couldock

Once Bitten

The eighteenth-century actor, Andrew Cherry, having been offered an engagement by a manager who had on a former occasion behaved not altogether well to him, wrote the following laconic answer to the manager's epistle:

Sir,—you have bit me once, and I am resolved you shall not make two bites of

A. Cherry

You Get What You Paid For

William Gillette was a young actor when he appeared in a play which contained a pathetic deathbed scene. The producer was not satisfied with Gillette's performance:

"This is ridiculous. Why, you actually laughed when you were sup-posed to be dying!"

"At the salary you pay," the actor retorted, "death is something to be greeted cheerfully."

Clash by Night

In 1941 Tallulah Bankhead starred with Lee Cobb in Clifford Odets's social drama Clash by Night. *This disastrous production was directed by Lee Strasberg and produced by Billy Rose. She called it the "ghast-liest experience of my career. I loathe a bully, and Rose is a bully through and through." Trouble began long before the show reached Broadway.*

According to her contract, she was to get top billing. When the show played Philadelphia, she saw a poster reading,

BILLY ROSE PRESENT
Tallulah Bankhead
in
Clash by Night

The printer had mistakenly omitted the "s" of "presents." She went to Rose and said, "Either you make up a new poster with my name on top—or the sign might as well read, Billy Rose Present, Tallulah Bankhead Absent."

In Detroit, at the next tryout, Lee Cobb went to Rose. "Billy, I'm very upset. Miss Bankhead's behavior on the stage is highly un-professional."

"What do you mean? Be specific."

Cobb explained that during his big speech in the opening scene of the second act in which, torn between love for her and hatred of her faithlessness, he gives in to his love and attempts to kiss her, Miss Bankhead would snap her fingers and say, under her breath, "Speed it up, you ham, speed it up."

The scene took place in a kitchen. Rose told Cobb that if he didn't like anything Miss Bankhead did he was to break up the act. "Smash the table," he advised Cobb, "break every dish."

"You mean it?"

"It's my idea. It's my dough. You heard my orders. Break it up."

That night, Cobb put on a show that almost tore down the walls of the theatre.

Miss Bankhead went to Rose. "Did you see what went on?" she said.

"That was done at my suggestion," Rose snarled. "Cobb has in-structions from me to break it up whenever you break him up."

"I'm in a nest of murderers," she moaned.

What Do You Say to a Naked Producer?

The most talked-about American producer between the two wars was undoubtedly Jed Harris. He was born in Vienna as Jacob Horo-witz and adopted the surname of Sam H. Harris, the Broadway pro-ducer; his first name came from one of his favorite books as a child, Jed the Poorhouse Boy. At twenty-eight he was called the Wonder Boy of Broadway, with four of the biggest hits on the Great White Way running simultaneously, netting him the enormous sum of five million dollars. At twenty-nine he announced his permanent retire-

ment; he moved to England where he became interested in cricket and British politics. The following year he was back in New York, with all his wealth wiped out in the stock market crash. He produced a series of Russian plays and light comedies which flopped, and although he later directed the premieres of two important American plays (Our Town and The Crucible), he had lost his touch as a producer. But his particular talent lay in losing friends and alienating influential people. After he demonstrated to Helen Hayes (in Coquette) that she could play roles other than comedy, Harris promptly sued when she wanted to leave the show to have a baby; this led to the clause in contracts that defined pregnancy as an act of God. After many years as Harris's general manager, Joe Glick quit and sent out an ornate card to his friends and business associates: "Joseph Glick takes great pride and pleasure in announcing that he is no longer associated with Jed Harris." Ben Hecht defined Harris's Jekyll-and-Hyde personality: "He seems to alternate between two phases. In one, he is an eighteenth-century English gentleman, quoting from Virgil and Shakespeare. In the other, he becomes Rasputin, the Mad Monk, snarling, baring his teeth and dripping venom." Harris seemed to know and enjoy the impact his personality had on others. In the reception area of his offices at the Selwyn Theatre building a sign read: "Please don't call Jed Harris a bastard." And over the door that led to his private office there was another warning: "Where the Grapes of Wrath Are Stored." George S. Kaufman was one of the many writers whom Harris alienated, after which he said: "Every playwright should have Jed Harris once—like the measles." The best-known Harris anecdote involves the same cast.

George S. Kaufman once came to see Harris. Harris was stark naked. They had a long conference on some revisions of *The Royal Family*, a comedy which Kaufman had written in collaboration with Edna Ferber. During the two hours, Harris didn't bother to put on any clothing. Finally, Kaufman rose to go. As he closed the door behind him, he said, "Pardon me, Jed, but your fly is open."

[50] ACTORS AS MANAGERS

An Economist

From the time of Burbage and Shakespeare to Wolfit, Gielgud, and Olivier, actor-managers ran theatres and companies, refuting the

modern canard that to be an artist one must prove to be fiscally ir-
responsible. At the beginning of the eighteenth century, the books
at Drury Lane were kept by the actor Thomas Doggett. Colley Cib-
ber, who was a fellow shareholder (with the more free-spending
Robert Wilks), describes what made Doggett such an excellent man-
ager.

Doggett, who was naturally an economist, kept our expenses and accounts to the best of his power within regulated bounds and modera-
tion. The expeditious care of doing us good, without waiting for our
consent to it, Doggett always looked upon with the eye of a man in
pain. In the twenty years while we were our own directors, we never
had a creditor that had occasion to come twice for his bill; every
Monday morning discharged us of all demands, before we took a
shilling for our own use.

And, from this time, we neither asked any actor, nor were desired
by them, to sign any written agreement (to the best of my memory)
whatsoever: the rate of their respective salaries were only entered in
our daily pay-roll; which plain record every one looked upon as good
as city security: for where an honest meaning is mutual, the mutual
confidence will be bond enough, in conscience, on both sides.

The Size of the House

Soon after the appearance of Garrick at Drury Lane Theatre, to
which he, by his astonishing powers, brought all the world, while
Rich was playing his pantomimes at Covent Garden to empty benches,
he met Garrick one morning at the Bedford Coffee House. Having
fallen into conversation, Garrick asked the Covent Garden manager
how much his house would hold, when crowded with company.
"Why, master," said Rich, "I cannot well tell; but if you will come
and play Richard for one night I shall be able to give you an ac-
curate account."

Do as the Boss Says

One night, John Kemble was performing his favourite part of Pen-
ruddock in *The Wheel of Fortune*. In one of the scenes he ought to
have been shaken violently by the party representing the character
he has wronged. This was done so feebly, although the actor (Mr.
Truman) had been a plodder in the Covent Garden company for

many years, that when the scene was concluded the Manager sent him to his dressing room and gave him the following piece of sensible advice: "Mr. Truman, you did not shake me in that scene so roughly as I expected; I fear, sir, that you remembered at the time that I was Manager. Sir, when you are playing with me, you must forget that: the next time we play that scene together I hope, sir, you will use me roughly, pull me about violently, and tear my clothes: 'tis proper, sir, and keeps up the cunning of the scene."

The Manager as Actor

James Planché had written for Elliston a sort of speaking pantomime called *Little Red Riding Hood*. On the first night everything went wrong in the mechanical department. When the performance was over, Elliston summoned all the carpenters and scene-shifters on to the stage, in front of a cottage scene, having a practicable door and window; leading Planché forward, and standing in the centre, with his back to the floodlights, he harangued them in the most grandiloquent manner, expatiating on the enormity of their offence, their ingratitude to the man whose bread they were eating, the disgrace they had brought upon the theatre, the cruel injury they had inflicted on the young and promising author by his side; then, pointing in the most tragical attitude to his wife and daughters, who were in his box, he bade them look upon the family they had ruined, and, burying his face in his handkerchief to stifle his sobs, passed slowly through the door of the scene, leaving his audience silent, abashed, and somewhat affected, yet rather relieved at being let off with a lecture. The next minute the casement was thrown violently open, and thrusting out his head, his face all scarlet with fury, he roared out, "I discharge you all."

Star Complex

An actor-manager was the center of a constellation of lesser actors whom he hired to revolve around him. He chose new plays entirely based on what role he would play in it, and often savaged old texts, to make his part proportionately bigger. All this was justified on commercial grounds, that audiences mainly came to see the star. Although less common in the theatre now, the modern heir of the actor-manager is the Hollywood superstar who has his or her own production com-

pany. Hesketh Pearson worked as a young actor with Sir Herbert Tree.

It was during a rehearsal of *Macbeth* that I noticed the grave difficulties which a producer who is also a "star" actor has to face. Tree was so much concerned with his own performance that nothing else seemed to matter. At one point, when Macbeth describes how he finds the dead King Duncan, he has to say:

> —there, the murderers,
> Steep'd in the colours of their trade, their daggers
>   Unmannerly breech'd with gore—

at which Tree broke off to complain "They won't be able to see me from that box. Will that gentleman oblige me by moving out of the way? Thank you."

Brief Negotiation

To an actor-manager only himself was indispensable.

Beerbohm Tree was once endeavoring to get a well-known actor back into his company. He invited the man to call and received him in his dressing-room as he was making up. "How much would you want to come back?" inquired Mr. Tree, busy with his paint pots. The actor named an exorbitant salary to which Tree merely retorted as he went on making up: "Don't slam the door when you go out, will you?"

Teaching an Author

An aspiring author once had an introduction to J. B. Buckstone, who received him in his lodgings near the Strand. With a quavering voice the young dramatist went on, while Buckstone was twirling the tassels of his dressing gown. The wit and poetry of the dialogue went for nothing. Meanwhile the embryo Shakespeare listened in vain for a word of commendation from the manager of the Haymarket. At last he said: "I am afraid that you do not care for my writing?" "Oh, yes," replied Buckstone, "I dare say the company will be very pleased with it, but I am waiting till I enter. You don't expect a hen to cackle over another hen's eggs, do you?"

Pinching Pennies

*Within living memory Sir Donald Wolfit typified the old kind of
actor-manager. Ronald Harwood based his play* The Dresser *on Wolfit, and in his biography chronicles the foibles of the last of this van-
ished breed.*

The company suffered from Wolfit's penny-pinching most of all when
it came to costumes. Good or bad actors will always seem better actors
when decently accoutred. Wolfit's actors wore darned tights, patched
doublets, frayed tunics, and wigs by Madame Gustave of Long Acre,
who insisted upon supplying them in three kinds: " 'alf-flow, Elizabethan and barbaric." Wolfit himself preferred these wigs with their
joints made of a broad band of material, requiring thick layers of
make-up to hide it, instead of a light, transparent gauze that was the
accepted method of most other wig-makers.

On occasion, he employed his meanness to gain an added advantage. In von Kleist's *The Broken Jug* he played the magistrate who
is guilty of the crime he is trying. During the course of the play, a
lunch recess occurs; the Magistrate and a visiting Councillor, played
by George Curzon, have a comedy scene downstage, while the witnesses, one of whom was played by Nan Munro, eat their lunch upstage. Miss Munro had apples in her lunch basket and, at one performance, took a bite—Wolfit reproduced the biting sound gut-
turally as "CHWAP"—that damaged a laugh Wolfit had hoped for.
The next morning he strode into his manager's office. "How much
are we spending on apples?" he demanded. The manager consulted
his files. "Three and six a week," he replied. "Too much. Cut them.
I'm not paying three and six a week for her to go CHWAP-CHWAP—
and kill my laughs!"

A Fine and Quiet Place

Very occasionally the star did not have the last word.

When Macready was performing in Chicago, he was unfortunate
enough to offend one of the actors. This person, who was cast for the
part of Claudius in *Hamlet,* resolved to pay off the star for many supposed offenses. So, in the last scene, as Hamlet stabbed the usurper, that
monarch reeled forward, and after a most spasmodic finish, stretched
himself out precisely in the place Hamlet required for his own death.

Macready, much annoyed, whispered: "Die further up the stage, Sir!"
The monarch lay insensible. Upon which, in a still louder voice, Hamlet growled: "Die further up the stage, Sir!" Hereon, Claudius, sitting up, observed: "I believe I'm King here, and I'll die where I please."

[51]   SPENDTHRIFTS

Powers of Persuasion

Despite the image of the producer as a "fat cat," most theatre managers have since time immemorial skirted on the edge of bankruptcy. A classic example was the congenial Richard Sheridan who employed his considerable wits to keep one step ahead of creditors.

Sheridan's first tricks were undoubtedly those by which he turned, harlequin-like, a creditor into a lender. This was done by sheer force of persuasion, by assuming a lofty indignation, or by putting forth his claims to mercy with the most touching eloquence, over which he would laugh heartily when his point was gained. He was often compelled to do this during his theatrical management, when a troublesome creditor might have interfered with the success of the establishment. He talked over an upholsterer who came with a writ for 350 pounds, till the latter handed him, instead, a cheque for 200 pounds. Once, when the actors struck for arrears of wages to the amount of 3000 pounds and his bankers refused flatly to advance another penny, Sheridan screwed the whole sum out of them in less than a quarter of an hour by sheer talk. He got a gold watch from Harris, the manager, with whom he had broken several appointments, by complaining that as he had no watch he could never tell the time fixed for their meetings.

Sometimes Sheridan leaned on colleagues.

Sheridan owed Mrs. Siddons a great deal of money. She went to him one morning with a friend, and entered the house, leaving this gentleman to walk up and down the street, and telling him that she had quite made up her mind not to leave the house without her money. After a long interval she came out again quite *rayonnante*. Well, said her friend, I hope you have succeeded. Yes indeed I have. Well, and how was it. Why, you see we had a great deal of conversation together—he showed me that he is under great difficulties; however, he has positively undertaken to pay me the whole debt next month, provided in the meanwhile I advance him fifty pounds. This I have done; so you see I have attained my object.

Accountancy

Herbert Tree was another actor-manager who was bored by financial details. Joseph Harker designed many of his extravaganzas.

Tree was a poor business man, and, what was more, he seemed to rejoice in the fact. Figures bored him. His definition of accountancy given to W. H. Lambert, a former general manager of His Majesty's Theatre, was characteristic of his attitude to this side of affairs. "Accountancy," he said, "is the art of disguising the true state of finance." When it came to talking about such matters he would usually yawn, gaze abstractedly out of the window, and in various other ways impress on you the hint that he wasn't interested.

Latterly he adopted the ruse of pretending that he had an urgent telephone call to make. Apologising for interrupting the caller's discourse, he would rise from his chair and, with a murmured "I do hope you'll excuse me for a moment," he would go out of the room. A few minutes later a taxi would be heard throbbing in the street below, after which a messenger would poke his head round the door with "Sir 'Erbert's compliments, and 'e 'as a most important engagement which 'e 'as only just remembered."

Cutbacks

The young Hesketh Pearson, later Tree's biographer, observed first-hand how the actor-manager tried to economize.

An earlier manager of his, Fitzroy Gardner, recorded that the expenses of running one show were considered uneconomical, some two hundred pounds a performance, and Tree was begged to make retrenchments. He spent a day in going through the accounts, at last spotted a reasonable saving, and suggested that in future the theatre green room should be supplied with *The Daily Telegraph* instead of *The Times,* a saving of one shilling a week. Gardner once took him to task over his personal expenditure, saying that he ought not to lunch every day at the Carlton; whereupon Tree led Gardner across the road to a confectioner's shop, ordered him a bun and a glass of milk, and left him alone to practice what he preached; after which Gardner did not decline Tree's invitations to lunch at the Carlton.

Moguls

Long before Hollywood moguls, producers and theatre managers had established certain standards of crassness. These are two stories from the early part of the century.

John B. Stetson of the Globe Theatre in Boston, a well-known theatrical producer who began his career as a pawnbroker, was one day watching the rehearsal of a passion play. After a while he turned to the stage manager and enquired, "Who are them fellows on the stage now?" "Those are the twelve apostles," replied the manager. "The devil they are," said J.B. vigorously. "What's the good of twelve on a stage this size? Let's have fifty."

The manager of the Sydney Theatre, whilst rehearsing a new play, overheard someone remarking that the perspective on the painted backdrop was wrong. Indignant, he at once sent for the scene painter and burst out at him: "I didn't limit you to expense in any way, so why the devil didn't you get the right perspective? Look sharp, my lad, and get another at once."

The Producer as *Auteur*

Apart from being the most prolific producer of his day, David Belasco, like many of his Hollywood descendants, also considered himself a writer. He worked in the grand manner.

He rarely sets his plays on paper with his own pen. Two secretaries take care of the mechanical part. He declaims passage after passage, acting out each character in detail, even going through the stage business. It is the duty of one secretary to take down the dialogue. The duty of the other is to record the action. He may work for months, even for years, on one play. Whenever he gets an idea, he makes a note of it and hangs it on the wall in his office. Later these notes are filed and indexed and cross-indexed. When he thinks he has collected enough material, he takes out the notes and starts reciting—that is, writing—his new play.

The keynote of his success, he believes, is his great power of concentration. While working on a play his mind is so occupied with it that his secretary has to help him cross the street to protect him.

He carries a briefcase on which is inscribed in gold letters: "The Play I Am Now Writing."

The Buck Need Not Stop Here

One of producer David Merrick's more celebrated flops was a play about Mata Hari. On opening night in 1968 at Washington's National Theatre, everything went wrong. When the beautiful bad actress in the title role was finally to be silenced by the firing squad, the moving wagon that was to bring on the executioners failed to move and had to be manually heaved on stage. Needless to say, the rifles also failed to fire, and when the curtain mercifully began to descend upon the dead heroine, she raised her head prematurely to see whether it had really fallen. As the audience dissolved into boisterous derision, Merrick stood up in the auditorium and was heard to say: "Anyone who wants this show for a buck can have it."

[52]   PROMOTION

Play-bills

Play-bills were very early in use; on the stationers' books is the following entry: "Oct. 1587, John Charlewoode, lycensed to him by the whole consent of the assistants, the onlye imprinting of all manner of bills for players, provided that if any trouble arise herebye, then Charlewoode to bear the charge." These play-bills were then affixed to the numerous posts which formerly encumbered the streets of the metropolis; hence the phrase, "posting bills," which is still retained. The following "merry jest" on this subject, is related by Taylor, the Water Poet: "Master Field, the player, riding up Fleet Street, at a great pace, a gentleman called him, and asked him, what play was played that day? He, being angry to be stayed on so frivolous a demand, answered that he might see what play was to be played on every post. 'I cry you mercy,' said the gentleman, 'I took you for a post, you rode so fast.'"

Travesties

The following is a copy of a curious playbill issued in the year 1793 by the manager of the Theatre Royal, Kilkenny:

Kilkenny Theatre Royal, by his Majesty's company of comedians. On Saturday, May 14, 1793, will be performed by command of several respectable persons in this learned metropolis, for the benefit of Mr. Kearns, the tragedy of "Hamlet!" originally written and composed by the celebrated Dan Heys, of Limerick, and insarted in Shakspere's works. Hamlet by Mr. Kearns (being his first appearance in that character), who, between the acts, will perform several solos on the patent bag-pipes, which play two tunes at the same time. Ophelia by Mrs. Prior, who will introduce several favourite airs in character, particularly "The Lass of Richmond Hill," and "We'll all be unhappy together," from the Reverend Mr. Dibdin's "Oddities." The parts of the King and Queen, by the direction of the Reverend Father O'Callagan, will be omitted, as too immoral for any stage. Polonius, the comical politician, by a young gentleman, being his first appearance in public. The Ghost, the Gravedigger, and Laertes, by Mr. Simpson, the great London comedian. The characters to be dressed in Roman shapes. To which will be added an interlude, in which will be introduced several sleight-of-hand tricks, by the celebrated surveyor, Hunt. The whole to conclude with the farce of "Mahomet the Imposter!" Mahomet by Mr. Kearns. Tickets to be had of Mr. Kearns, at the sign of the Goat's Beard, in Castle Street. The value of the tickets, as usual, will be taken (if required) in candles, bacon, butter, cheese, soap, &c., as Mr. Kearns wishes, in every particular, to accommodate the public. Note: No person shall be admitted into the boxes without shoes or stockings.

Irish Puffing

Kemble and Lewis chancing to be in Dublin at the same time, were both engaged by a theatre manager for one night's performance. Their announcement was coupled with the following delectable passage: "They never performed together in the same piece, and in all human probability, they never will again; this evening is the summit of the manager's climax. He has constantly gone higher and higher in his endeavours to delight the public; beyond this, it is not in nature to go."

The Plague

A manager named Harel was in charge of the Théâtre de la Porte
Saint-Martin in Paris during the 1832 cholera epidemic. He had just
produced a play called *La Tour de Neslé* when the plague emptied the
whole of Paris, not just the theatres. The enterprising manager sent
the following notice to newspapers: "One must note with astonishment that the theatres are the only public places where not a single
case of cholera has manifested itself among the spectators. We offer
this indisputable fact for scientific investigation."

Press Agent

*The press agent, as a distinct profession assisting a manager or a star,
appeared in the American theatre during the late nineteenth century.*

Among the press agents in the United States the leader is probably
a keen and ingenious person who rejoices in the unusual name of
A. Toxin Worm. To the profession Herr Worm—for he is by birth a
German—is known as Anti-Toxin Worm. It was he who was responsible for the unique press work which put Mrs. "Pat" Campbell in
the mouths of everybody during her recent visit to America. He was
quick to see the possibilities of Mrs. Campbell's little pet dog. Hundreds of other actresses have had pets quite as interesting, but certainly no other dog was so quickly made historic as was Pinky Panky
Po. Even in coining a name for the miserable little beast Herr Worm
showed positive genius. It was Worm also who, when his star was
playing at the Republic Theatre in New York, had load after load of
tanbark dumped on the streets surrounding the building, and then,
when the work was done, quietly disappeared. Forthwith came the
dramatic reporters inquiring anxiously the reason for this strange pro-
ceeding. Each of them was referred to Mr. Worm. Mr. Worm was
hard to find. Once found, he was reluctant to "give up." Finally he
told the story. Mrs. Campbell was extremely nervous. The noise on
the streets annoyed her greatly. He had had the tanbark put down so
that she might not be disturbed while acting. Newspapers all over the
country printed stories about it.

Pennies from Heaven

*Horace Collins was one of the early theatre publicists, specializing in
the field. He worked for Drury Lane, where his brother Arthur was*

general manager, and he freelanced for other London theatres. He was the press agent for George M. Cohan's play, Get-Rich-Quick Walling-ford, *when it transferred from New York to the Queen's Theatre in London, with its American star.*

Hale Hamilton was a good-looking actor, and he captivated the audience at his first appearance, but he was then unknown to the British public and the play hung fire. It was necessary to devise some method to bring the merits of the play to the attention of the public. As the play was all about money, I conceived the idea of distributing cardboard pennies; on one side of a disc was a reproduction of Queen Victoria's head as on a real old penny and on the other side the words: "Go to the Queen's Theatre."

I arranged for this imitation money to be dropped about the street and in refreshment bars. When lying on the pavement or on a counter the penny looked exactly like a coin and was invariably picked up and often used for practical jokes. In fact the "pennies" became so popular that publicans used to write in for such large supplies that we could not meet the demand.

Publicity Stunts

The best known and most off-beat promotion campaigns in recent years have been those of the New York producer, David Merrick.

The direction his career would take began to be evident with *Clutterbuck,* in 1949. After the play opened, Merrick paid telephone operators and bellboys to page "Mr. Clutterbuck" during the busy hours between five and six in the lobbies of midtown hotels. The show also trained Merrick in the intricacies of discount-ticket merchandising. Although *Clutterbuck* was a failure, it ran for six months on "two-for-one" tickets.

Five years were to elapse before Merrick had another show for Broadway, the musical *Fanny,* which featured a belly-dancer named Nejla Ates. This time Merrick had a Greenwich Village sculptor make a life-size nude statue of Miss Ates and one night he had it placed on a vacant pedestal in Central Park, being careful, of course, to scatter enough clues so that police and press could find their way to the spot in the morning.

For his next show Merrick hired an English cab with a set of dual controls fitted in the back seat. Behind a dummy wheel in front sat a live monkey grinning inanely at the dumbfounded pedestrians. The sign on the side of the cab read, "I am driving my master to see *The Matchmaker*."

When box-office business slowed for John Osborne's *Look Back in Anger*, Merrick paid $250 to a young woman to climb up on the stage from her planted location in a second-row seat and assault Kenneth Haig, the actor who was playing Jimmy Porter, an unfaithful husband. The newspapers, as Merrick intended, played up the story as a bizarre but real incident involving an inflamed playgoer overwhelmed by the emotion of a powerful play, and the uncertain life of the drama was extended seven months, by the producer's calculation. The more outré the joke, the better. For his French musical *Irma La Douce* Merrick had sandwich-board men walk the streets in portable cardboard *pissoirs*.

[53] THE BOX OFFICE

Paying the Audience

We are accustomed to relate theatrical success to doing business at the box office. But the ancient Greeks, who more or less invented our kind of theatre, thought that it was the audience who should be paid, like modern jurors.

In the Athens of Pericles there was a fund originally established to pay for war but which was later used to pay each citizen two obols to go to the theatre. One obol he used to cover his own needs, the other to give towards theatre construction, because there was still no permanent theatre built of stone at the time. Pericles introduced this state subsidy for the theatre because there were so many spectators and such fights over seats between citizens and aliens, and because the rich bought up all the seats so that the poor could not get in. So he ordered some of the funds received by the state to be turned over to citizens so that they could attend the theatre.

Losing Benefits

Benefit performances have been an institution in the theatre since the Restoration. As with modern fund-raisers, there was a special purpose involved, usually to help supplement the income of a deserving but in-digent actor or dramatist.

In one of Dryden's plays there was this line, which the actress endeav-oured to speak in as moving and affecting a tone as she could:

My wound is great—because it is so small.

After she spoke the line she paused, and looked very distressed. The Duke of Buckingham, who was in one of the boxes, rose immediately from his seat, and added in a loud ridiculing tone of voice

Then 'twould be greater, were it none at all,

which had such an effect on the audience, who before were not very well pleased with the play, that they hissed the poor woman off the stage, would never bear her appearance in the rest of her part, and as this was the second time only of its appearance, made Dryden lose his benefit night.

A Miser

Checking one's coat and hat in the theatre goes back at least to the late eighteenth century, as this story shows.

Richard Russel, Esq., had a renter's share at Drury Lane Theatre, where he used to go almost every evening. Notwithstanding his im-mense fortune, his penury was so great that rather than give a trifle to any of the women who attended in the box lobby to take care of the great coats, he used constantly to pledge his for a shilling at a pawn-broker's near the Theatre, and redeem it when the performance was over, which cost him one halfpenny interest.

Payment in Kind

Fred Ross, the nineteenth-century American actor:

I recall well a tour through the Northwest in 1881. We played the then small town of Astoria. As I did not appear for a little while after the opening of the play, I was asked to watch the gallery door to see we were not cheated there. Here for the first and only time did I see salmon taken in at the gallery ticket window in lieu of cash. Admittance to the gallery was twenty-five cents (or "two bits" as was usually the name for the coin in the West at the time). About nine o'clock, a wagon from the packing company came over and took the fish, paying a quarter for each. In this manner did the theatre get paid for admittance. It was surprising how many salmon were turned in.

How To Pay Off Authors

Arsène Houssaye:

Verteuil rarely opened his lips; when he did speak it was to the point. For instance, a mediocre author asked him one day for a box. "We must not refuse him," he said, "for he, more than any one else, has a claim on our gratitude." "Why?" I asked. "Because he has never sent us any plays."

Knitting

The Hungarian playwright Ferenc Molnár had a simple rule: "The fate of a play is decided by knitting. When the lady at the box office is knitting, the play is a flop. But when the prompter can get on undisturbed with knitting her pullover during the performance, then the piece is sure to be a great success."

"Comps"

One morning J. B. Buckstone was coming out of the theatre with his son "Roly," when a seedy-looking patron of the theatre approached him with a request for a moment's interview. Boiled down, the adulation of Buckstone and all his works into which the seedy-looking one plunged meant that he wanted an order for a free seat in the pit. The request was granted, whereupon the stranger was emboldened to ask why Buckstone did not "put on" another show like *Green Bushes*, which was the finest production ever seen at the Haymarket, and so on and so forth. By this time Buckstone's patience was exhausted. "Because," he exploded, as he took his son's arm, "all my time's taken up with writing orders for damned fools like you!"

He could be no less caustic in the written word where the "deadhead" (a term used then for anybody who did not pay) was concerned. On receiving a flowery request for a couple of free seats in the stalls he is alleged to have replied:

My dear Sir,—Your exceedingly kind inquiry after the health of my family and myself is, I hasten to assure you, highly appreciated. The letter conveying your kindly sentiments will ever be treasured; indeed, I have given instructions that it is to be preserved as an heirloom. With regard to your passing allusion to a couple of seats for Saturday evening next, I have to inform you with the profoundest regret that the house is booked up for the next eight years. Yours, etc.

Small Towns

Charles Hawtrey was touring in a small American town during the early part of the century when a man tried to get a free ticket, a courtesy that was traditionally extended to members of the profession. The would-be deadhead approached him in the lobby: "Are you Mr. Hawtrey?" The reply being in the affirmative, the fellow said: "Do you 'recognize' the profession?" "Are you an actor?" asked Mr. Hawtrey, scenting a little fun. The fellow said, "Yes." "Are you a tragedian?" "Yes." The dialogue went on: "Did you ever play *Julius Caesar?*" "Oh, yes." "*Hamlet?*" "Naw, I never played any of them small towns."

Try It Some Time

A company was playing *She Stoops To Conquer* in a small western town at the turn of the century when a man without any money, but wishing to see the show, stepped up to the box office and said: "Pass me in, please." The box office man gave a loud, harsh laugh. "Pass you in? What for?" he asked. The applicant drew himself up and answered haughtily: "What for? Because I am Oliver Goldsmith, author of the play." "Oh, I beg your pardon, sir," replied the other in a meek voice, as he hurriedly wrote an order for a box.

Invitation

The tradition of house seats, or "comps," goes back centuries. One of the best stories on the subject was often told by my grandfather when I was growing up in London.

George Bernard Shaw and Sir Winston Churchill were both irascible wits who liked to pester each other. Shaw once sent Churchill a couple of tickets for the opening night of one of his plays with the note: "Bring a friend—if you have one." The politician could not make it that evening, so he thanked the playwright for the invitation: "Dear G.B.S., I'd like to come to the second performance—if there is one."

Design

How To Work Miracles

The medieval drama of Europe grew out of Christian liturgy, like the Christmas plays that are still performed. Gradually these mystery or miracle plays outgrew the church, productions becoming more and more elaborate and taking over the entire town, as they still do every ten years in the German village of Oberammergau. The following description of miraculous stage effects is from the French town of Valenciennes.

At Whitsuntide in the year 1547, the leading citizens of the town presented the life, death, and Passion of Our Lord on the stage of the mansion of the Duke of Arschot. The spectacle lasted twenty-five days, and on each day we saw strange and wonderful things. The machines (secrets) of the Paradise and of Hell were absolutely prodigious and could be taken by the populace for magic. For we saw Truth, the angels, and other characters descend from very high, sometimes visibly, sometimes invisibly, appearing suddenly. Lucifer was raised from Hell on a dragon without us being able to see how. The rod of Moses, dry and sterile, suddenly put forth flowers and fruits. Devils carried the souls of Herod and Judas through the air. Devils were exorcised, people with dropsy and other invalids cured, all in an admirable way. Here Jesus Christ was carried up by the Devil who scaled a wall forty feet high. There He became invisible. Finally, He was transfigured on Mount Tabor. We saw water changed into wine so mysteriously that we could not believe it, and more than a hundred persons wanted to taste this wine. The five breads and the two fish seemed to be multiplied and were distributed to more than a thousand spectators, and yet there were more than twelve baskets left. The fig tree, cursed by Our Lord, appeared to dry up, its leaves withering in an instant. The eclipse, the earthquake, the splitting of the rocks and the other miracles at the death of Our Lord were shown with new marvels.

Setting the Scene

Movable scenery in England was introduced only after the Restoration. In the Elizabethan theatre cruder methods were employed which to-day might be called Brechtian.

The simple expedient of writing up the names of the different places where the scene was laid in the progress of the play, or affixing a placard to the effect upon the tapestry at the back of the stage, sufficed to convey to the spectators the intentions of the author. "What child is here," asks Sir Philip Sidney, "that coming to a play and seeing Thebes written in great letters on an old door, doth believe that it is Thebes?"

Machines

The earliest machines in the theatre were used by the Greeks: some kind of crane to bring on a god or supernatural character, hence the Latin phrase deus ex machina. *The eighteenth-century historian Thomas Chetwood describes the machine he brought to Ireland from England.*

When I came first from England, in the Year 1741, I brought over an experienc'd Machinest, who alter'd the Stage, after the Manner of the Theatres in France and England, and formed a Machine to move the Scenes regularly all together; but it is since laid aside, as well as the Flies above, which were made as convenient as the Theatre would admit.

Fifteen years later, Thomas Sheridan comments sarcastically concerning the installation at Crow-street, "of a new constructed Machine, which is to present to view eight different Sets of Scenes in the Space of one Minute," and adds that the "very quick firing of Scenes upon an Audience (borrowed no doubt from the late Improvements in the Prussian Artillery) may not perhaps be quite so pleasing, unless the Scenes are so bad as not to stand Examination."

A Bad Scenic Artist

Hopkins, the Drury Lane prompter, once recommended to Garrick a man whom he wished to be engaged as a mechanist, to prepare the scenery for a new pantomime. To this application Garrick returned the following answer:

I tell you what, Hopkins, the man will never answer the purpose of the Theatre. In the first place, he cannot make a moon. I would not give threepence for a dozen such moons as he showed me today; and his suns are, if possible, worse. Besides, I gave him directions about the clouds, and he made such as were never seen since the Flood. Desire the carpenter to knock the rainbow to pieces, 'tis execrable; his stars were the only things tolerable. I make no doubt of his honesty; but until he can make a good sun, moon and rainbow, I must dispense with his services.

D. Garrick.

Illusions

The illusions of the stage were much enhanced by Garrick's Alsatian scene-painter, Philip James de Loutherbourg, a man of genius in his way, and an eminent innovator and reformer in the matter of theatrical decoration. Before his time the scenes had been merely strained 'flats' of canvas, extending the whole breadth and height of the stage. He was the first to introduce set scenes and what are technically called "raking pieces." He invented transparent scenes, with representations of moonlight, rising and setting suns, fires, volcanoes, etc., and contrived effects of colour by means of silkscreens of various hues placed before the foot and side lights. He was the first to represent a mist by suspending a gauze between the scene and the spectator. For two seasons he held a dioramic exhibition of his own, called the Eidophusikon, at the Patagonian Theatre in Exeter Change, and afterwards at a house in Panton Square. The special attraction of the entertainment was a storm at sea, with the wreck of the "Halsewell," East Indiaman.

No pains were spared to picture the tempest and its most striking effects. The clouds were movable, painted upon a canvas of vast size, and rising diagonally by means of a winding machine. The artist excelled in his treatment of clouds, and by regulating the action of his windlass he could direct their movements, now permitting them to rise slowly from the horizon and sail obliquely across the heavens, and now driving them swiftly along according to their supposed density and the power ascribed to the wind. The lightning quivered through transparent places in the sky. The waves, carved in soft wood from models made in clay, coloured with great skill, and nightly varnished to reflect the lightning, rose and fell with irregular action, flinging the foam now here, now there, diminishing in size, and dimming in colour, as they receded from the spectator.

Proscenium

The theory that the proscenium was as a frame to the picture constituted by the efforts of the actors was much favoured by Samuel Whitbread, one of the managing committee of Drury Lane after its reconstruction; and it was at his instance that the grey curtain was placed in position unusually remote from the footlights, the performers being forbidden to mar the illusion by appearing in advance of the proscenium. Dowton, as the story runs, was the first actor who—like Manfred's ancestor in *The Castle of Otranto*—took the liberty of ceasing to be a picture, and of detaching himself from the gilded frame encompassing him. "Don't tell me of frames and pictures!" exclaimed the choleric comedian, "if I can't be heard by the audience in the frame, I'll walk out of it." The proscenium of Drury Lane was subsequently remodelled, and the performers brought nearer to the spectators.

A Crusader

Lee Simonson, one of the important scenic designers of the American theatre, paid this tribute to one of his colleagues.

Robert Edmond Jones, as an artist and as a person, was a unique combination of craftsman, romantic, mystic, and Puritan. His feeling for the materials he worked with and his skill in manipulating them were akin to those of our colonial craftsmen who gave a clear and enduring beauty to their silverware, chairs and chests, porticos and staircases, their steeples and weather vanes, frigates and figureheads. His profession was less a calling than a call, like the "call" that led some of his New England forebears to the pulpit. The soul to be saved was the theatre's. His aim, throughout his career, was not only to recover its pristine purity and splendor by his own efforts but also to inspire all workers in the theatre—authors, actors, directors, as well as fellow designers—to enlist in his crusade.

While planning a production Jones was as deliberately and shrewdly practical as a Yankee farmer pruning fruit trees or fertilizing a field before planting a crop. In designing his costumes, for instance, he assembled swatches of every bit of material to be used, often pinning down or basting costumes together for the dressmaker, or, if the need arose, as it did in *Caliban*, completing an array of hundreds of costumes with the aid of only a few assistants. He conscientiously absorbed source material, traveling to England to study the Tower of London at first hand for *Richard III*, spending several months in Venice before starting his first *Othello*, poring over the original Chinese documents of *Lute Song*. But these were mere preliminaries to the process of creation, or rather re-creation—the process of interpreting, intensifying, and refashioning every characteristic detail of architecture, the line and sweep of every costume, its encrustations and ornaments, until he achieved a vibrant pattern of life, texture, and form that sustained the play's dominant mood, heightened its pattern of emotions, and illuminated its inner meaning.

Blizzard by Belasco

The hit of the [1905] season was *The Girl of the Golden West*. Belasco's second-act blizzard was a sensation, "needing the services of thirty-two trained artisans, a kind of mechanical orchestra."

Why Not the Worst?

Although Belasco had vast scene-shops turning out every kind of scenery, he knew no limits in his search for realism.

When I produced *The Easiest Way* I found myself in a dilemma. I planned one of its scenes to be an exact counterpart of a little hall bedroom in a cheap theatrical boarding-house in New York. We tried to build the scene in my shops, but, somehow, we could not make it look shabby enough. So I went to the meanest theatrical lodging-house I could find in the Tenderloin district and bought the entire interior of one of its most dilapidated rooms—patched furniture, threadbare carpet, tarnished and broken gas fixtures, tumble-down cupboards, dingy doors and window-casings, and even the faded paper on the walls. The landlady regarded me with amazement when I offered to replace them with new furnishings.

The Road to Hell

For more than three decades, from the 1940s to the 1960s, Professor Nevill Coghill was the dominant figure of the theatrical scene in Oxford. His productions were famous for their imaginative but always scrupulously faithful interpretation of the text, and also for spectacular technical effects. Still remembered is his staging of A Midsummer Night's Dream *in the gardens of Worcester College, when Coghill laid pontoons under water in the lake so that Puck seemed to be gliding over it. He had inspired many hundreds of undergraduates to contribute their talents both to the theatre and to scholarship. I was privileged to be his friend at the end of his career when we were both at Merton College. It was during those years (1966) that he directed Richard Burton, his former pupil, in* Doctor Faustus. *The following description is from an earlier production of the play that Nevill Coghill directed in 1957.*

Throughout the play Marlowe has emphasized both the fascination and the danger of books, and here surely is the dilemma of renaissance man, fighting his way out of the middle ages, perfectly mirrored. Marlowe's solution is of course medieval and conventional. Nevill shifted the emphasis in Faustus's downfall from the oversimple, fatal contract-fulfillment, to the folly of excessive intellectual curiosity. The book-symbolism was developed and emphasized heavily at the end. Over the open trap on the forestage had been placed a huge book. At the climax of his desperation Faustus, seeing it for the first time, threw himself before it and began to turn the pages in search of one final answer. As each huge leaf rose and fell before his eyes it was seen to be perfectly blank. Under the extreme dramatic pressure of the moment this produced a thrill of terror starker than all the grimacing devils and looming black shapes of the previous action. The illusion of Academe was destroyed as devilish hands tore upwards through the pages to drag Faustus to Hell.

Indeed, on the first night, sparks from a smoke-puff set fire to the book and the audience enjoyed the unforeseen excitement of watching Faustus descend willy-nilly into real flames. The suspense was quickly broken as militant stage hands, uttering very corrupt text, shot fire extinguishers up through the gaping mouth of hell all over the bemused front-row audience.

When a Symbol Is Not a Symbol

When Sir John Gielgud appeared as Oedipus at the National Theatre in London in 1968, the set in Peter Brook's production was dominated by a gigantic golden phallus, thirty feet high. Coral Browne saw it and remarked, "Well, it's no one I know." Another giant phallus—beige this time—was used in a modern version of Aristophanes's *Lysistrata* staged in Cambridge, Massachusetts, in 1979. Midway through the opening performance, the wires supporting the phallus gave way, and, as if in symbolic gesture, it fell right across the stage knocking the leading lady to the ground.

[55] EXTRAVAGANZAS

Spectacle

Sir Herbert Tree's productions were the major theatrical events of their period. They were done with utmost splendour and realism. The wood near Athens in *A Midsummer Night's Dream* had rabbits running about in it; Olivia's Garden in *Twelfth Night* was carpeted with grass and filled with flowers and statuary; the opening scene of *The Tempest* showed a complete ship rocking in a sea the waves of which splashed over the deck and made many in the audience feel squeamish; the rustic scene in *The Winter's Tale* contained a real cottage, a real stream and waterfall, a willow-tree, reeds, and such like riparian devices; *King John* contained a still-life picture which exercised the ability of the entire company to keep still and look like a picture but did not forward Shakespeare's dramatic intent; in *Richard II* Tree rode through London on horseback, though Shakespeare was content with making another character mention the episode; while the return of Antony to Alexandria, described by Octavius Caesar in a short speech, was presented by Tree as a magnificent tableau, with surging crowds and processions of priests and military marches and the strewing of flowers and the clashing of cymbals and the dances of women and a general conglomeration of sound and colour. He was constantly criticized for the lavishness of his productions, and he once remarked: "Shakespearean scholars say I'm wrong in tempting people to come to the theatre and giving them a spectacle instead of Shakespeare. But I prefer a spectacle on the stage to spectacles in the audience."

Joy

Joseph Harker designed many of Tree's elaborate productions.

For cost and magnificence of mounting Tree's productions of *Henry the Eighth*, *Antony and Cleopatra*, and *Twelfth Night* have never, I suppose, been surpassed. I remember that just about the time he did *Twelfth Night* his financial affairs were bothering him somewhat. We lunched together one day at the Pall Mall restaurant, and then strolled back to the theatre, talking about the forthcoming show. Reaching the middle of the Haymarket, he stopped abruptly, quite oblivious, it seemed of the traffic. "Now, don't forget," he counselled me. "The keynote of this play is to be joy—joy—JOY," adding in an aside, as a sudden thought struck him—"with *economy*."

Gored by Gorse

One of the scenes in *Richard II* is laid on the Welsh coast, and Herbert Tree obtained a background with hills and in the foreground a mass of broom. To heighten the effect a quantity of real broom was to have been strewn on the stage, but unfortunately those responsible put down gorse. At the line, "For God's sake, let us sit upon the ground and tell sad stories of the death of kings," the lightly clad king threw himself on the ground—and the rest of the lines he uttered were not by Shakespeare.

Shifting Scenes

At the Lyceum, Irving was very extravagant—he had, indeed, no sense of money when he was striving for his effects. A big set he once devised involved a wait of twelve minutes in "striking" and subsequent re-setting. At rehearsal Irving said to the master carpenter: "You must manage that change in seven minutes, Arnott."

"I'm afraid it can't be done, Mr. Irving."

"Little deaf this morning, Arnott, eh?"

"No sir, only it can't be done with the men I've got."

"I didn't ask you how many men you had, Arnott. That change must be done in seven minutes."

And something like fifteen extra stage-hands were engaged for that change alone . . .

The Edifice Complex

Norman Bel Geddes once produced a play called *Siege* and was so optimistic about its chances that he spent a fortune for a massive set that showed four stories of an old Spanish fortress (this was the set that led George Jean Nathan to remark that Geddes had an edifice complex). When the critics completed their massacre of *Siege*, however, some of the pieces of the set had been blasted as far as Stamford. Undaunted, Geddes appeared at a masquerade party the very next night, dressed as an undertaker, with every one of the critics' requiems pinned to his right lapel.

A Show-stopper

The scenery for *Philomena* (1980) was sufficiently ugly for Walter Kerr to write that it was the first set he saw on Broadway which stopped its own applause.

Safari

The recent revival of Eva LeGallienne's *Alice in Wonderland* was designed by John Lee Beatty. The costumes were mostly made out of naugahyde. The concepts kept changing during rehearsals, requiring additional costumes to be made. After one of these requests, Beatty turned wearily to his assistant and sighed: "Oh dear, we will have to go out and shoot another nauga."

[56] PROPS

A Critical Prop

Vancauson, the celebrated maker of automata, had been entrusted with the manufacture of the asp in a play about Cleopatra. It hissed loudly as the actress playing the part placed it to her breast. A critic, being asked what he thought of the piece, replied drily, "I agree with the asp!"

Modesty

Mr. Johnson, the machinist of Covent Garden, viewing Chunee, the real elephant at Drury Lane, is reported to have said: "I should be very sorry, if I couldn't make a better elephant than that!"

Unfolding His Darker Purpose

Macready was once playing Lear at Nottingham, and requiring a map to enable him to arrange the division of his property among his daughters, mentioned it on the list of properties which would be required. The property man, however, not having had many intellectual advantages, mistook the word map for mop, and when the King, enthroned on full state, called for the map, a white, curly mop was placed in the hands of a "super" playing a noble, who, kneeling, presented it to the aged King. Macready is said to have rushed off the stage, dragging the unfortunate super and the superfluous mop with him amid roars of laugher.

Blood Donor

When playing Macbeth one night at Manchester, Macready's servant, who should have been in the wings with a bowl of cochineal which Macready used to smear on his hands to represent blood, failed to put in an appearance. Macready's exit was only a very momentary and very rapid one, and, finding that the blood he relied on for the next scene was not at hand, he rushed up to an inoffensive commercial traveller, who had been allowed by the special favour of his friend, the local stage manager, to come and watch the mighty star from the side, and without any warning struck him a violent blow on the nose, smothered his hands in the blood that flowed freely, and ran on to the stage again to finish the performance. When the curtain fell, he apologized to the victim for his apparent rudeness, as he put it, in the most courtly and chivalrous manner, presenting him with a five-pound note.

A Gift from the Wings

An unexpected arrival from the wings brought a confusion to Lillie Langtry one evening when she was playing in Camille. While she was on stage with her lover in the play, she noticed that the white camellia, which she was shortly to give to him, was not in its usual place. She managed to sidle towards the wings and whisper "My camellia!" One of the stagehands responded instantly, and, without looking at what she had been given, Mrs. Langtry returned to her lover, saying, "Take this flower, Armand. It is rare, pale, senseless, cold but sensitive as purity itself. Cherish it, and its beauty will excel the loveliest flower that grows, but wound it with a single touch and you shall never recall its bloom or wipe away the stain," with which she handed him a half-chewed stick of celery.

[57] SOUNDS

Nothing To Crow About

In Garrick's time, during the first scene of *Hamlet* it was customary for one of the performers to imitate the crowing of a cock, so that the Ghost might have practical cause for starting "like a guilty thing upon a fearful summons." We read, however, that the cock crowing "being often unskilfully executed, threw an air of ridicule over the performance," and was eventually dispensed with.

Yawning Musician

Music and drama have been closely allied since the Greeks, yet musicians and actors belong to different worlds.

Cervetto, the violoncello player, once ventured to yawn noiselessly and portentously while Garrick was delivering an address to the audience. The house gave way to laughter. The indignation of the actor could only be appeased by Cervetto's absurd excuse that he invariably yawned when he felt the greatest rapture, and to this emotion the address to the house, so admirably delivered by his manager, had justified him in yielding. Garrick accepted the explanation, perhaps rather on account of its humour than of its completeness.

Sound Cue

Macready was rehearsing Lord Byron's tragedy *Marino Faliero* at Birmingham, when he expressed considerable anxiety that there should be no mistake about the tolling of St. Mark's bell towards the end of Act IV. It is a very important incident in the play, as it is the agreed signal to inform him that his friends are in force, and comes just as Marino is being arrested by the guards belonging to the Council of Ten. Anxious to provide everything for the great actor, the Manager displaced his own official and undertook the duty himself. But alas! he was too zealous, and a good dozen lines before its time the warning bell was at hand, ruining the effect and completely discomposing the tragedian. As the drop descended Macready rushed from the stage, and, meeting the Manager, uttered the one syllable, "Beast!" The next morning's rehearsal was a little awkwardly carried on; at length the Manager said, "Last night, Mr. Macready—" "Oh, don't speak of it, Sir, it was a most painful affair," replied the actor. "Yes," continued the Manager, "and you called me a beast." "Did I indeed?" said Macready; "I am very sorry,—but you were a beast, Mr. S." And with an injured air the tragedian continued the rehearsal.

Thunder

One of the highlights of the film The Dresser *is the backstage view of the storm scene from* King Lear. *This description of the same scene is from the 1820s.*

Lee, manager of the Edinburgh Theatre, with a view to improving the thunder of his stage, ventured upon a return to the Elizabethan system of representing a storm. His enterprise was attended with results at once ludicrous and disastrous.

He placed ledges here and there along the back of his stage, and obtaining a parcel of nine-pound cannon-balls, packed these in a wheelbarrow which a carpenter was instructed to wheel to and fro over the ledges. The play was *King Lear*, and the jolting of the heavy barrow as it was trundled along its uneven path over the hollow stage, and the rumblings and reverberations thus produced, counterfeited most effectively the raging of the tempest in the third act. Unfortunately, however, while the king was braving, in front of the scene, the pitiless storm at the back, the carpenter missed his footing, tripped over one of the ledges, and fell down, wheelbarrow, cannon-balls, and all. The stage being on a declivity, the cannon-balls came rolling rapidly and noisily down towards the front, gathering force as they advanced, and overcoming the feeble resistance offered by the scene, struck it down, passed over its prostrate form, and made their way towards the foot-lights and the fiddlers, amidst the amusement and wonder of the audience, and the amazement and alarm of the Lear of the night. As the nine-pounders advanced towards him, and rolled about in all directions, he was compelled to display an activity in avoiding them, singularly inappropriate to the age and condition of the character he was personating. He was even said to resemble a dancer achieving the terpsichorean feat known as the egg hornpipe. Presently, too, the musicians became alarmed for the safety of themselves and their instruments, and deemed it advisable to scale the spiked partition which divided them from the pit; for the cannon-balls were upon them, smashing the lamps, and falling heavily into the orchestra. Meantime, exposed to the full gaze of the house, lay prone, beside his empty barrow, the carpenter, the innocent invoker of the storm he had been unable to allay or direct, not at all hurt, but exceedingly frightened and bewildered. After his unlucky experiment, the manager abandoned his wheelbarrow and cannon-balls, and reverted to more received methods of producing stage-storms.

But Would He Get Work?

Martin Harvey told a story about John Ryder, an elocution teacher who had at one time been Macready's leading man. He was on one occasion stage-managing a play in which a tremendous thunderstorm occurred. Ryder had called half-a-dozen special rehearsals of this storm, but he could not get the stage-hands to obtain enough noise out of boxes and cannon-balls. In the end he got exasperated and in a temper called out to the flyman: "That won't do at all! You must get more rattle."

As it happened a genuine and violent thunderstorm was in full blast in the heavens at the time, and it was after the "artillery of the clouds" had been doing its best that Ryder was the most dissatisfied. "Louder! Louder!" shouted Ryder. The flyman shouted in return, "Beg pardon, sir; that wasn't me. That was God Almighty." "Well," roared Ryder, "that may be loud enough for the Almighty, but it won't do for me."

[58] LIGHTING

Early Experiments

The Greek and Roman theatres were open air, and performances began in the morning. The public theatres in Elizabethan London

*performed in the afternoon and were partially exposed to the heavens.
But in the Renaissance courts of Europe there were indoor performances, which meant the beginning of stage lighting.*

Queen Elizabeth I almost always saw plays at night. The performances
started about ten o'clock and did not end until well after midnight,
which meant the use of artifical light—a development which did not
occur in the public theatres until seventy or eighty years later. There
were no fancy tricks in Elizabeth's time, but at the Court of James
I the first tentative experiments in coloured lights and deliberately
contrived groups of lights were made. Elizabeth was content with a
general blaze from huge candelabra, tall candle-sticks and flaming
torches which illuminated her as well as the players and helped warm
the draughty spaces of the palace.

Way to the Top

The use of candles involved the employment of candle-snuffers, who
came on at certain pauses in the performance to tend and rectify the
lighting of the stage. Goldsmith's Strolling Player narrates how he
commenced his theatrical career in this humble capacity: "I snuffed
the candles; and let me tell you, that without a candle-snuffer the
piece would lose half its embellishments." The duties of a candle-
snuffer were somewhat arduous. It was the custom of the audience,
especially among those frequenting the galleries, to regard him as
a butt with whom to amuse themselves during the pauses between
the acts, hurling missiles at the unfortunate candle-snuffer.

Hollow Crown

Winstone, a comic actor in the eighteenth century who sometimes
essayed tragical characters, appeared upon a special occasion as Richard III. He played his part so energetically, and flourished his sword
to such good purpose while demanding "A horse! A horse!" in the
fifth act that the weapon came into contact with a rope by which
one of the hoops of tallow candles was suspended, and the blazing
circle (not the golden one he had looked for) fell round his neck and
lodged there, greatly to his own discomfiture and to the amusement
of the audience. The amazed Catesby of the evening, instead of helping his sovereign to a steed, is said to have been sufficiently occupied
with extricating him from his embarrassing situation.

Keeping in Focus

Henry Irving:

It should be remembered that the style of our old actors was very much affected by their surroundings. . . . Naturally, a grand declamatory style was much more suited to a badly lighted stage than a manner full of artistic minutiae. This is what Hazlitt meant when he said that to be really appreciated, Kean's acting should be seen from the front row in the pit, which was then next to the orchestra. So limited was the radius of light that it was the great object of every player to get into what was called the "focus," so that his face might be clear to the audience. This also accounts for the habit, odd to us now, which actors had of constantly standing on the stage in a line.

One night Kean played the great scene in the third act of *Othello* with a power which astonished even his most devoted admirers. One of them, meeting him a day or two afterwards, complimented him on his performance. "You were wonderful the other night, Mr. Kean." "Was I?" said the tragedian. "Why, didn't you feel that you were?" "No. Can't say I remember anything particular." "Surely you must remember, Mr. Kean! On Thursday night when you seized Mr. —— by the throat, and got into such a fury, I thought you'd have killed him!" "Ha!" exclaimed Kean, brightening, "I remember now. Did I seem in a fury, eh?" "Oh, awful, sir, awful!" "No wonder. D—— the fellow, he tried to keep me out of the focus!"

The Actor's Face

W. Bridges-Adams, in one of his letters (1949) to Arthur Colby Prague, digresses into an illuminating passage about the evolution of lighting.

The chandeliers (perhaps even of Burbage at the Blackfriars) were there to shew the actors' figures, and the floats to shew their faces. God knows what perilous contraptions among the gauzes illumined the theophanies of Inigo Jones. With the merging of the apron and the scenic stage the rule held, and held for centuries: acting light and scenic light. I fancy Irving was to prove himself the greatest master of the art of blending the two so that the stage picture captured the imagination and the actor's face focussed it. Irving of course stuck to gaslight, subtler and more magical than the electric;

it restricted the painter's palette but was *alive* and imperceptibly a-quiver; it interposed a film of waving air between actor and spectator.

It was that child of the Lyceum, Teddy Craig, who was truly "no friend to actors"—with whom, in an unguarded moment, he professed himself willing to dispense. He was, I think, the first authoritative apostle of top-lighting, as it is known, and mostly loathed, by actors to-day; he was abetted alike by amateurs of design who lacked actors' sense and by the duller realists who pointed out that the sun and sky are overhead and the brightest thing in a daylit room must be the window. But the surrealist in us all tells us that the brightest thing in the stage-world is an actor's face; and the most expressive feature of that face are the eyes and mouth, lying respectively under the shadow of the brow and of the nose. Once, and only once, did Marie Tempest vail her judgment in this respect to a hubristic scene-designer—who hurried me to the play because it was coming off at once; she looked an expressionless eighty, and was dull. A few weeks earlier I had seen her at six feet distance across the floats: a vivacious thirty. Actors can't act in dark goggles and a Hitler moustache; and it may well be, as you suggest, that their facial powers are slowly becoming atrophied through disuse.

Selling the Sunset

David Belasco introduced hidden footlights to the theatre. "Lights are to drama what music is to the lyrics of a song. The greatest part of my success in the theatre I attribute to my feeling for colors, translated into effects of light." He recklessly squandered time and money on lighting effects. In his production of The Darling of the Gods *a single lighting effect lasted seven minutes. Here he describes another experiment.*

When I produced *The Girl of the Golden West*, I experimented three months to secure exactly the soft, changing colors of a California sunset over the Sierra Nevadas, and then turned to another method. It was a good sunset, but it was not Californian. Afterward I sold it to the producers of *Salomy Jane*, and it proved very effective and perfectly adjusted to the needs of that play.

[CHAPTER XII]

Directors

Why We Have Directors

In the course of repeatedly reflecting on the part of Romeo, and desirous of attaining to as great perfection as possible in the representation of it, it occurred to Mr. John Kemble that in that passage where Romeo in his despair approaches the house of the Apothecary, there had prevailed a great misconception as to the right manner of delivering it. Romeo says:

> And if a man did need a poison now,
> Whose sale is present death in Mantua,
> Here lives a caitiff wretch would sell it him.
>
> . . . .
>
> As I remember, this should be the house,
> Being holiday, the beggar's shop is shut.
> What ho! Apothecary!

As the passage had been always hitherto spoken, the player raised his voice in the "What ho! Apothecary!" to the pitch of "Milk below, maids!" Now, reasoned Mr. Kemble, could anything be more absurd? A man with all the marks of deep despair is seen looking about for an apothecary's shop; he is in search of some subtle poison, which it is death in this Apothecary to sell; and yet as if he wanted all the world to witness the purchase, he bawls out with Stentorian lungs, "What ho! Apothecary!" Nothing, as Mr. Kemble thought, could be more out of character, and he accordingly resolved to go a different way to work.

On his next representation of Romeo, when he came to the words, "As I remember, this should be the house," he lowered his voice to the meditative muttering of some midnight prowler; then in a side whisper, told us that "Being holiday, the beggar's shop was shut," and at length in a low sepulchral tone uttered the magic words, "What ho! Apothecary!" Thus far all was well; but unfortunately for Mr. Kemble's new and rational improvement Shakespeare happens

to have thought differently on the subject; and no sooner had Romeo
uttered in this low tone the words, "What ho! Apothecary!" than
Mr. Apothecary stepped forth and demanded, "Who calls so loud?"

The audience, as may readily be supposed, were instantly struck
by the strange incongruity, and burst into a general laugh. Mr.
Kemble was so disconcerted, that he could scarcely proceed with his
part, which he now learnt, by a mortifying exposure, could only be
performed well by attending to the part which others have to play
with him.

Taking Directions

One day at rehearsal Sir Herbert Tree asked a youthful actor to "step
back a little." The player did so. Tree eyed him critically and went on
rehearsing. After a time he repeated his request: "A little further
back." The youth obeyed. Surveying him, Tree went on with his work.
Shortly afterwards he again asked him to step still further back. "If I
do," expostulated the youth, "I shall be right off the stage." "Yes,"
said Tree, "that's right."

Directing

*In 1940 Gielgud played King Lear at the Old Vic and was instru-
mental in bringing in Harley Granville-Barker for a week of rehearsals.*

I never saw actors watch a director with such utter admiration and
obedience. It was like Toscanini coming to rehearsal—very quiet,
business suit, red eyebrows, and text in his hand. He filled every moment; so much so that people didn't even go to try on their wigs or
have a bun, or anything—they just sat there. I got actors and actresses,
from outside, friends of mine, to come and peek in, because I said,
"You really must see these rehearsals, they're something absolutely
extraordinary." And we would go in until quite late at night. I remember doing the death scene of Lear with him, and he began
stopping me on every word, and I thought every moment he'd say,
"Now stop, don't act any more, we'll just work it out for technical
effects." Not at all, he didn't say stop, so I went on acting and crying
and carrying on, and trying to take the corrections as he gave them
to me. And when I looked at my watch, we had been working on
this short scene for forty minutes. It was extraordinary that he had
the skill not to make you wild and not to exhaust you so much that

you couldn't go on; if you had the strength to go along with him, he could give you more than any person I ever met in my life.

Barker never talked much about mannerisms, but he used to make one aware that one could only do a certain amount and not try to do more. He got Lear within my orbit. He said to me, "Lear should be an oak, you're an ash; now we've got to do something about that."

Different Strokes

Laurence Olivier:

People who direct actors have different ideas as to what their part really is. When I was young, the director was very much of a martinet, rather a colonel, or a sergeant-major who roars. We all felt that Basil Dean was very, very unkind to us, and we were very frightened of him. Actually he wouldn't harm a fly, but he managed to get his effects out of us. I don't think he was ever happy unless he had the leading lady in tears at least once a day. Certainly he nearly had me in tears, when he was rehearsing me, several times.

Then there is the sort of director in whom you have complete faith. I remember the first time I worked with Michel Saint-Denis, I thought, "I'll believe in you, boy, whatever you say, I'll believe in you." He directed me in my first *Macbeth* in 1937, and for him, for me, for Lillian Baylis, for the Old Vic, for everybody concerned, it was utter disaster. But in spite of that, when he came to direct me in *Oedipus Rex* eight years later, again I found myself just putting myself in his hands, delighted to be. I still had utter faith; and that time, of course, it had a very splendid result.

Visual Effects

Hume Cronyn had this to say about Sir Tyrone Guthrie, whom everybody called Tony.

Tony loved visual effects. You remember the appearance of Richard in that coronation cape, a lovely theatrical effect? They practically had to push me on stage to get me started. I only weighed 130 pounds wringing wet, and I've got I don't know how many yards of velour trailing behind me with four people holding on to the train, and I've got to get the momentum of getting that started across the stage. And I can't remember whether it was in that scene, but one of those scenes was prefaced by the inevitable Tony Guthrie parade, people pouring out of the vomitories. There were the bishops and priests, and one of the priests stumbled carrying a magnificent jewelled cross and went to his knees; and then got kicked by the bishop behind him to get up to his feet. I mean, that's typical Guthrie.

Shy of Emotion

Michael Langham, who succeeded Sir Tyrone at both the Stratford Festival in Canada and the Guthrie Theatre in Minneapolis recalls the following about him.

"You're *feeling* it, you silly girl," he said to the actress playing Jessica in *The Merchant* at Stratford in 1956. "Your job is to make *us* feel it."

Olivier on Guthrie:

He seemed to me, in those days, to be a wee bit nervous of the intimacies, a bit shy of great human emotion. I may be misjudging him, but I remember in *Henry* V he would say to me and Jessica Tandy, "You two go and do the love scene by yourselves, will you, I can't be bothered with that."

Enthusiasm

Jessica Tandy on Guthrie:

He was putting on a pageant for some town in England, and there were hundreds of people all over the place and there was a woman reclining on the grass, you see, and he was all over the place with *all* these people and he finally came back, stepped over her and said, 'Isn't it fun putting on a play?" . . . You obviously felt he was enjoying it tremendously, and the enthusiasm was terrific.

Pace

Wolfit ignored the subtler nuances of supporting parts. Direction was given in general terms ("you must be more evil" or "more noble" or "less sympathetic") so that the peculiar traits of character were lost. . . . Wolfit's chief direction to his company was contained in one word that he had learned in his youth: "PACE!" "Pace, pace, pace!" he would bellow, which was his way, as it was so many actor-managers' before him, of getting the company to speak at unnatural speed, so that he could speak more slowly. He could be brutal and bullying to those who did not obey, or who asked the fatal question "Why?"

[60] TRADE SECRETS

So Much for Directing

James Agate:

Theatre consists of two great arts: acting and playwriting; and there is no third art necessary to coordinate them.

Tyrone Guthrie:

A director has but one task: to make each rehearsal so amusing that the actors will look forward to the next one.

The Rope Trick

In 1946 Harold Clurman was directing Maxwell Anderson's Truck-line Café.

I had cast a young actor of twenty-two. He had been recommended to me by Stella Adler who praised him highly as the most gifted of her students: Marlon Brando. I had never seen him on the stage but I trusted Miss Adler's judgment and went to "look him over" in John van Druten's *I Remember Mama* in which he played an adolescent. He was certainly interesting but the nature of his role in this play was so different from that of the returned G.I. in the Anderson play, who on learning of his wife's infidelity kills her, that I wasn't at all sure he would suit the part.

I had read him for the author, the producers (Elia Kazan and Walter Fried), and myself. He read poorly, his head sunk low on his chest as if he feared to divulge anything. Yet there could be no question: he was peculiarly arresting. We decided to use him.

He mumbled for days. I applied myself so strenuously to his

problem (I really couldn't determine what it was) that after a particularly arduous session—he listened attentively—I cried out, "All the actors here are witnesses: you will be a star someday and I shall demand that you support me when I'm a broken down old director." We all laughed. But he didn't improve.

The author's agent and wife suggested I recast the part. Anderson was a gentle and fair man and told me about this. "What do you wish me to do?" I asked. "Do what you think best," was his reply. I said I had faith in the boy and I would continue to work with him. But I was worried: the boy couldn't be heard beyond the fifth row.

His difficulty, it seemed, was that he could not give vent to the deep well of feeling which I sensed in him. He could not overcome some inner resistance: he would not "open up."

One day I asked everyone in the company to leave the stage and retire to the dressing rooms. I turned to Brando and said, "I want you to *shout* your lines." (For this I chose the crucial scene in which the young man tells how he drowned his unfaithful wife, whom he still loved.) Brando raised his voice. "Louder," I ordered. He complied. "Still louder," I insisted. This was repeated several times and my command for ever greater vocal volume began to exhaust the actor and to rouse him to visible anger. Then I yelled, "Climb the rope!" as I pointed to a rope which was hanging from the gridiron above the stage. Without hesitation he began climbing the rope while I urged him to keep shouting his lines. The other members of the cast came rushing onto the stage, alarmed at the terrifying sounds they had heard while still in their dressing rooms.

When Brando let himself down, he looked as if he were ready to hit me. "Now," I said quietly, "run the scene—normally." He recovered his poise and did as I bid him. He "spoke up"—effortlessly. In a few days he played the "moment" beautifully. On opening night—and every night thereafter—his performance was greeted by one of the most thundering ovations I have heard for an actor in the theatre.

How To Direct Shaw

Tyrone Guthrie saw Michael Langham's first production of The Doctor's Dilemma *in 1947.*

"All you can do with Shaw," said Guthrie, "is to fan the actors out in a semi-circle, put the speaker at the top, and hope for the best."

Advice

Laurence Olivier took over the direction of Eduardo de Filippo's *Philomena* from Franco Zeffirelli. Just before the opening in Baltimore he addressed the assembled cast on stage: "A word to the jockeys: don't let the horse get ahead of the rider."

[61] WORKING WITH ACTORS

Talking to Actors

In 1938 the notorious Jed Harris was directing Thornton Wilder's Our Town.

At the end of the first day's script reading, Jed smiled and moved his lips. The cast looked at him and then at one another. His lips were still moving but no sound emerged. The whisper had been reduced to pure breath.

A young actor in the company, William Roerick, assumed the responsibility of telling the others what he'd concluded, through lip reading and proximity, the director had said. "Mr. Harris says it's time for a break." Harris nodded and smiled and Roerick became his official whisper translator.

Sometimes, however, the director could be perfectly audible. "Tommy Ross," he said warningly to the actor playing Editor Webb. Ross was a stage veteran, a good actor but one tempted by old stage tricks. He was doing too much business with his hands; it was an old ploy designed to divert audience attention to himself. Harris said meaningfully, "I hate an actor who knows his *business*. I don't want any of your low comedy tricks in this play. It isn't that kind of play. If you do that once more I'm going to fire you and you are the best actor in America for the part."

Roerick remembered that because he thought it was the perfect way to deal with a misbehaving actor, threatening him but flattering him at the same time.

The Psychologist

Following the Second World War, Joan Littlewood created a new kind of collective with her Theatre Workshop which produced plays at London's East End.

The tremendous compliment she will pay to an actor is that she will give him complete and utter concentration. You know for the next few minutes, or an hour, or however long it takes, she is going to grapple with your problem. And everybody gets this—even if you are playing a big scene with a lot of people on the stage—everybody will get this terrific individual criticism. Some people who aren't used to such a close personal analysis of their work may find it harsh. After all, she's quite capable of saying to somebody: "You can't do that— it's beyond your capabilities." She's a great psychologist—if she thinks an actor needs putting down, she'll put him down. But she won't come the Boss-Director on you. If an actor has an idea and she has an idea, you have full time and opportunity to debate, try it out, and quite often a compromise is found. She is very willing to chuck out her idea if yours is better. She is always saying, "Don't let yourself be 'produced.' " In fact, I once heard her say, "The theatre will only triumph when all producers are dead!"

How To Play Opalescent Dawn

Sybil Thorndike:

Shaw and Gilbert Murray are the two men—not counting Lewis—that have been the guiding lights in my life. There was something god-like about Murray. I met him first in Manchester, when we were doing the *Hippolytus*, and Lewis was producing. I was playing a goddess and I thought, "Well, this is child's play, anybody can play these old goddesses." At a rehearsal I went up on the stage and I knew I could do the whole thing, and when I finished I thought, "Well, there!" I mean, this is what comes of long experience as an amateur: I can do it. Gilbert Murray came up to me and said, "Charming, my dear young lady, charming. Now what I want is opalescent dawn." I was knocked right flat to the bottom, and had to build up again.

Direction

Granville Barker once said to John Gielgud: "You've already shown me that—now show me something else."

Don't Underline

Michael Redgrave recounts The Three Sisters, *directed by Michel Saint-Denis.*

I had invented, during rehearsals, a bit of business where I went to sleep on a bolster, with my mouth open and breathing heavily; and this seemed to get a pleasing reaction from the audience. I remember Michel coming round after we'd been playing for about a week. And he said, "Do you know that moment when you do that? When you first did it, it was perfect. Now you are aware that you are moving the audience. Whenever you underline anything, which is what you are doing now, it is wrong. Anything that is underlined is bad art."

Lacking in Tact

The young Alec Guinness got one of his earliest breaks as Osric in the Hamlet *that John Gielgud directed at the Old Vic in 1934.*

I revered Gielgud as an artist and was totally glamourised by his personality, but he was a strict disciplinarian, intolerant of any slovenliness of speech and exasperated by youthful tentativeness. He was a living monument of impatience. At that time he was thirty years old, at the height of his juvenile powers and, with Richard of Bordeaux behind him (I saw him in the part fifteen times), commanded a huge following throughout the country. He held his emperor-like head higher than high, rather thrown back, and carried himself, as he still does, with ramrod straightness. He walked, or possibly tripped, with slightly bent knees to counteract a childhood tendency to flat-footedness. His arm movements were inclined to be jerky and his large bony hands a little stiff. A suggestion of fluidity in his gestures was imparted by his nearly always carrying, when on stage, a big white silk hankerchief. His resemblance to his distinguished old father was remarkable and he combined an air of patrician Polish breeding with Terry charm and modest theatricality. There was nothing he lacked, as far as I could see, except tact. His tactless remarks, over the decades, have joined the ranks of the happiest theatre legends of our time and, apart from their sheer funniness, they have always been entirely forgivable because they spring spontaneously from the heart without a glimmer of malice.

It was after a week of rehearsing *Hamlet* that he spoke "spontaneously" to me, with shattering effect. "What's happened to you?" he cried. "I thought you were rather good. You're terrible. Oh, go away! I don't want to see you again!"

I hung around at rehearsals until the end of the day and then approached him cautiously. "Excuse me, Mr. Gielgud, but am I fired?"

"No! Yes! No, of course not. But go away. Come back in a week. Get someone to teach you how to act."

Don't Mark Your Book

Alec Guinness on working with Tony Guthrie:

The first time I worked with Tony I learned a valuable thing. When I was a young actor it was the custom to mark our books, the moves, etc., and doing Shakespeare one had these little Temple editions. I'd worked with Gielgud and a lot of older actors, and it was the thing one did for entrances and exits and odd movement, down left or up right or whatever. I was marking my book one day and he said, "What are you doing?" I said, "Oh, marking in my moves." And he said, "Don't. If I give you a bad move or suggest a bad move to you, you won't remember it. And that's a very good thing. We'll think of another one. If I give you a good move, you'll remember it." And I have never marked a move or anything else since, in a script. And he was right. When I have directed myself, I have always tried to persuade actors to do that.

Terror

Peter Brook is known for spending weeks of rehearsals with improvisations. One of the best-known theatrical stories concerns his production of Seneca's *Oedipus* at the National Theatre. This was in 1968 during the height of the "Theatre of Cruelty" trend and Brook had made the distinguished cast go through many days of primal screaming, imitating various animals—everything except work on the text. One day he asked the actors to prepare a short improvisation based on the most terrifying experience they could possible imagine. The actors complied from their arsenal of inventive reactions. When it came to Sir John Gielgud's turn, he did nothing. The great actor stood there with his faraway, melancholy gaze until Brook asked whether there was nothing terrifying that he could think of. "Actually, Peter, there is," replied Sir John quietly: "we open in two weeks."

Acting by Numbers

Jason Robards, when confronted by an analytical director, will say, "Come on, man, do you want the sad face, the glad face, the fast face, or the slow face?"

Whatever Works

Laurence Olivier, directing *Philomena*, was having trouble with the priest's entrance in the last act. The actor in the role, Gabor Morea, went through some business to indicate his excitement, such as waving a handkerchief which he then used to wipe his brow. Olivier watched silently for a while, until his piercing "Wait!" sliced the air. "I've got it. You come in through that door," he told the actor, "you kiss the mezzuzah, and then go through into the other room." His assistant whispered: "Larry, this is a Catholic play; there is no mezzuzah." "You're right," replied Olivier, "but I did that in *The Merchant of Venice*, and it worked."

[62] DIRECTORS AND PLAYWRIGHTS

Collaboration

Jed Harris was working with Thornton Wilder on the original production of Our Town.

He was meanwhile still pressing Wilder for revisions. "You know what's missing from the play, Thornton? The moment when Emily and George first meet." Agreeing, Wilder sat down on a straight-back chair at the rear of the stage, and while rehearsals continued wrote a soda fountain scene for the young lovers. At the same time, downstage, Harris was inventing what would become one of *Our Town's* most memorable images, the funeral for young Emily: mourners standing at the cemetery, holding umbrellas. Those umbrellas would be remembered as vividly as anything Wilder wrote, and the playwright would acknowledge it.

Fifth Column

Jed Harris was notorious for collaborative rewriting of plays. According to his press agent, Richard Maney, "Jed's ego is so tremendous that, by the time he finishes getting a play revised, he convinces himself he is the real author. I am sure he's convinced he is the real author of Our Town, The Heiress, The Green Bay Tree, The Front Page, *and he even at times is of the opinion that he wrote* Uncle Vanya!" *Sometimes the magic did not work.*

Harris attempted to mold Ernest Hemingway's sole play, *The Fifth Column*, into an actable version. Harris was the seventh producer who had tried it. After Harris finally relinquished his option, somebody asked Hemingway what happened and he replied, tersely, *"Fifth Column,* sixth draft, seventh producer, eighth refusal."

Tolerance

One of the greatest influences on the contemporary theatrical scene has been George Devine, actor and director, who founded the English Stage Company at the Royal Court in London's Sloane Square. Since 1956 it became home to many of the best playwrights in the world today. The first of them was John Osborne, whose Look Back in Anger *began a revolution in British theatre.*

We disagreed about many things, after we'd started at the Royal Court. We used to have running skirmishes about Ionesco's plays and other French work. I used to say, "George, we're not going to do *another* of those, are we?" And he'd say, "Yes, dear friend, I'm afraid we *are.*" He thought they were good. I couldn't abide them. But he could contain my reaction patiently, even though he was not a patient man. He could contain and comprehend many things: that was one of his strengths. It wasn't that he was weak and compromising; he could be brutal and dismissive, and he went for what he wanted. But he had a special kind of tolerance. He suffered talent gladly.

Working with a Genius

In 1974 Peter Hall was directing Peggy Ashcroft and Alan Webb in Samuel Beckett's Happy Days.

Sam Beckett wandered in at 10:20. I asked him to talk to the cast. We discussed the set, the costumes. Then we began to go through the text. He had a few cuts and a few slight alterations. The primary one concerned the parasol that bursts into flames. This he said had never worked. The parasol is supposed to burn away because of the force of the unremitting sun. Sam has had trouble about that all over the world, with fire authorities and theatre technicians. He now asks that the parasol merely smokes and the material melts away like some kind of plastic under heat. He also, surprisingly, wants to cut an entire page of dialogue relating to the parasol. This disturbed Peggy because it is good and she has learnt it. And it also disturbed me because I think he's only cutting it out of a memory of all the difficulties of the past. I shall bide my time.

Exciting to be working with an absolute genius. The star-struck came out again for a few moments. The first time in ages.

Unusual Request

Basil Dean was directing in 1919 a play based on Sacred and Profane Love, *a novel by Arnold Bennett, which required a sensual actress in the leading role. Bennett was watching a rehearsal with growing dissatisfaction, then beckoned to Dean, who tells the story.*

"I d-d-don't like her," he stuttered, pointing at the actress. "She's too hard!" The scene went on a little longer and again he beckoned me forward, pointing his finger again at the actress: "Is th-th-that girl a v-v-virgin?" he asked, "I really don't know," I said. "I suppose so." A slight pause. Then Bennett: "Oh, c-c-can't th-th-that be altered?"

CHAPTER XIII

Audiences

The Good Old Days

Playgoing today is a solemn affair: many people put on their best clothes and are on their best behavior in the theatre. We owe this development to the middle classes which dominate audiences today. In ancient Athens most of the audience was pleasantly drunk, in honor of Dionysus, the patron god of the dramatic festivals. Elizabethan and Restoration audiences were also rowdy and inattentive, a tradition that continued to the end of the nineteenth century. Here is a description of English audiences by Dr. Moritz, a visiting German divine in 1782.

The winter theatres being shut, I twice attended that in the Haymarket. Often and often, whilst I sat in the pit, did a rotten orange or peel of an orange fly past me, or past some of my neighbours; and once one of them actually hit my hat, without my daring to look round for fear of another should come plump in my face. Besides this perpetual pelting from the gallery, which renders an English playhouse so uncomfortable, there is no end to their calling out and knocking with their sticks till the curtain is drawn up. I saw a miller's or a baker's boy, thus, like a huge booby, leaning over the rails and knocking again and again on the outside, with all his might, without being in the least ashamed or abashed. I sometimes, heard, too, the people in the lower or middle gallery quarrelling with those of the upper one. Behind me in the pit sat a young fop, who, in order to display his costly stone buckles with the utmost brilliancy, continually put his foot on my bench, and even sometimes upon my coat; which I could avoid only by sparing him as much space from my portion of the seat as would make him a footstool. In the boxes, quite in a corner, sat several servants, who were said to be placed there to keep the seats for the families they served, till they should arrive. They seemed to sit remarkably close and still; the reason of which was, I was told, their apprehension of being pelted; for if one of them dared but to look out of the box, he is immediately saluted with a shower of orange peel from the gallery.

Peanut Gallery

Olive Logan wrote this in 1870.

The "pit," which is so common in London, has for years had in American theatres no existence, except in the sole instance of the Old Bowery Theatre, where, until very recently, the odoriferous peanut was munched and the critical newsboy took his nightly sup of histrionic horrors.

The peanut is a production of Southern soil, and I believe is unknown in England—thrice happy in the ignorance; and as in German music halls "c-a-k-e-s—p-r-e-t-z-e-l-s" are hawked with sleepy perseverance, so in the Old Bowery Theatre an odious little ragamuffin carried about a ricketty basket containing apples, oranges and "candy," while above and before all, *bonne-bouche* intended for dirty *bouches*, "p-e-a-n-u-t-s" made vocal all the air. The "Bowery boy" might be jacketless, hatless and barefooted, but he purchased largely of the crisp-coated nut, and thereupon rose on the atmosphere a strange earthy odor, which no one who has once smelled it can ever forget.

How To Get a Good Seat

Once when Potier, the great French comic actor, was playing, the crowd was so great that a woman fell from the gallery into the pit. Everybody expected to see the woman carried dead from the theatre, but she had fallen upon a soft place, and beyond a few bruises, was unhurt. Her only answer to the expressions of sympathy that greeted her on all sides was, "Thank goodness, I have at last got a place where I can see and hear comfortably."

A Cat-Lover Is Upset

George Alexander was playing in the provinces, when a cat wandered on to the stage and attracted the attention of the audience. There was a fireplace on the stage, with red tinsel paper representing flames. Mr. Alexander handed the cat through this fireplace to a property man in the wings. Some lady in the gallery, evidently thinking that the flames were real and sympathising with the cat, expressed her indignation by hurling a ginger-beer bottle at Mr. Alexander.

Grand Guignol

A season of *Grand Guignol* was started in September 1920; Lewis Casson produced and Sybil Thorndike appeared in three of the five plays which made up the first programme. London's *Grand Guignol* became a success. . . . But most of the plays were strong meat in those days and hospital nurses were kept posted in the theatre ready to attend to any members of the audience who might be overcome by the horrific happenings enacted on the stage.

Editorials

The scene between Goneril and Lear had barely finished in an Old Vic production of *King Lear*, when Pett Ridge overheard a woman in the stalls saying to her husband, "Rather an unpleasant family these Lears."

A similarly outspoken patron at the Royal Court leant across to her friend during one of the tenser moments in *Macbeth* and bellowed in her ear, "So you see how one lie leads on to another lie!"

Realization

Ray Fry was playing the doctor in Ellis Rabb's production of A Streetcar Named Desire *at Lincoln Center.*

I had to wait all evening for my moment to carry Blanche, who was played by Rosemary Harris, off to the loony bin. I had to cross the entire width of the stage, then went into the house to pick her up before going back to cross the whole stage again on a long ramp. As I was carrying her away, past the front row, I heard a woman say very loudly: "My God, Harry, she's gone crazy!" Rosemary clamped down very hard on my arm and just before we turned upstage to ascend the ramp and finish the play, she said to me: "The poor dear just got it in time!"

Queens

One of Sarah Bernhardt's greatest triumphs was her Cleopatra which she brought to Victorian London.

She ended her performance with a magnificent *coup de théâtre*: systematically—and dramatically—she set about wrecking her palace and then collapsed among the debris. As the applause died away at the end of one performance, an elderly member of the audience was heard to remark to her companion, "How different, how very different from the home life of our own dear queen."

Almost a century later an actor emerged from Wyndham's Theatre in London at the end of a performance of the American homosexual comedy *The Boys in the Band* and remarked: "How different, how very different from the home life of our own dear queens."

Fairies

When Joan Greenwood was appearing as Peter Pan, Hermione Gingold went to see the show and, at one point in the evening, made a modest contribution to the entertainment. In the scene in which Peter saves the life of Tinkerbell by asking the audience if they believe in fairies, rising above the cries of "yes" from the children rang the mellow Gingold tones: *"Believe* in them, darling? I *know* hundreds of them!"

[64] APPLAUSE: REAL AND FAKED

Roman Audience

In the ancient Roman theatres the audience testified their applause or censure by cheers or hisses, and espoused the pretensions of different actors with so much warmth, that the representation was often interrupted, and quarrels ensued which terminated in bloodshed. Such, indeed, was the partiality of the people to theatrical amusements, that every eminent player had his party; and their absurd factions rendered the theatre a constant scene of riot and disorder. Persons of the highest rank took part in these brawls, which were, at length, carried so far, as to attract the attention of the senate; and in the reign of Tiberius, the players were, in consequence, banished from Italy.

Moved to Tears

Irving used to delight in telling a story of his early days in which he was very much the criticised party. One night when playing Hamlet, he noticed an old lady in the front row of the pit dissolved in tears, and delighted at this apparent appreciation of his acting, he sent round word that he would like to see her after the performance. When she arrived, Irving said, "Madam, I perceived that my acting moved you very much." "Indeed it did," said the old lady. "You see, I've a young son myself play-acting somewhere up in the north, and it broke me up to think that he might be no better at it than you."

Clap-trap

Leigh Hunt described in 1807 the technique of getting an audience to clap before the days of "applause" signs. The actor he praises is Alexander Pope, who lived a hundred years after the more famous poet.

There is an infallible method of obtaining a clap from the galleries, and there is an art known at the theatre by the name of clap-trapping, which Mr. Pope has shown great wisdom in studying. It consists of nothing more than gradually raising the voice as the speech draws to a conclusion, making an alarming outcry on the last four or five lines, or suddenly dropping them into a tremulous but energetic undertone, and with a vigorous jerk of the right arm rushing off the stage. All this astonishes the galleries; they are persuaded it must be something very fine, because it is so important and so unintelligible, and they clap for the sake of their own reputation.

Canned Applause

During the nineteenth century it was common in the French theatre to plant in the audience people who were paid to applaud in the right places, and with their enthusiasm create a success. They were called "claqueurs" or the "claque," and they were the human equivalents of the canned laughter we have on television comedy. When Arsène Houssaye was appointed director of the Comédie Française in the 1850s he met the leader of the claque, M. Vacher.

Verteuil, when presenting to me the heads of various departments, from the scene painters down to the candle-snuffers, had overlooked one. That one introduced himself. I beheld a philosopher, with a knowing smile, a broad forehead, a sharp eye, and a bright face. "Monsieur le directeur, I have been for many years the leader of criticism." "Above all, the leader of enthusiasm," I said. "Allow me, I am just; when I applaud with our cows—I mean with my men—it is to show the public that it should applaud." "Why do you say your cows? Is it because of your name?" [V*acher* is French for cowherd.— Trans.] "Yes, it is because of my name; but also because the public would applaud in the wrong places if I did not drag them away from the drinking troughs round the corner and lead them hither with a leash; but, when I have them in battle array, they obey like one man, at the slightest signal, and Heaven alone knows how many battles we have won when they were already half lost. The *sociétaires* are well aware of it." M. Vacher spoke like a small Napoleon. I told him that he had come at the very moment when I was thinking of suppressing the *claque*. "Oh, monsieur, don't do that. If you only knew how we prevent authors and, above all, actors from becoming demoralized! M. Samson himself could not go on acting amidst a freezing silence." "M. de Molière managed to play without a *claque*." "Monsieur le directeur, I know my theatrical history nearly as well as you do. In those days there was a pit that knew how to seize its opportunity. In our days there is no longer a pit. What are all those curious idlers that come? Provincials, who have lost their way hither, who would be capable of hissing the most striking situations or of applauding at random. I have studied the spirit of all the authors, as I have studied the acting of every Comedian, here at the Odéon and on the Boulevards. You will not be able to do without us for the next fifty years, when the public may be educated up to it. Remember, monsieur le directeur, the saying of Beaumarchais, 'How many idiots go to the making of a public?' "

I was about to defend my opinion against a critic of such experience when Rachel happened to come in. She nodded to Vacher, and condescended to shed the light of her smile on him. "Behold!" she said, "not the leader of the *claque*; but the leader of success. No feast is complete without Vacher." Vacher bowed and went away, saying, "I beg of the director to study my art of acting as he would study that of any Comedian."

That very same evening I watched him at his work. He worked with both his eyes and his hands. He had assumed the interested look of a paying spectator. He directed the maneuvers of "his cows" without anyone being the wiser for it. It was truly the master's eye.

Fainting as an Art

The excellence of an actor on the Yiddish stage in former years was measured by the volume of sobs and tears he elicited from the audience. In order to ensure success, it was customary for dramatic actors to instruct their valets to hire a woman or two, who should faint at each performance at an appropriate time. Bessie Thomashefsky, the famous star of the Yiddish stage, tells this episode.

An aged woman, who was hired to faint during a performance, dozed off in her seat in the balcony. Suddenly she awoke from her slumber, peered quizzically at the stage, and began to faint. It was just at the beginning of a comic scene, when the audience was expected to burst forth in an uproarious laughter, and the fainting was entirely uncalled for. An elderly lady, however, perceiving that somebody in the audience had fainted, came to the conclusion that the scene on the stage must be extremely tragic, and she fell into a swoon herself. The noise and confusion that followed this ill-timed display of emotion nearly broke off the performance. The Thespian was so frenzied with rage that he could hardly say his lines. After the show, the tragedian took his servant to task for his carelessness in employing help. "Idiot!" he thundered. "Couldn't you get a woman intelligent enough to know when to faint? Instead of boosting me, you have nearly busted me." "Sir," said the servant humbly, "I apologize, and from now on I shall dress like a woman, and do the fainting myself."

At the next performance the faithful man was on the job, in woman's apparel, and sure enough, he fainted at the most tragic scene. The ushers, however, knowing that it was not fainting but feinting, made no move to proffer any succor to the stricken person. They stood at their respective stations and looked at the prostrate form with a broad grin. Whereupon a few kind-hearted women carried the limp body into the restroom, sprinkled cold water on "her" face, and proceeded to strip "her" clothes. Soon these benevolent ladies discovered to their horror the true gender of the object of their attention.

[65] THEY STAYED AWAY IN DROVES

Throwing Out the Audience

When cholera broke out at Paris, in 1832, the panic spread so widely through the city that the theatres were almost deserted, and the actors had to play to a few hundred francs. The Odéon on a particular night found one solitary spectator waiting for the raising of the curtain. It was in vain that he was offered the price of his admission back and was implored to leave the house; he stood upon his rights and demanded to have the play acted. So, perforce, the curtain rose and the piece commenced, every performer doing his very worst. This was too much for the auditorial unit, who at last expressed his disapproval in that sibilation dear to the indignant playgoer. His behaviour was more agreeable to the actors, however, than theirs was to him, for immediately charging him with interrupting the piece, the people in front ejected the solitary spectator and the performance concluded. This is the only occasion on record in which the management chucked out the whole audience.

And Hissing Back

At about the same time there was once so pitiful an audience in the theatre at Weimar that the number could be expressed by one figure. The assemblage was not only small, but discontented, and hissed continuously, whereupon the Manager brought his full company upon the stage and hissed down his public.

End of the Line

A small touring company found itself playing to a small audience in a small town in Yorkshire. When the time came for the curtain to go up, the audience was found to consist of only two men. Going on the stage, the manager said, "I am very sorry to disappoint you, but we really cannot play to such a small house. Here is your money back. You'd better go home." "Sorry," said one of the audience, "we can't take it and we can't go. We're the bailiffs in possession."

It Was Better in Yiddish

Sir Laurence Olivier was giving an outdoor performance of *Othello* on his American tour. During the first intermission he was stopped at the door to his portable dressing room by a distressed woman who wanted directions to the bus leaving for New Haven. "But why," asked Sir Laurence, "aren't you staying for the remainder of the performance?" "Frankly," the lady explained, "I saw it years ago back in Brooklyn. It was in Yiddish and it hurts me to hear how much it loses in translation."

[66] INTERRUPTIONS

Why Shoot Her?

On one occasion, when the famous Ned Shuter was to have appeared, Thomas Weston made his first appearance at Drury Lane as a substitute for him. The celebrated Mrs. Clive had possession of the stage, but when Weston entered in the place of the popular favourite, he was met with cries of "Shuter! Shuter!" When he attempted to speak, the pit and gallery renewed their cries of "Shuter! Shuter!" Shuter had been advertised, and they would have none other. Weston kept quite calm, and when at last a lull occured he pointed at Mrs. Clive and said, as though he quite misunderstood the cause of the interruption: "Why should I shoot her? She plays the part very well."

This little pleasantry completely turned the tide of favour, and secured for him a patient hearing.

What Was the Question?

Carles was the name of an actor who suffered an amusing experience while playing Hamlet at an East End theatre. He was in the habit of taking some refreshment during the evening, and this was sent in regularly at 8 o'clock from a tavern opposite the stage door. A new boy being sent for the first time with the usual "pint of ale, a crust, and cheese," with instructions to give it to Mr. Carles. Seeing no one about, and hearing Carles upon the stage, which was on a level with the street, saying solemnly: "To be or not to be," the boy walked on to the astonished actor with the words: "To be, to be sure, sir; pint o' ale and a crust." Needless to say, Hamlet kicked the boy, ale and crust almost into the street, but solemnity was never restored that evening. Whenever Hamlet entered, the audience smiled audibly. Mrs. Siddons was the victim of a similar interruption on one occasion.

A Farewell Hiss

On the night of Mrs. Siddons's retirement from the stage, she withdrew, much affected with the sympathy of the audience, but, as the curtain fell, one of those sounds followed, from some enemy of the great actress, which penetrates the ear amid a thousand plaudits. Mrs. Siddons caught the tone, and turning startled to Bannister, asked, "Can that be a hiss?" "No," said Bannister, "it is a hys-teric."

How To Deal with an Unruly Audience

One night when John Kemble was performing at some country theatre one of his favourite parts, he was much interrupted, from time to
time, by the squalling of a young child in one of the galleries. At
length, angered by this rival performance, Kemble walked with solemn
step to the front of the stage, and, addressing the audience in his
most tragic tones, said, "Ladies and Gentlemen, unless the play is
stopped the child cannot possibly go on."

Hissed to Death

Olive Logan, writing in 1870, gives the following sad tale.

Fullerton was an actor in a Philadelphia theatre, many years ago. A
cabal was formed, it seemed, for the purpose of driving him from the
stage. It began early in the season, and the disturbance increased
nightly, until at length, some eight or ten different disturbers, distributed through the house, contrived to confuse and distract the performer who happened to appear in the same scenes with Fullerton.
Every effort possible was made to ascertain the cause of this continued
persecution, but in vain. A nervous man at all times, poor Fullerton
became nearly incapable of all effort. His terror and agony on entering
the stage were truly pitiable. At length his little courage gave way,
and repeated shocks brought him to the very edge of insanity. On
the evening of the 29th of January, after acting the Abbé del Epée,
with less exhibition than usual of outrage from his persecutors, he
left the theatre, in apparently good spirits, for his lodgings, as he
stated. Not having arrived there, search was made, after some hours,
but no tidings could be heard. On the following morning his body
was found floating near one of the wharves on the Delaware. His
persecutors had hissed him to death.

Quick on His Feet

When Barry Sullivan, the Irish tragedian, was playing Richard III
one night, and the actor came to the lines, "A horse! A horse! My
kingdom for a horse!" some merry wag in the pit called out: "And
wouldn't a jackass do as well for you?" "Sure," answered Sullivan,
turning like a flash at the sound of the voice, "come around to the
stage door at once!"

Go Sleep with the Fishes

One of John Barrymore's performances was repeatedly punctured by outbursts of coughing, so when he came back for the second act, the actor reached inside his coat and pulled out a large fish. "Here you damned walruses," he shouted, tossing the fish into the audience, "busy yourselves with this, while we go on with the play."

Potent Threat

Anyone who has been to a school matinee knows how dreary it is to watch a play with a captive audience. It can also be hell for the actors, as Gyles Brandreth describes a school matinee.

During the 1974 production of *Macbeth* at Stratford-upon-Avon I saw Nicol Williamson give an impressive performance at a school matinee. Unfortunately most of the young audience were more interested in talking to each other than in watching the play. After a while Williamson could tolerate the chattering no longer. He threw down the stool he was holding, turned to the audience and told them to "Shut up!" saying that he could be earning thousands of pounds a week making a film in America, but had chosen instead to come and act in this great play, by a great playwright, in a great theatre for next to nothing so they could damn well be quiet while he was doing it—especially as there were some adults in the audience who had *paid* for their tickets and who wanted to hear what he was saying. If there was so much as another whisper he threatened to start the play from the beginning and would go on doing it again and again from the beginning until everybody was quiet. The rest was silence.

[67]   RIOTS

Riots have often broken out in the theatre. This is hardly surprising, when one thinks how few other occasions bring together a volatile mix of a thousand or more people and make them listen to stories of great passions. I remember from my own childhood in Budapest, on the eve of the Hungarian revolution, the audience demonstrating at Richard III when he confessed to being a villain: they were unac-

cept cept ...

customed to such frankness from their own leaders. *The eighteenth,
nineteenth, and early twentieth centuries in England and Dublin were
particularly riotous. Some riots were set off by young, drunk gentlemen,
such as the Irish rake who insulted Thomas Sheridan, the dramatist's
father, or sometimes the occasion was a genuine grievance against the
management. In the latter category were the notorious O.P. (Old
Price) riots when John Kemble tried to raise ticket prices in the re-
built Covent Garden Theatre pit from 3s 6d to 4s, and boxes from
six to seven shillings. This caused sixty-six nights of continuous rioting, until Kemble backed off and apologized to his public. Here follow a few scenes from the turbulent history of the theatre.*

Ways To Handle Riots

1721 is remarkable in dramatic history as the first year in which
soldiers appeared as guards in the theatre. A certain noble Earl,
whether Scotch or Irish the record does not say, much addicted to the
wholesome and inspiring beverage of whiskey, was behind the scenes,
and seeing one of his friends on the other side among the performers,
crossed the stage; of course, was hissed by the audience. John Rich,
who was on the side that the noble Earl came to, was so provoked
that he told his Lordship "not to be surprised if he was not allowed
again to enter." The drunken Peer struck Mr. Rich a slap on the
cheek, which was immediately returned, and his Lordship's face being
round, and fat, and sleek, resounded with the smack of his blow.
A battle royal ensued, the players on the one side, and that part of
the aristocracy then behind the scenes on the other.

In the end, the players being strongest, either in number or valour,
thrashed the gentlemen, and turned them all out into the street,
where they drew their swords, stormed the boxes, broke the sconces,
cut the hangings, and made a wonderful riot. Quin came round with
a constable and watchmen from the stage, charged the rioters, and
they were all taken into custody, and carried in a body before Justice
Hungerford, who then lived in the neighbourhood, and were bound
by him over to answer the consequences. They were soon, however,
persuaded by their wiser friends to make up the matter, and the manager got ample redress. The King, on hearing of the affair, was indignant, and ordered a guard to attend the theatres, a warning monument of a lord drinking too much whiskey.

Enemy Talent

In 1755, Garrick, as manager of Drury Lane, staged *The Chinese Festival*, a production by one Noverre, a citizen of Switzerland. After the arrangements were made and a troupe of French dancers were provided, Englishmen suddenly found themselves at war with France. Feeling ran high against all foreigners, and certain "patriots" accused Garrick of bringing in enemy talent to crowd his own countrymen off the stage. On November 18, 1755, friends of idle English performers disturbed and overpowered that part of the audience which was enjoying the entertainment and caused a thousand pounds of damage to the house. They then laid siege to Garrick's own home to sack it. Though Garrick's domicile escaped untouched, the rioting put an end to the production, and three days later, Garrick appeared before the audience and declared that if more disturbance arose while he was speaking, he would give up the stage.

The Astor Place Riot

The worst riot in the history of the theatre took place in New York City, on May 10, 1849, outside the Astor Place Opera House. It was the culmination of an ugly rivalry between William Macready and Edwin Forrest. The incident had a long and complicated incubation.

Edwin Forrest, the rising star of the American stage and William Charles Macready, a veteran of the London theatre, became fast friends when Forrest made his debut at Drury Lane in 1836. Indeed, Forrest wrote to a friend that Macready "has behaved in the handsomest manner to me. Before I arrived in England he had spoken of me in the most flattering terms, and on my arrival, he embraced the earliest opportunity to call upon me, since which time he has extended to me many delicate courtesies and attentions, all showing the native kindness of his heart, and his great refinement and good breeding."

In 1843 Macready came to the United States, played a successful series of engagements, and was well received everywhere. The two or three weeks that he was acting in New York he made his headquarters at the home of the Forrests, and the American tragedian, with exceedingly fine feeling, refused urgent invitations from several managers to appear in rival houses at the time of Macready's visit to other cities. Notwithstanding all this, however, Macready went back to England full of a corroding jealousy of Forrest. The press, by constantly comparing the two actors, had succeeded in making both of them self-conscious, and though Macready probably had little to do with the harsh criticism which greeted Forrest, when the American next visited London, a bitter professional jealousy had been aroused between them.

Then Forrest did a really outrageous thing to Macready when the latter was playing Hamlet in Edinburgh. While the Englishman was careering across the stage, flourishing his handkerchief above his head and acting his conception of the mad prince as he spoke the lines:

> They are coming to the play; I must be idle.
> Get you to a place—

Forrest gave vent to a deep and prolonged hiss as a sign of his profound disapproval of this "business." The right of a spectator to express his condemnation of a player by hissing was then unquestioned, and had Forrest not been a brother-actor in notoriously unfriendly relations with Macready, nothing would have been thought of the matter. The charge of professional jealousy Forrest contemptuously dismissed; but he could not have failed, in his most sincere moments, deeply to regret that he had not been restrained, that unhappy night at Edinburgh, by feelings of professional courtesy.

At this time in Britain and later in New York, however, it seems to have been a case of the pot calling the kettle black. For although Forrest steadfastly refused to have anything to do with an organized opposition to Macready, when the Englishman made his second visit to America he did not disdain to enter into a war of words with his rival, thus fanning to a flame a fire already fierce. The English articles *pro* and *con* had all been copied in America, it must be recalled, and had naturally lost nothing by the process. So when Macready began his closing engagement in New York, in May 1849, the elements of a storm were at hand. For the Bowery boys loved Forrest scarcely less than they loved a fight.

Macready's third and last American engagement began in September 1848. When he performed *Macbeth* in Philadelphia, Forrest's native city, he had to do it almost in dumb show, amidst occasional showers of nuts and rotten eggs; but he played through the part and at the end addressed the audience, pledging his sacred word of honour that he had never shown any hostility to "an American actor." This called forth a public letter from Forrest, in which he confessed boastfully to having hissed Macready at Edinburgh but denied any part in the organized opposition which had been shown the visitor; he added, with superfluous offensiveness, that *his* advice had been to let "the superannuated driveller alone."

A plan for hissing Macready from the stage, upon his appearance in New York, had been submitted to Forrest. The latter refused, of course, to countenance the conspiracy. But this did not prevent the theatre from being crowded with the Englishman's enemies when, on May 7, 1849, he began his engagement at the Astor Place Opera House. The play was obliged to proceed amid a tumult of yells and hisses, and at the end of the third act the performance stopped, and the visiting star returned to his hotel. His desire was to set sail at once for England, but in response to the urgent wishes of his friends he agreed to make one more attempt to play, and on May 10 *Macbeth* was advertised.

Upon the opening of the doors that night, the theatre filled almost instantly with people who were favourable to the actor, nearly all others being excluded; but Macready's enemies did not by any means go quietly home. Instead they filled the streets and waited for the most favourable moment to precipitate their attack. That moment soon came outside the theatre, as it had already come inside. Stones were hurled against windows of the building, smashing them to atoms, and at one time it seemed as if destruction of the entire edifice was inevitable. Macready himself barely escaped with his life by being hurried out of the front door in disguise and helped to make his way through the crowd. Meanwhile the militia had been called out, and when orders to disperse had been greeted by the angry crowd with yells and hoots of derision, the soldiers were bidden to close their columns and fire. The result was that one hundred and thirty-four rioters were killed outright, and over a hundred wounded; while the remainder of the now-sobered mob dispersed into the darkness.*

Rocking the Cradle

In February 1926 Sean O'Casey's *The Plough and Stars* at the Abbey Theatre raised the audience to a passion. On the fourth night the passion exploded into a full-scale riot. While part of the audience stormed the stage to attack the cast, another section waged war on the rioters themselves. Lennox Robinson recalled a friend of his hurl-

---

* The casualty figures were certainly exaggerated by the sensational press of the day. Modern historians (for example, Alan S. Downer in *The Eminent Tragedian*) estimate between seventeen and twenty dead, with "uncounted number of wounded."

ing her shoe at one of the rioters "and with unerring feminine aim, hitting one of the players on the stage."

W. B. Yeats called the police and then went on stage to try to quell the audience. He remembered the riot that had greeted J. M. Synge's play, *The Playboy of the Western World* when it had appeared in the same theatre for the first time nineteen years before, and bellowed at the audience, "You have disgraced yourselves again, you are rocking the cradle of a new masterpiece." Every subsequent performance was supervised by the police.

[68] REALITY AND ILLUSION

Unexpected Help

One of the guards assigned to prevent rioting at an English theatre during the eighteenth century once got carried away.

When John Banks's play *Earl of Essex* was performed, a soldier, who stood sentinel on the stage, entered so deeply into the distress of the scene that, in the delusion of his imagination, upon the Countess of Nottingham's denying the receipt of the ring, which Essex had sent by her to claim a promise of favour, he exclaimed, " 'Tis false! she has it in her bosom!"—and immediately seized the mock Countess to make her deliver it up.

Sailors to the Rescue

A common incident in the nineteenth-century theatre was the breaking of stage illusion by members of the lower classes, whose education omitted Plato's theory of mimesis. The interesting fact is that such people, unlike those today, would be going to theatre at all.

Harriet Mellon was acting a distressed maiden, persecuted for debt by a heartless tradesman, at a Liverpool theatre. She declared herself to be without a friend in the world with such effect as to bring a sailor from the gallery, climbing down from tier to tier in sight of the people and bounding over the orchestra to her defence upon the stage.

A similar incident occurred during the performance of *El Hyder* at the Liverpool Amphitheatre, where Edward Stirling, playing the part of Tom, single-handedly engaged seven Frenchmen in a rocky defile, and a desperate fight ensued. In this case a sailor climbed down from the gallery, threw off his jacket, and taking his place by the side of Mr. Stirling, knocked down his unhappy supers, saying: "I'd stand by you, messmate; seven to one ain't fair nowadays."

Jack Gallagher, a grizzly-bearded old-time boatswain's mate, had never been in a theatre; so some of the officers thought they would give him a novel treat, and at the same time have a little amusement themselves. The old tar was given five dollars, with directions about getting his ticket. Jack dressed himself up in his best mustering clothes, and went on shore, securing a prominent seat in the front row of the stalls. The play was H.M.S. *Pinafore,* and it was very amusing to see the expression on Jack's face as the travesty on a sailor's life went on. Mingled feelings of surprise and disgust evidently filled his breast, for he looked on the play as intended for a true representation of life on board ship. He sat quietly on, critically taking in the spectacle before him, until the scene changed to a vessel's deck, with the crew engaged in furling sail. To Jack the efforts of the play-sailors were so absurd and so ill-directed that he could restrain himself no longer, but burst out with: "Avast, there, ye land-lubbers! Who ever see a tops'l furled without passing in the leeches first? Get a pull on yer buntlines, and take down the slack of yer buntwhip. Ye're a lot of cowboys and sojers, that's what ye are!" Jack's speech was unintelligible in its details to most of the audience, but his manner was so earnest and his feelings so thoroughly wrought up that the whole house took in the situation at once and burst into a loud roar of laughter and applause.

Back to the Future

One night as Mrs. Siddons was playing Isabella (in *The Fatal Marriage*) and had uttered the words by which she used to pierce all hearts, words uttered on discovering her first husband in whose absence she had remarried: "Oh, my Biron! My Biron!," a young Aberdeenshire heiress, Miss Gorden of Gight, sent forth a scream as wild as Isabella's; and taking up the words in a hysterical frenzy was carried out still uttering them. Next year the impressible young lady was wooed and won by a Byron, the Honourable John of that name, by whom she became the mother of one more famous than the rest, Lord Byron, "lord of himself, that heritage of woe."

Out of Africa

Late in 1985, Canadian critics Don Rubin and Pat Keeney visited Dakkar for the first African meeting of the World Encyclopedia of Contemporary Theatre. After a long day of discussions they were invited to a production at the National Theatre of Senegal. As they walked from their hotel, Keeney and Rubin were assaulted at every corner by beggars who tried to grab the foreigners' attention with loud wails, and their ankles with gnarled and leprous arms. Finally, the two shaken critics managed to reach the Daniel Sorano Theatre, the entrance of which was surrounded by still more beggars, with horribly sad eyes and disfigured faces. Fighting their way inside, the Canadians found the whole lobby occupied by beggars, who somehow managed to get into the auditorium: there were beggars sitting between the aisles all the way up to the stage, which had no curtain. The visitors wondered how the beggars would be cleared from the stage before the performance; they also felt an acute sense of embarrassment at the thought of being entertained in the midst of all this misery. Only when the lights went down did the critics realize that the beggars both inside and outside the theatre were playing roles in an award-winning show about the useful role of beggars in society. This point was brilliantly brought home by this realistic portrayal, though Rubin and Keeney are not sure to this day whether it was done by actors playing beggars or by real beggars who could also act.

Hi, Mom

Judi Dench was playing Juliet at the Old Vic in 1961. It was in Act III, scene ii, where she is told by the Nurse that Romeo has killed Tybalt and been banished. Coming to the end of the long emotional speech in which Juliet defends Romeo, Judi Dench asked, "Where is my father and my mother, nurse?" "Here we are darling. Row H," came a cry from the stalls.

[69] FIRST NIGHTS

Socrates Takes a Bow

When Aristophanes presented his satire on Socrates in his play *The Clouds*, the philosopher attended the opening. The theatre was crammed full with Greeks because of the Dionysian festival, but there were also great numbers of foreigners. The Athenians immediately recognized the mask worn by the actor representing Socrates, but the foreigners did not know who was being satirized, so they were making a great deal of noise, asking who on earth was this Socrates? When the noise reached Socrates, who had a prominent seat, he decided to stand up and that is how he watched the entire play.

Uneven Contest

On the first night of Shaw's *Arms and the Man*, April 21, 1894, the actors, who could make neither head nor tail of the business, played with anxious seriousness, and were rewarded with a crazy success. The audience laughed immoderately at nearly everything. Unfortunately, the actors, convinced by the laughs that this strange piece must be a farce, began to play for them on the conventional farcical comedy lines; and the first-night success was never repeated. Shaw had planned all the laughs unerringly, but only as responses to an earnestly sincere performance. When the performance became comic the play lost its hold. But the only hitch on the first night was when Bernard Gould, now famous as Sir Bernard Partridge of *Punch*, had to make a remark about the Bulgarian army. By a slip of the tongue he applied it to the British army; and this was more than Golding Bright, then an unknown lad in the gallery, could bear. He hissed. When Shaw took his call as author at the end amid tremendous applause, young Bright heroically sent forth a solitary "Boo." Shaw, at the height of his practice as a mob orator, seized on the interruption to make a speech. "I quite agree with you, my friend," he said, "but what can we two do against a whole houseful of the opposite opinion?"

Post-mortems

Having to go backstage and "congratulate" someone on a bad performance is one of the professional hazards that most theatre people dread. Here are some tips on how to handle the situation with aplomb.

W. S. Gilbert burst into an actor's dressing-room after a dire performance and exclaimed: "My dear chap! Good isn't the word!"
And when Sir Herbert Tree played Hamlet in 1892 Gilbert said to

him after the first performance, "My dear fellow, I never saw anything so funny in my life, and yet it was not in the least vulgar."

Hume Cronyn confided in an interview how he has solved this eternal problem with a technique he perfected through his long career: "I walk into the dressing room, look my colleague straight in the eye, I put my hand on his or her shoulder, and I say with a broad, friendly smile: 'How about you?' The actor has no idea, of course, what I meant, but that is usually the end of the discussion."

Achievement

For many a year, Mr. Richard Maney—Broadway's super-publicist and master of sparkling jargon—has entered an actor's dressing room after an opening to say merely, "Well, nobody got hurt."

How It Feels

A premiere for the playwright is rather like childbirth for the father. It is the actors who go through labor, while the author paces up and down outside, like in the old novels, waiting for the first signs of life. Here is R. C. Sherriff's brief description of the opening of Journey's End.

The night it was produced I was all over the theatre, running up to the gallery, walking round the pit, standing in a box. I couldn't sit down; I must have walked five miles in the theatre that night. I couldn't bear to look at the audience—I remember thinking they looked like the robots in *R.U.R.* standing outside the wire. When the curtain fell and there was no applause I was pained, but thrilled, too.

Michael Langham relates how Tyrone Guthrie persuaded him not to attend his own first night.

It was my debut at the Vic and I was just entering the auditorium when I heard a pistol shot behind me. It was due to Tony's large hands coming together and producing a sound greater and more arresting than any hand-clap I've ever heard. (Guthrie's rehearsals were sporadically peppered with such gun-fire.) He was standing in the lobby. "Where are you going?" "To watch the play," I answered defensively, feeling I've been caught red-eyed in an act of voyeurism. "*Not* very intelligent. Your own rhythm is beating faster at the moment than anyone else's in London; you'll find the whole thing unbearably slow. Come up to the office and distract yourself with some designs that just arrived." My face must have betrayed a degree of frustration, for he added, "We can always slip in at the back every now and then to watch the showy bits."

I had a pleasant evening. Had I followed my instincts, it would have been miserable. It was, as Tony knew, my first show in London.

Author! Author!

Any curtain-speech at a tottering premier is usually a mistake. We think of curtain-fall on Noël Coward's *Sirocco* (1927) when everyone was booed for ten minutes, and Frances Doble, forced to speak, could only quaver that it was the happiest night of her life: something that, at this remove, has an uncommon pathos. But one speech, that of William Douglas Home, after *Ambassador Extraordinary*, his message-from-Mars invention, is remembered now for its courage.

It arrived on a midsummer night (June 30, 1948) at the Aldwych Theatre. The gallery waited until the cast had lined up, and until Raymond Lovell, as the Foreign Secretary, had stepped forward to answer some friendly applause. Here the booing burst in its raucous curtain lecture. Upstairs they were crying "Rubbish!," a favourite gallery-word. It was then that the author appeared: staring for a shocked half-minute before it let drive again. William Douglas Home, as a Parliamentary candidate used to hecklers, advanced in an unhurried way to the front of the stage and looked out into the house with interest. So this was a theatre, he seemed to be thinking; that, no doubt, would be the gallery. The noise was deadlier now, and Home spoke conversationally to the booers: "I like heckling. Please go on. We have the night before us." A voice yelled: "You're here to be judged." Home disregarded it. He looked down for a moment to summon his thoughts, and a photographer leapt out and took a picture. "Thank you, sir," said the dramatist with a polite bow. By then he had the right form of words to praise the cast, and he did so, gracefully unhurried, with no attention whatever to the rumblings overhead. Having settled this matter, he added: "I hope some people have enjoyed the play." He lifted his head, and the words cracked like a lash against the front of the gallery: "As for the others, it doesn't much matter whether they like the play or not—because if they don't learn the lesson of compromise, taught to-night, in six months' time that gallery won't be here." The voice was Home's, but behind it one could hear the words of Kean at the Royal Coburg long before. The gallery appeared to sense this. In a renewed hubbub he looked round again, and moved, almost casually, into the wings: "Far and away," said Harold Hobson, "the most dramatic event of the evening."

Diagnosis

Ralph Richardson once electrified a first-night audience and other members of the cast by stepping out of character in mid-scene and turning towards the auditorium with the question, "Is there a doctor in the house?" Somebody in the audience stood up. "Doctor," said Sir Ralph, "isn't this play awful?"

CHAPTER XIV

Critics

Collector's Items

Walter Kerr on *Hook and Ladder:* "It is the sort of play that gives failure a bad name."

Robert Benchley on *Perfectly Scandalous:* "It is one of those plays in which all the actors unfortunately enunciated very clearly."

George S. Kaufman reviewing a comedy: "There was scattered laughter in the rear of the theater, leading to the belief that somebody was telling jokes back there."

Robert Garland, after seeing *Clash by Night*, a flop by Clifford Odets, asked in his review about this once powerful playwright: "Odets, where is thy sting?"

Kenneth Tynan on a musical: "It contains a number of those tunes one goes *into* the theatre humming."

Unkindest Cuts

Bernard Shaw reviewing Herbert Tree as Falstaff in 1896: "Mr. Tree wants one thing to make him an excellent Falstaff, and that is to get born over again as unlike himself as possible . . . Mr. Tree might as well try to play Juliet."

Dorothy Parker on Marion Davies: "She has two expressions—joy and indigestion."

Reviewing a show in which both the plot and the two starring performers seemed to him soapy and weak, Alexander Woollcott wrote two lines: "In the first act *she* becomes a lady. In the second act *he* becomes a lady." And writing about another ill-fated Broadway open-

273

ing, Woollcott suggested that the leading man "should have been gently and firmly shot at sunrise."

Bernard Levin reviewing Paul Scofield in his famous role as Sir Thomas More in Robert Bolt's *A Man for All Seasons* wrote: "His face frozen, his voice dull and level except at the end of a sentence, when the pitch falls like a bad violinist's 'glides,' he makes every line sound like a platitude and extinguishes every spark of fire that Mr. Bolt manages to blow into brightness. Towards the end, when he is bowed and grey but unbroken, Mr. Scofield comes into his own, for grayness is then needed. But until then, his playing bores the doublet and hose off me."

James Agate on Charles Laughton's Henry VIII at Sadler's Wells in 1933: "Mr. Laughton came to Sadler's Wells with all his blushing film vulgarities thick upon him."

A critic commenting on Siobhan McKenna's voice in the *Sons of Oedipus*, in 1977: "Miss McKenna's normal stage voice is exactly half-way between a goose-girl and a whole company of keening mourners."

Brooks Atkinson on a British actress with the first name of April, giving a guest performance in America: "Oh, to be in England, now that April's here."

Wolcott Gibbs: "Miss Mendelssohn, as the demented governess, gave a notable display of continental acting technique, which seems to have quite a bit in common with professional wrestling."

A Pack of Cards

As dramatic critic of the Denver Post (Tribune, *according to some sources*), *Eugene Field reviewed a performance of* King Lear *briefly.*

"Last night Mr. Creston Clarke played King Lear at the Tabor Grand. All through the five acts of the Shakespearean tragedy he played the king as though under the premonition that someone was about to play the Ace."

I recall an elegant variation on the above by James Barber, critic of the Vancouver Province *in the late 1960s. Reviewing a rather campy production of* Hamlet *at the University of British Columbia, he wrote:* "There was a full house at the Frederick Wood Theatre last night: four queens and an ace."

Stage Fight

John Forster, *critic of* The Examiner *and a friend of William Macready wrote of Edwin Forrest's Macbeth during his second visit to England.*

Our old friend Mr. Forrest afforded great amusement to the public by his performance of Macbeth on Friday evening at the Princess's. Indeed, our best comic actors do not often excite so great a quantity of mirth. The change from an inaudible murmur to a thunder of sound was enormous; but the grand feature was the combat, in which he stood scraping his sword against that of Macduff. We were at a loss to know what this gesture meant till an enlightened critic in the gallery shouted out, "That's right, sharpen it!"

An Ideal Review

On Saturday, July 9, 1783, Mrs. Siddons, about whom all the world has been talking, exposed her beautiful, adamantine, soft and lovely person, for the first time in Smock-alley theatre, in the bewitching, melting, and all-tearful character of Isabella. From the repeated panegyrics in the impartial London newspapers, we were taught to expect the sight of a heavenly angel; but how were we supernaturally surprised into the most awful joy, at beholding a mortal Goddess? The house was crowded with hundreds more than it could hold—with thousands of admiring spectators who went away without a fight. This extraordinary phenomenon of tragic excellence!—this star of Melpomene!—this comet of the stage!—this sun of the firmament of muses!—this moon of blank verse!—this queen and princess of tears!— this Donnellan of the poisoned bow!—this empress of the pistol and dagger!—this chaos of Shakespeare!—this world of weeping clouds!— this Juno of commanding aspects!—this Terpsichore of the curtains and scenes!—this Proserpine of fires and earthquakes!—this Katterfelts of wonders! exceeded expectation, went beyond belief, and soared above the powers of description. She was nature itself—She was the most exquisite work of art—She was the very daisy, primrose, tuberose, sweetbriar, firze-blossom, gilliflower, wall flower, cauliflower, auriculus, and rosemary—in short she was the bouquet of Parnassus.

Where expectation was raised so high it was thought she would be injured by her appearance; but it was the audience who were injured. Several fainted even before the curtain drew up, but when she came to the scene of parting with her wedding ring, oh! what a sight was there! the very fiddlers in the orchestra albeit unused to the melting mood, blubbered like hungry children crying for their bread and butter; and when the bell rang for music between the acts, the tears ran from the bassoon players' eyes in such plentiful showers, that they choked the finger stops, and making a spout of the instrument, poured in such torrents on the first fiddler's book, that not seeing the overture was in two sharps—the leader of the band actually played in one flat. But the sobs and sighs of the groaning audience, and the noise of the corks drawn from the smelling bottles, prevented the mistake between the flats and sharps being discovered. 109 ladies fainted—46 went into fits, and 99 had strong hysterics. The world will scarcely credit the truth when they are told that 14 children—5 old women—10 taylors—6 common councilmen, were actually drowned in the inundation of tears that flowed from the galleries, lattices, and boxes, to increase the briny pond in the pit. The water was three feet deep, and the people that were obliged to stand up on the benches, were in that position up their ankles in tears.

Another View of the Same Event

At the time necessary for her entrance, she kept the audience waiting for ten minutes, or more, without any business going forward—a measure very impolite and very improper. The acting of Mrs. Siddons is truly great, tho' it sometimes bears the appearance of being preconceived, which will always reduce the desired effect. Mrs. Crawford's acting has not so much grandeur, but my feelings prompt me to imagine it partakes more of nature; Mrs. Crawford has an eye totally destitute of fire and meaning, but her voice is full of harmony. Mrs. Siddons has an eye labouring with expression, but her voice is confined, and not agreeable and would be dissonant if not managed with less than her judgment: she had infinite difficulty to conquer a whining monotony she possesses, and which her brother, Mr. Kemble, is troubled with, to a degree, in so much that many of his most capital scenes appear spiritless—not from a deficiency knowledge, but a want of power.

Soul of Wit

Alexander Woollcott here describes the wittiest woman of her generation.

Shortly after the armistice, Dorothy Parker was made dramatic critic of *Vanity Fair*, from which post she was forcibly removed upon the bitter complaints of sundry wounded people in the theatre, of whose shrieks, if memory serves, Billie Burke's were the most penetrating. In protest against her suppression, and perhaps in dismay at the prospect of losing her company, her co-workers, Robert E. Sherwood and Robert Benchley, quit *Vanity Fair* at the same time in what is technically known as a body, the former to become editor of *Life*, and the latter its dramatic critic.

Since then Mrs. Parker has gone back to the aisle seats only when Mr. Benchley was out of town and someone was needed to substitute for him. It would be her idea of her duty to catch up the torch as it fell from his hand—and burn someone with it. I shall never forget the expression on the face of the manager who, having recklessly produced a play of Channing Pollock's called *The House Beautiful*, turned hopefully to Benchley's next *feuilleton*, rather counting on a kindly and even quotable tribute from that amiable creature. But it seems Benchley was away that week, and it was little Mrs. Parker who had covered that opening. I would not care to say what she had covered it with. The trick was done in a single sentence. "*The House Beautiful*," she had said with simple dignity, "is the play lousy."

And more recently she achieved an equal compression in reporting on *The Lake*. Miss Hepburn, it seems, had run the whole gamut from A to B.

Brief Beefs

In the 1920s, the *Sun*, an extremely outspoken paper in England, gave one of the shortest notices on record. The play, produced by Penley, was entitled *Mr. Symkin*. "Globe Theatre. *Mr. Symkin*. Good God. What piffle."

Alexander Woollcott's review for a play called *Wham!* read "Ouch!" (There is one briefer still written by a London critic at the turn of the century. The morning after the opening of a show called *A Good Time*, his assessment in the paper read: "No.")

A clever notice that appeared a few years ago in an American paper dealt with a performance of *Uncle Tom's Cabin*; it reported that "there were fifty in the cast and ten real bloodhounds. The dogs gave an excellent performance, but received little support from the rest of the company."

Cleopatra

Tallulah Bankhead enjoyed a good rapport with the New York critics especially in the early part of her career when she was an unofficial member of the Algonquin Round Table. Heywood Broun ribbed her indifferent performance in The Exciters, *with a friendly: "Don't look now, Tallulah, but your show's slipping." But when she slipped badly in a revival of* Antony and Cleopatra, *the critics had a field day.*

On Armistice Day, 1937, I received the worst critical lambasting I ever experienced. There was no dissenting verdict. My old friend Richard Watts, Jr., wrote in the New York *Tribune*: "Miss Bankhead seemed more a serpent of the Suwannee than of the Nile." John Mason Brown, later to caress me with superlatives, mowed me down: "Tallulah Bankhead barged down the aisle as Cleopatra and sank. As the serpent of the Nile she proves to be no more dangerous than a garter snake." "Miss Bankhead played the Queen of the Nil," spit out George Jean Nathan, then took time out to warn the compositors that "Nil" was no typographical error.

Pith

The late Kenneth Tynan, whom Olivier recruited to be the National Theatre's first literary advisor, was the most expressive of Britain's postwar critics.

Of Noël Coward: "Forty years ago he was Slightly in *Peter Pan*, and you might say he has been wholly in *Peter Pan* ever since."

He spoonerized the Rodgers and Hammerstein musical *Flower Drum Song* as "The World of Woozy Song," referring to another Oriental show on Broadway called *The World of Suzie Wong*.

Of Ralph Richardson's voice: "Something between bland and grandiose; blandiose perhaps."

The Master as Critic

In the theatre almost everybody is a critic, and most theatre people of course know much more about their craft than their reviewers. Noël Coward was famous for his off-hand "bitchicisms."

On seeing an actress play Queen Victoria in the provinces: "Her Victoria made me feel that Albert had married beneath his station."

Griffith Jones was once in a play with a fourteen-year-old infant "prodigy" who was on stage throughout most of the play and, despite critical acclaim, firmly sank it. Coward visited the play on second night: "Two things should have been cut. The second act and that youngster's throat."

Discussing with James Dow the theatre of the late 1950s: "Since the war a terrible pall of significance has fallen over plays."

Colleagues

To Howard Dietz, about his new play *Between the Devil*, George Kaufman said, "I understand your new play is full of single entendre."

[71] FEUDS AND SQUABBLES

Physical Reaction

Piron the critic did not relish all of Voltaire's dramatic productions, and Voltaire was angry with Piron for not approving them. Voltaire, however, knowing the overwhelming force of Piron's opinion, called upon him one day with a new piece, which he thought had been labored into such a state of perfection as to defy all criticism. "There," said he, "my good friend, do me the favor to read that; I will call for it in two days, and request your candid opinion of it."

Voltaire called upon his friend. "Well, have you read it?" "Yes." "What do you think of it?" "I think it will be hissed." "You are mistaken," said Voltaire, "the manager has accepted it. Go with me to the theatre a week from today and see the representation." They went; the performance began, proceeded very heavily through two acts, in the third act the scenery met with some applause; the last two acts, from the hard efforts of the actors, passed quietly, and the curtain dropped. Voltaire jogged his companion, who appeared half-asleep, "Now, my good friend, you find you were mistaken." "Not much," replied Piron. "Yes," said the other, "you thought the piece would be hissed." "My dear sir," rejoined Piron, "how can people hiss when they yawn?"

Combat unto Death

In the 1890s Bernard Shaw was an established critic and a struggling playwright. He waged a long campaign to get a play of his staged at the Lyceum, where Sir Henry Irving and Ellen Terry presided over the higher drama. Shaw alternated between flattering and attacking Irving in his roles; while Irving tried to string Shaw along by offering to option his play, The Man of Destiny, *with no intention of producing it, but hoping to buy also the critic's favor. Shaw declined and never forgave Irving for not producing him. His belated revenge came when in 1905 he was invited to Irving's state funeral.*

As a playwright of consequence Shaw received a ticket for the Abbey ceremony from George Alexander, who was greatly relieved when it came back with this note: "I return the ticket for the Irving funeral. Literature, alas, has no place at his death as it had no place in his life. Irving would turn in his coffin if I came, just as Shakespeare will turn in his coffin when Irving comes."

Boredom Becomes Electra

Alexander Woollcott was not fond of Eugene O'Neill. The latter's trilogy, Mourning Becomes Electra *had already been running for twenty weeks when finally, in February 1932, Woollcott wrote about it. To make no secret of his sentiments he called the piece "a grumbling and belated review of the remorseless and venerated trilogy by the same sacred cow who wrote* Strange Interlude."

To a woman I know, lunching one day last fall at the Colony Club, there floated from the near-by table a fragment of conversation that was as tantalizing as a bit of lamplit melodrama glimpsed through a tenement window by a passing elevated train. It was evidently a chat across an omelette by a man and woman each of whom had recently been to see that glum three-decker by Eugene O'Neill called *Mourning Becomes Electra*. The man could not pretend that he had enjoyed it, and indeed he was muttering mutinously because all the town was ringing, like some overworked welkin, with its praises. The woman, as she completed the ritual of the finger-bowl and drew on her gloves, interrupted with a single question put to him in a voice that was fairly Arctic in its superiority. "Just tell me this, my dear," she said, "has there ever been any incest in your family?" The reply was a mere mumble, but from the context the eavesdropper could gather that the man was disavowing all knowledge of any such *contretemps* under his ancestral roof. "Ah!" cried the woman, with a triumphant pounce on his bashful admission, "then you simply cannot begin to appreciate *Mourning Becomes Electra*."

Against the *Times*

Banning the critic from the theatre is a recurrent fantasy of the frustrated producer. Years ago the Shuberts banned Alexander Woollcott, then the New York *Times* critic, from their theatres in a feud that was dragged through the courts, aroused national interest, and lasted a year. Woollcott had mildly disapproved of a "not vastly amusing" French farce entitled *Taking Chances*, put on by the Shuberts in March 1915. Review tickets for the Shuberts' next opening were pointedly sent not to Woollcott but to Carr Van Anda, the *Times*'s managing editor, with a request that another critic be assigned. Clearly the *Times* had to stand up for its rights. Woollcott went but was stopped at the door, and the lawyers entered the case. The *Times* won an injunction restraining the Shuberts from barring its critic and threw out all Shubert advertising. Many months later the Shuberts won a reversal of the original decision of the Appellate Division, but it was the loss of the important advertising outlet that eventually persuaded the Shuberts to drop the quarrel. By Christmas of 1916 the Shuberts had mellowed enough to send the *Times* critic a box of cigars. Woollcott's closing line on the incident was: "The whole thing went up in smoke."

In the aftermath of the incident, Aleck confided to a friend: "They threw me out, and now I'm basking in the fierce white light that beats upon the thrown."

A Critic's War

For years Robert Benchley carried on a war with the notorious Broadway hit *Abie's Irish Rose*. He wrote: "People laugh at this every night, which explains why democracy can never be a success. Where do people come from who keep this going? You don't see them out in the daytime." And returning to it: "In another two or three years, we'll have this play driven out of town." Near the close of the play's record run (1922–27) Benchley posted a prize for the best critical comment on the show. Harpo Marx won with: "No worse than a bad cold."

Benchley had to write single-line summaries of Broadway shows. He once summed up *Abie's Irish Rose* as "Hebrews 13:8." A look at the Bible revealed the reference was to the line "Jesus Christ, the same yesterday, and today, and forever."

[72] GETTING EVEN

The Nature of the Beast

Kenneth Tynan described the critic as "a man who knows the way but can't drive the car." Others have been less kind.

Irish dramatist Brendan Behan: "Critics are like eunuchs in a harem. They're there every night, they see it done every night, they see how it should be done every night, but they can't do it themselves."

And as Christopher Hampton, British playwright, once said: "Asking a working actor what he thinks about critics is like asking a lamp-post how it feels about dogs."

A Young Man from Caracas

Critics are often accused of writing about what they have not experienced. A few years ago *Los Angeles Times* drama critic Dan Sullivan took a sabbatical and enrolled in a year of courses at Stanford where he learned about acting and technical aspects of the theatre. He fared better than his colleague Marco Antonio, a young critic with a rising reputation in his native Venezuela. He too was eager to widen his critical horizon by gaining first-hand experience of acting. Not long after he let this be known, one of the theatres in Caracas offered him a small part in a domestic farce. Being a handsome man, Marco Antonio played the small but important part of the lover, and the piece ended with the cuckolded husband shooting him as the curtain fell. After two weeks of performances, the prop man either forgot to take out the cleaning brush from the barrel of the rifle, or else deep in his subconscious he remembered that there was a critic on stage. At any rate, when the husband fired the shotgun the brush went straight through Marco Antonio's heart. The curtain dropped on schedule, the audience applauded as usual—totally unaware until the next morning that in the eternal battle between critics and practitioners the score was evened for a moment.

A Critical Horse

Irving was putting on one of his Shakespearean pageants in which it was necessary that he should be mounted. A horse was accordingly obtained from a firm which specialized in providing animals for stage purposes, and Irving, who was not much of a horseman, anxiously enquired if it was quiet. "It's as quiet as a lamb," was the reassuring answer; "it's just finished an engagement at His Majesty's Theatre carrying Mr. Beerbohm Tree in *Richard II*." At this moment the horse yawned. "Ah!" said Irving, "he's a bit of a critic too, I see."

Wit and Venom

Tallulah Bankhead:

It was through Alex Woollcott that I won my first citation as a wit. Aware of my concern with the stage, Alex asked me if I would like to attend an opening night performance. Would I? I'd have attended any performance with anyone. The opening was Maeterlinck's *The Burgomaster of Stilemonde*, one of the Belgian's minor inventions. At the end of the first act I turned to my escort to say, "There's less in this than meets the eye."

But Tallulah kept her real opinion of Woollcott for her autobiography, which appeared after his death.

He was vindictive, shockingly petty in a feminine fashion, given to excesses when expressing his preferences or his prejudices. He probably endorsed more second-rate books than any man of his time. To him the acting nobility was confined to Minnie Maddern Fiske and Harpo Marx. In condemnation of a play or an actor he could be downright vicious. Mr. W. was an emotionalist who rarely succumbed to the chill demands of logic. Woollcott was less a critic than an amusing hysteric.

How They Took It

Mrs. Bancroft:

I was once much impressed by a small child's criticism. He watched for a long time, silently and attentively, a scene of great emotional interest between two people. When asked what he thought of it, he answered: "I like that one best." "Why?" "She speaks like telling the truth, the other speaks like telling lies." What criticism can be finer than this? One was acting straight from the heart, the other from not even next door but one to it.

Sir Michael Redgrave:

Actors and creative artists instinctively resent criticism of any kind; they really like lots and lots of praise. I have noticed, looking back at the reviews of plays that I thought had been rather unfairly attacked, that on the whole I have agreed with the consensus of critical opinion.

Diana Rigg appeared nude in Ronald Millar's Abelard and Heloise. *In his review John Simon wrote: "Diana Rigg is built like a brick mausoleum with insufficient flying buttresses." Miss Rigg recalls her feelings in her entertaining book about critics,* No Turn Unstoned.

I remember making my way to the theatre the following day, darting from doorway to doorway and praying I wouldn't meet anyone I knew. The cast behaved with supreme tact and pretended they hadn't read the review.

Don't Tangle with a Critic

There can be few people working in the theatre who have never been stung by a critic. The temptation to sting back is enormous, but usually the critic has the last word.

As a play reviewer Heywood Broun was usually gentle, but one actor's performance so displeased him that he was moved to classify the young man, Geoffrey Steyne, as the worst actor on the American stage. Steyne sued, but the case was dismissed. The next time Broun reviewed a play in which Steyne appeared, he made no mention of the actor until the last sentence, which read, "Mr. Steyne's performance was not up to its usual standard."

Thin Bottom

The play was *A Midsummer Night's Dream*, and Mr. Arthur Wood took the part of Bottom. Mr. Wood was a very clever actor, but a little over-sensitive to criticism, and when a local paper suggested certain modifications in his playing of the part, he wrote a very indignant letter to the editor. This was duly published by the paper with the sly comment: "Mr. Wood seems rather thin-skinned about his Bottom."

The Correct Response

Noël Coward, when the critics called his work thin, replied: "Very well—from now on I will write nothing but very fat plays for fat critics." He once described New York drama critics Brooks Atkinson and Walter Kerr as the "unhidden persuaders," and said: "I read all the notices, but remember only the good ones." And: "I can take any amount of criticism, so long as it is unqualified praise."

[73] CRITICS ARE HUMAN

Bad Playwrights

Shaw began as a bad novelist and a good critic. The other great drama critic in late nineteenth-century London was William Archer, who introduced Ibsen to English audiences and wrote an influential treatise on playwriting. Critics may know more than anybody else about what is wrong with a play, but writing a successful one takes a different talent. Shaw went on to become one of the most influential dramatists of the past hundred years; this episode shows how very nearly he might have given up.

In their British Museum days William Archer and Bernard Shaw used frequently to discuss the drama, and some time in 1885 Shaw confided to Archer that though he was no good at construction he was nothing less than a genius at writing dialogue, on which Archer confided to Shaw that though he was useless at dialogue there was very little he did not know about construction. This seemed an admirable basis for collaboration. A perfect plot by Archer, sustained by the brilliant dialogue of Shaw, would score a bull's eye. So thought Archer and so thought Shaw. With such a number of good plots crying aloud to be used, Archer was naturally not foolish enough to invent one himself; he took what he required from an early play by Emile Augier, worked it up in the Parisian manner, provided it with a comic heroine, a serious heroine, and a noble-hearted hero, placed the scene of Act I in a hotel garden on the Rhine, and handed the scenario to Shaw.

Some weeks elapsed. Archer thought that Shaw had forgotten all about the play and did not remind him of it. Besides, Shaw was apparently composing an elaborate treatise, for Archer saw him every day at the Museum "laboriously writing page after page of the most exquisitely neat shorthand at the rate of about three words a minute." Some six weeks after the completion of the scenario Shaw staggered Archer by saying: "Look here, I've knocked off the first act of that play of ours and haven't come to the plot yet. In fact, I've forgotten the plot. You might tell me the story again." Archer stifled his annoyance and again carefully described the plot. Shaw thanked him warmly, left him, and three days later reported: "I've written three pages of the second act and have used up all your plot. Can you let me have some more to go on with?" Archer sternly reminded him that the plot was an organic whole, and that to add to it was like giving a few additional arms and legs to a statue already provided with the necessary limbs. Shaw tried to reassure him and offered to read the first two acts when he had finished the second. Archer consented, and when the time came listened with a puzzled frown to Act I and fell fast asleep during Act II. When he woke up he told Shaw exactly what he thought of him and declared the collaboration at an end. A fellow-dramatist, Henry Arthur Jones, to whom Shaw also read the unfinished play, reminded him that "sleep is criticism," but kept awake in the hope of being rewarded by a thrill, and at the conclusion of the performance asked, "Where's your murder?" Shaw, concluding that play-writing was not his job, flung the unfinished work on his pile of discarded manuscripts and thought no more about it.

Influence

"The articles signed "G.B.S." in *The Saturday Review*," said James Agate, "made me determine that one day I would be a dramatic critic"; and Max Beerbohm admired Shaw "beyond all other men" as a dramatic critic: "I never tire of his two volumes. He was at the very top of his genius when he wrote them."

Self-defense

James Agate wrote this in 1932.

When a play is crashingly dull the critic has only two resources. One is sleep, in justification whereof I shall quote William Archer's dictum that the first qualification for a dramatic critic is the capacity to sleep while sitting bolt upright.

Arousal

Professor Brander Matthews was a great stickler for proprieties. At an opening night he had gone to review a play. The next day he was asked for his opinion by one of his students at Columbia University.

"Well, gentlemen," said Professor Matthews, "the play was in four acts, and I was there as the guest of the author. After the first act the audience sat silent and I applauded. After the second act I sat quiet while the audience hissed." The professor took a long-drawn and reminiscent pull at his cigarette, then held it at arm's length and flicked off the ashes.

"And the third act?"

"Well, gentlemen," and there was a gleam of satisfaction in the professor's eye, "after the third act I went out and bought standing room and came back and hissed too."

Tears

The contentious Jed Harris took on critics as well. His story about Brooks Atkinson and the first production of Our Town *is typical and probably untrue to the last word.*

The New York *Times* critic half humorously said he'd read that Harris had been knocking drama critics. "I told him it wasn't so in his case," Harris recalled. "I said I thought he wrote beautifully but that I wished the critics knew more about the facts of theatre, the real business of putting a play on. I said, 'You fellows ought to come to rehearsal once in a while,' and then I invited him over to watch the first run-through of *Our Town*. To my surprise he agreed. I put him in the balcony so that none of the company would see him. Of course they would have been scared to death. But as it turned out, that first run-through was a magnificent performance. I never saw a better one. After it was over, I went up to see him. Tears were running down his cheeks. He said to me, 'You so and so. You ruined the opening night for me.' "

CHAPTER XV

Theatre and Society

Whipped

The emperor Augustus Caesar had the actor Epiphanus whipped three times around the palace and banished for daring to give a performance in his presence on a public holiday.

Getting Busted

The Puritan revolution in England managed to close down the theatres after 1642. The players had to go underground.

Playgoing had now become as a vice or a misdemeanour, to be prosecuted in secret—like dram-drinking. During a performance of Fletcher's tragedy of *Rollo, Duke of Normandy*, in which such excellent actors as Lowin, Taylor, Pollard, Burt and Hart were concerned, a party of troopers beset the house, broke in about the middle of the play, and carried off the players, accoutred as they were in their stage dresses, to Hatton House, then a prison, where after being detained some time, they were plundered of their clothes and dismissed. The clothes worn by the players upon the stage were of superior quality— fine dresses were of especial value in times prior to the introduction of scenery—and the loss was hard to bear. The public, it was feared, would be loath to believe in the merits of an actor who was no better attired than themselves. But at length it became too hazardous, as Kirkman relates, in the preface to *The Wits, or Sport upon Sport* (1672), "to act anything that required any good cloaths; instead of which painted cloath many times served the turn to represent rich habits."

Censorship

From Tudor times strict censorship was exercised on the English stage by an official of the Court, variously known as the Master of the Rev-

els, *the Lord Chamberlain, and the Examiner of Plays. All unpro-*
duced scripts had to be submitted and licensed by this censor, who
vigorously excised scenes or suggested changes in lines. There were at-
tempts in the eighteenth century to change or abolish censorship, but
in fact the Lord Chamberlain's office exercised its arbitrary power,
against which there was no appeal, until 1968.

Colley Cibber tells an amusing anecdote of what happened to himself
when he presented his version of *King Richard the Third*, as altered
from Shakespeare, to receive licence of the Master of the Revels. The
whole first act was expunged without sparing a line of it. This extraordinary conduct induced Cibber to apply to him for a speech or two,
that the other four acts might limp on with a little less absurdity. No;
he had an objection to the whole act, and among other reasons he assigned was that the distresses of King Henry the Sixth, who is killed
by Richard, would put weak people too much in mind of King James,
who was then living in France, and whom the nation had banished
for his tyranny! This arbitrary folly did not, however, last many years;
for by the patent which George I granted to Sir Richard Steele and
his assigns, of which Cibber was one, the patentees were freed from
the thraldom of the Master of the Revels, and made sole judges of
what plays might be proper for the stage, without submitting them to
the approbation of any other person whatever. But it ought to be
mentioned that this exemption was soon followed by a new law, by
which the power of licensing plays was given to a person duly au-
thorised—a law which occasioned an universal murmur in the nation,
and was complained of in the public papers; in all the coffee-houses of
London it was treated as unjust, and contrary to the liberties of the
people.

Costumes by the Lord Chamberlain

In 1874 *Offenbach's* Vert-Vert *was produced at the St. James's The-*
atre in London.

It was a disastrous first night—under-rehearsed, with a boisterous audience in front—and it ended in chaos. Even a troupe of French
dancers with *La Riperelle*, "a scandalous dance in scanty clothes,"
failed to stem the debacle. Their dance and dresses, later when the
show was somewhat pulled together, caused trouble with the Lord

Chamberlain who ordered the costumes to be lengthened. He was tricked into saying what should be done to them and the manager announced the new costumes as "designed by the Lord Chamberlain!"

Convincing the Censor

In 1909 there was one of the periodic debates in the House of Commons about the Censor.

In his evidence before the Censorship Committee, Granville-Barker told how the Salvation Army lent their uniforms for the Court Theatre production [of Shaw's *Major Barbara*] and how the Censor, before licensing the play, had asked him whether the feelings of the Army would be outraged by its being put upon the stage: "I was fortunately able to tell him that we had been in communication with the Salvation Army, and that so far from their feelings being outraged, they regarded it, I may say, as an excellent advertisement—to use the term 'advertisement' in its very best sense. Had I not been able to assure Mr. Redford [the Censor] of that, he might, I think, easily have been unwilling to license the play."

Shaw's comment was: "Redford did not care a rap about the feelings of the Salvation Army. It was 'My God, why hast thou forsaken me?' that frightened him. He asked whether they were not the last words of Christ on the cross. Barker assured them that they were in the *Psalms*. He then gave in."

Protest

In 1925, the young Noël Coward's play Fallen Angels, *starring Tallulah Bankhead, created a sensation at the Globe Theatre in London.*

On August 29, the last night of the run, notorious public protestor Mrs. Charles Hornibrook visited the theatre. This odd lady had recently parted company with the London Council for the promotion of Public Morality and was operating on her own. At the end of the second act, she stood up in her box. "Ladies and Gentlemen, I wish to protest. This play should not go unchallenged." In the disturbance that followed, there were hoots from the gallery, the orchestra struck up with "I Want To Be Happy" and Mrs. Hornibrook was gently guided out of the theatre.

A Word to the Puritans

If the Theatre were to be shut up, the Stage wholly silenced and suppressed, I believe the world, bad as it is now, would be ten times more wicked.

La Motte

[75] CHURCH AND STAGE

Irreligious Theatre

From the early days of the Christian Church, there were violent attacks on the pagan theatre. Beginning with Tertullian in the second century, the Early Fathers of the Christian Church were writing tireless tirades against the theatre and the acting profession. This is a typical sentence from St. Augustine, who was a great connoisseur of forbidden pleasures and seems to be speaking here from experience: "Stage-plays are the most petulant, the most impure, impudent, wicked, unclean, the most shameful and detestable atonements of filthy Devil-gods."

When the Church won the battle, the curtain came down on the European stage for a thousand years. But even during the medieval period, in the great age of faith, the Church seemed to need theatre and the result sometimes was a curious mixture of the sacred and the profane.

In France, at different cathedral churches, there was a Bishop or an Archbishop of Fools elected; and in the churches immediately dependent upon the papal see, a Pope of Fools. These mock pontiffs had usually a proper suite of ecclesiastics, and one of their ridiculous ceremonies was to shave the precentor of Fools upon a stage erected before the church in the presence of the populace, who were amused during the operation by his lewd and vulgar discourses accompanied by antics equally reprehensible. They were mostly attired in the ridiculous dresses of pantomime players and buffoons, and so habited entered the church, and performed the service accompanied by crowds of laity in masks, representing monsters, or with their faces smutted to excite fear or laughter, as occasion might require. Some of them personated females and practised wanton devices.

During divine service they sang indecent songs in the choir, ate rich puddings on the corner of the altar, played at dice upon it by the side of the priest while he celebrated mass, incensed it with smoke from old burnt shoes, and ran leaping all over the church. The Bishop or Pope of Fools performed the service habited in pontifical garments, and gave his benediction; when it was concluded, he was seated in an open carriage; and drawn about to different parts of the town followed by a large train of clergy and laymen, and a cart filled with filth, which they threw upon the populace assembled to see the procession. These licentious festivities were called the December Liberties. They were always held at Christmas time, or near to it, but not confined to one particular day, and seem to have lasted through the chief part of January.

Comedy

Molière's play about the religious hypocrite Tartuffe *touched some of the powerful ecclesiastics in France so close to the nerve that they prevailed upon Louis XIV and managed to keep the play off the stage for five years. Molière concluded a spirited defense in the preface to the published version of the play.*

Let me finish with the words of a great prince on the comedy *Tartuffe*. Eight days after it had been banned, a play called *Scaramouche the Hermit* was presented to the court. The King, on his way out, said to this great prince: "I should really like to know why the persons who make so much noise about Molière's comedy do not say a word about Scaramouche." To which the prince replied: "Because the comedy of Scaramouche makes fun of Heaven and religion, which these gentlemen do not care a hoot about, while Tartuffe makes fun of them, which they cannot bear."

The Actor and the Archbishop

Archbishop Tillotson was very well acquainted with Betterton, and continued that acquaintance even after he was in that high station. One day, when Betterton came to see him at Lambeth, that prelate asked him how it came about that after he had made the most moving discourse that he could, was touched deeply with it himself, and spoke it as feelingly as he was able, yet he could never move people in the church near so much as the other did on the stage. "That," says Betterton, "I think is easy to be accounted for: it is because you are only telling them a story, and I am showing the facts."

[76] POLITICS AND THE THEATRE

Too Moved To Stay

Most theatregoers remember how Hamlet put on a play to "catch the conscience of the king." There is a true story from the fourth century B.C. when an actor's art had a similar effect.

Alexander, the tyrant of Phera, had the reputation of being the most heartless of men. He went to see the tragic actor Theodoros perform the part of Merope in a Euripides play. The actor lived his role with such force that the tyrant burst into tears and left the theatre. Later he apologized to Theodoros and explained that he did not mean to offend him: "I had to leave because I was ashamed that I should have been so moved by the sufferings of actors but not by my fellow citizens."

Conspiracy

Beaumont and Fletcher, having concerted the plan of a tragedy over a bottle, settled which parts of the play they should respectively take. "Well," said Fletcher, "it shall be so: you manage the rest, and I'll undertake to kill the king." These words were overheard and they were presently made prisoners; but having it in their power easily to prove that they only meditated the assassination of a theatrical monarch, the whole went off in a jest.

Lincoln's Death

There had been an unsuccessful attempt on the life of George III in May 1800 inside the Drury Lane Theatre. But the most notorious political event that took place in a theatre was the assassination of Abraham Lincoln in 1865 by the actor John Wilkes Booth. April 14, 1861, was the day that the Union flag was struck down by the Confederates at Fort Sumter; four years of Civil War later, this was the date that the national flag was unfurled on the same spot once more. It was an important date for the recently re-elected President. Here is a contemporary and official account of the fateful events later that day.

It was announced in the papers of the morning of the 14th of April that President Lincoln and Lieutenant General Grant would be in attendance at Ford's Theatre on that evening. General Grant was not present, and the President, in the kindness of his heart not wishing to disappoint the people, reluctantly went.

At half-past eight o'clock, Mr. Lincoln, accompanied by Mrs. Lincoln, Miss Harris, and Major Rathbone, entered the theatre. The play, Taylor's *Our American Cousin*, was "going smoothly." Dundreary was telling why a dog wags his tail, and the enthusiastic reception of Mr. Lincoln drowned the point of Dundreary's conundrum. When he reached the door of the private box, the President turned and bowed in acknowledgment of the greeting, and then followed Mrs. Lincoln into the box.

The President, as usual with him, had no guard. The box occupied by the presidential party consisted of the two upper boxes on the right-hand side of the audience, which, by the removal of a partition, had been thrown into one. In the corner furthest from the stage sat the President. The box was decorated with the flag he loved so well, hanging around him and his friends in graceful festoons, relieved by a back ground of lace. Where the flags met, an engraving of Washington in a gilt frame was placed.

All went smoothly behind as before the scenes, the presence of the President awaking emulation among the people of the company. Towards the beginning of the second scene of the third act, John Wilkes Booth, son of the celebrated actor of the same name, visited this exclusive domain, to which his profession of actor was an open sesame. He entered by the back door of the theatre, and left very soon, leaving that back door open. He had evidently ridden to the theatre, for ere entering he left his horse in the alley.

Madame Mountchessington has left the stage to Asa Trenchard, with the remark: "You don't understand the manners of good society. That alone can excuse the impertinence of which you are guilty." Trenchard answers, "I guess I know enough to turn you inside out"; and the audience clap their hands and laugh in glee. Mrs. Lincoln joins in the laugh—a pistol shot, sharp and clear, is heard. The words *Sic semper tyrannis* ["May all tyrants die thus"] are whispered— "Revenge for the South" is added, a white face "covered with a night of hair," lighted by two black, shining eyes, is seen between the

President's box and the stage; a moment passes; it drops. A form crouches as it falls, then rises in histrionic attitude, in its hand a knife, whose newly polished surface reflects the numerous gas jets. Three seconds—nay, two—and it is gone.

Still as the hush that follows a prayer in the chamber of the dying, the audience sit spell-bound, it may have been, for two seconds; a tall man jumps upon the stage, and he too disappeared, while a voice in the audience at last utters the name of the assassin—"John Wilkes Booth."

The audience were not at all alarmed by the report of the pistol in the box. It was supposed by most to be part of the business of the piece; and it was not till the marble face and gleaming dagger were seen descending from the box that a suspicion of the truth flashed upon them. When Booth was named as the man, some few cries of "Hang him!" were raised; but though the audience left their feet, they seemed bereft not only of all power of action, but even all power of thought. A vacant, doubting look was stamped upon each face; and it was not till Miss Harris called to Miss Keene for some water, and a few gentlemen had ascended the stage, that the mind of the audience seemed to take in understandingly the deed, and all the horror of the deed they had witnessed. All spoke but no one said anything. Exclamation followed exclamation, till at last Miss Keene stepped forth, and waving her arm, besought them to be calm and retain their seats. At last, on repeated requests to leave the theatre, made by several gentlemen, the audience rolled, rather than walked out, leaving the theatre, in which they had witnessed a tragedy unequalled in atrocity or magnitude of consequences since the murder of the first Caesar.

Realism

When Raymond Massey scored his huge success playing the title role of *Abe Lincoln in Illinois*, he was so lifelike and earnest that George Kaufman remarked: "Massey won't be satisfied until he's assassinated."

Politics

The playwright Robert Sherwood was speechwriter to Franklin Delano Roosevelt. After a successful campaign speech in Philadelphia, Sherwood complimented the President on his "timing" in delivering certain lines. "Do you think Alfred Lunt could have done it better?" asked F.D.R. "Yes," said Sherwood. F.D.R. roared with laughter.

Witch Hunt

Years before Senator Joe McCarthy became a name that will live in infamy in the annals of American democracy, the Congress of the United States managed to kill off the largest social experiment of taking theatre to the masses. The Federal Theatre project gave employment to eight thousand people during the Depression and brought, mainly free, a vast array of classic and new works to millions of people. It was ended by an act of Congress on June 30, 1939, after less than five years. Hallie Flanagan, director of the Federal Theatre, describes her experience on December 6, 1938, before the House Committee to Investigate Un-American Activities.

I was sworn in as a witness by Chairman Dies, a rangy Texan with a Cowboy drawl and a big black cigar. I wanted to talk about Federal Theatre, but the Committee apparently did not. Who had appointed me? Harry Hopkins. Was that his own idea or did somebody put him up to it? I said I had no knowledge of any recommendations made in my own behalf; I said that while the Committee had recently been investigating un-American activity, I had been engaged for four years in combating un-American inactivity. The distinction was lost on the Committee.

Mr. Starnes took a different tack: Did I consider the theatre a weapon? I said the theatre could be all things to all men. "Do you see this?" Congressman Starnes suddenly shouted, waving a yellow magazine aloft. "Ever see it before?" I said it seemed to be an old Theatre Arts Monthly. This described a meeting of workers' theatres in New York in 1931. Hadn't I been active in setting them up? No. I had never been connected in any way with workers' theatres. I wrote a report on such theatres for Theatre Arts Monthly under the title "A Theatre Is Born." This theatre, however, was not born through me; I was simply a reporter.

How about these plays that had been criticized by witnesses before the Committee? Were they propaganda? For communism? "To the best of my knowledge," I told the Committee, "we have never done a play which was propaganda for communism; but we have done plays which were propaganda for democracy, for better housing . . ."

How many people had we played to so far? Twenty-five million people, a fifth of the population. Where did our audience come from? Was it true that we "couldn't get any audiences for anything except communist plays?" No. The list submitted would show our wide audience support. Back to the article, "A Theatre Is Born," and the phrase where I had described the enthusiasm of these theatres as having "a certain Marlowesque madness."

"You are quoting from this Marlowe," observed Mr. Starnes. "Is he a Communist?"

The room rocked with laughter, but I did not laugh. Eight thousand people might lose their jobs because a Congressional Committee had so pre-judged us that even the classics were "communistic." I said, "I was quoting from Christopher Marlowe."

"Tell us who Marlowe is, so we can get the proper references, because that is all we want to do."

Allies

Before America entered the war, Noël Coward was both a spy and good-will ambassador from Churchill to Roosevelt, both of whom insisted when they met him that Coward sing "Mad Dogs and Englishmen." In 1944 these close allies all but fell out over the song.

At a dinner party given by Churchill on board H.M.S. *Prince of Wales* in honour of President Roosevelt on the evening following the signing of the Atlantic Charter, the two world leaders became involved in a heated argument as to whether "In Bangkok at twelve o'clock they foam at the mouth and run" came at the end of the first refrain or at the end of the second. It was Roosevelt who got it right; told later by Coward that he'd been wrong, Churchill murmured, "England can take it."

Foreign Aid

The opening of the new building of the Shaw Festival on Niagara-on-the-Lake was attended by a great many Canadian dignitaries. Prime Minister Pierre Elliott Trudeau also invited Mrs. Indira Gandhi, the Prime Minister of India, who happened to be on a state visit to negotiate a grain deal with Ottawa. Despite the glittering gala, the production was something less than exciting, and as the two prime ministers left the theatre, one political wag was overheard to say:

"Mrs. Gandhi came to us for wheat; it is a pity that we should be giving her this chaff."

[77] ROYALTY

Royal Mistress

The best-known British royals who had intimate relations with actresses were Charles II ("Let not poor Nell starve," he was supposed to have said on his deathbed about Nell Gwyn) and Edward VII when he was Prince of Wales. But the most enduring relationship between an actress and a prince took place in the earlier part of the nineteenth century.

Mrs. Jordan lived for many years with George III's younger son, the Duke of Clarence, who later became King William IV, and they had ten illegitimate children, all of whom were officially acknowledged and eventually ennobled.

For some unknown reason, Mrs. Jordan has never had the same appeal to the British public as Nell Gwyn, although she was a far better actress, a much more domesticated mistress, and incomparably less of a burden to the public treasury. In fact Mrs. Jordan earned large sums of money, most of which she spent on keeping the Duke and their enormous brood.

The Duke did make her an allowance—a modest one of £1000 a year—and when George III heard of it he testily ordered his son to reduce it by half. No actress, he felt, was worth more than £500 a year. The Duke took this news to Mrs. Jordan, who replied by seizing a Drury Lane playbill and pointing to the words, "No money returned after the rising of the curtain."

Same Plot, Different Ending

Oddly enough one of Shakespeare's plays about royalty—*Richard II*, written in 1595, dealing with the King who was deposed in 1399, imprisoned and murdered—became a factor in the absurd attempt by the Earl of Essex to lead a revolt against the Queen's counsellors in 1601. His confederates had the far-fetched idea that if *Richard II* could be acted in public just before the revolt, it would influence people in their favour. They bribed the Lord Chamberlain's company to stage it on Saturday night, February 7, the night before the abortive coup d'état, but it is fairly clear that the players had no knowledge of the plot, or of the real reasons which prompted a group of nobles to give them an unexpected £10.

The story of the play came out at the inquiry on February 18, but the Queen [Elizabeth I] was so little worried by it that she allowed the Lord Chamberlain's Men to act at Court six days later, and kept them as her favourite actors for the rest of her life.

Three Georges

Acting was the only art which George the First even pretended to admire; he was very fond of ordering the King's company down to Hampton Court, and understood and enjoyed political allusions of such plays as *Henry VIII*, which he was careful to explain to the Prince of Wales. George the Second enjoyed the play hugely, and was never so happy as when watching a piece of the Restoration, with all its indelicacies restored to the acting version by his own royal command. The audiences of George the Third had the satisfaction of his Majesty's presence on very frequent occasions, but always to witness plays of the greatest innocence. It must have been very cheerful to hear his Majesty's hilarity ring round the house at the smallest joke; we know he would laugh himself almost into apoplexy when the clown in the pantomime stole the goose or sat on the baby. He was so easily pleased that the actors sometimes made "gag" for his especial benefit. They would make sly jokes at his Majesty's agricultural pursuits, and his Majesty would take the point with delight, and chuckle from the royal box, "Hee, hee; good, they mean my sheep."

One-Track Mind

During the summer of 1755 Garrick had planned several schemes for the entertainment of the town, and among other means of giving them effect, invited a distinguished dancer to perform in a ballet which he had splendidly conceived. This artist was a Monsieur Noverre, who arrived in London with a band of no less than a hundred other performers, and immediately began to make preparations for his corps to exhibit. But they became the object of the malice and ridicule of all the wits about town. The indignation of the lower orders was kindled, that such a number of Frenchmen, as they call all foreigners, should be brought among them. Still Garrick thought that this patriotic prejudice might be allayed, and as the King, George II, had never seen him act, he so contrived it that on the night when the dancers were to make their first appearance, his Majesty was induced to command his own performance of *Richard III*.

When the tragedy was over and the dancers entered, no respect was paid to the royal presence, all in the theatre was noise, tumult, and commotion. The King was amazed at the uproar, but being told that it was because the people hated the French, he smiled and withdrew. On that occasion a gentleman, one of the most celebrated wits of the time, who had been in attendance on his Majesty, went afterwards to the green room, and Garrick, anxious to know how the King had been pleased, inquired what his Majesty thought of Richard. "I can say nothing on that head," replied the courtier, "but when the actor told Richard,—'The Mayor of London comes to greet you,' he roused himself, and when Taswell entered, buffooning the splendid annual, his Majesty said, 'Duke of Grafton, I like dat Lord Mayor'; and when the scene was over his Majesty exclaimed again, 'Duke of Grafton, dat is a good Lord Mayor'; and when Richard was in Bosworth-field, roaring for a horse, his Majesty said, 'Duke of Grafton, will dat Lord Mayor not come again?'"

He's Been Wrong Before

George III was a theatrical lowbrow without even George II's fine taste in music. His father, Prince Frederick, had once conceived a scheme for sponsoring a London season of all Shakespeare's plays to be produced at the rate of one a week, but son George had no high opinion of the poet. "Was there ever such sad stuff as a great part of Shakespeare?" he asked once, "only one must not say so!"

He thought Garrick "a great fidget who could never stand still," but he liked Mrs. Siddons and agreed to her appointment as "preceptress in reading to the Princesses." Yet Mrs. Siddons committed the greatest of all theatrical sins so far as he was concerned: she made him cry. Like George IV, who said he could not bear "the harrowing of the heart" that Kean's Othello gave him, George III could not stand any hint of tragedy in a play. He went to see a comedy called *The Mysterious Husband* which unexpectedly changed mood in the last act and ended with a harrowing death scene. In the midst of this, the King was heard saying to his wife in a loud voice, "Charlotte, don't look—it's too much to bear!" By royal request, the play was never done again.

A House Divided

Drury Lane has two signs that can still be seen over the doorways on either side of the foyer. One is marked "King's Side" and the other "Prince's Side." These date back to an evening when George III and his eldest son both attended the theatre. The King hated his son, and when they met in the foyer he suddenly lunged forward and smacked the Prince in the face. There was a scurry of nobles to pull the old man back, and one suspects that it was an astute publicity agent who there and then labelled the doorways and asked the respective parties to keep to opposite sides of the foyer in future.

Family Drama

Napoleon was partial to private theatricals, and the Bonaparte family used to cast pieces, sharing the parts between them. It was not in accord with the dignity of an Emperor to act, but he would be present at the entertainments. Lucien, his brother, was playing one evening in the palace at Neuilly the role of Zamore in *Alzire*. Napoleon strongly reprimanded him for appearing in costume not historically correct: "When I am striving to build up a taste for good manners and decency, the members of my family, at least, should throw no obstacle in the way of my projects."

She Could Be Amused

Queen Victoria adored the theatre all her life—as a young girl when it represented almost the only view she had of the warm, exciting world outside the cold confines of Kensington Palace; and as an old, old lady when she could forget her personal sadness in the laughter and music of Gilbert and Sullivan.

The theatre was the one place where she would readily excuse minor lapses from dignity, and laugh even if the joke were a little against herself. When she arrived at a theatre, it was the custom for the manager to meet her at the entrance and walk backwards as he held lighted candles aloft and guided her to her box. John Buckstone, the great comedian and manager of the Haymarket, was doing this one evening when the draught from an open door blew out the candles and left them all in darkness. Involuntarily he uttered one of his famous tag lines, "Now just look at that!" The Queen laughed, and allowed him to guide her on through the dark passage by hand.

Another time, walking backwards in front of her, he tripped and fell flat on his back. Once again, all he could say was, "Now just look at that!" The Queen roared with laughter.

Children's Play

Queen Victoria instilled her love of the theatre in her children from an early age.

Upon a certain occasion, Balmoral Castle was full of grown-up guests, and one evening the children were allowed to come into the drawing-room and encouraged to give one of their plays. A make-believe scene was hastily arranged by means of chairs and settees, representing supposedly the courtyard of a Norman castle. The Prince of Wales, as a gallant knight, came prancing in on horseback, just returning from the Crusades. In the courtyard he found his lady wife—the Princess Alice—and her ladies drawn up to receive him, while on near-by seats were arranged as spectators a fine array of dolls, male and female, supposedly children of the knight and his lady. The brave knight recounted his adventures with much pomp of language; at the end of the recital his wife advanced with her ladies to deliver the keys of the castle as its chatelaine. After some equally high-flown language the lady stepped back a pace or two, and swept the array of dolls with an all-inclusive gesture, saying: "And we, too, my lord, have not been idle during your absence!"

The Real Thing

Gertrude Lawrence was starring in a London play that was honored by a visit from King George VI and his Queen. As Queen Elizabeth [now the Queen Mother] entered the Royal Box, the entire audience arose to acclaim her. Miss Lawrence, watching from the wings, murmured, "What an entrance!" Noël Coward, on tiptoe behind her, added, "What a part!"

A tag to the above is a story about Miss Julie Harris when she was waiting to be presented to Queen Elizabeth II at the Kennedy Center in Washington. Watching the Queen move down the reception line, Miss Harris whispered to a fellow actor: "I could play her better than that."

The National Theatre

From Peter Hall's diaries:

Friday, 25 January 1974

Breakfast at the Savoy with a gentleman from the Post Office who is in charge of the commemorative stamps issues. What stamps should be issued for the National Theatre opening? I suggested three ideas. First, the building. Second, the building as part of the nation rather than as part of the metropolis. Third, Olivier. The man said they had great trouble in putting living persons on stamps unless they were members of the Royal Family.

Tuesday, 11 February 1975

As we were presented, the Queen asked me when the National Theatre would open. I said I didn't know. The Queen Mother asked when the National Theatre would open. I said I didn't know. The Prince of Wales asked me when the National Theatre would open. I said I didn't know. At least they all knew I was running the National Theatre.

Bring on the Clowns

"I think you are even more famous than I am," said Kaiser Wilhelm, in one of his few gracious moments when he was introduced to Grock. "Why not?" said the celebrated clown. "I'm funnier."

[78] SOCIAL STATUS

Bed-Makers

Molière was a frequent visitor to the court of Louis XIV. One day he came into the royal bedroom and finding a chamberlain there making up the royal bed, he offered to help. "What? That I would share my work with a low comedian? Never!" the chamberlain exclaimed and left the room. Another chamberlain overheard this conversation. He was a cultivated man and a bit of a poet himself. Seeing the dramatist standing there, wounded in his pride, he went up quickly to him and said, "Monsieur, would you do me the great honor of making up the King's bed with me?"

A Prince of Players

James Quin was dining one day at a party in Bath; a nobleman present, who was not illustrious for the brilliancy of his ideas, exclaimed, "What a pity it is, Quin, my boy, that a clever fellow like you should be a player!" Quin flashed his eye and replied, "What would your Lordship have me to be—a Lord?"

Unimpeachable Character

Colley Cibber commented on a well-known fellow actor of the late seventeenth century: "His character as a gentleman could have been in no way impeached, had he not degraded it by being a celebrated actor."

Climbing Up the Ladder

Cibber was the first actor admitted into the exclusive White's Club. A little later Garrick was not only accepted but was sought out by high society. His former teacher, Samuel Johnson, is cited by Boswell.

Sir, it is wonderful how little Garrick assumes. No, sir, Garrick *fortunam reverenter habet.** Consider, sir, celebrated men such as you have mentioned have had their applause at a distance; but Garrick had it dashed in his face, sounded in his ears, and went home every night with the plaudits of a thousand in his cranium. Then, sir, Garrick had under him a numerous body of people, who, from fears of his power, or hopes of his favour, or admiration of his talents, were constantly submissive to him. And here is a man who has advanced the dignity of his profession. Garrick had made a player a higher character.

Don't Let Her Marry an Actor

The daughter of a nobleman once discovered a strong passion for John Kemble, which led her father to inform the actor that he had taken effectual means to prevent any such union, but that if Mr. Kemble would relieve him of the duty of acting sentinel over his daughter by marrying some other lady within a fortnight, he would present him with four thousand pounds. Kemble accepted the terms and married Mrs. Brereton, but the money was never paid.

* "Holds his fortune in reverence."

Knighted

*Today there are always at least a dozen members of the British the-
atre who are dames and knights. Laurence Olivier was the first to be
made a peer, but the tradition is less than a century old. Macready
felt bitter when the young Queen Victoria knighted the first musician,
Henry Rowley Bishop in 1842, and wrote the following in his diary.*

This mere idealess administerer to the pleasures of a sense—as Carlyle
says, what does it all *mean?*—is honoured according to Court and Government diction, while men who have enriched the minds of their
fellow-men with new thoughts, have quickened and elevated kind and
noble feelings by the effects of their intellect and imagination are
passed by. Agh! I am sick of the whole rotten mass of stupid corrup-
tion.

*It would take more than another fifty years before Henry Irving be-
came the first British actor to be knighted. He resisted the honor for
a dozen years, when the idea was first floated; finally he accepted it on
behalf of the whole profession.*

Irving was human enough to be gratified on his own account, but he
was pleased mainly because he saw it as a symbolic recognition of the
fact that actors and actresses were not "rogues and vagabonds," but
no worse (even if no better) than any other group of men and women.
    This knighthood was a very special honour, conferred on a profes-
sion rather than an individual, and that is undoubtedly the way Queen
Victoria regarded it. She rarely spoke at an investiture, outside the
set formula, but as she knighted Irving at Windsor Castle on July 18,
1895, she said to him, 'We are very, very pleased."

Arise, Mr. Coward

On October 28, 1931, the King and the Queen attended Noël Coward's patriotic new musical *Cavalcade* at the Theatre Royal, Drury
Lane. During the second interval, the author was presented to the
King and a rumour flashed round the auditorium that he had been
knighted, there and then, in the Royal Box.

*Noël Coward was finally knighted by that King's granddaughter in
1970.*

Worker's Paradise

In 1973 the Stratford Festival of Ontario was touring the Soviet Union as the National Theatre of Canada. Critic Don Rubin traveled with the company to file reports for the Canadian Broadcasting Corporation. The day after *King Lear* opened in Moscow, Rubin asked William Hutt, the well-known actor who played Lear, to sit down for a radio interview. None of the public rooms in their hotel were quiet enough, so Rubin suggested that Hutt come to his room for the taping.

As soon as the actor entered the critic's room, he was astonished: "How come that you can get a suite at least four times the size of my room?" he asked ominously. "I'm supposed to be the bloody star of this company, while you . . ." "I honestly don't know," said Rubin, "when we arrived, this is the room I was assigned. I'd happily exchange it with you after our interview . . ." By now the actor was rushing out the door and down the staircase to lodge his complaint with the manager at once. The Soviet manager did not know any English, and by the time the company interpreter was fetched, Hutt had worked himself into a passion approaching the storm scene in *King Lear*. He demanded in his beautifully modulated voice an explanation why he, a veteran star, should be discriminated against, especially in favor of a young critic.

The manager listened to the interpreter, then the two had a little discussion, after which the interpreter turned to Hutt:

"I think I understand the reason now. The manager says that Mr. Rubin here is simply traveling with the company; he is nothing more than an observer. But you, Mr. Hutt, you are a worker, and we wanted to honor you by giving you a real worker's room."

The star was left speechless for once: never in his life had he been called—or treated as—a worker before.

CHAPTER XVI

Backstage

The Classics

*Most theatres develop their own personalities and traditions, espe-
cially if they continue as long as the Comédie Française. Arsène
Houssaye, its director in the middle of the nineteenth century, describes how the rituals are kept alive.*

Every year the Comédie Française remembers her gods. It indulges, if
only for a few moments, in meditation, and celebrates a mass to Corneille and to Molière. The youngest poets are asked to furnish a dramatic poem, an ode, or a scenic trifle, the better to celebrate the com-
memoration, just as tenors and baritones from the Opéra are asked to
come to Sainte-Clotilde or Saint-Roch to sing the *Dies Irae* and the
Requiem at a funeral mass. Only the other day we kept the anniversary of Pierre Corneille. The bust of our great poet was there, as on
an altar, in the center of that stage of which he is one of the gods. On
his brow lay the immortal laurel wreath. All his latest interpreters, or
rather the whole company of the theatre, stood reverently grouped
around him and the Tragic Muse, grasping the Sybillic palm-branch,
recited stanzas in honour of the author of *Le Cid*. The lines were by
M. de Banville; they were delivered by Mlle. Rachel. Corneille must
have been pleased.

The Relic

George Frederick Cooke drank himself to death in New York, and
was buried there. When Edmund Kean visited America some years
after, he caused the body to be taken up and removed to another
place, where he erected a monument over it. In the transition from
the old grave to the new, Kean abstracted one of the toe-bones of the
great actor, which he preserved as a relic and brought back with him
to England. On his return the Drury Lane company went to meet
him at Barnet, in order to grace his entry into the metropolis. Elliston

313

led the procession, the other actors following according to rank. On encountering Kean, they were about to welcome him, when he stopped them. "Before you say a word, my merry men," said he, with a serious air, "Behold! Fall down and kiss this relic! This is the toe-bone of the greatest creature that ever walked the earth—of George Frederick Cooke. Come, down with you all, and kiss the bone." The little black relic, not unlike a tobacco-stopper, was produced. Elliston, between doubt and reverence, fell upon his knees and kissed it. Stout Stephen Kemble dropped down with difficulty; then another came, and another, and actor after actor followed, from the beginning to the end of the line, till all had performed the ceremony.

This ridiculous relic was preserved for many years by Kean with the greatest reverence, until one day Mrs. Kean, in a moment of passion, flung it from the window into a dry well in the Duke of Portland's garden. Kean never knew the culprit, but after a long search, he gravely and sadly observed to his wife, "Mary, your son has lost his fortune. In possessing Cooke's toe-bone he was worth £10,000; now he is a beggar."

No Respect

The Gielgud-Burton production of Hamlet *ran for 185 performances, which set a new record for the play in America. It also broke a taboo.*

We are still playing to absolute capacity at the Lunt-Fontanne and could continue to do so through the coming fall season, but Richard Burton has had enough . . . Edwin Booth played Hamlet for 100 performances. Barrymore stopped at 101, for which some members of the Players' Club never forgave him. Not because he *stopped* but because he didn't stop at 99, out of respect for Booth.

Tradition

Tallulah Bankhead:

Playing Hamlet or another of Shakespeare's classic heroes is no guarantee of immortality. You have this on the authority of an actress who risked his Cleopatra only to escape by a hair the fate of Custer. Alec Guinness, one of the most brilliant actors of our time, in 1951 set himself up as Hamlet in London. Mr. Guinness is a thinker as well as an actor—a fusion encountered as seldom as Halley's comet. After much consideration, he decided to play the Dane with a beard. He won't do it again. The hue and cry was deafening. You can't play ducks and drakes with tradition in England. Had David Garrick or Sir Henry Irving or Beerbohm Tree profaned Hamlet with whiskers? No! Then let's have no more of such hanky-panky!

The Gypsy Robe

Gypsy refers to the singing and dancing chorus of the big musicals; the gypsies are the toughest, most hard-working, most fiercely dedicated bunch of professionals on Broadway. The Gypsy Robe is a dressing gown covered with souvenirs of previous musicals, and is passed from one company to another. On the first night of a new musical, the current owner brings it to the theatre and presents it to a gypsy in the new show. It can be given to anybody, man or woman. The lucky recipient will put on the robe and parade round the stage so that everybody can see it. Sometimes the company will assemble on the stage to witness the ritual, sometimes the Gypsy will visit all the dressing rooms so that everybody can see it and touch it for luck.

The Gypsy keeps the robe in his dressing room until the next Broadway musical opens. He then pins or sews some small souvenir of his own show. It might be a program, a photo of the star, or a piece of costume or a small prop, appropriately marked with the name of the show and the date. He will then take it round to the new theatre and pass it on to the Gypsy of his choice. To receive the Gypsy Robe is a colossal honor, though nobody knows who will get it until it arrives.

The history of the Robe is interesting. It started in October 1950 with a chorus singer, Florence Baum, who was appearing in *Gentlemen Prefer Blondes*. She had in her dressing room a white satin gown trimmed with maribou. One of the dancers, Bill Bradley, admired it, and as a rather camp little joke asked permission to wear it backstage to cheer up the other gypsies. The show was a huge success and a week later he sent it round to his friend, Arthur Parrington, who was due to open in *Call Me Madam*. Attached to it was a note saying that this was the famous Gypsy Robe and that to wear it backstage and thus show it to everybody would bring good luck to the show. Arthur Parrington obediently followed the instructions and was delighted that *Call Me Madam* was a huge success also. From then it went to Forrest Bonshire in *Guys and Dolls*, and so the new superstition was kicked off to a flying start. During the years that followed, the original Robe became so encrusted with souvenirs that it began to fall to pieces, and though the wardrobe mistress of *Can Can* in 1953 did her best to sew and darn it together, it finally disintegrated in 1954 and was presented to the Drama Collection at Lincoln Center where it is occasionally put on show.

Enter Ghost

In the old days of touring stock companies, actors referred to salary day with the phrase "when the Ghost walks." The phrase was said to originate from the days of Booth.

A company of players producing a Shakespearean repertoire were in desperate straits when they one day announced a performance of *Hamlet* in a small town. Salaries had been unpaid for many weeks, and there was much dissatisfaction in the company. All went well with the performance until Hamlet's line about his father's ghost: "Perchance 'twill walk again." Here the ghost broke into the scene from off-stage with the loudly-voiced answer: "Nay, 'twill walk no more until its salary is paid."

[80] TOIL AND TROUBLE

Theatrical Superstitions

It is hard to imagine another profession where so many superstitions are observed as in the theatre. Actors have always kept a considerable variety of mascots and charms around their person or in dressing rooms. I came across all the traditional objects—piglets, ivory, and "witches' root" (whatever that might be), love-knots, three-leaved clovers, children's teeth, horse-shoes. Chimney sweeps are of course lucky, so the great Eleonora Duse once accosted a blackened chimney-sweep in broad daylight to borrow his broom and sweep for a premiere. Girardi, the clown, before going on stage, always touched with the tips of his fingers a wide assortment of charms. And the playwright Sardou, who never had a flop, always wrote with a white scarf around his neck. It had been given to him by a Chinaman. In China, white is the color of mourning and by the contorted logic of most superstitions, Sardou believed that by wearing it, he could ward off bad luck.

Katharine Hepburn still crosses herself when she crosses the Martin Beck Theatre where she had flopped in The Lake more than half a

*century ago. And there is a strong belief that certain rituals or talis-
mans will keep a show running, as when Georgia Simmons distributed
"conjure pennies' to her fellow cast members in* All the Way Home,
*which the Shuberts were ready to close after three nights; after sev-
eral reprieves the play ran* 333 *performances and won the Pulitzer
Prize in* 1961. *Some actors observe a tradition that is supposed to date
back to Booth: they do not unpack their makeup box until after the
notices appear. There used to be also an initiation ceremony for young
actors who were told by their elders to piss into their dressing-room
washbasin. The following brief catalogue is taken from a little essay
on stage superstitions published in America at the turn of the century.*

Some actors insist that all their stage shoes must be kept on the floor.
If they were put on a table or in a cupboard it would ruin them. But
in some theatres keeping shoes on the floor is almost as bad, for rats
like leather and many a good pair of shoes has been ruined by them.

Almost every player has some little piece of jewelry or wearing apparel which is his or her mascot. Some people are superstitious about
an old wig band and will use it again and again, having repeated new
wigs attached to the same old band. One actress at the Illinois Theatre, in Chicago, was discovered in tears because something had become of her old hare's foot with which she applied rouge to her cheeks.

Here are some more bad luck signs: a yellow clarinet in the orchestra; to pass through a funeral; to pass another actor on the stairs; to
speak the "tag"—that is, the last line of a play—at a rehearsal; to look
through the hole in the curtain to count up the house.

The Tag Line

*The tradition of not rehearsing the "tag" or last line in a play is said
to go back to Elizabethan times. But it did not bring luck to the
young Ellen Terry.*

I played Julia in *The Rivals* very ill; it was too difficult and subtle for
me—ungrateful into the bargain—and I even made a blunder in bringing down the curtain on the first night. It fell to my lot to finish the
play—in players' language, to speak the "tag." Now, it has been a superstition among actors for centuries that it is unlucky to speak the
"tag" in full at rehearsal. So during the rehearsals of *The Rivals* I followed precedent and did not say the last two or three words of my
part and of the play, but just "mum, mum, mum!" When the first

night came, instead of dropping my voice with the last word in the conventional and proper manner, I ended with an upward inflection, which was right for the sense, but wrong for the curtain.

The unexpected innovation produced utter consternation all round me. The prompter was so much astounded that he thought there was something more coming and did not give the "pull" for the curtain to come down. There was a horrid pause while it remained up, and then Mr. Buckstone, the Bob Acres of the cast, who was very deaf and had not heard the upward inflection, exclaimed loudly and irritably: "Eh! eh! What does this mean? Why the devil don't you bring down the curtain?" And he went on cursing until it did come down. This experience made me think more than ever of the advice of an old actor: "Never leave your stage effects to chance, my child, but rehearse, and find out all about it!" How I wished I had rehearsed that "tag" and taken the risk of being unlucky!

Superstitious Actresses

A nineteenth-century periodical in Leipzig reported the following superstitions by famous actresses of the time.

Josephine Gallmeyer is always tardy in her dressing-room, because she believes it brings her bad luck to be punctual. Frederike Grossmann always executed three scrapes with her right foot before stepping on the stage. Therese Tietjens believed that the person would speedily die who shook hands with her over the threshold at parting. Rachel and Mars claimed to have celebrated their greatest successes immediately after they had met a funeral. The petite Déjazet always made her entrance with a tiny seed in her mouth, which she would throw away as soon as she had to open her lips. Once she dropped the seed from her mouth when the Marquis de V. made a proposal of marriage to her, and she rejected him for fear of an unhappy marriage. A story is also told of a Viennese tragedienne who never plays unless she has a white mouse in her bosom, which some claim to have often seen peeping from his singular hiding place.

Auspicious Opening

Similar beliefs have held sway in otherwise widely different countries as the following passage shows by Vladimir Nemirovitch-Dantchenko, who was co-founder, with Stanislavsky, of the Moscow Art Theatre.

October 14 was definitely settled as our opening day. This date was due to a gypsy woman. I never indulged in superstition, nor in "pre-destination from on high," yet nowhere did superstition rule with such power as in the theatre. And the circumstances and the whole activity of the theatre are so constituted as to cause human beings to yield to it; it would be beyond me to make a count of all the numerous instances that came within my experience . . .

Gneditch once wrote a one-act play called *Foul Weather*, which was not at all bad. Just as it was about to be put on in St. Petersburg, before the raising of the curtain, Svobodin, the actor who was to play the chief role, died behind the wings; so the play was abandoned. Later I wanted to present it at one of my school performances, but during a rehearsal the brother of the leading actress met with a tragic death. Many years went by. Somehow I happened to ask our actress Muratova, who was engaged in the school of the Art Theatre, "What do you intend to put on next?" She replied: "I've just distributed among my pupils their parts for Gneditch's *Foul Weather*. Do you know, it's a very good play." Involuntarily, I cried out; though right after that I laughed. And, of course, I made no explanation for my outcry. But this time, again, the play did not go on, because, as it happened, Muratova herself died.

When we produced Maeterlinck's *The Intruder*, things went wrong from the start, and the play had no success. During every performance something happened: either the curtain refused to close, or the iron curtain collapsed, or the understudy of the leading lady fell dangerously ill. The actors began to implore us to take the play off.

I conceived the idea of producing *Faust*, having Stanislavsky in mind for the role of Mephistopheles. Stanislavsky smiled, shrugged his shoulders, and said: "But I must tell you, I've wanted to play Mephistopheles quite a number of times, but each time I tried it some kind of misfortune took place in my family."

The landlord of our theatre, Stchukin, a simple merchant, who would not even destroy rats for fear of vengeance, brought a gypsy woman to me in order that she might foretell on what day the theatre should be opened. In response to my jesting tone he touched my shoulder and said: "Believe me, there'll be 'antoniasm'—instead of 'enthusiasm.' " The gypsy gave me a list, as she expressed it, of "decisive" days, which meant dangerous or risky days. And she said: "When you begin a big business, remember this: take a day that's of 'no particular account' "; by which she meant that it mustn't be a Saturday, a Sunday, a Monday; "take a kind of middle figure," i.e. not a five, or a ten, or a fifteen. So Stchukin and I chose for the opening day a Wednesday, the 14th of October; and, oddly enough, it was revealed years afterwards, the famous Small Theatre of Moscow had had its opening 74 years before also on Wednesday, October 14.

Someone Should Tell NBC

Joseph Harker, the famed scenic designer of the turn of the century almost came to grief once.

In designing the scenery for *Chu Chin Chow* I overlooked the fact that peacocks were tabu in stage circles, and included them in a scheme of decoration for some panelling. Realising almost at the last moment before delivering the scenes that I had made a blunder, I painted out the peacocks and substituted turkeys!

There is perhaps no superstition more widely adhered to in theatre-land than that which holds that peacocks are harbingers of evil, though I know some others that are only a little less firmly believed in. There are few actresses, for example, and perhaps still fewer actors—for I believe the men are even more superstitious than the women—who would cheerfully resign themselves to occupying a dressing room numbered 13. Whistling in a dressing-room, again, is considered by some to be unlucky, the only way of conciliating the gods who have been offended in this way being for the whistler to turn about three times—turn completely round, that is—leave the room for a minute, and re-enter, taking care to knock thrice on the door before doing so!

Here I am reminded that David Belasco, the great American producer, will not in any circumstances tolerate the use of flowers of any arresting colour, notably red, in his productions, because he believes, doubtless for the soundest of reasons, that they distract attention. I remember seeing a play in Paris in which some mirrors were conspicuous objects in a boudoir scene. They were not important in the sense that the action of the piece depended on their existence in the scene, but were merely adjuncts, or intended as such, to the interior represented. As it happened, however, they obtruded on one's notice to the extent of monopolising a very large share of the attention that should have been given to the play; they reflected every light in the house, completely ruining the effect not only of the scene, but of the act. To obviate this the mirrors, in most theatres, would have been frosted, or soaped—the latter a very common device.

Break a Leg

The British actor Richard Huggett has written a fascinating book about theatrical superstitions. He explains the reasons behind the rituals of strange wishes for opening nights.

To wish good luck to another person, so they say, is to part with it yourself. It also means that you are inviting the hostile and rather contemptuous intervention of the gods if you draw attention to your desperate need for fortune. I knew one neurotic actor who would go quietly berserk if anybody wished him good luck, or sent a telegram, or tried to give him a first-night present. He would creep on stage by a back entrance, avoiding like the plague meeting or even seeing anybody on the way.

In recent years a curious and rather repulsive tradition borrowed from the Continent has grown up of offering gruesome first-night wishes like "break a leg" or "fall down backward" or just a stream of good-natured obscenities. But usually actors say pleasant, encouraging things like "be brilliant" or "enjoy yourself" or "have a marvelous time." A popular greeting much quoted by wits is Dorothy Parker's famous telegram to Uta Hagen, "a hand on your opening and may your parts grow bigger," and in America "knock them for a loop" has gained wide currency.

Among the older actors a popular greeting was "skin off your nose" and this according to Tenniel Evans has a special significance. It apparently referred to the bad old days, before Mr. Leichner came to our rescue, when makeup was crude, coarse, and untested and when applied it invariably had a disastrous effect on the skin which started to peel off in patches. This is why the actors in the early part of the nineteenth century could always be identified by their blotchy complexions. So if you said "skin off your nose," you were in effect hoping that the actor would be in a position where he must continue to apply his makeup; in other words, to be in work, and that is the best wish you can extend to any actor.

Bad Luck

Noël Coward once informed the press that the only superstition he had ever had was that it was bad luck to sleep thirteen in a bed. Before the opening of his play *Waiting in the Wings* in 1960, Marie

Lohr went to Saint Mark's Church and prayed long and hard for a good first night. On the way to the theatre she slipped and broke her arm. "No good deed ever goes unpunished," was Coward's comment.

The Scottish Play

Richard Huggett's book on theatrical superstitions is called The Curse of Macbeth, *because this tragedy is considered so unlucky that it is hardly ever called by name inside the profession. People usually refer to it with such euphemisms as "that play," "the unmentionable," or "the Scottish play." It is supposed to be bad luck to quote from the play or to use any sets, costumes, or props from a production. The play partly acquired its evil reputation because of the witches and partly because tradition traces a long line of disasters back to its premiere on August 7, 1606, when Hal Berridge, the boy actor playing Lady Macbeth, was said to have died backstage during the performance. Michael Billington mentions, among others, mishaps associated with the following productions at the Old Vic: in 1934 four actors played Macbeth in a single week: Malcolm Keen (lost his voice), Alistair Sim (bad chill), Marius Goring (sacked by Lilian Baylis), and John Laurie; in 1937 Laurence Olivier's first Macbeth had to be postponed three days after a change of directors and because the death of Lilian Baylis; in 1954, the portrait of Lilian Baylis crashed down on to the bar during opening night. The 1980 production starring Peter O'Toole became infamous as an artistic disaster; it was referred to as "The Harry Lauder Show," after the Scottish music-hall comedian. William Redfield wrote of a* Macbeth *mishap:*

The actor playing Macbeth died in the midst of an opening night: I do not mean he gave a bad performance; I mean he plain dropped dead. Mr. Geoffrey Toone, who played Banquo on Broadway with Michael Redgrave and Flora Robson, was nearly dispatched one evening during the second scene with the Three Murderers. An over-zealous Third Murderer shoved a dagger into Mr. Toone's ear. Later, Mr. Toone was discovered sitting at his dressing-room table, his ear heavily bandaged, and staring at himself in the mirror. He was murmuring, "He's too keen, that chap. He's just too keen."

Voodoo *Macbeth*

In 1935 John Houseman was put in charge of the Negro Theatre Project of the Works Progress Administration and he hired the twenty-year-old Orson Welles to direct an all-black Macbeth *at the Lafayette Theatre in Harlem. They decided to set the play in early nineteenth-century Haiti and, as Houseman describes in the first volume of his memoirs, they stressed the supernatural aspects of the play.*

We had chosen the cast together: Jack Carter, the creator of Crown in the original *Porgy*, was the Thane, with Edna Thomas as his murderous lady. For the Macduffs we had Maurice Ellis and Marie Young; J. Louis Johnson was the Porter, Canada Lee was Banquo and Eric Burroughs (a graduate of London's RADA) played Hecate, a composite figure of evil which Welles had assembled out of fragments of witches' lines and to whose sinister equipment he presently added a twelve-foot bullwhip. Our supernatural department was very strong at the Lafayette. In addition to the witches and sundry apparitions called for by the Bard, we had a troupe of African drummers commanded by Asadata Dafora Horton (later minister of culture of the Republic of Sierra Leone). Except for their leader, who had a flawless Oxford accent, they spoke little English: the star of the troupe, Abdul, an authentic witch doctor, seemed to know no language at all except magic. Their first act, after they had been cast in *Macbeth*, was to file a formal requisition for five live black goats. These were brought into the theatre by night and sacrificed, hugger-mugger, according to approved tribal ritual, before being stretched into resonant drum skins.

The music for the production was composed by Virgil Thomson, who had problems with the voodoo spells.

One day, after Orson, Virgil, and I had been auditioning their voodoo numbers, we complained to Asadata that his chants did not sound evil enough. Virgil, as usual, got right down to the point.
    "Are those really voodoo?"
    "Oh, yes. Yes, indeed, Sirs. That is absolutely real, authentic voodoo."
    "They don't sound wicked enough."
    "Sirs, I . . ."
    "Sometimes for the theatre you have to exaggerate."
    "I am sorry, Sirs. You can't be any more wicked than that!"
    . . . Finally Asadata admitted what those chants of his really were: they were strong spells intended to *ward off* beriberi—not to induce it. He dared not give us the real thing, he explained. It might have worked.

In fact, the production was a tremendous success, a hallmark in the history of American Theatre. Even after its ecstatic opening, the spells continued to ward off evil. When the whole Negro Theatre was attacked by Percy Hammond, the drama critic of the Republican Herald Tribune, as "one of Uncle Sam's experimental philanthropies" which "gave us last night an exhibition of deluxe boondoggling," he failed to reckon with the consequences.

Early in the afternoon of April 15, the day of the Macbeth reviews, Orson and I were formally visited in my office by Asadata Dafora Horton and his corps of African drummers, including Abdul, the authentic witch doctor. They looked serious. Asadata was their spokesman. They were perplexed he said, and desired guidance. He then produced a sheaf of clippings from which he detached the *Herald Tribune* review. He had read it to his men he declared, and it was their opinion and his, that the piece was an evil one. I agreed that it was.

"The work of an enemy?"

"The work of an enemy."

"He is a bad man?"

"A bad man."

Asadata nodded. His face was grim as he turned to his troupe, to Abdul in particular and repeated what I had said. The men nodded, then silently withdrew. Excited by waves of praise and a line a block long at the box office, we quickly forgot both them and Percy Hammond. We stayed for the night's performance, which was better played and no less enthusiastically received than the first. We thanked the company, had a brief, violent personal row on the sidewalk over the *Times* notice in which my name had been coupled with Orson's as director, then went home to get some sleep.

It was reported to us by our disturbed house manager when we arrived at the theatre around noon of the next day that the basement had been filled, during the night, with unusual drumming and with chants more weird and horrible than anything that had been heard upon the stage. Orson and I looked at each other for an instant, then quickly away again, for in the afternoon paper which we had picked up on our way uptown was a brief item announcing the sudden illness of the well-known critic Percy Hammond. He died some days later—of pneumonia, it was said.

[81] GHOST STORIES

Ghosts of Drury Lane

W. Macqueen-Pope was a theatre historian and author of several books on Drury Lane, where he worked for many years.

There is a story of a screaming woman in the green room and back-stage. That sound can certainly be heard—or something very like it—but it is a trick of the wind. When poor Clifford Heatherley died with tragic suddenness in *Crest of the Wave* many of the company swore they saw his ghost on the stage that night. He played the Ghost of Henry VIII and many were certain they saw him.

Richard Huggett:

[Another ghost at the Theatre Royal] is clearly a former actor be-cause he confines his activities to the stage and the dressing rooms and contrives to make his presence felt in many different ways. On first nights he goes to the dressing rooms and helps the suffering ac-tors on with their clothes. . . . Betty Jo Jones, the American actress, who was in the original *Oklahoma!* company in 1947, told the thea-tre's publicity director W. Macqueen-Pope, that one evening she was playing a small scene upstage. It was a comedy scene, she was young and inexperienced, and, in addition, the wide-open spaces of the Drury Lane are death to comedy. Suddenly she felt a pair of hands grip her and steer her, firmly but gently, down to the foot-lights. This is where she was forced to play out her scene, much to the bewilderment of others on the stage. She was later asked for an explanation, but nobody believed her when she told them what had actually happened. The second night the same thing happened. She was standing upstage, ready to start her small comedy scene, when the hands propelled her down to the footlights, and the scene which had been coldly received started to get laughter. The following night it happened again, and with the confidence born of experience, she played her scene and was rewarded with a round of applause.

Happy Ghost

In The Lost Theatres of London, *historian Joe Mitchenson describes the ghosts of the Royalty Theatre, demolished in 1953.*

The ghost of a lady of the Queen Anne period, who had been murdered and found in the basement of one of the original houses, was
said to descend the stairs and disappear in the middle of the vestibule.

A similar story involved the ghost of a gypsy girl with a tambourine,
who appeared only when the orchestra was playing. Her presence was
explained by the reputed discovery of a body entombed in a hollow
wall at the time of one or other of the re-constructions of the theatre.

These stories have had long currency in the annals of haunted theatres but they are insignificant compared with the definite first-hand
evidence of the appearance of Fanny Kelly herself, as late as 1934,
when a lady in Victorian costume was seen by the present author
seated in the prompt side box at a rehearsal of *Murder in Motley*.
This was but one of her many reputed appearances, wandering gently
and happily, in daylight around the theatre, observed by attendants,
actors and playgoers alike.

Spooky

Lincoln's Inn Theatre in London was closed in 1732.

The last piece performed was, it was said, *Harlequin and Dr. Faustus*, and the company included a whole troupe of stage friends. When
the final performance was over, and the time came for the payment
and dispersal of the company, there remained over "a supernumerary
demon," the real article presumably, for he asked no wages but "flew
up to the ceiling, made his way through the tiling and tore away one-
fourth of the house." This was surely a good reason for closing the
rest of the edifice.

Minimalism

Samuel Beckett is a very shy and private man. He rarely grants interviews and avoids television in particular. Martin Esslin recalls that
during one of Beckett's productions in London the BBC prevailed
upon him and filmed a half-hour with the playwright in the theatre.
Beckett seemed very ill at ease with the camera, and sure enough,
when the film was developed, they found absolutely nothing on it.

[82] SCANDALOUS GOSSIP

God Stand Up for Bastards!

The notion of Sir William D'Avenant being more than a poetical child only of Shakespeare was common in town, and Sir William himself seemed fond of having it taken for the truth.

Shakespeare, in his frequent journeys between London and his native place, Stratford-upon-Avon, used it to lie at D'Avenant's, at the Crown in Oxford. He was very well acquainted with Mrs. D'Avenant; and her son, afterwards Sir William, was supposed to be more nearly related to him than as a godson only. One day, when Shakespeare was just arrived, the boy was sent for from school, and a head of one of the colleges, who was pretty well acquainted with the affairs of the family, met the child running home and asked him whither he was going in so much haste: the boy said, "To my godfather, Shakespeare." "Fie, child," says the old gentleman, "why are you so superfluous? Have you not learnt yet that you should not use the name of God in vain?"

William the Conqueror

Another famous and probably apocryphal story about the prolific Shakespeare comes from an actor of his company, Nicholas Tooley, who noted the following in his diary under March 13, 1601.

Upon a time when Burbage played Richard III, there was a citizen grew so far in liking with him that before she went from the play she appointed him to come that night unto her, by the name of "Richard the Third." Shakespeare, overhearing their conclusion, went before, was entertained, and at his game ere Burbage came. Then, message being brought that Richard the Third was at the door, Shakespeare caused return to be made, that William the Conqueror was before Richard the Third.

Owning Up to It

There were many actresses following the Restoration who led lives more interesting off stage than on it. Several of them became royal or aristocratic mistresses. Mrs. Oldfield was widely supposed to have had an affair with George Farquhar, the playwright, and to have been

*the "Penelope" of his amatory correspondence. She lived successively
with Arthur Manwaring, "one of the most accomplished characters
of his age," and General Churchill: by each she had a son.*

Mrs. Oldfield acquired a graceful carriage in representing women of
high rank, and expressed their sentiments in a manner so easy, natural, and flowing, that they appeared to be of her own general utterance. Notwithstanding her amorous connexions were publicly
known, she was invited to the house of women of fashion, as conspicuous for unblemished character as elevated rank. Even the royal family
did not disdain to see Mrs. Oldfield at their levees. George the Second
and Queen Caroline, when Prince and Princess of Wales, often condescended to converse with her. One day the Princess told Mrs. Oldfield she had heard that General Churchill and she were married: "So
it is said, may it please your royal highness," replied Mrs. Oldfield,
"but we have not owned it yet."

Not in Garbo's Version

Queen Christina of Sweden was at the comedy one day with Queen
Anne, the mother of Louis XIV. She lolled in a posture so indecent
that her feet were higher than her head; she showed what ought to
be concealed by even the least modest of women.

The Queen Mother told many ladies that she had been sorely
tempted to slap her, and that she would have done so if the place
had not been public. Mlle. de Montpensier, who did not like Christina because, she said, "this Queen of the Goths did not see fit
to return the visit I paid her," says also that she saw Christina at the
comedy one day dressed like a man, except for a skirt, sitting in the
middle of the theatre, hat on head, her legs raised and crossed.

Ample Flesh

Most of the great actresses in the reign of Le Roi Soleil were superb
creatures who in addition to harmony of countenance had the pleasant and thoroughly appreciated grace of abundant flesh. Mme. Raisin, says Bois-Jourdain, "had plenty of bosom and was extremely gar-
nished with haunches, which endeared her to the Great Dauphin,
son of Louis XIV. Despite his devoutness, he permitted himself the
indulgence of taking her as a mistress, for he loved good cheer and
ample flesh. He gave her a child (Mlle. Fleuri), somewhat absent-

mindedly perhaps, for it is claimed that his favorite habit was to substitute for the procreative enjoyments a more piquant one offered him
by the beautiful nipples of the indulgent Mme. Raisin. He never lay
with his mistress on Friday, and sent her that day to her pacified
husband, the actor Raisin but made her promise strict abstinence.
La Raisin took advantage of this weekly rest not to fast but to give
herself to her other lover, the poet Campiston, who was also a gour-
met of luxurious breasts."

Memories

Arsène Houssaye:

Mlle. Georges came to ask me yesterday to give a performance for
her benefit. "You'll save me from starving," she said. I looked at her
in surprise for she wore a magnificent hat and feathers and primrose
kid gloves. "You are thinking how well all this still becomes me, are
you not, my dear Director?" she asked, smiling.

Thereupon she took a small glass from her pocket and looked at
herself mincingly. I became thoroughly alarmed, for she looks seventy-
five when she speaks, and eighty when she smiles. She proposed to me
to edit her *Memoirs*. I took her at her word there and then, and
tried to gather material for the chapter on Napoleon. "Is it true that
he sent for you long after midnight, and that he forgot that you were
there until morning, absorbed as he was in the map of Europe?"
"Pure slander," she replied with dignity. "He knew what was due to
me and what was due to him. His map of Europe. I was his map of
Europe."

Mlle. Georges made her last bow to the public in that performance
for her benefit. She played *Rodogune*. They filled her money-box—
no small matter—consequently the seats fetched fabulous prices. The
Emperor paid for his seat right imperially. King Jerome paid for his
right royally with a thousand-franc note. "Alas!" remarked the great
tragic actress, "I preferred the times when he sent me 'love notes' "—
for Mlle. Georges had known all the crowned heads of the Imperial
family.

Streaking

On December 17, 1913, during a performance at the Opéra Royal, a
man appeared suddenly in the costume of Adam before the fall, ran

down the center aisle jostling some spectators, and stood in front of the orchestra, gravely "conducting." He was the chauffeur of one of the automobiles waiting outside the theatre. The performance was not even interrupted as he was hustled off to the asylum.

Where Are They Now?

The most famous and enduring burlesque show in the history of the theatre is the Folies-Bergère. It began in 1869 and after some changes became a fixture of Paris nightlife in the mid-1880s. Early in our century, the final number was called The Living Curtain, *composed of twenty unclad—and purportedly female—bodies. A historian of the French theatre, looking at a photograph of* The Living Curtain, *followed up on what became of the twenty.*

A close examination of the portraits necessitates one sad revision. Three of the faces are indubitably the faces of men. Let us face it. The Folies-Bergère caters to all tastes.

One of the three female impersonators murdered a female member of *The Living Curtain* of a previous production when he found her in the bed of a banker whom he was planning to blackmail on his own account. Another joined a Jesuit order. The third became a bookseller without license on the Seine—the books he sold being the popular pornography of the day.

Of the seventeen legitimate females, six graduated into high-class brothels and were never heard of again. Two married industrialists, one a manufacturer of toys, the other of motor-cars. Two established successful dress shops, the back rooms of which were used for rendezvous between their expensive women clients and men they were not married to. Two committed suicide and were buried in unhallowed ground at the public expense. One wrote a bawdy novel which became the bestseller of the day. Four married ordinary men, joined churches and raised families. The seventeen women yielded among them ninety-six abortions and eleven children.

CHAPTER XVII

Disasters and
Beyond

It Brought the House Down

When Sir Charles Sedley's comedy of *Bellamira* was performed, the roof of the theatre fell down, by which, however, few people were hurt except the author. This occasioned Sir Fleetwood Shepherd to say, "There was so much fire in his play, that it blew up the poet, house and all." "No," replied the good-natured author, "the play was so heavy that it broke down the house, and buried the poor poet in his own rubbish."

America's Sweetheart

One of the most popular child actors in the middle of the nineteenth century was a teenage idol called Miss Mary Marsh, who toured with the Marsh Juvenile Troupe.

The entire company was composed of children. As they died—and the mortality rate among them was remarkable—or as they grew too large for the troupe, their places were filled by other precocious infants, engaged by their clever manager in his strollings from town to town.

Little Mary Marsh was an uncommonly attractive child, bright-eyed, graceful, fresh, and fair. The boy between eight and fifteen in her audiences who did not succumb to her loveliness was only fit for treason, stratagem and spoils. The passion the child inspired in the breasts of her adorers was a pure one, and, except in the neglect of a prosy lesson or two, it did no harm. Her memory is still kept green in the hearts of many practical men of to-day, who unblushingly confess to a filling of their boyish eyes and a quivering of their boyish lips when the sad story of her untimely and dreadful death was told here. While playing in one of the Southern cities, her dress took fire from the footlights and she was fatally burned, living but an hour or two after the accident occurred.

Spectre

In a performance of *The Burning Bridge* at the Surrey Theatre, Henry Kemble got his long robes so entangled in a set piece that he pulled down with it every morsel of scenery on the stage, with the exception of some orange trees, discovering only bare walls and flooring. At the conclusion of the play, a female spectre had to rise from a lake surrounded by mist, an effect in these primitive times, produced by lamps placed behind gorgons, and surrounding the figure. When the machine had nearly mounted to the flies, one of the gorgons took fire, and the spectre's dress was presently in a blaze. The spectre, a man, strove hard to get rid of his gear, and in doing so disclosed to the audience that he was a Scotsman with a kilt on, being cast for the part of Waverley which was to follow. The humour of the situation once more obscured the serious nature of the predicament, to extricate himself from which the terrified actor jumped from a great height to the stage, and seriously injured himself.

Sheridan Loses a Theatre

Drury Lane was a mine of wealth to Sheridan, and with a little care might have been really profitable. The lawsuits, the debts, the engagements upon it, all rose from his negligence and extravagance. But Old Drury was doomed. On February 24, 1809, soon after the conclusion of the performances, it was announced to be in flames. Rather it announced itself. In a few moments it was blazing—a royal bonfire. Sheridan was in the House of Commons at the time. The reddened clouds above London threw the glare back even to the windows of the House. The members rushed from their seats to see the unwonted light, and in consideration for Sheridan, an adjournment was moved. But he rose calmly, though sadly, and begged that no misfortune of his should interrupt the public business. His independence, he said—witty in the midst of his troubles—had often been questioned, but was now confirmed, for he had nothing more to depend upon. He then left the House, and repaired to the scene of conflagration.

Not long after, Kelly found him sitting quite composed in "The Bedford," sipping his wine as if nothing had happened. The musician expressed his astonishment at Mr. Sheridan's sang-froid. "Surely," replied the wit, "you'll admit that a man has a right to take his wine by his own fireside." But Sherry was only drowning care, not disregarding it. The event was really too much for him, though perhaps he did not realize the extent of its effect at the time. In a word, all he had in the world went with the theatre. Nothing was left either for him or the principle shareholders. Yet he bore it all with fortitude, till he heard that the harpsichord, on which his first wife was wont to play, was gone too. Then he burst into tears.

Free at Last

The great fire which destroyed Covent Garden in 1807 also set free Mother Goose.

The goose was a very light and airy affair made of basket-work covered with down and feathers. In this, little bandy-legged Leonard used to waddle up and down the stage in the most natural manner. While the theatre was burning, the immense draught of heated air took Goosey from her perch in the property-room and drew her swiftly through the window, when with extended wings she soared aloft and sailed gracefully over the heads of the admiring crowd, away across Bow Street and Long Acre and on towards Lincoln's Field.

It Is the Cause

Olive Logan, writing in 1870, mentions one of the hazards to audiences.

A woman in Saginaw, Michigan, was some months ago taken insane while witnessing a play, and carried out of the theatre to a lunatic asylum. A wag suggested that the reason she went mad was because the acting was so bad.

Near Miss

Forbes-Robertson was nearly killed by a careless carpenter during a rehearsal of *Caesar and Cleopatra* on the stage of a Liverpool theatre. In the middle of one of Caesar's speeches a hammer fell from the grid missing Robertson by inches. He merely paused for a second, looked up, said quietly, "Please don't do that again," and continued his speech.

Physical Proximity

Actors moving about on a crowded stage are prone to all the mishaps and injuries that afflict dancers and acrobats. But, more than these other performers, they also have to portray grand passions convincingly on stage. Inevitably accidents happen with daggers and rapiers, resulting even in death. Sometimes the injuries are invisible to the audience and inaudible to the afflicted.

Patrick Tovatt tells the story of when he was playing in *Long Day's Journey into Night* with A.C.T. in San Francisco, his colleague and good friend David Grimm struck him as required by the text, but somewhat carelessly that his left eardrum was shattered. They specially rehearsed it so that Grimm would hit Tovatt on the right side for the rest of the run, carefully avoiding the ear, so that at least he would hear his cues. Things went well until a year later the production was revived and on the last night of a lengthy tour Grimm forgot himself and shattered Tovatt's other ear.

Adale O'Brien was in a production of The Trojan Women *that Jon Jory directed at the Long Wharf Theatre in New Haven.*

A certain young lady who was playing Cassandra had a tendency to become very frustrated if she felt her scene was not going well, so she would use the frenzy of her part to strike whoever happened to be standing next to her on stage. David Spielberg, the young actor playing Talthybius, had sustained half a dozen of these maulings and even discussed the problem with some of us older actors:
   "What shall I do?"
   "Hit the bitch back," growled Martin Macguire playing Menelaus.
   "I can't do that," said Spielberg, out of an old-fashioned sense of chivalry perhaps. Instead, he went on to devise his own revenge. One night Cassandra was almost hysterical, feeling totally alienated from the audience, and mid-scene she brought her arm practically from the floor to take a swing at Talthybius, scoring a direct hit at his mouth with the back of her hand. The young man could feel the blood dripping from his cut lip, and without missing a beat he turned to a couple of sentinels up on the parapets of Troy: "Guards, take her away!" And the two extras grabbed the astonished actress and dragged her off stage with half her scene still to come.

Revenge

Occasionally an actor is so overcome by his own passions, rather than following those of the script, that tragedy ensues. Macklin's temper killed a fellow-actor over a wig; William Terriss, a much-loved actor of the late Victorian era, was assassinated at the stage door of the Adephi in London by a disgruntled extra. But the Grand Guignol of such stories was reported in newspapers; it comes from Japanese-occupied China in the 1930s, a town called Dairen in Kuantung province.

After an astonished silence, the audience burst into wild applause. They had just witnessed the end of a sad love scene, most convincingly acted by Liu Shu-Ku, famous for his female roles and another well-known actor. Suddenly a third performer rushed on stage from the wings, brandishing a dagger. Shouting revenge he stabbed both lovers to death. Then he strode downstage and plunged the knife dramatically into his own heart. After the applause died down, it took the audience some moments to realize that these deaths were too real. As the bodies were cleared, they learned that the assassin was an actor who had been recently dismissed from the company. By committing suicide on stage he might have imagined that he was murdering theatre itself.

[84] ANIMAL STUNTS

A Fatal Trap

In one scene of a piece entitled *The Fire Worshippers* at the Surrey Theatre one of the actors had to ride across the stage on a live camel adorned with gorgeous trappings. Suddenly an open trap gave way beneath its weight, and the poor animal was the next moment lying wedged in the aperture with its neck broken. The actor saved himself by leaping off. The play had to proceed, and a new piece was to follow, but it was impossible to extricate the unfortunate beast, which presently expired, having had the chief situations performed over his body, while men were busy below cutting him out piecemeal.

Starring Horse

A representation of Corneille's tragedy of *Andromeda* in 1682 occasioned great excitement in Paris owing to the introduction of a real horse to play the part of Pegasus. The horse was generally regarded as a kind of Roscius of the brute creation, and achieved an extraordinary success. Adorned with wings and hoisted up by machinery, he neighed and tossed his head, pawed and pranced in mid-air after a very lively manner.

Mazeppa

By the early nineteenth century there was an entire genre of equestrian drama, and special buildings, called hippodromes, were erected later to house them. In 1861 the boyish-looking sex-star Adah Isaacs Menken took on Mazeppa, a perennial favorite with audiences, in which she was strapped on to a supposedly wild stallion and carried off stage. Often no male equestrians could be found to perform the stunt and a dummy was used instead. Adah approached Captain John P. Smith, a producer of such attractions.

"I found her nervous and anxious," wrote the Captain, "full of trepidation, as she dressed or rather undressed for the part. I assured her there was no danger and that she had only to hold on like grim death, and the mare 'Belle Beauty' would do the rest."

The Captain was, however, too sanguine in his expectations. The mare, who had been trained to a specific routine, was upset by changes made by Adah. Nervous and fidgety, as the mare ran up the inclined runway, her foot slipped and she plunged off, falling with a terrible crash to the stage below with Menken strapped to her back. Smith was terrified. He was certain that his star had been killed. "We lifted Menken, pale as a ghost, nearly lifeless, the blood streaming from her beautiful shoulder. Then with the help of the tackle, we raised 'Belle Beauty.'"

After both woman and mare had recovered from their fall, rehearsals were resumed and the mare successfully carried the beauty on her back up the steep runway, built like a spiral so that everyone in the audience would have a long view of so much alluring charm.

Hamlet's Dog

*The Victorian actor Frederick Warde got his early chance as a
stage manager in Leeds. The staple was melodrama, Shakespeare,
and animal acts. Or sometimes a mixture.*

The star for the week was a "Dog-man," that is to say, he brought
with him two trained dogs that appeared in the play. They seized
the villain when he was attacking the hero, rescued the heroine in
distress, brought in the lost will at the critical moment, or something
of that sort. The play was *The Forest of Bondy, or the Dog of Mon-
targis*. It was to have run for the week, but it did not please. The
proprietor sent for me and instructed me to change the bill. I knew
the star had no repertoire, so I asked what play he would suggest. He
replied: "Give 'em some Shakespeare, put up *Hamlet*."

I found our Dog-man star and told him of the manager's suggestion. He was delighted with it. Said he: "A good idea. Use the
dogs,—Hamlet's dog, let him sieze the King in the last act." I inquired if he had ever played Hamlet. He replied, "No, but that's all
right, I'll wing the beggar," meaning that he would read over the
lines in the wings and then go on and speak them before they had
left his memory.

As Hamlet speaks considerably more than a thousand lines, this
was a startling proposition. However, I called a rehearsal for the following morning. Our Dog-man came with a book of the play he had
bought on his way to rehearsal. He separated the uncut leaves with
a letter opener and began to read the part. Its length surprised him,
and turning to me he remarked in a strong Cockney dialect, "The
bloomin' Dane cackles, don't he, Cully?" He floundered through the
first scene until he reached Hamlet's soliloquy beginning, "Oh, that
this too too solid flesh would melt," etc. That was too much for him.
He admitted defeat and departed abruptly, taking his dogs with him.
We substituted stock plays to fill out the week.

[85] FALLING SETS

*It has been said that people will always go to see live performances
simply on the chance that, on their particular night, the sets might
come crashing down. My own long wait finally came to an end during
a recent visit of the Grand Kabuki to Los Angeles; the curtain of*

Royce Hall at UCLA was brought down and after ten minutes the performance resumed to applause. Many anecdotes of theatrical disasters portray the set as the real antagonist.

Balcony Scenes

Lady Benson tells a story of playing once in *Romeo and Juliet*, in which the balcony was composed of dress baskets. She had been warned that the construction was so flimsy that she must not walk about, but forgetting this in the excitement of the play, she moved to and fro, with the result that she was thrown into Romeo's arms, balcony and all.

A more laughable balcony scene occurred during a run of *The Gladiator*, when Spartacus, having overcome his opponent in the arena, looks up at the spectators seated in an elevated gallery for the signal "thumbs down." The occupants in the gallery consisted of some twelve supers and about as many minor members of the company, who were correctly dressed as to the top half of their bodies, but were wearing trousers or skirts beneath, hidden by the parapet of the gallery. Unfortunately, one night the floor of the gallery collapsed, with the result that thumbs down became feet up as some twenty-four trousered or stockinged legs were waving wildly in the air.

Convicted

In a trial scene Bransby Williams appeared at the dock habited in the ordinary manner from the waist up, but, to save time later, his lower limbs were already dressed as a convict. This was concealed by a portion of the dock, consisting of a canvas screen, which he held before him. When it came to the point where the judge passed sentence, he forgot to keep hold of the screen, and throwing up both his hands, exclaimed, "I am innocent, my lord, innocent, I swear it." Down went the screen, showing his legs already encased in trousers well marked with the broad arrows. The conflict between this evidence of guilt and his statement of innocence was too much for an audience that rocked with laughter.

Locked Doors

At one point in *The Three Musketeers* the Queen has given a private audience to D'Artagnan when the King is heard coming. Thereupon the lady-in-waiting, played in a production at the Lyceum by Eva Moore, tries to smuggle the hero out by a private door, and on finding it locked from outside, hammers wildly at it, crying, "Locked! Locked! My God, what shall I do?" On one particular evening, however, the locking had been omitted, and when Miss Moore hurled herself at it crying, "Locked, locked," she fell headlong through, leaving two feet and legs very much in view for the entertainment of the audience.

A somewhat similar accident once befell Clarice Mayne, who, however, was saved by immediate inspiration. She was supposed to be a prisoner in a room and, having tried all the doors only to find them locked, had to return to the centre of the stage moaning, "They are all locked, how can I escape?" Unfortunately as she did this one of the doors flew open and she had no choice but to walk out, an action that might have spoilt the whole plot had she not returned at once saying, "I cannot escape that way; there are armed men in the passage," and to give colour to her statement one or two stage hands at once tramped heavily up and down just out of sight.

The *Mayflower*

On September 20, 1920, three hundred years and two weeks to the day after the original Pilgrim Fathers had set out from Plymouth for the New World, the curtain rose on a musical play written to mark the historic anniversary. The setting was the Surrey Theatre, London (since demolished), the play *The Mayflower* by W. Edward Stirling and Alfred Hayes.

Determined to make their drama life-like, the authors portrayed the embarkation as realistically as possible and decided to leave nothing to "imaginary puissance." As one critic recorded, the management had been able to afford only "a very small, unseaworthy-looking vessel." Restricted as they were, the Pilgrim Fathers could do nothing but stand huddled on the deck and sing.

By the end of the first act the good ship was under full sail for the wings, when the hero, the last of the faithful band, arrived on the wharf and, diving into the water, started to haul himself up the ship's side to join his fellows. His zeal spelt disaster. Her delicate balance thrown, the *Mayflower* began to list unnervingly and then turned turtle, crashing to the stage with a sickening crunch casting Pilgrim Fathers as far as the footlights.

The curtain came down on this catastrophic scene and the audience sat in stunned silence until word filtered through from the prompt-corner that there were no casualties. When the curtain rose on Act II the *Mayflower* had made a miraculous recovery and the stage revealed the intrepid band firmly planted in New Plymouth—a sight which would have brought sighs of relief from the anxious audience, had not the first line been: "Let us give thanks to God who hath brought us safely across the ocean." Beneath waves of laughter, *The Mayflower* sank without trace.

Don't Call Me

Victor Jory was playing at the beginning of his career in a stock company. The manager had brought in a Broadway actor to star as the Caliph in one of those Eastern extravaganzas now mercifully lost in the sands of time. The sets were huge twenty-four-foot flats and fancier than usual. Jory, delivering a message to this Eastern potentate, noticed that one of the flats had begun to sway ominously, so he got up, went and propped it up with his body. The other actor, not realizing the situation, was surprised to see him gone and urgently whispered upstage: "Come back down, Victor." Victor tried frantically to signal why this would not be a good idea. After a couple more attempts to bring him down, whispered between cues and speeches, the Caliph left his throne, walked upstage, grabbed Jory's arm and dragged him downstage, closely followed by a twenty-four-foot flat, which dislodged several others, with one of them falling right through the two actors, who stood there with the set around their necks. At which point the Broadway actor looked accusingly at young Victor, stepped out of character and uttered in front of a rather large audience something not quite suitable for printing.

Paranoia

Donald Wolfit was quick to cry "conspiracy" when things went wrong. In *King Lear*, he played the storm scene standing against an eighteen-foot obelisk, which required holding in position by a man standing behind it, and thus hidden from the audience. Just before the Coronation, in 1953, the task was carried out by a patriotic stage-hand who had begun to celebrate the forthcoming event somewhat in advance of others. On the line "Strike flat the thick rotundity o' the world!" the stage-hand hiccoughed and lurched forward, causing the obelisk to strike hard the back of Wolfit's head. The actor, being enormously strong, finished the scene supporting both the obelisk and the patriot, by then paralytic. When Wolfit came into the wings, he was limping (the bump on his head was concealed by his wig and he did like his injuries to be *seen*). With furtive glances over his shoulder, the madness of Lear still upon him, he cried hoarsely at his stage director, "Pam, Pam, Binkie Beaumont* has sent men to kill me!"

[86]   EMBARRASSMENTS

The Buried Majesty of Denmark

During the time of Mr. Garrick's performance in Goodman's-fields, the stage rose so much from the lamps to the back scenery, that it was very difficult for a performer to walk properly on it, and unfortunately it was then the custom to introduce their ghosts in a complete suit, not of gilt leather, but of real armour. The dress for this august personage was one night, in honour of Mr. Garrick's Hamlet, borrowed from the Tower, and was consequently rather too ponderous for the ghost of the royal Dane. The moment, therefore, he was put up at the trap door, unable to keep his balance, he rolled down the stage to the lamps, which catching the feathers of his helmet, the ghost seemed in danger of being consumed by mortal fires, till a gentleman roared from the pit, "Help! help! the lamps have caught the cask of your spirits, and by G——— if the iron hoops fly, the house will be in a blaze." The attendants ran on the stage, carried off the ghost, and laid him in a water tub.

Old Bloopers

Mrs. Langtry at one performance said to her stage lover: "Let us retire and seek a nosy cook."

An actor at the Queen's Theatre, Manchester, turned "Stand back, my lord, and let the coffin pass," into "Stand back, my lord, and let the parson cough."

Charles Calvert, one of the most painstaking readers on the stage, was playing Henry V at the Prince's Theatre, Manchester, and he had

* Binkie Beaumont at H. M. Tennant was one of London's most powerful theatrical producers.

to say to one of his old soldiers that instead of going to battle he should have a "good soft pillow for that good white head." What he did say was "a good white pillow for that good soft head."

A well-known actor who has often been applauded by New York theatregoers, in one of his speeches intended to say, "Royal bold Caesar," but forgot himself in his excitement and said: "Boiled rolled Caesar, I present thee with my sword."

A nervous, excited young actor exclaimed: "Dare to harm one head of her hair, and the last moment shall be your next."

New Bloopers

Ray Fry:

Marie Christiansen in the production of *I Remember Mama* gathered all of us around her, including the young Marlon Brando, and said words to this effect: "Now children, because you have been all so good today, Mr. Thorkelson will read to you from *The Sale of Two Titties*."

Larry Hugo played Joey in Shaw's *Misalliance* in San Francisco. The actress in the role of Hypatia had been on a severe diet for several weeks with dubious results. In the last act, instead of the line "I obviously fascinate Patsy, and Patsy fascinates me," he said "I obviously pascinate Fatsy and Fatsy pascinates me." And, as if to rub it in, he said it not once, but three times.

Missing Parts

Esmé Percy lost his glass eye one night while he was on stage in his big scene in *The Lady's Not for Burning*. The rest of the company, led by John Gielgud and Richard Burton, were transfixed with horror. Percy called out in a frantic whisper, "Oh, do be careful, don't tread on it, they cost £8 each," and it was left to Richard Leech, a doctor as well as an actor, to step forward and retrieve it.

A comic policeman playing in a pantomime with Whimsical Walker hit the comedian so hard over the head with his truncheon that Walker's false teeth fell out and dropped into the orchestra pit, landing in the string section and hitting one of the violinists in the eye. And the late Courtenay Thorpe, handicapped after a gun accident and continuing his career with a false limb, was once criticized by a weary stage-manager, "That hand is singularly wooden in its gesture, sir."

"Well," replied Thorpe, "that may be because it is made chiefly of wood."

Debacle

One of the artistic disasters that I recall in the theatre was the opening night of Lee Strasberg's production of The Three Sisters *during the World Theatre Season of 1965. The London theatre world was eagerly awaiting an introduction to the famous Method, and the Aldwych was filled to capacity with practically every star of the British stage.*

There was little time in London to get acclimated to the raked stage of the Aldwych Theatre (the actors had to sit tilted awkwardly forword on rented antique furniture that could not be adjusted to the incline), or to work out the myriad technical problems of the production. The lighting was so poor, the actors had difficulty seeing one another. Two days before the opening Tamara Daykarhanova was knocked down in an accident, suffering a fractured arm.

But none of these problems can explain away the debacle of opening night, which was the result of "an unbelievably self-indulgent performance," in the opinion of many observers. "The calamity was Sandy Dennis," reported Strasberg. "With her nervous tics, you couldn't watch it." The artistic director had had enormous fights with her during rehearsals, but there was no ridding her of the stuttering mannerism that particularly irritated the critics. Kim Stanley, usually a tower of strength according to Strasberg, fell to pieces. She moved at a lethargic pace and indulged in interminable pauses. "She waddled on the stage . . . I don't know what she did," Strasberg remembers sadly. The curtain went up late, and the show took almost four hours because of the delays between the acts and during the scenes. The expectant English audience was greatly dismayed by what they saw, and many left before the final curtain. When Miss Dennis came out in the third act and said, "Oh it's been a terrible evening," someone yelled out, "It sure has been!" and the remaining spectators burst into laughter. The curtain came down to a shower of boos and catcalls, which stunned the cast. Laurence Olivier came backstage to comfort the actors with his supportive presence and helped cushion the blow of the catastrophic opening by sweeping the company off to a party prepared for them at which they proceeded to drink "heartily."

Not His Strong Suit

Adam Tarn was a distinguished dramaturg at the Contemporary Theatre in Warsaw and editor of the theatre journal Dialog *when, in 1968, a wave of anti-semitism drove him from his native Poland. He went into exile in Canada. As a fellow eastern European I invited him to visit the Vancouver Playhouse where I was dramaturg at the time. I took him to see a production of a Cuban play,* The Criminals, *which had been staged on our second or experimental stage by John Juliani, the major avant-garde director in Canada during the 1960s. It was one of those affairs where each audience member went through an obstacle course and finally watched the show from a cocoon-like isolation cell. Afterwards, seeing that Tarn, close to seventy, had not enjoyed the three-hour performance, I made some excuse that it was, after all, an experimental production. This provoked the following story from Tarn.*

A man went to see his tailor to order a suit. The tailor took all the usual measurements around the waist, the arms and the length of the legs and told his customer to come back in a week to try on the suit. A week passed and the man returned. The tailor brought out his nearly completed work, but when the man tried on the suit he found one leg was quite a few inches shorter than the other, one shoulder was padded and the other was not, and most curiously, the jacket had three arms. "What's the meaning of this? This suit doesn't fit at all." The tailor proudly replied: "Ah yes, sir, but you don't understand: this is my experimental suit."

If Only He Knew

Speaking of Poles and experimental theater, Bill Woodman recalls the first visit Jerzy Grotowski made to New York City in 1968. As always, the Polish director restricted attendance to just a few dozen people.

We were crammed into the tiny airless foyer of a converted church in Greenwich Village, waiting to be seated. The cream of New York theatre had turned out to see the work of this famed guru: I remember rubbing up against Hal Prince, Jerome Robbins, Joe Papp. As we waited, while trying to breathe, Nina Foch said to me: "If only Mr. Grotowski knew what was happening here, he would be mortified." I happened to look up and high above the lobby there was a sort of loggia, where Jerzy Grotowski was standing and looking down on this distinguished group, with a smile of immense satisfaction on his face.

[87] AND THE SHOW WENT ON

Pain

Sarah Bernhardt:

I remember that one day when I was playing Posthumia, an old blind woman of eighty, in *Rome Vaincue*, five minutes before going on the stage I was gripped with such agony that I rolled about the corridor sobbing. M. Perrin, the manager of the Comédie Française, sent for a doctor in a great fright. Suddenly during an abatement of the pain I heard the line that gave me my cue. I leapt up. I adjusted my white wig. And before the manager had recovered from his surprise, I had parted the curtain of the Hall of Judgment. My face racked by suffering, my forehead knit by the will to suffer no longer, all my being trembling under the sting of the agonies I had just cast out of me, made such an impression upon the public that they stamped with enthusiasm on my appearance.

I said my lines. I screamed my prayer. My shriveled hands sought for the support that my blind eyes could not see. I left the stage sustained by the applause of the audience, but on the threshold of my dressing room, the pains returned, and gripped me so violently that I lost consciousness.

The Fire-Marshal's Nightmare

The following story from the nineteenth century demonstrates, among other things, what actors had to do to acquire "sense-memory" before Stanislavsky came to the rescue.

The first night on which the musical romance of *Lodoiska* was performed, the last scene had a very natural and fine effect, from the real danger of Mrs. Crouch, the heroine, when she appeared in the blazing castle. The wind fanned the flames rather too near the place where she was stationed; she felt them, but could not retire without spoiling the scene. With true fortitude she maintained her situation at the hazard of her life, until Mr. Kelly, alarmed for her safety, flew hastily to snatch her from danger, when his foot slipped, and he fell from a considerable height. She then uttered a scream of terror, but providentially he was not hurt by the fall, and in a moment caught her in his arms. Scarcely knowing what he did, he turned to the front of the stage with rapidity and undissembled terror. Mrs. Crouch, actually scorched by the flames, and alarmed at first by Mr. Kelly's fall and then at his precipitancy, was nearly insensible of her situation; but the loud plaudits which they received from the audience, who thought their acting uncommonly excellent, roused them from their apprehensions for each other, and at the same time convinced them of the effect, which they found was far superior to any studied scene, as their danger and their fears were well timed, and perfectly in character. They profited therefore ever after from that involuntary scene, by imitating, as closely as possible, their real fears in those they were obliged to feign.

I'm All Right, Jack

Bill Woodman recalls in the 1950s that Jack Bittner was fighting a knight in one of the *Henry VI* plays at the Antioch Shakespeare Festival; the knight lost his footing on a stairway and fell down into some shrub. Jack peered over into the shrub and without missing a beat called out: "Art thou all right, knight?"

Go On Without Me

Jon Jory was directing Marat/Sade *at Louisville in 1971.*

There was this very old character actor, now deceased, with a marvelous stage presence. He was still in very good shape, walking ten miles a day. He had done a fine job as one of the inmates. About a week after the show opened, I looked in on a performance, and scanning the stage for his presence (it was one of his scenes) I realized that the old man was missing. Fearing something had happened, I rushed backstage to check whether the stage manager was taking care of him. Nobody there had noticed his absence. I found him in his dressing room calmly reading a book.

"How are you, Bob?" I greeted him.

"Oh fine, thank you."

"You're not feeling ill?"

"No, not at all," he replied.

"I don't mean to upset you," I said, "but a performance is going on upstairs, one of your scenes."

"Oh, yes, yes, I know, Jon. But you see," he explained kindly, "there are several sections of this play that I do not really approve of. I didn't want to upset you on opening night so I carried on like a trouper, but after that, I thought it best that when I did not approve of a scene, I should simply leave the stage."

[88] WHAT IT'S ALL ABOUT

Meditation on a Theme (c. 1825)

The world is the stage—men are the performers—chance composes the piece—fortune distributes the parts—the fools shift the scenery—the philosophers are the spectators—the rich occupy the boxes—the powerful have their seat in the pit, and the poor sit in the gallery—the fair sex present the refreshments—the tyrants occupy the treasury benches—and those forsaken by Lady Fortune snuff the candles—Folly makes the concert—and Time drops the curtain.

If I Could Only Do That

Many actors came from a theatrical family and wanted to go on the stage from a very early age. Few remember the actual moment when the desire moved towards a decision, the way Sir Ralph Richardson did.

I remember how the desire to act did really click, just in one moment; I can remember it vividly. I went to the Theatre Royal in Brighton and I saw Sir Frank Benson playing Hamlet. Even as a boy I read a great deal of Shakespeare, and so I knew the play fairly well. I'll always remember when the ghost appeared and he said, "Remember me," and Benson took his sword and he scratched it on the stage, there was a terrible noise, the sword moving across the floor of the stage—it was a wonderful, weird effect. "Remember me," the ghost said. It sounded like Vengeance, it sounded like Hell, where the ghost came from. It absolutely mesmerized me. "My God," I thought, "if I could do that. That's the job for me, sheer magic. Oh, goodness, if I could touch something like that," and my heart was really beating quite wildly. "Oh, oh," I thought, "if only I could be an actor, if only I could have a sword and scratch it on the floor, I wouldn't ever want to do anything else."

Kindling a Fire

Lewis Casson and Sybil Thorndike were famous for their productions of Greek drama in the Gilbert Murray translations.

We took these plays to the mining towns. And I remember the authorities saying, "Oh, are you taking tragedies down to the poor miners?" Lewis said, "I know the Welsh people, I am a Welshman, they like a tragedy." And do you know, we were playing in an old little place, and the audience was electric. They were sitting on the edge of their seats, playing the parts themselves. And one miner came round after *Medea*, which is a bit of a pill, and he said, "This is the play for us. It kindles a fire." And what more do you want to do in the theatre but kindle a fire?

I like to think that I've helped to make living people feel, in themselves, that they are working toward some better existence. I've had a very full, very rich life, with exciting work to do, all the time, and a lovely happy life in the home, and if I've made people understand more about human beings by what I've done in the theatre, then that will give me satisfaction. In fact, as the old miner said of *Medea*, "I would like to feel that I've kindled a fire."

Peace

W. Bridges-Adams was artistic director of the Shakespeare Memorial Theatre following the First World War.

After one performance, I received upon the stage a delegation from the Académie Française. In welcoming them (bearing very much in mind that Stratford could play as big a part in fostering world peace as Geneva) I said that it was a remarkable thing that throughout the war the bitterness of national hatreds could not stop Wagner from being played in London, nor Shakespeare from being played in Berlin; and that when a little time had elapsed, and old wounds were a little healed, I hoped I should have the privilege of welcoming upon that stage the representatives, not only of some, but of *all* nations, in the name of our common heritage in Shakespeare. It was a reckless thing to say at such a time, but to my amazement and relief was welcomed with a perfect storm of applause.

Rank

After the fall of France in June 1940, Louis Jouvet tried to carry on producing plays at Aix-en-Provence in the unoccupied zone. The Nazi authorities censored his plans, so he accepted an invitation to take his troupe to tour Switzerland.

Before receiving official sanction to depart, he was required to call on Lieutenant Raedeker of the German army. Arriving at eight in the morning, he was requested to wait. After several hours of waiting, Jouvet lost patience, got up, and said to one of the attending officers: "I am leaving. Tell your commander that if he is a lieutenant in the German army, I am a general in my profession."

Physician, Heal Thyself

Jean-Gaspard Deburau, the white-faced Pierrot immortalised by Jean-Louis Barrault in the film *Les Enfants du Paradis*, was a melancholy man. In one of his long neurotic depressions he went to see a highly recommended doctor called Ricod, who, after a thorough examination earnestly advised him: "I know of only one proven remedy for this type of melancholy. You must go and see a performance by the clown Deburau and, I guarantee, you will feel much better. The actor looked at him sadly and sighed: "It seems then that I must die of this malady, because I am Deburau."

He died in fact as a result of falling on stage. His funeral was said to have been attended by every beggar, thief, whore, and seamstress in Paris.

Bibliography

Sources Cited

Anonymous. *Fun for the Million, or, The Laughing Philosopher*. London, 1835.

Anonymous. *Through the Stage Door*. Chicago, 1903.

Anonymous. *Wit and Humor of the Stage*. Philadelphia, 1909.

Aye, John. *Humour in the Theatre*. London: Universal Publications, n.d. (1932/33).

Baker, H. Barton. *History of the London Stage and Its Famous Players*. London, 1904.

Baker, Roger. *Drag: A History of Female Impersonation on the Stage*. London: Triton, 1968.

Bankhead, Tallulah. *Tallulah—My Autobiography*. New York: Harper & Bros., 1952.

Barrow, Andrew. *Gossip 1920–1970*. New York: Coward, McCann, 1979.

Beauman, Sally. *The Royal Shakespeare Company: A History of Ten Decades*. London: Oxford University Press, 1982.

Bedford, Paul. *Recollections and Wanderings of Paul Bedford*. London, 1864.

Belasco, David. *The Theatre Through Its Stage Door*. New York: Harper & Bros., 1919.

Benson, Constance. *Mainly Players*. London: Thornton Butterworth, 1926.

Bernhardt, Sarah. *The Art of the Theatre*. Trans. by H. J. Stenning. New York: Dial Press, 1925.

Bevan, Ian. *Royal Performance*. London: Hutchinson, 1954.

Boswell, James. *The Life of Samuel Johnson*. London: J. M. Dent, 1906.

Brandreth, Gyles. *Great Theatrical Disasters*. London: Granada, 1982.

Bruce, John (ed.). *The Diary of John Manningham, 1602–3*. London, 1868.

Bulliet, C. J. *Venus Castina: Famous Celestial Impersonators, Celestial and Human*. New York: Bonanza, 1956.

Burton, Hal. (ed.). *Great Acting*. London: BBC, 1967.

Cerf, Bennett. *Shake Well Before Using*. Simon & Schuster, 1948.

———. *Good for a Laugh*. Garden City: Hanover House, 1952.

———. *The Sound of Laughter*. Garden City: Doubleday, 1970.

Cibber, Colley. *An Apology for the Life of Mr. Colley Cibber*. Critical edition by Edmund Bellchambers. London, 1822.

Clurman, Harold. *On Directing.* New York: Macmillan, 1972.

Cole, Toby, and Helen Chinoy. *Directors on Directing.* 2nd ed. Indianapolis: Bobbs-Merrill, 1976.

Coleman, John. *Fifty Years of an Actor's Life.* London, 1904.

Coleridge, Samuel Taylor. *Table Talk and Omniana.* London, 1888.

Collins, Horace. *My Best Riches.* London: Eyre & Spottiswoode, 1941.

Colman, George (the Younger). *Random Records.* London, 1830.

Connelly, Marc. *Voices Offstage.* New York: Holt, Rinehart, 1968.

Cook, Dutton. *A Book of the Play.* London, 1876.

————. *On the Stage.* London, 1883.

Craig, Edward Gordon. *Henry Irving.* London: Longman's, 1930.

Crawford, Mary Caroline. *The Romance of the American Theatre.* New York: Halcyon House, 1940.

Davies, Thomas. *Dramatic Miscellanies.* London, 1784.

Dean, Basil. *Seven Ages.* London: Hutchinson, 1970.

Deschanel, Emile. *La Vie des Comédiens.* Bruxelles, n.d. (19th c.).

D'Israeli, Isaac. *Curiosities of Literature.* New York, 1865.

Doran, Dr. John. *"Their Majesties' Servants."* London, 1864.

Drennan, Robert E. *The Algonquin Wits.* Secaucus, N.J.: Citadel, 1968.

Elliot, W. G. *In My Anecdotage.* London: Philip Allan, 1925.

Engelbach, Arthur H. *Anecdotes of the Theatre.* London: Grant Richards, 1914.

The Entertainers. London: Harrow House, 1980.

The Era Almanack or Playgoer's Portfolio. London (annual).

Findlater, Richard (ed.). *At The Royal Court.* Ambergate, England: Amber Lane Press, 1981.

Fitzgerald, Percy. *The World behind the Scenes.* London, 1881.

Flanagan, Hallie. *Arena.* New York: Duel, Sloan & Pearce, 1940.

Frohman, Daniel. *Encore.* New York: Lee Furman, 1937.

Galt, John. *Lives of the Players.* London, 1831.

Garfield, David. *The Actors Studio: A Player's Place.* New York: Macmillan, 1980.

Gelb, Arthur, and Barbara Gelb. *O'Neill.* New York: Harper & Row, 1962.

George, Daniel. *A Book of Anecdotes.* England: Hulton, 1957.

Gilliland, Thomas. *The Dramatic Mirror.* London, 1808.

Gottfried, Martin. *Jed Harris: The Curse of Genius.* Boston: Little, Brown, 1984.

Grattan, T. C. *My Acquaintance with the Late Edmund Kean.* London, 1833.

Green, Abel, and Joe Laurie, Jr. *Show Biz: From Vaude to Video as Seen by Variety.* New York: Henry Holt, 1951.

Gorelik, Mordecai. *New Theatres for Old.* New York: Samuel French, 1940.

Guiness, Alec. *Blessings in Disguise.* London: Hamish Hamilton, 1985.

Guthrie, Tyrone (with Robertson Davies and Grand Macdonald). *Renown at Stratford.* Toronto: Clarke, Irwin, 1953.

Hall, Sir Peter. *Diaries.* Harper & Row, 1984.

Halle, Kay. *The Irrepressible Churchill.* New York: Facts-on-File, 1985.

Hampton, Christopher. Introduction to *Tales from the Vienna Woods,* by Ödön von Horváth. London: Faber & Faber, 1977.

Hardwicke, Sir Cedric. *A Victorian in Orbit: The Irreverent Memoirs of Sir Cedric Hardwicke*. Garden City: Doubleday, 1961.

Harker, Joseph. *Studio and Stage*. London: Nisbet, 1924.

Harrison, G. B. *Elizabethan Plays and Players*. London: Routledge, 1940.

Harwood, Ronald. *Donald Wolfit*. London: Secker and Warburg, 1971.

Hay, Julius. *Born 1900*. London: Hutchinson, 1974.

Henry, Lewis C. *Humorous Anecdotes about Famous People*. Garden City: Halcyon Press, 1948.

Hodson, James Lansdale. *No Phantoms Here*. London: Faber & Faber, 1932.

Hone, William. *Ancient Mysteries Described*. London, 1823.

Houseman, John. *Run-Through*. New York: Simon & Schuster, 1972.

Houssaye, Arsène, *Behind the Scenes of the Comédie Française*. Trans. and edited by Albert D. Vandam. Philadelphia, 1889.

Huggett, Richard. *The Curse of Macbeth, With Other Theatrical Superstitions and Ghosts*. Chippenham, England: Picton, 1981.

The Humourist. London, 1892.

Hunt, Leigh. *Dramatic Essays*. London, 1807.

Hutton, Laurence. *Curiosities of the American Stage*. New York, 1891.

Irving, Henry. *The Drama: Addresses*. London, 1893.

Kennedy, Harold J. *No Pickle, No Performance*. New York: Doubleday, 1977.

Knapp, Bettina Leibowitz. *Louis Jouvet: Man of the Theatre*. New York: Columbia Univ. Press, 1957.

Laughs from Jewish Lore. New York: Hebrew Publishers, 1954.

Lawlor, John, and W. H. Auden. *To Nevill Coghill from Friends*. London: Faber & Faber, 1966.

Lawrence, Jerome. *Actor: The Life and Times of Paul Muni*. New York: Samuel French, 1974.

Little, Stuart W., and Arthur Cantor. *The Playmakers*. New York: W. W. Norton, 1970.

Logan, Olive. *Before the Footlights and Behind the Scenes*. Philadelphia, 1870.

McClure, J. B., *Entertaining Anecdotes*. Chicago, 1880.

Mackinnon, Alan. *The Oxford Amateurs*. London, 1910.

Macqueen-Pope, W. *Pillars of Drury Lane*. London: Hutchinson, 1955.

Mander, Raymond, and Joe Mitchenson. *The Lost Theatres of London*. Taplinger, N.Y., 1968.

Marks, Edward B. *They All Had Glamour*. New York: Julian Messner, 1944.

Mason, R. Osgood. *Goodwin's Sketches and Impressions*. New York, 1887.

May, Robin. *The Wit of the Theatre*. London: Leslie Frewin, 1969.

Meyer, Michael. *Ibsen: A Biography*. Garden City: Doubleday, 1971.

Miles, Alfred H. *The New Anecdote Book*. London, n.d. (c. 1906).

Moore, Thomas. *Memoirs of the Life of the Right Hon. Richard Brinsley Sheridan*. London, 1825.

Morgan, John De. *In Lighter Vein*. San Francisco, 1907.

Morley, Sheridan. *A Talent To Amuse*. Boston: Little, Brown, 1985.

Moseley, Roy. *My Stars and Other Friends*. London: Heinemann, 1982.

Nagler, A. M. *A Source Book in Theatrical History*. New York: Dover, 1959.

Nass, L., and G.-J. Witkowski. *The Nude in the French Theatre*. Boar's Head Books, n.p. 1953.

Nemirovich-Danchenko, V. I. *My Life in the Russian Theatre*. London, 1936.

Nichols, John. *Literary Anecdotes of the Eighteenth Century*. London, 1812–16.

Nobles, Milton. *Shop Talk*. Milwaukee, n.d. (19th century).

O'Keeffe, John. *Recollections of the Life of John O'Keeffe*. London, 1826.

Oppenheimer, George. *The Passionate Playgoer*. New York: Viking, 1962.

Oxberry, William. *The Actor's Budget*. London, 1820.

Patten, William. *Among the Humorists and After-Dinner Speakers*. New York, 1909.

Pearson, Hesketh. *Bernard Shaw*. London, 1942.

————. *The Last Actor-Managers*. New York, 1950.

Pendleton, Ralph (ed.). *The Theatre of Robert Edmond Jones*. Middletown: Wesleyan Univ. Press, 1958.

Percy, Sholto, and Reuben Percy. *The Percy Anecdotes*. London, 1821–23.

Pirchan, Emil. *Bühnenbrevier*. Vienna: Verlag Wilhelm Frick, 1938.

Plutarch's Lives. The "Dryden Plutarch" revised by Arthur Hugh Clough. London: J. M. Dent & Sons, 1910.

Plutarch's Morals. Translated, corrected, and revised by William Goodwin. Boston, 1870.

Redfield, William. *Letters from an Actor*. New York: Viking, 1967.

Révész, Tibor. *Bölcsek Mosolya*. Budapest: Gondolat, 1960.

Reynolds, Frederick. *The Life and Times of Frederick Reynolds*. London, 1826.

Richards, Dick. *The Wit of Noël Coward*. London: Leslie Frewin Publishers, 1968.

Rigg, Diana. *No Turn Unstoned*. London: Hamish Hamilton, 1982.

Ritoók, Zsigmond. *Szinház és Stadion*. Budapest: Gondolat, 1968.

Robertson, W. Graham. *Life Was Worth Living*. New York: Harper & Bros., 1931.

Rogers, Samuel. *Recollections of the Table Talk of Samuel Rogers*. New York, 1856.

Rosenfeld, Lulla. *Bright Star of Exile*. New York: Thomas Y. Crowell, 1977.

Ross, Frederick G. *Memories of an Old Theatrical Man*. Berkeley: Friends of the Bancroft Library, Univ. of California, 1977.

Rossi, Alfred. *Astonish Us in the Morning: Tyrone Guthrie Remembered*. London: Hutchinson, 1977.

Russell, W. Clark. *Representative Actors*. London, n.d. (19th century).

Ryan, Richard. *Dramatic Table Talk*. London, 1825.

Sigaux, Gilbert. *Un Siècle d'Humour Théâtral*. Paris: Les Productions de Paris, 1964.

Skinner, Otis. *Footlights and Spotlights*. New York: Blue Ribbon Books, 1924.

Skolsky, Sidney. *Times Square Tintypes*. New York: Ives Washburn, 1930.

Smith, H. Allen. *The Compleat Practical Joker*. Garden City: Doubleday, 1953.

Smith, Sol. *Theatrical Management in the West and South for Thirty Years*. New York, 1868.

Speaight, Robert. *A Bridges-Adams Letter Book*. London: Society for Theatre Research, 1971.

Spence, Joseph. *Observations, Anecdotes, and Characters of Books and Men*. Ed. by Edmund Malone. London, 1820.

Stirling, Edward. *Old Drury Lane*. London, 1881.

Stockwell, La Tourette. *Dublin Theatres and Theatre Customs*. Kingsport, Tennessee: Kingsport Press, 1938.

Teichmann, Howard. *George S. Kaufman: An Intimate Portrait*. New York: Atheneum, 1972.

Terry, Ellen. *The Story of My Life*. London, 1908.

Timbs, John. *English Eccentrics and Eccentricities*. London, 1877.

Toll, Robert C. *On with the Show*. New York: Oxford Univ. Press, 1976.

Toole, J. L. *Reminiscences of J. L. Toole . . . as Chronicled by J. Hatton*. London, 1889.

Trewin, J. C. *The Night Has Been Unruly*. London: Robert Hale, 1957.

Ujváry, Sándor von. *Ferenc Molnár, der lachende Magier*. Vaduz: Verlag Interbook, 1965.

U.S. Department of State. *The Assassination of Abraham Lincoln, and Attempted Assassination of W. H. Seward*. Washington D.C.: Government Printing Office, 1866.

Vandenhoff, George. *Dramatic Reminiscences*. London: 1860.

Wallack, Lester. *Memoirs of Fifty Years*. New York, 1889.

Warde, Frederick. *Fifty Years of Make Believe*. New York: International Press Syndicate, 1920.

Webster, Margaret. *The Same Only Different*. New York: Alfred A. Knopf, 1969.

Wharton, Grace, and Philip Wharton. *The Wits and Beaux of Society*. New York, 1861.

Woollcott, Alexander. *The Portable Woollcott*. New York: Viking, 1942.

Young, Julian Charles. *A Memoir of Charles Mayne Young*. London, 1871.

Zolotow, Maurice. *No People like Show People*. New York: Random House, c. 1951.

Reference Works

Allen, J. T. *Stage Antiquities of the Greeks and Romans and Their Influence*. London, 1927.

Ayres, Alfred. *Acting and Actors; Elocution and Elocutionists*. New York: Appleton, 1894.

Baker, David Erskine. *Biographia Dramatica, or A Companion to the Playhouse*. London, 1812.

Billington, Michael. *Theater Facts and Feats*. Enfield, Middlesex: Guinness Superlatives, 1982.

Bordman, Gerald. *The Oxford Companion to American Theatre*. New York: Oxford Univ. Press, 1984.

Brook, Donald. *A Pageant of English Actors*. London: Rockliff, 1950.

Clinton-Baddeley, V. C. *All Right on the Night*. London: Putnam, 1954.

Collier, John Payne. *The History of English Dramatic Poetry to the Time of Shakespeare*. London, 1831.

——. *Memoirs of the Principal Actors in the Plays of Shakespeare*. London, 1846.

Cowan, Lore. *Are You Superstitious?* London: Leslie Frewin, 1968.

Fuller, Edmund. *Thesaurus of Anecdotes.* New York: Crown, 1942.

Hartnoll, Phyllis. *The Oxford Companion to the Theatre.* New York: Oxford Univ. Press, 1983.

Lawrence, W. J. *Old Theatre Days and Ways.* London: George G. Harrap, 1935.

Mantzius, Karl. *History of Theatrical Art in Ancient and Modern Times,* New York, 1903–21.

Matthews, Anne. *Anecdotes of Actors: With Other Desultory Recollections.* London, 1844.

Mencken, H. L. *The American Language.* 4th ed. New York: Knopf, 1936.

Muir, Frank. *An Irreverent and Thoroughly Incomplete Social History of Practically Everything.* New York: Stein & Day, 1976.

New York Times Directory of the Theater. New York: Arno Press, 1973.

Richards, Dick. *The Curtain Rises . . .* London: Leslie Frewin, 1966.

Rigdon, Walter. Ed. *The Biographical Encyclopaedia & Who's Who of the American Theatre.* New York: James H. Heineman, 1966.

Sellar, R. J. B. *Sporting and Dramatic Yarns.* London: T. Fisher Unwin, 1925.

Ward, Adolphus William. *A History of English Dramatic Literature.* London, 1875.

Zeska, Philipp. *Spektakel Müssen Sein, oder Kleines Theater-Bestiarium.* Wien: Neff Verlag, 1968.

Interviews

Ashcroft, Peggy. BBC interview (1965/66)

Boutsikaris, Dennis (1984)

Coward, Noël. BBC interview (1965/66)

Englund, Claes (1986)

Esslin, Martin (1984)

Fry, Ray (1984)

Gielgud, John. BBC interview (1965/66)

Huddle, Elizabeth (1985)

Jory, Jon (1984)

Keeney, Patricia (1986)

Kranes, David (1984)

Lessac, Arthur (1985)

Linney, Romulus (1984)

Neville, John (1986)

O'Brien, Adale (1984)

Olivier, Laurence. BBC interview (1965/66)

Phillips, John (1984)

Redgrave, Michael. BBC interview (1965/66)

Richardson, Ralph. BBC interview (1965/66)

Ross, Duncan (1984)

Rubin, Donald (1986)

Smith, Cotter (1984)

Thorndike, Sybil. BBC interview (1965/66)

Tovatt, Patrick (1984)

Vanderbroucke, Russell (1984)

Sources

1. Curtain Raisers

ACTOR AND LIAR   Plutarch: *Life of Solon*
THE GREATEST ROMAN   Percy and Percy: *Anecdotes*
NOT ALTOGETHER FOOL   Russell: *Representative Actors*
THE KING'S JESTER   Galt: *Lives of the Players*
LORD, WHAT FOOLS   D'Israeli: *Curiosities of Literature*
A VALUABLE ACTRESS   Percy and Percy: *Anecdotes*
METHUSALEH   Galt: *Lives of the Players*
DECLAMATION   George: *A Book of Anecdotes*
TAKING OFF   Russell: *Representative Actors*
DIGESTION   Rogers: *Recollections*
THE WAGES OF SIN   Cibber: *An Apology*
PERSONALITY   Bernhardt: *The Art of the Theatre*
NATURAL ACTING   Anon.: *Fun for the Million*
ENVY   Russell: *Representative Actors*
THIN ICE   Zolotow: *No People Like Show People*
JEALOUSY   Rogers: *Recollections*

2. Art and Passion

RULES   Ryan: *Dramatic Table Talk*
A STRIKING ACTOR   D'Israeli: *Curiosites of Literature* and Ryan: *Dramatic Table Talk*
A STRICT OBSERVER   Galt: *Lives of the Players*
HIS VERY STICK ACTED   Rogers: *Recollections*
MOVE OTHERS   Ryan: *Dramatic Table Talk*
NO FEELINGS, PLEASE   Craig: *Henry Irving*
GOOD ACTING   Bernhardt: *The Art of Theatre*
SIMILE   Coleridge: *Table Talk*
A CHAMELEON   Russell: *Representative Actors*
ACTING SIMPLIFIED   Aye: *Humour in the Theatre*
PASSION   Russell: *Representative Actors*
IT'S CALLED ACTING   Mr. William Woodman

359

3. Physique

SHORT GIANTS   (a) *The Era Almanack* (1882); (b) Henry Irving in *The Era Almanack* 1881
TOO TALL   BBC interview in Burton: *Great Acting*
TOO THIN   Hutton: *Curiosities of the American Stage*
AND FAT   Hardwicke: *A Victorian in Orbit*
TOO MUCH   *The Era Almanack* 1876
COMIC NOSE   Bernhardt: *The Art of the Theatre*
OVERDRAWN   Oxberry: *The Actor's Budget*

4. Learning

THE GREAT TRADITION   Pearson: *The Last Actor-Managers*
THE SCHOOL OF LIFE   Benson: *Mainly Players*
THE MASTER   Morley: *A Talent To Amuse*
LEARNING TO LAUGH   BBC interview
CURED OF THE GIGGLES   *Ibid.*
ACTING SCHOOL   BBC interview
PRICELESS ADVICE   Cerf: *Shake Well Before Using*
SHAMED INTO SCHOOL   Mr. Duncan Ross
THE GOLDEN RULE   Lawrence: *Actor*

5. Entrances

MR. SMITH IS STAGE-STRUCK   Smith: *Theatrical Management*
GETTING STARTED   Hodson: *No Phantoms Here*
GETTING A BREAK   BBC interview
GETTING HIRED   BBC interview

6. Child Actors

THE INFANT PHENOMENON   Doran: *"Their Majesties' Servants"*
AND THE BUBBLE BURSTS   Percy and Percy: *Anecdotes*
A DWARF   Harker: *Studio and Stage*
GETTING ON   Logan: *Before the Footlights*
LIFE BEGINS   Miles: *The New Anecdote Book*

7. Struggles

DARNED SOCKS   Galt: *Lives of the Players*
A RAKE'S PROGRESS   *Ibid.*
MORE BAILIFFS   *Ibid.*
THE ACTING LIFE   Miles: *The New Anecdote Book*
CHRISTMAS ON STAGE   Webster: *The Same Only Different*
ACTOR'S LUCK   Cerf: *Shake Well Before Using*

8. The Great Role

LADY MACBETH   Webster: *The Same Only Different*
THE ROLE OF HER LIFE   BBC interview

BUILDING A PART   BBC interview
WHOSE ROLE IS IT ANYWAY?   Redfield: *Letters from an Actor*
WORK-OUT   Mr. John Neville
CAMP   Richards: *The Wit of Noël Coward*

9. Old Age

AGE CANNOT WITHER   Hardwicke: *A Victorian in Orbit*
THE OLD TROUPER   Galt: *Lives of the Players*
BRING ME A PICKLED ELEPHANT   Wallack: *Memories of Fifty Years*
WHEEL OF FORTUNE   Cerf: *Shake Well Before Using*
MRS. PAT   Brandreth: *Great Theatrical Disasters*

10. Retirement

MRS. WOFFINGTON REPENTS   Galt: *Lives of the Players*
REMEMBRANCE   Rogers: *Recollections*
CONTENTMENT   Toole: *Reminiscences*
GIVE MY REGARDS   Zolotow: *No People Like Show People*

11. Exit Lines

THE EPILOGUE   Russell: *Representative Actors*
DEATH SCENE   Percy and Percy: *Anecdotes*
LUCID INTERVAL   Ryan: *Dramatic Table Talk*
HERITAGE   Deschanel: *La Vie des Comédiens*
FAREWELL DREAM   Miles: *The New Anecdote Book*
TRIBUTE   Russell: *Representative Actors*
EPITAPHS   (a) Oxberry: *The Actor's Budget;* (b) and (c) Ryan: *Dramatic Table Talk*
FINAL RESPECTS   Hardwicke: *A Victorian in Orbit*

12. Rehearsals

LESSON   Coleman: *Fifty Years of an Actor's Life*
HER OWN AUDIENCE   Houssaye: *Behind the Scenes*
GETTING HIS POINT ACROSS   Ryan: *Dramatic Table Talk*
LOW FORM   Brandreth: *Great Theatrical Disasters*
DOUBLE ENTENDRE   *Ibid.*
FREUDIAN SLIP   BBC interview; tag, Brandreth: *Great Theatrical Disasters*
BIG BAD WOLFIT   Harwood: *Donald Wolfit*
THE CLASH OF TITANS   Redfield: *Letters from an Actor*

13. Nerves

CONTEMPT   Brandreth: *Great Theatrical Disasters*
FOREKNOWLEDGE   Robertson: *Life Was Worth Living*
COPING   Huggett: *The Curse of Macbeth*

Who's Noivous?   Redfield: *Letters from an Actor*
Sleeping   Bernhardt: *The Art of the Theatre*

14. Lines

When in Rome   G. Edwards in *The Era Almanac* 1876
The Prompter   Engelbach: *Anecdotes of the Theatre*
Too Much Help   Webster: *The Same Only Different*
Lapse   Bernhardt: *The Art of the Theatre*
Memory   (a) Galt: *Lives of the Players*; (b) and (c) Russell: *Representative Actors*
Association   *The Era Almanack* 1882
Acting by Rote   Anon.: *Fun for the Million*
Adapting Shakespeare   Brandreth: *Great Theatrical Disasters*
Leveling   Miles: *The New Anecdote Book*
Word Perfect   BBC interview and Richards: *The Wit of Noël Coward*

15. In the Vineyards of the Lord

The Old Excuse   Percy and Percy: *Anecdotes*
The Morning After   Grattan: *My Acquaintance with the Late Edmund Kean*
What Greatness   Smith: *Theatrical Management*
Me? Drunk?   Hardwicke: *A Victorian in Orbit*
Playing Drunk   Ryan: *Dramatic Table Talk*
Unusual Role   *The Humourist*
A Prayer   Zolotow: *No People like Show People*

16. Pulling Legs

Ad Lib   Smith: *The Compleat Practical Joker*
A Sneezing Actor   Owen Fawcett in *The Era Almanack* 1878
Alas, Poor Yorick!   Vandenhoff: *Dramatic Reminiscences*
Corpsing   Ryan: *Dramatic Table Talk*
Easy Bet   Benson: *Mainly Players*
Closing Nights   Brandreth: *Great Theatrical Disasters*
Actors' Jokes   Aye: *Humour in the Theatre*
Agents   Mr. John Phillips

17. Crowds and Extras

Comic Relief   Rigg: *No Turn Unstoned*
Anything for Money   Aye: *Humour in the Theatre*
The Tedium Is the Message   Huggett: *The Curse of Macbeth*
Compliment   Ross: *Memories of an Old Theatrical Man*
Crowd Scene   Webster: *The Same Only Different*
Thanks   Anon.: *Wit and Humor of the Stage*

18. Amateurs

QUINTESSENTIAL   Hodson: *No Phantoms Here*
A VERY GOOD FISHMONGER   Ryan: *Dramatic Table Talk*
ATTACKING THE PROMPTER   Edward Spencer in *The Era Almanack* 1880
OXFORD AMATEURS   Mackinnon: *Oxford Amateurs*

19. Careers

HOW TO GET AHEAD   Fuller: *Thesaurus of Anecdotes*
AND SO HE BECAME A PLAYWRIGHT   Galt: *Lives of the Players*
A LADY OF FASHION   Hutton: *Curiosities of the American Stage*
CAREER CHOICE   BBC interview
THERE IS A TIDE   *The Entertainers*

20. Success and Failure

FAME   (a) Davies: *Dramatic Miscellanies* and Harrison: *Elizabethan Plays and Players*; (b) Miles: *The New Anecdote Book*
OVERNIGHT SUCCESS   Bedford: *Recollections and Wanderings*
HOW TO TAKE A FLOP   Fuller: *Thesaurus of Anecdotes*
SOME DON'T FLY   *Ibid.*
IMAGINATION   Drennan: *Algonquin Wits*
AND I CAN FAIL AGAIN   Green and Laurie: *Show Biz*
GIVING UP   Ryan: *Dramatic Table Talk*

21. Generosity and Modesty

READY MONEY   The Saints of the Stage in *Cornhill Magazine* 1867
THEIR BROTHERS' KEEPERS   Bedford: *Recollections and Wanderings*
MARTYRDOM   Reynolds: *The Life and Times of Frederick Reynolds*
CAMARADERIE   Ross: *Memories of an Old Theatrical Man*
KIND TO STAGEHANDS   Webster: *The Same Only Different*
MY FUR LADY   Guinness: *Blessings in Disguise*

22. Rivalries

ENVY   Miles: *The New Anecdote Book*
MEANNESS   Russell: *Representative Actors*
HE KNEW   Miles: *The New Anecdote Book*
FAMOUS WHISPER   Woollcott: "The First Mrs. Tanqueray" in *The Portable Woollcott*
TO A YOUNG ACTRESS   Cerf: *Shake Well Before Using*
MIAOW   *Ibid.*

23. Private Lives

FICKLE LOVE   Ryan: *Dramatic Table Talk*
FAMILY FEUD   Wharton and Wharton: *The Wits and Beaux of Society*

FREQUENT FATHER   Russell: *Representative Actors*
RECOGNITION SCENE   Ryan: *Dramatic Table Talk*
IRVING'S WIFE   Huggett: *The Curse of Macbeth*
IRVING'S ACTRESSES   Webster: *The Same Only Different*
CARTHARSIS   BBC interview
MY DAUGHTER ELECTRA   Rosenfeld: *Bright Star of Exile*

24. Eccentricities

STRANGE DAUGHTER   Timbs: *English Eccentrics and Eccentricities*
THAT WAY MADNESS LIES   Grattan: *My Acquaintance with the Late Edmund Kean*
DELUSION   Timbs: *English Eccentrics and Eccentricities*
NO JOY   Pearson: *The Last Actor-Managers*
A GOOD REASON   Huggett: *The Curse of Macbeth*
SHAKESPEARE BEFORE SWINE   Fuller: *Thesaurus of Anecdotes*
NOTHING IN EXCESS   Mr. Don Rubin
HOW TO PREVENT A LONG RUN   Hodson: *No Phantoms Here*
CARNY KNOWLEDGE   Interview with an anonymous actor who hopes to continue working with Mr. Papp.

25. Theatre Talk

EXEUNT OMNES   "J. H." in *The Era of Almanack* 1878
LINGO   Mencken: *Dictionary of the American Language*, quoting from the *New York World*
ACTOR-TALK   BBC interview

26. Provincial Players

GO AND BLOW YOUR NOSE   Ryan: *Dramatic Table Talk*
KILL THAT ACTOR   John S. Clarke: "Theatrical Incidents" in *The Era Almanack* 1874
HEE-HAW   Nobles: *Shop Talk*

27. Stock Theatre

MIXED UP   Edward Compton: "Theatrical Anecdotes" in *The Era Almanack* 1881
STOCK JOKE   Fuller: *Thesaurus of Anecdotes*
EXPERIENCE   Webster: *The Same Only Different*
UNMIXED DOUBLES   (a) Harwood: *Donald Wolfit*; (b) Robin May: *The Wit of the Theatre*
FORCED TO TOUR   *Ibid.*
THE LAVATORY PLAYERS   BBC interview
THE EARTH MOVED   Anon.: *The Wit and Humor of the Stage*

28. Boondocks

A HUMAN PROP   Plutarch: *Life of Crassus*
SON OF A GUN   Warde: *Fifty Years of Make Believe*
ONE-NIGHT STAND   Anon.: *The Wit and Humor of the Stage*
THE AMERICAN TOUR   Webster: *The Same Only Different*
THE SECRET OF SUCCESS   Connelly: *Voices Offstage*

29. Landlords and Landladies

THE IMPORTANCE   Edward Compton, "Theatrical Anecdotes" in *The Era Almanack* 1881
SCOTTISH SABBATH   Benson: *Mainly Players*
FLEAS   *Ibid.*
MORE FLEAS   Harker: *Studio and Stage*
GOOD ADDRESS   Drennan: *Algonquin Wits*

30. The Physical Actor

OUT OF CONTROL   Lucian: *De Saltatione*
PRESENCE   Young: *A Memoir of Charles Mayne Young*
PHYSICAL FEATS   (a) Cook: *On the Stage;* (b) D'Israeli: *Curiosities of Literature*
MANNERISMS
SUIT THE ACTION   Pearson: *The Last Actor-Managers*
EPILEPSY   Mr. Martin Esslin
POETRY AND MOTION   BBC interview
HOW HE GOT SLAPPED   Fuller: *Thesaurus of Anecdotes*

31. Mimicry

PARMENON'S PIG   Plutarch: *Of Banquets*
STICK TO COWS   Ryan: *Dramatic Table Talk*
POWER OF MIMICRY   Anon.: *Fun for the Million*
BURLESQUE   Miles: *The New Anecdote Book*
INSPIRATION   BBC interview
MIMESIS   Redfield: *Letters from an Actor*

32. Methods and Method

BLOCKING   Ryan: *Dramatic Table Talk*
AN ACTOR PREPARES   Galt: *Lives of the Players*
UNDERACTING   Ryan: *Dramatic Table Talk*
SLEEPWALKING   Redfield: *Letters from an Actor*
HOW DID I DO THAT?   BBC interview
ALIENATION   BBC interview
STANISLAVSKY   BBC interview
THE METHOD   Garfield: *The Actors Studio*
FRENZY   Kennedy: *No Pickle, No Performance*

33. Tricks of the Trade

MASKING   Webster: *The Same Only Different*
ACT IN YOUR PAUSES   Hardwicke: *A Victorian in Orbit*
LESS IS MORE   BBC interview
RELAXING   BBC interview
ENJOY WHAT YOU DO   BBC interview
TRAINING THE AUDIENCE   J. B. Buckstone: "Actors and Audiences" in *The Era Almanack* 1874
HOW TO WIN   BBC interview

34. Voice

WHEN IN DOUBT   Hardwicke: *A Victorian in Orbit*
LOSING IT   BBC interview
COCAINE AND MENTHOL   Bankhead: *Tallulah*
VELVET   BBC interview
SHAW'S ADVICE   BBC interview
HE DID IT HIS WAY   Mr. Arthur Lessac
BREATHING   Bernhardt: *The Art of the Theatre*
THE MASTER'S VOICE   Richards: *The Wit of Noël Coward*

35. Costumes

THE FAITHFUL DRESSER   Ryan: *Dramatic Table Talk*
ANACHRONISMS   O'Keeffe: *Recollections*
HOW DID IT GET THROUGH CUSTOMS?   Miles: *The New Anecdote Book*
MRS. CAMPBELL   Webster: *The Same Only Different*
CLOTHES   Pendleton: *The Theatre of Robert Edmond Jones*
ANATOMY   BBC interview
SHAKESPEARE'S CRAFT   Harwood: *Donald Wolfit*
THE DRESSING ROOM   Moseley: *My Stars and Other Friends*
TIGHTS   Morley: *A Talent to Amuse*

36. Wigs

BLACK AND WHITE   Cook: *A Book of the Play*
A HISTORIC WIG   *Ibid.*
LOSING IT   *Ibid.*
BEARD   Rigg: *No Turn Unstoned*
CARROT   *Ibid.*

37. Makeup

SPECIAL EFFECTS   *Aeschyli Vita*
NOT JUST MAKEUP   Pearson: *The Last Actor-Managers*
GREASE-PAINT   Harker: *Studio and Stage*
CONTRAST   Robertson: *Life Was Worth Living*
PERFECT DISGUISE   Patten: *Among the Humorists*

BLOOD   Hardwicke: *A Victorian in Orbit*
NOSES   Brandreth: *Great Theatrical Disasters*
BEYOND MAKEUP   Lawrence: *Actor*

38. Impersonation

BOY ACTRESSES   see C. J. Bulliet: *Venus Castina* and Roger Baker: *Drag*
LADIES' PET   Cibber: *Apology*
SHAVING THE QUEEN   *Ibid.*
VICE VERSA   Ryan: *Dramatic Table Talk*
THE IDEAL WOMAN   Toll: *On with the Show*

39. It Starts with Them

THE FATHER OF TRAGEDY   Percy and Percy: *Anecdotes*
SOPHOCLES   *Ibid.*
A CLASSICIST   *Ibid.*
WHO STOLE FROM WHOM?   Stirling: *Old Drury Lane*
PLAGIARISM   (a) Ryan: *Dramatic Table Talk*; (b) and (c) Drennan: *Algonquin Wits*
A GENTLEMAN   Wharton and Wharton: *The Wits and Beaux of Society*
FRANK WORDS   Gorelik: *New Theatres for Old*
EDUCATION OF A DRAMATIST   Hodson: *No Phantoms Here*
SYMBOLISM   Drennan: *Algonquin Wits*
HELPFUL ADVICE   BBC interview
NARRATIVE DRAMA   Hay: *Born 1900*
HOW TO BECOME A PLAYWRIGHT   Cerf: *Good for a Laugh*

40. How They Worked

EXIT PURSUED BY A BEAR   Ryan: *Dramatic Table Talk*
FAST WORK   Percy and Percy: *Anecdotes*
KEEPING UP   Aye: *Humor in the Theatre*
HOW I WROTE THIS PLAY   Pearson: *Bernard Shaw*
JOURNEY'S START   Hodson: *No Phantoms Here*
SLOW WRITER   Teichmann: *George S. Kaufman*

41. Getting a Hearing

LITERARY MANAGER   Galt: *Lives of the Players*
IF ONLY HE KNEW   Percy: *Anecdotes*
WHAT DID I DO TO DESERVE THIS?   Nichols: *Literary Anecdotes*
BAD PLAYS   Cook: *On the Stage*
MIGRAINE   Houssaye: *Behind the Scenes*
HOW TO AVOID READING PLAYS   E. Manuel in *The Era Almanac* 1875
EARLY SHAW   Pearson: *Bernard Shaw*
HOW TO GET PRODUCED   Cerf: *Good for a Laugh*

42. Drama and Trauma

A Tragedy Called Europe   Ryan: *Dramatic Table Talk*
Fiasco   Révész: *Bölcsek Mosolya*
Curt Rejection   Fuller: *Thesaurus of Anecdotes*
Competition   Skolsky: *Times Square Tintypes*
The Old Story   *Ibid.*
Tryout   Teichmann: *George S. Kaufman*

43. Playwright in the House

Interpretation   Révész: *Bölcsek Mosolya*
Sneak Previews   Ryan: *Dramatic Table Talk*
Brogue   *Ibid.*
Because He Moves in Mysterious Ways   Pearson: *Bernard Shaw*
Shaw's Advice   BBC Interview
Gnashing of teeth   Meyer: *Ibsen*
No Leading Lady   Aye: *Humor in the Theatre*
On a Clear Day   Richards: *The Wit of Noël Coward*
Deep Cuts   Gelb and Gelb: *O'Neill*
Expert Advice   Cerf: *Shake Well Before Using*
Playwright to the Rescue   Mr. Cotter Smith
Wish You Were Here   Teichmann: *George S. Kaufman*

44. Dramatic Endings

Greek Tragedies   Various sources
Grave Dispute   Anon.: *Fun for the Million*
Fate   From Christopher Hampton's introduction to *Tales from the Vienna Woods* by Ödön von Horváth
A Broken Heart   Mr. Martin Esslin
Last Wish   Teichmann: *George S. Kaufman*
Exaggerated Rumor   Ms. Elizabeth Huddle
Obituary   Dan Sullivan: Los Angeles *Times*, Feb. 26, 1983

45. The Text

Human Nature   Mr. Romulus Linney
Rewriting the Play   Webster: *The Same Only Different*
How To Tell What Shakespeare Wrote   Harwood: *Donald Wolfit*
Playwright's Protest   Mr. Martin Esslin
Perspective   Redfield: *Letters from an Actor*

46. Shakespeare and His Cult

Throw Them the Bard   Ryan: *Dramatic Table Talk*
Bathos   Oxberry: *The Actor's Budget*
Obscure Shakespeare   Elliot: *In My Anecdotage*
Our Shakespeare   Beauman: *The Royal Shakespeare Company*
Ye Olde Tent   Guthrie: *Renown at Stratford*

WOODEN O   Baker: *History of the London Stage*
TRAGIC FLAW   Teichmann: *George S. Kaufman*

47. Literary Figures

FOUND OUT   Percy and Percy: *Anecdotes*
THE COMPANY OF MUSES   *The Humourist*
LIFE CLASS   Skinner: *Footlights and Spotlights*

48. Good Producers

THE GENERAL'S SECRET   Xenophon: *Memorabilia*
THE THRIFTY PRODUCER   Plutarch: *Life of Phocion*
THE MANAGER'S STRATAGEM   Galt: *Lives of the Players*
DUBIOUS ETHICS   Frohman: *Encore*
GOD'S FAVORITE   Hodson: *No Phantoms Here*
BLOODY THOUGHTS   BBC interview

49. Misers and Tyrants

AN UNPOPULAR MANAGER   Webster: *The Same Only Different*
A MANAGER OUTWITTED   *The Era Almanack* 1884
POKER   Nobles: *Shop Talk*
ONCE BITTEN   Ryan: *Dramatic Table Talk*
YOU GET WHAT YOU PAID FOR   Henry: *Humorous Anecdotes*
CLASH BY NIGHT   Zolotow: *No People Like Show People*
WHAT DO YOU SAY TO A NAKED PRODUCER?   *Ibid.*

50. Actors as Managers

AN ECONOMIST   Cibber: *An Apology*
THE SIZE OF THE HOUSE   Ryan: *Dramatic Table Talk*
DO AS THE BOSS SAYS   *Ibid.*
THE MANAGER AS ACTOR   Baker: *History of the London Stage*
STAR COMPLEX   Pearson: *The Last Actor-Managers*
BRIEF NEGOTIATION   Patten: *Among the Humorists*
TEACHING AN AUTHOR   *The Era Almanack* 1884
PINCHING PENNIES   Harwood: *Donald Wolfit*
A FINE AND QUIET PLACE   Brandreth: *Great Theatrical Disasters*

51. Spendthrifts

POWERS OF PERSUASION   Wharton and Wharton: *The Wits and Beaux of Society* and George: *A Book of Anecdotes*
ACCOUNTANCY   Harker: *Studio and Stage*
CUTBACKS   Pearson: *The Last Actor-Managers*
MOGULS   Aye: *Humour in the Theatre*
THE PRODUCER AS AUTEUR   Skolsky: *Times Square Tintypes*
THE BUCK NEED NOT STOP HERE   Mr. David Kranes

52. Promotion

PLAY-BILLS   Ryan: *Dramatic Table Talk*
TRAVESTIES   *The Era Almanack* 1882
IRISH PUFFING   Percy and Percy: *Anecdotes*
THE PLAGUE   Sigaux: *Un Siècle d'Humour Théâtral*
PRESS AGENT   Anon.: *Through the Stage Door*
PENNIES FROM HEAVEN   Collins: *My Best Riches*
PUBLICITY STUNTS   Little and Cantor: *The Playmakers*

53. The Box Office

PAYING THE AUDIENCE   Ulpianus: *Commentary on Demosthenes*
LOSING BENEFITS   Spence: *Observations*
A MISER   Ryan: *Dramatic Table Talk*
PAYMENT IN KIND   Ross: *Memories of an Old Theatrical Man*
HOW TO PAY OFF AUTHORS   Houssaye: *Behind the Scenes*
KNITTING   Ujváry: *Ferenc Molnár*
"COMPS"   Harker: *Studio and Stage*
SMALL TOWNS   Anon.: *Wit and Humor of the Stage*
TRY IT SOME TIME   *Ibid.*
INVITATION   Also found in Halle: *The Irrepressible Churchill*

54. The Scenic Art

HOW TO WORK MIRACLES   Nagler: *A Source Book in Theatrical History*
SETTING THE SCENE   Cook: *A Book of the Play*
MACHINES   Stockwell: *Dublin Theatres*
A BAD SCENIC ARTIST   Ryan: *Dramatic Table Talk*
ILLUSIONS   Cook: *A Book of the Play*
PROSCENIUM   Oxberry: *An Actor's Budget*
A CRUSADER   Lee Simonson: "Legacy" in Pendleton: *The Theatre of Robert Edmond Jones*
BLIZZARD BY BELASCO   Cerf: *Good for a Laugh*
WHY NOT THE WORST?   Belasco: *The Theatre Through Its Stage Door*
THE ROAD TO HELL   John Cox: "On a Production of Dr. Faustus" in Lawlor and Auden: *To Nevill Coghill from Friends*
WHEN A SYMBOL   Brandreth: *Great Theatrical Disasters*

55. Extravaganzas

SPECTACLE   Pearson: *The Last Actor-Managers*
JOY   Harker: *Studio and Stage*
GORED BY GORSE   Aye: *Humour in the Theatre*
SHIFTING SCENES   Webster: *The Same Only Different*
THE EDIFICE COMPLEX   Cerf: *Shake Well Before Using*
A SHOW-STOPPER   Mr. Dennis Boutsikaris
SAFARI   Mr. Russell Vanderbroucke

56. Props

A CRITICAL PROP   *The Era Almanack* 1876
MODESTY   Colman: *Random Records*
UNFOLDING HIS DARKER PURPOSE   Miles: *The New Anecdote Book*
BLOOD DONOR   Engelbach: *Anecdotes of the Theatre*
A GIFT FROM THE WINGS   Brandreth: *Great Theatrical Disasters*

57. Sounds

NOTHING TO CROW ABOUT   Cook: *On the Stage*
YAWNING MUSICIAN   Cook: *A Book of the Play*
SOUND CUE   *The Era Almanack* 1881
THUNDER   Cook: *A Book of the Play*
BUT WOULD HE GET WORK?   Anon.: *Wit and Humor of the Stage*

58. Lighting

EARLY EXPERIMENTS   Bevan: *Royal Performance*
WAY TO THE TOP   Cook: *A Book of the Play*
HOLLOW CROWN   *The Era Almanack* 1882
KEEPING IN FOCUS   Irving: *The Drama*
THE ACTOR'S FACE   Speaight: *A Bridges-Adams Letter Book*
SELLING THE SUNSET   Belasco: The Theatre Through Its Stage Door

59. The Good, the Bad, and the Ugly

WHY WE HAVE DIRECTORS   Percy and Percy: *Anecdotes*
TAKING DIRECTIONS   Fuller: *Thesaurus of Anecdotes*
DIRECTING   BBC interview
DIFFERENT STROKES   BBC interview
VISUAL EFFECTS   Rossi: *Astonish Us in the Morning*
SHY OF EMOTION   *Ibid.*
ENTHUSIASM   *Ibid.*
PACE   Harwood: *Donald Wolfit*

60. Trade Secrets

SO MUCH FOR DIRECTING   Redfield: *Letters from an Actor* and Mr. Martin
   Esslin
THE ROPE TRICK   Clurman: *On Directing*
HOW TO DIRECT SHAW   Rossi: *Astonish Us in the Morning*
ADVICE   Mr. Dennis Boutsikaris

61. Working with Actors

TALKING TO ACTORS   Gottfried: *Jed Harris*
THE PSYCHOLOGIST   Cole and Chinoy: *Directors on Directing*

How To Play Opalescent Dawn   BBC interview
Direction   Redfield: *Letters from an Actor*
Don't Underline   BBC interview
Lacking in Tact: Guinness: *Blessings in Disguise*
Don't Mark   Rossi: *Astonish Us in the Morning*
Terror   Oral tradition
Acting by Numbers   Redfield: *Letters from an Actor*
Whatever Works   Mr. Dennis Boutsikaris

62. Directors and Playwrights

Collaboration   Gottfried: *Jed Harris*
Fifth Column   Zolotow: *No People Like Show People*
Tolerance   Findlater: *At The Royal Court*
Working with a Genius   Hall: *Diaries*
Unusual Request   Dean: *Seven Ages*

63. Manners and Morals

The Good Old Days   Charles J. Stone: "Audiences of a Century Ago" in
      The Era Almanack 1872
Peanut Gallery   Logan: *Before the Footlights*
How To Get a Good Seat   *The Era Almanack* 1875
A Cat-Lover   Miles: *The New Anecdote Book*
Grand Guignol   Mander and Mitchenson: *The Lost Theatres of London*
Editorials   Brandreth: *Great Theatrical Disasters*
Realization   Mr. Ray Fry
Queens   Brandreth: *Great Theatrical Disasters*
Fairies   *Ibid.*

64. Applause: Real and Faked

Roman Audience   Percy and Percy: *Anecdotes*
Moved to Tears   Aye: *Humour in the Theatre*
Clap-trap   Hunt: *Dramatic Essays*
Canned Applause   Houssaye: *Behind the Scenes*
Fainting   *Laughs from Jewish Lore*

65. They Stayed Away in Droves

Throwing Out the Audience   *The Era Almanack* 1881
And Hissing Back   *Ibid.*
End of the Line   Aye: *Humour in the Theatre*
It Was Better in Yiddish   Cerf: *The Sound of Laughter*

66. Interruptions

Why Shoot Her?   Miles: *The New Anecdote Book*
What Was the Question?   *Ibid.*

FAREWELL HISS   *The Era Almanack* 1872
HOW TO DEAL WITH AN UNRULY AUDIENCE   (a) Moore: *Memoirs of Sheridan;*
    (b) Ryan: *Dramatic Table Talk*
HISSED TO DEATH   Logan: *Before the footlights*
QUICK ON HIS FEET   Anon.: *Wit and Humor of the Stage*
GO SLEEP WITH THE FISHES   Henry: *Humorous Anecdotes*
POTENT THREAT   Brandreth: *Great Theatrical Disasters*

67. Riots

WAYS TO HANDLE RIOTS   Galt: *Lives of the Players*
ENEMY TALENT   *Ibid.*
THE ASTOR PLACE RIOT   Crawford: *The Romance of the American Theatre*
ROCKING THE CRADLE   Brandreth: *Great Theatrical Disasters*

68. Reality and Illusion

UNEXPECTED HELP   Ryan: *Dramatic Table Talk*
SAILORS TO THE RESCUE   Miles: *The New Anecdote Book*
BACK TO THE FUTURE   Mason: *Goodwin's Sketches and Impressions*
OUT OF AFRICA   Ms. Patricia Keeney
HI, MOM   Brandreth: *Great Theatrical Disasters*

69. First Nights

SOCRATES   Ailianos: *Diverse Stories*
UNEVEN CONTEST   Pearson: *Bernard Shaw*
POST-MORTEMS   Brandreth: *Great Theatrical Disasters;* Mr. Don Rubin
ACHIEVEMENT   Redfield: *Letters from an Actor*
HOW IT FEELS   (a) Hodson: *No Phantoms Here* (b) Rossi: *Astonish Us in
    the Morning*
AUTHOR! AUTHOR!   Trewin: *The Night Has Been Unruly*
DIAGNOSIS   Rigg: *No Turn Unstoned*

70. Famous Reviewers and Infamous Reviews

COLLECTOR'S ITEMS   Various sources
UNKINDEST CUTS   Various sources
A PACK OF CARDS   Fuller: *Thesaurus of Anecdotes*
STAGE FIGHT   Aye: *Humour in the Theatre*
AN IDEAL REVIEW   *Theatric Magazine* 1806
ANOTHER VIEW OF THE SAME EVENT   *Dublin General Post*, July 10, 1783
SOUL OF WIT   Woollcott: "Our Mrs. Parker" in *Some Neighbors*
BRIEF BEEFS   Various sources
CLEOPATRA   Bankhead: *Tallulah*
PITH   Various sources
THE MASTER AS CRITIC   Richards: *The Wit of Noël Coward*
COLLEAGUES   Teichmann: *George S. Kaufman*

71. Feuds and Squabbles

PHYSICAL REACTION   Révész: *Bölcsek Mosolya*
COMBAT UNTO DEATH   Pearson: *Bernard Shaw*
BOREDOM BECOMES ELECTRA   Woollcott: *Program Notes*
AGAINST THE *Times*   Little and Cantor: *The Playmakers*
A CRITIC'S WAR   Bordman: *The Oxford Companion to American Theatre*

72. Getting Even

THE NATURE OF THE BEAST   Brandreth: *Great Theatrical Disasters*
A YOUNG MAN   Mr. Claes Englund
A CRITICAL HORSE   Aye: *Humour in the Theatre*
A WIT AND VENOM   Bankhead: *Tallulah*
HOW THEY TOOK IT   (a) Miles: *The New Anecdote Book*; (b) BBC interview
DON'T TANGLE WITH A CRITIC   Drennan: *Algonquin Wits*
THIN BOTTOM   Aye: *Humour in the Theatre*
THE CORRECT RESPONSE   Richards: *The Wit of Noël Coward*

73. Critics Are Human

BAD PLAYWRIGHTS   Pearson: *Bernard Shaw*
INFLUENCE   *Ibid.*
SELF-DEFENSE   Rigg: *No Turn Unstoned*
AROUSAL   Fuller: *Thesaurus of Anecdotes*
TEARS   Gottfried: *Jed Harris*

74. Enemies of the Stage

WHIPPED   Rigg: *No Turn Unstoned*
GETTING BUSTED   Cook: *A Book of the Play*
CENSORSHIP   Cibber: *Apology*
COSTUMES BY THE LORD CHAMBERLAIN   Mander and Mitchenson: *The Lost Theatres of London*
CONVINCING THE CENSOR   Pearson: *Bernard Shaw*
PROTEST   Barrow: *Gossip 1920–1970*
A WORD TO THE PURITANS   Percy and Percy: *Anecdotes*

75. Church and Stage

IRRELIGIOUS THEATRE   Hone: *Ancient Mysteries Described*
COMEDY   Molière: Preface to *Tartuffe*
THE ACTOR AND THE ARCHBISHOP   Spence: *Observations*

76. Politics and the Theatre

TOO MOVED TO STAY   Ailianos: *Diverse Stories*
CONSPIRACY   Ryan: *Dramatic Table Talk*
LINCOLN'S DEATH   U.S. Dept. of State: *The Assassination of Abraham Lincoln*

REALISM Teichmann: *George S. Kaufman*
POLITICS Drennan: *Algonquin Wits*
WITCH HUNT Flanagan: *Arena*
ALLIES Morley: *A Talent To Amuse*
FOREIGN AID Mr. Don Rubin

77. Royalty

ROYAL MISTRESS Bevan: *Royal Performance*
SAME PLOT *Ibid.*
THREE GEORGES *Ibid.*
ONE-TRACK MIND Galt: *Lives of the Players*
HE'S BEEN WRONG BEFORE Bevan: *Royal Performance*
A HOUSE DIVIDED *Ibid.*
FAMILY DRAMA McClure: *Entertaining Anecdotes*
SHE COULD BE AMUSED Bevan: *Royal Performance*
CHILDREN'S PLAY Anon.: *Wit and Humor of the Stage*
THE REAL THING Cerf: *Good for a Laugh*
THE NATIONAL Hall: *Diaries*
BRING ON THE CLOWNS Hardwicke: *A Victorian in Orbit*

78. Social Status

BED-MAKERS Révész: *Bölcsek Mosolya*
A PRINCE OF PLAYERS Galt: *Lives of the Players*
UNIMPEACHABLE CHARACTER Cibber: *Apology*
CLIMBING UP THE LADDER Boswell: *Life of Samuel Johnson*
DON'T LET HER MARRY AN ACTOR Miles: *The New Anecdote Book*
KNIGHTED Bevan: *Royal Performance*
ARISE, MR. COWARD Barrow: *Gossip 1920–1970*
WORKER'S PARADISE Mr. Don Rubin

79. Customs and Traditions

THE CLASSICS Houssaye: *Behind the Scenes*
THE RELIC George: *A Book of Anecdotes*
NO RESPECT Redfield: *Letters from an Actor*
TRADITION Bankhead: *Tallulah*
THE GYPSY ROBE Huggett: *The Curse of Macbeth*
ENTER GHOST Anon.: *Wit and Humor of the Stage*

80. Toil and Trouble

THEATRICAL SUPERSTITIONS Anon: *Through the Stage Door*
THE TAG LINE Terry: *The Story of My Life*
SUPERSTITIOUS ACTRESSES McClure: *Entertaining Anecdotes*
AUSPICIOUS OPENING Nemirovich-Danchenko: *My Life in the Russian Theatre*

SOMEONE SHOULD TELL NBC   Harker: *Studio and Stage*
BREAK A LEG   Huggett: *The Curse of Macbeth*
BAD LUCK   *Ibid.*
THE SCOTTISH PLAY   Billington: *Theater Facts and Feats* and Redfield:
      Letters from an Actor
VOODOO *Macbeth*   Houseman: *Run-Through*

81. Ghost Stories

GHOSTS OF DRURY LANE   McQueen-Pope: *Pillars of Drury Lane*
HAPPY GHOSTS   Mander and Mitchenson: *The Lost Theatres of London*
SPOOKY   *Ibid.*
MINIMALISM   Mr. Martin Esslin

82. Scandalous Gossip

GOD STAND UP FOR BASTARDS!   Spence: *Observations*
WILLIAM THE CONQUEROR   Bruce: *Diary of John Manningham*
OWNING UP TO IT   Bevan: *Royal Performance*
NOT IN GARBO'S VERSION   Nass and Witkowski: *The Nude in the French
      Theatre*
AMPLE FLESH   *Ibid.*
MEMORIES   Houssaye: *Behind the Scenes*
STREAKING   Nass and Witowski: *The Nude in the French Theatre*
WHERE ARE THEY NOW?   *Ibid.*

83. Occupational Hazards

IT BROUGHT THE HOUSE DOWN   Percy and Percy: *Anecdotes*
AMERICA'S SWEETHEART   Hutton: *Curiosities of the American Stage*
SPECTRE   Fitzgerald: *The World behind the Scenes*
SHERIDAN LOSES A THEATRE   Wharton and Wharton: *The Wits and Beaux of
      Society*
FREE AT LAST   Oxberry: *The Actor's Budget*
IT IS THE CAUSE   Logan: *Before the Footlights*
NEAR MISS   Pearson: *The Last Actor-Managers*
PHYSICAL PROXIMITY   Mr. Patrick Tovatt and Ms. Adale O'Brien
REVENGE   Pirchan: *Bühnenbrevier*

84. Animal Stunts

A FATAL TRAP   Fitzgerald: *The World behind the Scenes*
STARRING HORSE   Ryan: *Dramatic Table Talk*
MAZEPPA   Marks: *They All Had Glamour*
HAMLET'S DOG   Warde: *Fifty Years of Make Believe*

85. Falling Sets

BALCONY SCENES   Aye: *Humour in the Theatre*
CONVICTED   *Ibid.*

LOCKED DOORS *Ibid.*
THE *Mayflower* Brandreth: *Great Theatrical Disasters*
DON'T CALL ME Mr. Jon Jory
PARANOIA Harwood: *Donald Wolfit*

86. Embarrassments

THE BURIED MAJESTY OF DENMARK *The Era Almanack* 1882
OLD BLOOPERS Morgan: *In Lighter Vein*
NEW BLOOPERS Mr. Ray Fry
MISSING PARTS Brandreth: *Great Theatrical Disasters*
DEBACLE Garfield: *The Actors Studio*
NOT HIS STRONG SUIT Personal recollection
IF ONLY HE KNEW Mr. William Woodman

87. And the Show Went On

PAIN Bernhardt: *The Art of the Theatre*
THE FIRE-MARSHAL'S NIGHTMARE Percy and Percy: *Anecdotes*
I'M ALL RIGHT, JACK Mr. William Woodman
GO ON WITHOUT ME Mr. Jon Jory

88. What It's All About

MEDITATION ON A THEME Ryan: *Dramatic Table Talk*
IF I COULD ONLY DO THAT BBC interview
KINDLING A FIRE BBC interview
PEACE Speaight: *A Bridges-Adams Letter Book*
RANK Knapp: *Louis Jouvet*
PHYSICIAN, HEAL THYSELF *The Entertainers*

The author wishes to express his thanks to the following publishers, writers and their representatives.

Aitken & Stone Ltd., for permission to reprint from *Sir Donald Wolfit* by Ronald Harwood and from *Born 1900* by Julius Hay.

Amber Lane Press and Mr. John Osborne, for permission to quote from *At the Royal Court*, edited by Richard Findlater.

Thornton Butterworth Ltd., for permission to reprint from *Mainly Players* by Constance Benson.

Mr. John Casson, on behalf of the late Dame Sybil Thorndike.

Century Hutchinson Publishing Group Ltd., for permission to reprint from *Royal Performance* by Ian Bevan and *Astonish Us in the Morning: Tyrone Guthrie Remembered* by Alfred Rossi.

Citadel Press, for permission to reprint from *The Algonquin Wits* by Robert E. Drennan.

Columbia University Press, for permission to reprint from *Louis Jouvet: Man of the Theatre* by Bettina Leibowitz Knapp.

Rupert Crew Ltd., for permission to reprint from *Pillars of Drury Lane* by W. Macqueen-Pope.

Richard Curtis Associates, Inc., for permission to reprint from *Letters from an Actor* by William Redfield.

Mr. Laurence Evans of International Creative Management Ltd., on behalf of Lord Olivier, Sir John Gielgud, Dame Peggy Ashcroft, and Lady Richardson for the late Sir Ralph Richardson.

Eyre & Spottiswoode, Ltd., for permission to reprint from *My Best Riches* by Horace Collins.

The Friends of the Bancroft Library, University of California at Berkeley, for permission to reprint from *Memories of an Old Theatrical Man* by Frederick Ross.

Grafton Books, for permission to reprint from *Great Theatrical Disasters* by Gyles Brandreth.

Robert Hale Limited, for permission to reprint from *The Night Has Been Unruly* by J. C. Trewin.

Harrow House Editions, for permission to quote from *The Entertainers*, © Harrow House Editions, London.

Holt, Rinehart & Winston, for permission to reprint from *Voices Offstage* by Marc Connelly and *Showbiz: From Vaude to Video* by Abel Green and Joe Laurie, Jr.

Mr. Richard Huggett, for permission to quote from his book, *The Curse of Macbeth*.

Michael Imison Playwrights Ltd., on behalf of the estate of Noel Coward.

Alfred A. Knopf, Inc., for permission to reprint from *The Same Only Different* by Margaret Webster, and *The American Language*, fourth edition, by H. L. Mencken.

Jerome Lawrence, for permission to reprint from his book *Actor: The Life and Times of Paul Muni*.

Christopher Mann Ltd., on behalf of Sir Michael Redgrave.

Mr. Tom Milne, for permission to quote from his and Clive Goodwin's article "Working with Joan," which appeared in *Encore* VII (July-Aug. 1960).

Mr. Roy Moseley, for permission to reprint from his book, *My Stars*.

James Nisbet & Co. Ltd., for permission to quote from *Studio and Stage* by Joseph Harker.

Octagon Books, for permission to reprint from Mordecai Gorelik, *New Theatres for Old*.

The Society of Authors, for permission to reprint from *Bernard Shaw: Extracts from Letter to Hesketh Pearson* 1918.

Taplinger Publishing, for permission to reprint from *The Lost Theatres of London* by Raymond Mander and Joe Mitchenson.

Mr. Howard Teichmann, for permission to quote from his book, *George S. Kaufman*.

A. P. Watt Ltd., on behalf of Michael Holroyd, for permission to include selections from *The Last Actor-Managers* by Hesketh Pearson.

Portions of the following books appear through the kind permission of the publishers or representatives:

The Actors Studio: A Player's Place reprinted with permission of Macmillan Publishing Company. Copyright © 1980, 1984 by David Garfield.

Arena by Hallie Flanagan reprinted by permission of Harold Matson Company, Inc. Copyright 1940 by Hallie Flanagan. A Hawthorn book. Reprinted by permission of E. P. Dutton, a division of NAL Penguin Inc.

Bernard Shaw by Hesketh Pearson reprinted with permission of Collins, London.

The Compleat Practical Joker by H. Allen Smith reprinted by permission of Harold Matson Company, Inc. Copyright 1953 by H. Allen Smith, 1980 by Nelle Smith.

Footlights and Spotlights by Otis Skinner reprinted by permission of Macmillan Publishing Company, copyright 1924 by Macmillan Publishing Company, renewed 1952 by Mrs. Alden S. Blodget (Cornelia Otis Skinner).

Henry Irving by Edward Craig reprinted with permission, © Edward Craig. Published by David McKay Company, Inc.

Ibsen: A Biography by Michael Meyer reprinted by permission of Harold Ober Associates Incorporated. Copyright © 1967, 1971 by Michael Meyer.

Jed Harris: The Curse of Genius by Martin Gottfried, copyright © 1984 by Martin Gottfried. By permission of Little, Brown and Company.

Laughs from Jewish Lore reprinted by permission of the publisher, Hebrew Publishing Company, copyright © 1954. All rights reserved.

My Life in the Russian Theatre by Vladimir Nemirovitch-Dantchenko. Reprinted with the permission of the publishers, Theatre Arts Books, New York.

A short extract from the piece by John Cox reprinted by permission of Faber and Faber Ltd. from *To Nevill Coghill from Friends* by John Lawlor and W. H. Auden.

No People like Show People reprinted by permission of William Morris Agency, Inc., on behalf of the author; copyright © 1951 by Maurice Zolotow.

Index